D0991688

HQ 782 .J64 1984
**Johnson & Johnson Pediatric Round
Table (11th : 1984)**
 Play interactions : the contribution of
play materials and parental

Play Interactions

The Johnson & Johnson
Pediatric Round Table Series

The Johnson & Johnson Pediatric Round Table series of publications was initiated in 1974. Its objective is to bring together the world's outstanding scientists and medical and health care specialists to review current child development research and explore the innovative edge of pediatric concepts and programs. *Play Interactions: The Contribution of Play Materials and Parental Involvement to Children's Development* is the first title in this series to be published by Lexington Books.

Play Interactions

*The Contribution of Play Materials
and Parental Involvement to
Children's Development*

Proceedings of the eleventh
Johnson & Johnson **Pediatric Round Table**

Edited by

Allen W. Gottfried
California State University, Fullerton

Catherine Caldwell Brown

Sponsored by

Johnson & Johnson
BABY PRODUCTS COMPANY

Lexington Books
D.C. Heath and Company/Lexington, Massachusetts/Toronto

HQ
782
J64
1984

Library of Congress Cataloging in Publication Data
Main entry under title:

Play interactions.

(Johnson & Johnson pediatric round table series)
Includes index.
1. Play—Congresses. 2. Child development—
Congresses. 3. Parent and child—Congresses.
4. Toys—Social aspects—Congresses. I. Gottfried, Allen W.
II. Brown, Catherine Caldwell. III. Series:
Johnson & Johnson Baby Products Company pediatric
round table series.
HQ782.P518   1986   305.2'3   85–45463
ISBN 0–669–11797–8 (alk. paper)

Copyright © 1986 by Johnson & Johnson Baby Products Company

All rights reserved. No part of this publication may be reproduced
or transmitted in any form or by any means, electronic or mechanical,
including photocopy, recording, or any information storage or retrieval
system, without permission in writing from the publisher.

Published simultaneously in Canada
Printed in the United States of America
International Standard Book Number: 0–669–11797–8
Library of Congress Catalog Card Number: 85–45463

The paper used in this publication meets the minimum requirements of
American National Standard for Information Sciences—Permanence of
Paper for Printed Library Materials, ANSI Z39.48–1984.

The last numbers on the right below indicate the number and date of printing.

10 9 8 7 6 5 4 3 2 1

95 94 93 92 91 90 89 88 87 86

Contents

Foreword

T. Kerry McCarter
Johnson & Johnson Baby Products Company

I am often asked: "Why is Johnson & Johnson, a child-*care* company, entering the *toy* business?" My answer is that our products *look* like toys and *play* like toys, but they are actually skill-enhancing implements! Well-designed play materials are important to children's development, and care and development are closely linked to children's overall well-being.

That's why Johnson & Johnson is pleased to sponsor the Pediatric Round Table Series. As a company committed to children's well-being, we have a critical interest in the progress of child development research. We look to this work to give caregivers guidance in helping children to reach their full potential. By offering each child an improved chance to reach his full potential, child development research offers nothing less than a better world. And, practically speaking, we look to this research to guide our efforts in providing effective supporting products.

Yet, this is a new field, born of the twentieth century. It is difficult to see where current child development research will lead. It is possible that thirty years from now we will look back and see current research as the vacuum tube of child development. It may lead to unseen frontiers, as did personal computers and satellite communications. Certainly, if anyone can provide important insights and breakthroughs, it is the contributors to this book.

Introduction

Allen W. Gottfried

P lay is an intriguing, ubiquitous, and developmentally significant phenomenon. The nature of play, its determinants, and its consequences have received scholarly explanation for a number of centuries. Over the years, scientists from various disciplines have asked questions about play, ranging from the reasons for its existence and its meaning in phylogeny to what it tells us about cognitive and social development in humans. Play is by no means a trivial and simple set of behaviors. It is a complex multidimensional sequence of behaviors that change considerably with age in process and morphology, particularly during infancy and the early childhood years.

Like many other psychological constructs, play is easier to recognize and to observe than to define. One of the major obstacles to deriving an established or acceptable definition is that no single behavior or set of behaviors encompasses the many forms of play. There is exploratory play, in which the infant or young child examines via manipulation the characteristics of objects. Functional play involves sensorimotor practice or what may be called playful repetition. In constructive play, the young child attempts to create something, such as pictures, forms, or objects. There is play that does not include objects and play that is object-oriented. Object-oriented play may involve a single object, multiple objects, or combinatory object play. Play activities may be unstructured (free play) or structured (organized by another person, such as a parent or teacher). There are solitary play, parallel play, and social play. Pretense or imaginative play itself comes in a variety of forms. It can be verbal or nonverbal, solitary or social. There is also a mature form of play, common in older children and adults, called games-with-rules.

Although a definition of play is difficult to derive, there is consensus on the common characteristics of play behaviors (Rubin, Fein, & Vandenberg, 1983). First, play is intrinsically motivated rather than extrinsically motivated. Play behaviors occur for their own sake rather than as a result of external demands or reinforcements. Second, the focus of play is on the activity itself and not on the outcome or consequence of the activity. Third, object-oriented play is not simply exploratory behavior but involves what the young child can do with an object. Fourth, in play is the derivation of imposing novel meaning on objects and events. Fifth, there is the freedom in play to be nonrule-based, particularly in pretend play. Sixth, in play, the young child is actively involved in the activity. There is a seventh characteristic I would like to add to this list, the affective component of pleasure. Pleasure is both inherent in the play activity itself and a result of play activities as evidenced in the satisfaction, laughter, and joy seen in children during and immediately after play. Hence, the young child is not only the director and performer of play activities but also a spectator who provides positive or pleasurable self-feedback.

Culture and family clearly influence the content and style of play. Toys, which are integral and important vehicles of play, and technological changes in society and education have a substantial impact on children's play interests and activities. Within and across varying environments, researchers have delineated developmental progressions of play during children's early years. These progressions can be briefly summarized: (1) from simple object manipulation to engaging in object relationships, (2) from actions with real objects to actions with imaginary objects, (3) from sensorimotor to abstract forms of play (for example, pretend play), (4) from self-centered play to play that includes others, and (5) from solitary to social interactive play and social pretense. In the progression of object play, initially the infant will reach for and manipulate a single object. Subsequently, the child will play with multiple objects simultaneously, for example, banging blocks together or using one to maneuver another. At a more advanced level, the child will display combinatory play with different objects in a spontaneous and appropriate way, such as feeding a doll with a bottle or shoveling sand into a dump truck.

Another transition, related to object play, takes the child from functioning with actual objects to activities in which the child employs substitute objects and then imaginary objects. This is known as decontextualization. Within the social realm of pretense, the child's play is initially egocentric or focused only toward himself or herself, then gradually comes to include others. Upon young children's entry into toddler and nursery groups, there is another social progression that is obvious. Initially children's play is solitary and individualistic. In the process of socialization, children will engage in similar parallel play and gradually will participate in intense social interactive and sociodramatic play. It is noteworthy that progressions in children's play are not mutually exclusive of each other. They are integrated and to some degree confluent developments.

For young children, play is a special interaction with the environment. It is a unique way to learn about the world and a creative way to express their knowledge, enact their representations of experiences, and display psychological advances in many domains. The various forms of play and their progressions are highly informative in terms of what they tell us about developmental maturity as well as emerging functions. Evidence indicates that play is related to children's social, emotional, and intellectual development. It is an important indicator of children's language and symbol systems, and of the meanings children give to persons, places, and events. It is also an index of children's imagination, curiosity, motivation, preferences, interests, and persistence.

Since play contributes to and reflects so many aspects of psychological development, it is not surprising that play has numerous practical implications. Curricula in early childhood education programs throughout the world are built around play. Whether in structured, semistructured, or unstructured settings, play provides ways of evaluating parent-child and peer relationships, and of examining children's perceptual skills and motor dexterity. For a number of years, play has been a valuable tool in clinical assessment and treatment. Play is a rich organizing construct that has furnished a wealth of knowledge about young children's development.

The Johnson & Johnson Pediatric Round Table conference (held October 7–10, 1984) from which this book is derived was devoted to children's play and how toys or play materials and parental involvement in play contribute to young children's development. At the conference, scholars had the opportunity to present current theories, speculations, and empirical findings on play. The Round Table was conceptualized into five sections: (1) origins of play, (2) play and developmental processes, (3) social significance of play, (4) parent-child interaction in different populations, and (5) consequences of play materials and parent-child interaction.

Play Interactions provides a comprehensive and insightful analysis of young children's play interactions. Part I, on the origins of play, addresses issues concerning the adaptive value of play and humans as myth makers, the emotional basis of and affective template representation in pretend play, and the search for universal play behaviors across diverse cultures. Part II deals with cognitive, linguistic, and motivational processes of play. The chapters in part II describe developmental progressions from infancy through the early childhood years; relationships between play and language with implications for symbolic development; cognitive, competence, and attribution approaches to intrinsic motivational aspects of play; and the exciting new phenomenon of computer play. Part III elaborates on the construct of play by examining the role of social processes. The chapters in part III focus specifically on social representation in symbolic play, play within the family context, peer play interactions in preschool settings, and socioeconomic correlates of pretend play. Part IV addresses parent-child interactions and the applications of play and toys in clinical populations. Part V deals with interactions within the home environment. Extensive research programs on the cognitive, social, emotional, and educational outcomes of home stimulation and parent-child interactions are presented. Finally, part VI provides an overview of play interactions, including an integrative analysis of current longitudinal investigations in North America demonstrating that play materials and parental involvement are two of the most potent and pervasive home environmental factors related to young children's developmental status.

Play Interactions

Part I
The Origins of Play

1
Beyond the Ethology of Play

Brian R. Vandenberg

W hen I first became interested in studying the topic of play, I felt that it was essential to begin with biology, since a psychology of play that was not grounded in biology would likely be limited if not flawed. This led me to explore the ethological and comparative research on play, whose main objective is to identify the adaptive functions of play. I find it intriguing that the adaptive benefits of play are not obvious. No primary drives such as hunger, thirst, or sex are satisfied, and play seems to be the antithesis of goal-directed, problem-solving abilities that are so clearly essential to the survival of any species (see, for example, Vandenberg, 1978).

This has led to speculation that the adaptive functions of play are more indirect, that through play, important cognitive and social skills are stimulated that enhance the probability of a species' survival. Much of the research on play with animals, and with humans as well, has investigated this indirect link. However, the strength of the data supporting such a link is open to debate. Smith (1982), for instance, in an exhaustive review of this topic, concludes that the data fail to point to any identifiable adaptive benefit of play. This conclusion is troubling, since play is a pervasive behavior displayed by a wide number of species. Play must have significant adaptive value; otherwise, selective pressures would have eliminated it from the repertoire of animals long ago.

We are left with a conundrum. We can either assert that play has adaptive value because it exists—a circularity that is disquieting—or we can argue about the relative merits of the research that addresses its indirect contribution to more obviously adaptive functions—a position that *begins* with the assumption that play is, at best, a biological epiphenomenon.

However, this conundrum may be the result of the way we researchers have conceptualized the problem. Perhaps it points out the limitations of using a biological approach for understanding behavioral and psychological phenomena. Evolutionary theory and the concomitant emphasis on adaptation serve as the premise upon which ethological and comparative approaches are built. But what if we started at a different point? What if we began our investigation of humans by asking "What are the features of a being that is capable of creating a theory of evolution and interpreting the world almost exclusively from this vantage point?" This turns the process of investigation on end: evolutionary theory, instead of providing the assumptive framework for gathering data, becomes an important datum in itself. The answer to the question "What are the characteristics of a being that would create evolutionary theory?" entails a different approach to human life than is involved in an ethological perspective. It also has very different implications for our understanding of play. I'd like to sketch briefly what some of these are.

Myth and Reality

The datum of evolutionary theory suggests that humans are myth-making beings who create reality through belief in stories they have constructed about reality. By "myth," I don't mean "mistake," as it has come to be used in modern terminology, but myth in the sense of a belief system that orders and gives meaning to life. Perhaps the most pervasive myth of our culture is the myth of science, of which evolutionary theory is a part.

We cannot easily gain insight into our own myth systems, and it is only when we come into contact with another, foreign myth system that we can begin to see the reality of our own. Unfortunately, we are prone to relegate the myth systems of others to the realm of fantasy, and to reify our own as reality. As Brian Sutton-Smith has pointed out, "The cosmic constructions of ideology and religion are seen as ultimate meanings without which none of the rest make sense. Other people's religions or ideologies are, of course, often designated as mere 'fairy tales,' mere 'child's play'" (Sutton-Smith, 1980, p. 12). The reification of our myths to the status of reality reflects a basic tendency of the human mind to "constitute the world in such a way that it appears independent of our own constitution" (Yalom, 1980, p. 222). This explains why it is difficult to take science or evolutionary theory as a datum to be explained, rather than as a system for explaining.

I would like to elaborate briefly this view of humans as myth-making beings, and then use this perspective as a framework for thinking about children's play.

Hypnosis and the placebo effect are two phenomena that give empirical support to this theory of humans as myth makers. Both of these phenomena are quite remarkable. For example, under hypnosis major surgery can be performed without anesthetics with no signs of pain, and various warts and fungus growths, for which there are no easy cures, can be eliminated (Crasilneck & Hall, 1975). The placebo effect is quite powerful. It has been demonstrated, for instance, that for many people suffering acute pain, a sugar pill that is believed by the sufferer to be a powerful analgesic can be just as effective as morphine, one of the most powerful of pain killers (Hilgard & Hilgard, 1975).

What is it about hypnosis and the placebo effect that is responsible for these results? Both have several important features in common. Consider the process of hypnosis: One individual, sometimes a stranger, frequently holding a position of status or power, skillfully tells another person a story about reality. The narrative is different from what is commonly considered reality: "your hand is anesthetized" or "you feel no pain in your tooth." A similar process occurs in the placebo effect: a person of status or power leads the subject to believe that the administered treatment is a potentially powerful curing agent, when in "reality" it is not. In both cases, if the subject comes to believe the story, he responds as if the story were true, and thereby creates the reality he believes in. I think this reveals a fundamental epistemological axiom of human functioning: that through belief in stories about reality, we create our reality.

This does not imply that reality is a personal, solipsistic construction that is independent of an external world. There is a world independent of our imagination of it, and it does have forceful consequences that cannot be ignored. Many potential stories can be used, but to be viable, they must be responsive to the demands of the external world. But the particular stance we take toward the world and ourselves, and the way we sift and selectively interpret the facts of the world are strongly influenced by the stories we believe about the nature of reality.

Two facts about hypnosis require further analysis. First, not everyone can be hypnotized. This could be taken as evidence that disproves the universality of humans as myth makers. However, closer inspection of the reasons why people can or cannot be hypnotized deepens our understanding of how myths operate. Considerable research has been undertaken to identify what the critical factors are that differentiate those who can be hypnotized from those who cannot. The only factor that has been consistently found is the ability to become engrossed in fantasy (Bowers, 1976). For example, those who are likely to become involved in a movie or a book to the point of being oblivious to their surroundings are more likely to be hypnotized. Stated in a different way, those capable of investing *belief* in another reality are more hypnotically suggestible. This difference points to the importance of *belief* in myths. It is not enough to be able to understand an alternative story about reality, to have the cognitive skills necessary to comprehend the symbolic content of a story. An investment of emotional commitment of belief that brings the story to life is also required. This is evident in the placebo effect as well. Only when the person believes that the treatment can help is the treatment beneficial. If this belief is undermined, in even the subtlest of ways, then the power of the placebo is lost.

Thus, the individual not only must possess the requisite cognitive and symbolic abilities necessary to create and understand complex myths, but also must make the emotional commitment of belief. Only when these aspects are brought together does a story have *meaning* for the individual. It is through belief that a myth becomes reified, that it becomes ours, and gives meaning to our lives.

A corollary property of belief is hope. Hope is the forward-looking component of living meaningfully within a life myth that links past and present with an anticipation for the future. To lose hope, to lose the basis for emotional commitment to life, is to lose life itself. Indeed, the loss of hope has been cited as a cause of death among concentration camp victims (Frankl, 1959), for those grieving over the loss of a loved one (Epstein, Weitz, Roback, & McKee, 1975), and for those suffering from a life-threatening illness (Kubler-Ross, 1969).

Another fact about hypnosis is that children are more easily hypnotized. Although little research on hypnosis with children has been done, the existing data indicate that hypnotic susceptibility is inversely correlated with age (Gardner & Olness, 1981). This suggests that as children grow into adulthood, the boundaries between reality and fantasy become more entrenched, and it becomes increasingly difficult to entertain, in a believing way, alternative myths. To function as mature adults, we need our myths. Children's reality, on the other hand, is much more labile. They can more quickly reinvest belief in alternative realities. While this ability enables children to be good hypnotic subjects, the permeability of the fantasy reality dichotomy makes confident action in the world difficult. The process of development could be construed, in this framework, as the process of becoming rooted in the various myths of the culture.

What might be some of the factors that affect this development? Increasing cognitive and symbolic sophistication enables the child to comprehend and use the complex myths of the culture. But this is only one component; the other component is the investment of emotional belief in a myth. This belief is facilitated through *trust* in the caregivers, which enables the child to invest confidently in the cultural myths that are transmitted to the child by the parents. A strong sense of self and self-esteem comes from confidence in one's own efficacy within a trusted cultural myth system about reality.

Unfortunately, I cannot further elaborate this approach here, and I realize that it is necessarily incomplete. However, I would like to use this briefly sketched perspective as a basis for discussing children's play.

Human Play

The ethological, comparative, and biological perspectives on play have had considerable direct and indirect influence on the way play in humans has been studied. The most direct influence has been in the research on play and problem solving. The rationale for studying the link between play and problem solving and the design for much of the research is derived from work with nonhuman primates (Vandenberg, 1980). The play-training studies, and research examining the effects of play on social, linguistic, and perspective-taking abilities, draw more subtly on these perspectives, implying that play's developmental importance is to be found in the way it stimulates other, more obviously adaptive skills.

However, the view of humans as myth-making and believing beings suggests that reality, for humans, is a trusted fantasy. To be human and to live in a meaningful way within a culture requires living in and through a very sophisticated, abstract system that is largely imaginary. To be incapable of fantasy is to be barred from human culture. Thus, in fantasy play, children are displaying their human capacity as myth-making beings who create imaginary worlds that structure, energize, and give meaning to experience. The myths and fantasies of childhood are not eroded by the onset of logic and reason; rather, they are replaced with more sophisticated adult myths about the importance of logic and reason. Ironically, the mythical belief in logic and reason by adults has led to the myth that adults have no myths. This perspective suggests that it is fantasy, not logic, that is the fundamental adaptive quality in humans.

Myth making and believing necessarily entail cognitive, symbolic, and social abilities. But where ontological priority is placed is crucial. A biological framework of adaptation is likely to stress the primary importance of these cognitive, social, or symbolic abilities, which are enhanced through play. The perspective I offer assumes that play is a manifestation of the fundamental properties of myth, and that cognitive, social and symbolic abilities are concomitant aspects of myth making. The importance of play and fantasy are not to be found in their indirect stimulation of cognitive skills and problem solving; rather, play and fantasy are central features of what it means to be human, and problem-solving skills are a spin-off of the ability to imagine.

The ethological perspective also has led to the term *practice play,* which has been commonly used in describing certain types of children's play. This term was derived from watching young animals playfully perform actions they would later use in serious contexts as adults. A kitten stalking and attacking a ball of yarn would be an example of this. Its human counterpart can be found in children playing house and playing at other adult activities that they might take on in the future. However, the tense excitement that accompanies much of children's play implies that it is more than a mere practice session. For example, a 4-year-old friend of mine frequently pretends that she is a cheerleader. She dances, jumps, and twirls in youthful imitation of her older heroines. We might be tempted to speculate that she is practicing a role that she may later adopt. However, it is still unclear why she has picked this particular role to practice and why she plays it with so much gusto. A clue to a more complete explanation is that her mother was a cheerleader and has talked to her daughter about it. Thus, her daughter is attempting to construct a possible future for herself as she plays with a myth about maturity and adulthood that has been presented to her by her mother. In its meaning, immediacy, and emotional richness, her play is closer to hope than rehearsal.

Thus, children's dramatic play is more developmentally related to adults' hopeful anticipations about their future than to the ritualistic practicing of skills and roles. It is not a mere practice session for the development of cognitive, social, or linguistic skills. Rather, it is a highly charged dramatic enactment of a potential future. Certainly, cognitive, social, and linguistic skills are required for such enactments. But if we examine play exclusively within these frameworks, particularly as a stimulant to these skills, we are likely to overlook play's relation to myth, meaning, and hope, and lose sight of its centrality in human life.

I'm sure that many ethologists would be cautious, if not skeptical, about using the term *hope* to describe practice play. After all, how much sense does it make to say that a kitten playing with a ball is involved in hope? But this criticism raises the question that is the focus of my discussion: What starting point should be used for understanding play in humans? The ethological approach is basically reductionistic, since understanding of human functioning is derived from an analysis of the lowest common factors among species. But such an approach is likely to hinder our understanding of the unique features of human play. The approach I advocate begins with an analysis of what features are uniquely human. This approach places ontological priority on the existence of hope, myth, and meaning. These attributes are not to be derived from analyses of other species but are starting points for understanding humans, and an approach that excludes them necessarily diminishes that understanding.

There are other features besides hope that are involved in children's play. In dramatic play among peers, for instance, children play with myths of the culture. This results in the children's further rooting themselves in the cultural myths while exerting control over the myths and freeing themselves from them. For example, children playing house reenact and playact the myths associated with family membership, but they frequently alter the script. New twists are introduced as the script is bent to the desires of the children. Perhaps more favorable child-oriented behaviors are assumed by the "mommy" and "daddy" players, or the children in the play family are more angry, demanding, and powerful than the parents. This tension between the myths imposed from without and the exertion of personal control in shaping one's interpretation and use of the myths reflects the poles of a dialectic relationship between the individual and his culture. Through play, the child socialized into a general cultural framework while developing a unique individuality with a distinctly personal matrix of life history and lived meanings.

Trust is an important element in children's play. When infants play with their caregivers, considerable trust is involved. Adults are likely to toss the infant into the air, make ghoulish faces at him, emit strange sounds and shrieks, and play with parts of the infant's body. The activities are playful because they are incongruent *and* because they are performed with a trusted caregiver. If such activities were to be performed by a stranger, the infant would become extremely frightened, even to the edge of terror. When there is trust between the adult and the infant new realities can be safely embraced. Such play reinforces the link between child and parent, thereby strengthening the child's grounding in the parent's myth world. At the same time, it encourages the exploration of new alternatives outside the usual rituals of action and gives tacit support to the growth of the child as a unique individual who will create his own personal version of the cultural myths.

Most of children's social play, however, is conducted with peers, not adults. Unlike play with adults, peer play involves a power relationship among equals. This can be both liberating, since the child is freed from the submissive role in the play, and threatening, since now the child must negotiate his identity and social power with others who are also jostling for stature and influence. In fact, I would like to suggest that the watching child trying to negotiate entry into an ongoing play round is undergoing a paradigmatic event that reveals many important features of human life. For such a child, an invitation into the playing group is more than just an opportunity to play; it is an issue of existence. To be outside the group is to be a nonentity; to join the play is to be accorded an officially sanctioned identity and status within a group of trusted and trusting players. This goes to the heart of the process of socialization: one must be able to play the game with others, to share a common framework, and to trust that others will also. Thus, humans derive meaning through play and develop a sense of belonging and rootedness by sharing the trust of others.

Brian Sutton-Smith (1984) has pointed out that the usual psychological theories of play present a middle-class, sanitized view of children's play. The darker, more hostile and aggressive sides of peer play has been generally ignored. Part of the reason why we researchers have overlooked the negative aspect of play behavior is because it does not fit into our model of play as a stimulant for the cognitive, social, and symbolic abilities that are necessary to succeed in school. However, if peer play is seen as the siren call of individuality, as a place for negotiating one's identity with equals, then a different picture emerges. The sense of efficacy that peer play affords is sometimes purchased at the expense of adult norms. Indeed, it is the opposition to adult norms that gives some peer play its thrill. For instance, the attraction of some delinquent acts, like joy riding in a stolen car, could be considered a form of play whose excitement is derived from the undoing of adult norms and values. Furthermore, with issues of power, identity, status, and trust at stake, peer play among children may sometimes take a vicious turn; after all, why should children act differently from adults?

Finally, I'd like to address the relation between cultural myths and toys. Our culture is a materialistic one that places a great deal of emphasis on ownership. Status and identity are closely linked to one's ability to possess scarce, expensive, and coveted objects. The *St. Louis Post-Dispatch* was quite cooperative in publishing an article on business in the Sunday magazine section that illustrates my point:

> In our society, the money you make, more than any other single factor, is an indicator of individual worth. And in business it is a measure by which everyone is judged. For *this reason alone,* every working person should strive to maximize his or her salary in any given position. (Burdick & Mitchell, 1984, p. 6. italics added)

Children do not escape this myth. Indeed, it could be argued that one's developmental status is, in part, defined by ownership of objects: a tricycle is a must for a preschooler, one's first two-wheeler is a major rite of passage, to be a teenager without a stereo is to suffer developmental arrest, cars are a requirement of the late teens, and entrance into adulthood is not complete until one owns a house. Within this framework, toys sometimes take on greater importance than mere playthings; they can also be objects of status. Many parents have endured constant badgering from their children to buy a desired toy, only to see the toy abandoned a week after it is purchased. What is important in these instances is not the toy per se and the play it is intended to prompt but the ownership of the toy. The Cabbage Patch doll craze reflects some of this emphasis. The press to acquire one was fueled not only by the need to have a cute doll, but also by the status and identity implications of owning or not owning one.

To summarize, our understanding of play is very closely tied to the theory we adopt about humans. Ethological approaches, with their attendant emphasis on biology, focus on identifying the adaptive features of play. The approach I have sketched suggests that myth, meaning, and hope are fundamental aspects of human life and that play is an important manifestation of these phenomena.

References

Bowers, K.S. 1976. *Hypnosis for the seriously curious.* New York: Norton.

Burdick, T., & Mitchell, C. 1984. The raise-getting game and how to win it. *St. Louis Post-Dispatch PD,* October 7:6.

Crasilneck, H.B., & Hall, J.A. 1975. *Clinical hypnosis: Principles and applications.* New York: Grune & Stratton.

Epstein, G., Weitz, L., Roback, H., & McKee, E. 1975. Research in bereavement: A selection and critical review. *Comprehensive Psychiatry* 16:537–546.

Frankl, V.E. 1959. *Man's search for meaning.* New York: Pocket Books.

Gardner, G.G., & Olness, K. 1981. *Hypnosis and hypnotherapy with children.* New York: Grune & Stratton.

Hilgard, E.R., & Hilgard, J.R. 1975. *Hypnosis and the relief of pain.* Los Altos, Calif.: Kauffman.

Kubler-Ross, E. 1969. *On death and dying.* New York: Macmillan.

Smith, P.K. 1982. Does play matter? Functional and evolutionary aspects of animal and human play. *The Behavioral and Brain Sciences* 5:139–184.

Sutton-Smith, B. 1980. Some sources of play theorizing. In K.H. Rubin (Ed.), *New directions for child development: Children's play.* San Francisco: Jossey-Bass.

Sutton-Smith, B. 1984. Recreation as folly's parody. *TAASP Newsletter* 10:4–13.

Vandenberg, B. 1978. Play and development from an ethological perspective. *American Psychologist* 33:724–738.

Vandenberg, B. 1980. Play, problem solving and creativity. In K.H. Rubin (Ed.) *New directions for child development: Children's play.* San Francisco: Jossey-Bass.

Yalom, I. 1980. *Existential psychotherapy.* New York: Basic Books.

2

A Cross-Cultural Perspective on Child-Structured Play Activities and Materials

Helen B. Schwartzman

One of the purposes of anthropology is to use the study of other cultures to further ethnographers' understanding of their own societies. The study of unfamiliar cultures throws into relief aspects of one's own culture that may be taken for granted. Anthropology is based on a premise that is nicely summarized in the proverb "It is hardly a fish that can discover the existence of water" (Kluckhohn, 1949). In this chapter studies of child-structured play are used to examine a number of ideas about children's play that are (or are about to be) taken for granted by individuals concerned with issues in child development. In particular, ideas about the contribution of play materials and parental involvement to child development will be considered. The specific givens examined here include:

1. Work precludes play for children who assume economic responsibilities at an early age, because this does not allow them legitimate, uninterrupted time for play.
2. Children who come from economically disadvantaged families will play less frequently and less imaginatively than do children from more advantaged circumstances and/or "complex" cultures.
3. Peer groups are natural and important socialization experiences for all children.
4. Children must have sufficient and appropriately structured space and toys allotted to them by adults in order to play successfully; and adults must model, and/or facilitate the development of, specific types of play.

The implications of this critique for the design of play materials and environments are specifically considered at the end of this chapter.

Child-structured Play

It is important first to define what is meant by child-structured play. I have suggested recently (Schwartzman, 1983) that although children's play has been classified and categorized from a number of different perspectives, one division that has been neglected is a contrast between child-structured and adult-structured play. I define *child-structured play* as the play (and toys) of children which they create on their own and often out of the sight of adults. Team games, sports, board games, and other highly structured games which adults have introduced to children, which may or may not require adult supervision, are referred to as *adult-structured play*. One of the most important differences between these two play forms is that adult-structured play has been greatly studied in laboratories, schools, playgrounds, and so on, while the child-structured play has been investigated only infrequently.

Certainly the most extensive study of the child-structured play of Western children is Iona and Peter Opie's collection of English children's street games, *Children's Games in Street and Playground* (1969). (Interesting and relevant material is also available in the Opies' earlier study, *The Lore and Language of Schoolchildren,* 1959). In the 1969 study, the Opies state that their concern is

> solely with the games that children aged 6–12 play of their own accord when out of doors, and usually out of sight. We do not include, except incidentally, party games, scout games, team games, or any sport that requires supervision; and we concentrate for the most part on the rough-and-tumble games which, though they may require energy and sometimes fortitude, do not need even the elementary equipment of bat and ball. We are interested in the simple games for which, as one child put it, "nothing is needed but the players themselves." (p. v)

Given these criteria, the Opies collected and catalogued over 150 games; these include chasing games, catching games, seeking games, hunting games, racing games, dueling games, exerting games, daring games, guessing games, acting games, pretending games. All of these games demonstrate what children can do using themselves as the major "implements" in a game, or using very simple materials (such as cans, sticks, and stones) or structures (walls, streets, fields) in creating the game.

The Opies also performed an analysis of games diminishing or growing in popularity over the last fifty years in Britain. This analysis revealed that the games whose decline was most pronounced were those that were the best known to adults and the most likely to be promoted by them. The games that were flourishing or increasing in popularity were those that adults did not feel comfortable in encouraging (for example, knife throwing, chasing in the dark) or those in which adults were least proficient (for example, ball bouncing, rope skipping).

In discussing play environments, the Opies suggest that when children play in a restricted space (such as a playground), their behavior is more aggressive and hierarchical than when they play in the streets and "wastelands," where they are said to act in a more cooperative, egalitarian, and thoughtful manner. But the authors note that their street play always seems to get children in trouble with adults because of the places they choose for play and the fact that they seem to want

> deliberately to attract attention to themselves, screaming, scribbling on the pavements, smashing milk bottles, banging on doors, and getting in people's way. A single group of children were able to name twenty games they played which involved running across the road. (p. 11)

Perhaps children are more likely to explore their individual relationships with each other when interacting in restricted environments, and when in an open environment group relationships (we–other, adult versus child) assume prominence.

The Opies are particularly critical in this book of the view that contemporary children can no longer entertain themselves and that traditional games have been extinguished or are in the process of dying out. They argue (and their collection substantiates this) that this is not happening, but that it may become a reality.

> Nothing extinguishes self-organized play more effectively than does action to promote it. It is not only natural but beneficial that there should be a gulf between the generations in their choice of recreation . . . If children's games are tamed and made part of school curricula, if wastelands are turned into playing fields for the benefit of those who conform and ape their elders, if children are given the idea that they cannot enjoy themselves without being provided with the "proper" equipment, we need blame only ourselves when we produce a generation who have lost their dignity, who are ever dissatisfied, and who descend for their sport to the easy excitement of rioting, or pilfering, or vandalism. (p. 16)

In most non-Western cultures the opportunities for children to engage in self-organized play are greater because they are frequently considered to be competent at an earlier age than Western children and therefore there are fewer watchful eyes on their behavior. Along with this, play is often defined as a behavior that does not need to be watched and strictly supervised, organized, or promoted by adults. Play is generally seen as natural, and while it may be actively discouraged in some societies (see, for example, Feitelson, 1954, 1977), it is usually tolerated or ignored.[1]

Questioning Current Assumptions about Children's Play

When the above reports and observations of child-structured play are examined in detail, I believe they force us to question a number of assumptions about play made by Western researchers and educators. These are considered below and then related to design issues.

1. *Play does not occur (or occurs less frequently) when children must assume child-care and other economic responsibilities at an early age.* The basic assumption here is that children must have "legitimate time" (see Singer, 1973) or relatively long undisturbed periods of time for play (especially imaginative play) to develop. The ethnographic literature suggests, however, that children develop ingenious ways to combine their work with their play. These ways provide them with enough time to engage in play and still carry out their work responsibilities, whatever they may be. For example, Okinawan children living in the village of Taira studied by Maretzki and Maretzki (1963) were expected to take care of their younger siblings, but the behavior of their young charges did not interfere with their involvement in play.

> H. [an 8-year-old girl], carrying her baby sister on her back, is playing on the beach. She straightens up suddenly with a wry expression on her face. "She urinated, wet," she exclaims, standing up and spreading her dress at the back, which is completely soaked. The baby is bare-bottomed and crowing happily at the older children playing around her. The older sister waves her dress briefly in the wind, then squats to continue her play. When asked if she was not going home to change, she explains that she would dry soon enough, and, as for the baby, she was dry. The day is warm and windy and the dress dries off rapidly. (p. 470)

More recent cross-cultural research on child development (e.g., Harkness & Super, 1983) specifically relates children's play activities to their work responsibilities. In their investigation of a rural Kipsigis community in Kenya, Harkness and Super suggest that "children's playing often takes place in the context of work" (p. 10). They provide several examples of how Kipsigis children integrate their work and play, for example initiating a game of tag while watching the family cows or climbing a tree while looking after a younger sibling suggesting that children who are required to work by their parents do not give up play, but merely restructure and learn different contexts and opportunities for play.

2. *Children from disadvantaged families and/or living in less economically complex societies will play less frequently and also less imaginatively than children from more economically advantaged families living in economically complex societies.* This argument has been advanced by a number of psychologists and educators (see Feitelson & Ross, 1973; Feitelson, 1977; Singer, 1973; Smilansky, 1968) who have developed play-training or play-tutoring programs especially for urban disadvantaged children who are believed to be deficient in their display of imaginative play abilities. A critique

of these studies is explicitly formulated in Schwartzman (1984), but it can be noted here that when studies have been made in contexts that are familiar and not threatening to the children (neighborhoods as opposed to schools or laboratories) these deficiencies are frequently not evident, although there are differences in play style as well as content (see Labov, 1972). These children's self-structured play is often highly imaginative and creative, unlike the stilted and nonimaginative behavior that they apparently produce when tested in artificial contexts. The creation of ingenious and self-designed toys by lower income children and by non-Western children also demonstrates this point.

3. *Peer groups are natural and important socialization experiences for all children.* The research of Konner (1975) with the !Kung Bushmen suggests that peer groups as identified by Western researchers, are not universal social experiences for all children, and in fact may be maladaptive group experiences. Because of the practice of long birth spacing and the small group size of the Bushmen, children interact in multiaged as opposed to same-age peer groups. Konner argues that multiage groups may be the more common experience for children in the history of mankind. He also suggests that researchers' ideas about peer relations in infancy and early childhood may be greatly distorted and highly culture-specific because they

> are almost entirely an artifact of laboratory investigations of child care conditions in advanced industrial states. In this context we can begin to understand the bizarrely inept form of social behavior which we know in the laboratory and nursery as "parallel play" and "collective monologue." (p. 122)

The impact of multiage groups on !Kung children's play is also described by Draper (1976), who argues that such groups discourage competitive play because there are not enough children to "fill out" a team and the players are at very different levels of motor skill, motivation, and cognitive development and therefore find it unrewarding and frustrating to engage in games that involve intense competition, rules, and complex strategy.

4. *Children must have sufficient and appropriate space and toys allotted to them by adults to engage in particular types of play.* In this view, play space, toy ownership, and the presence of manufactured toys are assumed to provide the proper stimuli for play, particularly imaginative play (see Feitelson, 1977).[2] The importance of proper play space was of particular concern to early play reformers such as Gulick (1920) and Curtis (1915), who believed that there was an absence of play among urban immigrant and lower working-class children in large U.S. cities because they lacked privacy and space to store play objects. The problems of children doing nothing or "fooling around" instead of engaging in constructive play were more generally attrib-

uted to the phenomena of immigration and urbanization. The play reformers developed the playground movement as a means to encourage proper play and to discourage rowdy behavior and "teach children leadership and cooperation, develop skills and health, and encourage imagination and creativity" (Mergen, 1980, p. 198). Play leaders who knew how and when to organize and structure children's activities on the playground were believed to be particularly important in achieving these ends. Henry Curtis, who was the first supervisor of playgrounds in Washington, D.C., suggests:

> Play for any high development always requires good camaraderie and leadership. The American city, which has mixed up Jews and Greeks and Italians and Slavs in a single community, has worked strongly against the development of that sense of trust and affection which is essential to highly organized and frequent play. (Curtis, in Mergen, 1980)

The impact of schools, supervised playgrounds, and the introduction of organized sports on New Zealand children is specifically considered by Sutton-Smith in *A History of Children's Play: The New Zealand Playground 1840–1950* (1981). This book is particularly useful to consider because it documents over a period of 110 years the impact of adult-introduced play materials and activities on children's development, and especially on their abilities to be physically and emotionally self-reliant.

When the ethnographic literature is reviewed with these ideas in mind, it suggests that in most societies children do not have their own private space (at least not interior space) or an assemblage of ready-made toys that are theirs alone, as is typical of middle-class American children, and yet they are able to construct active play lives for themselves. The processes of migration, immigration, and urbanization have mixed numerous groups in countries all over the world, and yet urban children in cities as different as Lusaka, New York, and Port-au-Prince are able to transform various types of environments into play areas of their own design using what may seem to be useless and even dangerous space and materials (such as trash heaps and abandoned buildings) in very creative ways. In a similar way, children are able to use whatever materials are available to create a variety of playthings.

Child-designed Toys

Children probably create toys for themselves (or use materials in the environment as toys) in all societies.[3] It is assumed that Western children (especially middle-class children) will be creative and ingenious in their designs, but are they? What about non-middle-class and non-Western children? And what types of contexts and what types of materials facilitate or inhibit a creative, imaginative, and self-organized use of materials and space?

Unfortunately, there is not much systematic research to use in answering these questions because of the tendency for investigators to study play in artificial contexts and with the use of ready-made and adult-designed toys. There are, however, a few interesting reports in the ethnographic and folk-lore literature. The majority of descriptions of child-designed toys are brief reports included in anthropologists' monographs. For example, Cora DuBois reports the following in her study of Alorese children:

> Children play a great deal. Girls emphasize food-gathering activities and cooking; boys emphasize hunting. It is noteworthy that the children have many games and toys, some of which are very ingenious—for example, a pressure squirt gun that is fashioned of bamboo. (1944, p. 59)[4]

The Maretzkis' report that the children of Taira in Okinawa meet the "minimum of equipment" with a "maximum of inventiveness and enthusiasm" in their play (1963, p. 536). Stones, peas, or seeds may be used as marbles; empty cartons are trucks and boats; cabbage leaves become helmets; and bamboo pieces are daggers.[5] These descriptions suggest that the anthropologists are themselves somewhat surprised by the children's inventiveness (perhaps this is a reflection of the ethnographers' culture, which supports the view that creativity and inventiveness will only occur when fostered by adults with proper space and materials).

More detailed studies of non-Western children's self-organized and self-designed toys are available in Lorna Marshall's (1976) ethnography of the !Kung Bushmen, which includes one chapter on the topic of play and games. Marshall describes the children's ingenuity in manufacturing a variety of objects for play, for example a toy gun made out of a reed, a "camera" carved out of a tuber, "autos" made from tubers, and bulbs modeled after the Marshalls' jeeps and accompanied by motor sounds imitated by the boys who specialized "in the roar of low gear pulling out of heavy sand" (p. 342).

The indigenous play and toy objects of Chama (Tacanan) Indian children in northern Bolivia are described in detail by Shoemaker (1964). These children are said to spend many hours creatively shaping toys from the raw materials of the jungle, but the ethnographer reports that they do not play group games (only one, a free-for-all tag played with one leg tied up, was observed). The children's ability to use a variety of materials for playful purposes is demonstrated in this unusual report.[6] Papaya and banana leaves are used for umbrellas and for playhouse roofs. Large, soft leaves are used as toy cups; these may also be pressed against the teeth and popped like bubble gum or cupped in one hand and popped with the other like a paper bag. Juice from the *kwasosa* tree is blown into durable soap bubbles. Small reeds are cut in differing lengths and slit on one side to make variously toned whistles. Younger children string bracelets of colored seeds, alligator teeth, and tiny shells, and they mold simple objects from clay. They also stick feathers in light-weight peeled lemons that resemble shuttlecocks and make balloons from elastic fungus pods.

The older boys make models of canoes, airplanes, and launches which they whittle from balsa wood. Whistling tops which spin on hard wood pegs are made from little gourds. Intricate clocks, animals, and other objects are carved from hard lumps of clay. The boys hunt using bows made from palm strips and slingshots made of crude rubber. They also use reeds to make toy guns with a firing range of 30–45 feet and enough force to kill lizards. The boys were also inspired by the anthropologist's two-way radio to make one of their own using a thread line and two matchbox receiver-transmitters.

Jackson (1964) also presents a description of the native toys of the Guarayu Indians of central eastern Bolivia. These toys consisted of items used in their original form as taken from the jungle or fashioned out of materials at hand. Artificial lips are made by pressing on bright orange-red blossoms from the *tuinani* tree which are double and crescent shaped. Small canoes are simulated by using large pods of the *pinomini* palm, and children pull each other around in them on the ground. Playhouses are built with short sticks, and several miniature items are used in house play, including small-sized baskets and hats woven from palm fronds, small water pots made from pottery clay, small dolls and animals modeled from clay or whittled from mahogany wood, other dolls fashioned from corn husks and cast-off rags, bows and arrows made from palm, and small guns made from a hollow piece of cane with a stiff trigger of dry palm to shoot off the ammunition of dry corn kernels or small stones.

What happens to the play of non-Western children when they grow up in an urban rather than rural environment? Leacock (1971), reporting on the play and self-designed toys of African children living in Lusaka, the capital of Zambia, suggests that children naturally and unself-consciously demonstrate their knowledge and use of a variety of social and cognitive skills in play. For example, the organization of roles and role relationships and the ability to count scores are demonstrated in games; the ability to understand and use volume, area, and linear measurements is displayed in water play and the construction of numerous toy objects; and language and dramatic skills are demonstrated in the construction and performance of stories and songs. The most interesting material in this report describes the children's (generally boys') creation and demonstration of numerous toy objects.

> Boys are ingenious at finding and making do with available materials. . . . The most characteristic of African toys is the wire car. These are models of cars and trucks that most boys start making at eight or nine. They are from one to two feet long, and made of heavy wires bent into shape and bound together with finer ones. . . . Boys are most commonly seen running up and down with their cars, pushing them along from a standing position. A long heavy wire, bent into a circle at the driving end, is attached at the other end

to the front axle of the car in such a fashion that the boy steers the car by turning the wheel in his hand. . . . After a boy decides which type of car or truck to build, he straightens and cuts lengths of heavy and light wire. . . . finishing touches—a front seat, driver, and steering wheel—may be added. No tools are used; none but hammerstones are available. (pp. 64–65)

Adult-designed Toys and Play Space

The toy inventions described so far appear to indicate a high degree of resourcefulness, creativity, and ingenuity on the part of children who do not grow up in environments with vast numbers of manufactured toys and carefully designed playgrounds at their disposal. Unfortunately, there are few systematic studies of child-designed toys of Western, middle-class children, again because of the tendency for researchers to study these children in adult-structured environments, using adult-designed toys as stimuli for the investigation of particular types of behaviors (see especially the numerous doll play and toy preference studies, for example, Levin & Wardwell, 1971). That Western children use natural materials as well as their own toys in creative and imaginative ways is documented in fiction and biographies as well as in psychologists' "naturalistic" reports of their own children's activities (see Piaget, 1951), but there is no systematic research tradition here.

For Western and particularly for American children there are, however, a variety of studies of relationships between particular types of toys and/or play environments (generally adult-designed) and specific types of behavior. These studies reflect American researchers' (and parents') interest in improving the behavior of children by manipulating the external environment. Included are the early observation and experimental studies conducted in the 1930s examining the effect of particular types of toys on children's behavior. For example, Van Alstyne (1932) noted, in a study of preschool-aged children's use of play materials, that play objects such as dishes, dolls, wagons, and telephones encouraged conversation between children, whereas materials such as clay, scissors, puzzles, and books fostered a more passive type of cooperation. Parten (1933) also investigated the use and choice of play materials and play activities evidenced by a group of preschool children by using a one-minute time-sampling technique. She found that these children most frequently played in groups of two, that the size of the play groups increased with age, that two-thirds of the groups were unisexual, and that playing house was the most social type of play engaged in by these children (that is, it required complex social adjustments, negotiations, and cooperation), whereas sand play and constructive work with clay, paper, beads, and paints, involved the children in parallel and generally nonsocial play activities. A similar study conducted by Updegraff and Herbst (1933) suggested, however, that play with clay produced more sociable and cooperative behavior than play with blocks.

A more recent example of this particular type of approach appears in Doyle's (1976) use of the concept ecological niche in his study of American preschool children. He differentiates between *single-niche play settings* (those that encourage solitariness or competitiveness by the presence of props such as puzzles and bicycles) and *multiple-niche play settings* (those that foster sociality and cooperation by the presence of props such as teeter-totters). Doyle suggests that if preschools wish to emphasize sociality, cooperation, and sharing and to deemphasize antisocial behavior such as name-calling, competition, quarreling, and fighting, then the number of multiple-niche settings should be increased while the number of single-niche settings should be reduced. On the other hand, it could be argued that competition *is* a social skill in American society, and that a reduction in settings that encourage this behavior, while pleasing to teachers and reformers, is not in tune with current cultural realities.

It was also during the 1930s that investigations began of the effect of playground design on children's play activities. For example, Johnson (1935) found that playgrounds with less equipment encouraged both social contact and conflict among children, whereas playgrounds with more equipment encouraged individual play and discouraged both social contact and conflict. Since then there have been numerous studies of the effects of playground design and play material on children's behavior (for example, Gramza, 1970). One interesting study to mention in relation to the investigations discussed above is Scholtz and Ellis' (1975) examination of American 4- and 5-year-old children's preferences for toys and equipment *or* peers. The investigators found that after repeated exposure to a particular play environment (specifically designed toys and play equipment) the children became bored with the toys and increasingly preferred to play with their peers. Perhaps material objects, no matter how well designed, can never be as interesting or novel as the presence of another person.

American children's preference for sex-typed toys has been investigated by a number of researchers and the results are fairly predictable, with boys choosing (investigator defined) "masculine" objects such as soldiers or trucks, and girls choosing "feminine" toys such as dolls (see Garvey's 1977 discussion of these studies). One interesting study of this type is that by Rheingold and Cook (1975). They made an inventory of the private rooms of ninety-six children (aged 1–6) from American middle-class families and found that parents created sex-stereotyped environments for their children. For example, boys' rooms contained more toy animals and objects related to science (magnets, puzzles, spaceships), while girls' rooms contained more dolls (particularly female and baby dolls), as well as doll houses (equipped with stoves, tea sets, and so on, and frequently decorated with floral wallpaper, ruffles, lace and frills). Most striking of all was the difference in the number of vehicles found in boys' rooms (375) in comparison to girls' (17). None of the girls in this sample, no matter what their age, owned a wagon, bus, motorcycle, boat, or trailer. (Perhaps this suggests that girls, in the parents' opinion, are not going anywhere.) Rheingold reported, however, that in her laboratory young girls spent as much time as boys playing with trucks and other vehicles. It appears that these parents were creating environments that reflected their own interests, which were not necessarily those of their children.

The impact of sex differences on children's environmental competence as displayed in constructive play has been investigated by Saegert and Hart (1978). In this study of New England middle-class children, it was found that boys modified the landscape more frequently and more effectively than girls. Boys built physical structures more frequently than girls, and while some girls built houses, forts, and so on, they manipulated the environment less in doing so. Girls were more likely to modify spaces in their imagination, so that bushes became "walls," branches of trees were "shelves," and rocks were used as seats. Boys (after the age of 7) built forts, tree houses, and other structures with walls, windows, seats, and even roofs. When girls built such structures they did not create walls; instead they put considerable effort into the elaboration of the interior with drapes, bottles, pots, pans, and so on. Boys "made many more models in the dirt, manipulated streams with dams and channels, made and managed gardens, built sled runs and jumps, and in general made their mark on the landscape more than girls" (p. 163). Indeed, it is possible to see in this behavior (and in films that Hart has also recently made depicting some of these activities; see Schwartzman, 1978, pp. 336–37) a striking demonstration of the Western and American view of man versus nature. In this play building of dams and superhighways, skyscrapers and stripmining, we see both the creative and potentially destructive results of this worldview.

Anderson and Mitchell (1978), in a study comparing the type and number of toys in the possession of children from poor and wealthy families in Denmark at the turn of the century, found that there were indeed great differences between the groups. Poor children (rural and urban) possessed almost no purchased toys, while wealthy children had an array of such toys at their disposal, such as rocking horses, tin soldiers, wooden forts, dominos and other games, dolls, and trundle hoops. The authors found, however, that though they were able to document an enormous difference in the possession of purchased toys, these differences "implied few or no real differences in play habits" (p. 129). The reasons for this are several: (1) mechanical toys lost their novelty value quickly; (2) toys were made at home by parents for children or by children for themselves; and (3) much play took place without the use of toys or equipment at all.

Children from every milieu were accustomed to using whatever was at hand as props for playing. The leaves of fall, swept into piles on four sides, made a kind of room familiar to many. . . . Rich or poor, children played store, selling sand, pebbles, berries, and leaves for money made of paper. Rich as well as poor brought chestnuts home in the fall to polish and fit with toothpicks for the creation of farms and zoos. (p. 130)

The authors suggest that "when the use of purchased play material is examined in the context of materials and facilities as a whole, differences melt into practices shared by all" (p. 131).

The most interesting recent research on toys and their influence on behavior attempts to answer questions such as: Do minimally structured, highly ambiguous toys or objects produce more imaginative play actions (as opposed to some other form of activity), or does the reverse occur? What types of toys do children seem to prefer, minimally structured or highly structured objects? In a study by Pulaski (1970) it was found that children measured as high in fantasy using Singer's (1973) rating scales preferred minimally structured toys (such as clay and blocks), whereas children measured as low in fantasy preferred highly structured toys (such as dolls and trucks). Pulaski also reported that children aged 5–8 produced more pretend or imaginative stories when toys were minimally structured. In a Danish experiment, children were offered the choice of playing in either a room with mechanical toys or in one with simply building blocks. For the first few days, the room with the mechanical toys was the most popular; however, after that the children preferred the room with simple toys (Hegeler as reported in Anderson and Mitchell, 1978). In my own research of preschool children's imaginative play (see Schwartzman, 1976, 1978) in a Chicago day care center, I found, based on an analysis of twenty group make-believe play events collected during a two-month time period, that approximately 75 percent of the events involved the use of blocks in the construction of the event rather than the more structured and seemingly realistic doll house materials (for example, stove, refrigerator, chairs, table, tea cups).

Studies of younger children (2-year-olds), however, suggest that this relationship between minimally structured toys and imagination may be reversed. Fein (1975) analyzed play as the process whereby children make object and activity substitutions or transformations, for example the child pretends to drink from a cup, or pretends to feed a toy horse. Pretense is discussed here as a symbolic transformation that permits one thing to be treated *as if* it is another. Fein suggested that when objects are "highly prototypical" (a "cuplike" cup, or a detailed miniature representation of a horse) some transformational activity is still necessary in the play use of the objects. For example, a cup must be treated as if it is full, or an inanimate horse must be treated as if it is animate. However, when material is less prototypical, more substitution/transformations are required. In this study, she found that an easy transformation (toy animal to living animal) can support a more difficult one (empty shell to full cup) and that with such support the functional relation between two objects can be maintained. The principle appears to be that the process whereby one thing is used to symbolize another initially requires a relatively prototypical context which serves to anchor the transformation. (p. 295)

At this age, therefore, more structured toys (highly prototypical or realistic) appear to increase instances of pretending and to facilitate pretending with less-structured toys. Recent research (for example, Elder & Pederson, 1978; Mann, 1984; Ungerer, Zelazo, Kearsley, & O'Leary, 1981; Watson & Fisher, 1977) also supports the relationships suggested by Fein between developmental level, toy realism/nonrealism, and pretense in adult-structured environments.

Designs for Children's Play

I have examined a number of assumptions about play made by Western researchers and educators. There are other cultural givens that are not specific to play and games, but that nevertheless influence individuals involved with child development issues. The first, discussed some time ago by Margaret Mead (see Mead & McGregor, 1951), is the American and Western concern with fixing and improving children by manipulating the external environment, by providing the "right" materials and the "right" models for behavior. This is supported as well by a belief that "the conditions of living are improvable: materially, biologically, and socially. Improvement means betterment, and betterment means progress" (Hoebel, 1966, p. 499).

What I suggest is not that we should (or even could) shed our culture's concern with improvement, change, and design, but only that we recognize that: (1) an interest in design and improvement is itself situated in a cultural context; and (2) certain designs for play may teach children lessons that we may not wish them to learn.[7] It is for this reason that I have used cross-cultural research on child-structured play to question specific ideas about play and games that are now taken for granted by many researchers, educators, parents, and others. It is important to ask in formulating any type of design for play, including materials design and interactional design:

1. What type of play do the children for which this design is intended naturally engage in most frequently? What type of play will this particular design support—child-structured or adult-structured play? How does it do this?

2. Does the design promote resourcefulness, self-sufficiency, and self-organization? Or does it encourage reliance on adults or highly structured

toys, equipment, and space? Does the environment reward or frustrate a creative and inventive use of materials?

3. Does the design promote peer or multiage group play? Which experience do we wish to promote?

4. Is the design premised on any unexamined beliefs about what types of play specific groups (such as children from certain cultures or social classes) can or cannot engage in? How do these beliefs influence the design? What will this design teach children about themselves? What does it teach teachers? Parents?

5. Is the design premised on the idea that play should occur in a separate time and space from other activities? Does such a design support a sharp (and possibly artificial) dichotomy between play and work, or play and everything else? Do we want children to learn to divide activities in this fashion, or would it be better for children to learn that play and work are integrated? How (or can) play materials and environments "teach" either view?

I think that everyone involved with studies of or designs for chidren's play experiences a type of "be spontaneous" paradox (see Bateson, 1972) in their activity. How can we study, plan, or design for a type of behavior that is, in part, characterized by spontaneity but which paradoxically resists deliberate plans, design, and organization? How do we encourage playfulness without preempting it? How can we understand play without missing the point?

Notes

1. I have reviewed the nature and extent of child-structured play in a variety of cultural settings in more detail elsewhere (see Schwartzman, 1978, 1983). In these discussions, reports of child-structured play in Asia, Oceania, Central and South America, North America, Africa, the Near East, and Europe are considered.

2. For example, Feitelson notes that "during 12 months of observations in 75 households of Kurdish Jews, not a single instance of toy ownership was recorded" (1977, p. 9). A more problematic expression of this view is offered by Frank and Teresa Caplan (1973), who suggest that cultures without manufactured toys produce unimaginative children and adults and contribute to a lack of economic development. For example, they state that "if more Indian children were exposed to active free play with sturdy playthings, it is our belief that India may be able to put itself into the twenty-first century" (p. 233).

3. It is important to note here that I believe there is a tendency to define play and imagination by the presence or absence of objects (that is, toys) and this has led researchers to exclude consideration of other activities as play. Especially neglected is children's speech play, which is a well-developed activity among young children,

adolescents, and adults in many cultures (and requires no objects, manufactured or otherwise). This form of imaginative play will not be considered here but has been discussed in detail by Kirschenblatt-Gimblett (1976; also see Schwartzman, 1978, pp. 283–299).

4. It is interesting to compare these descriptions of Alorese children's creativity and ingenuity in play with suggestions made by Trude Schmidl-Waehner (a psycho-analyst who examined the children's drawings collected by DuBois) that there was evidence of poverty-stricken relationships and a noticeable lack of creativity exhibited in the drawings. The drawings were not natural to the children while the play, of course, was.

5. In the Fischer's (1963) ethnography of the New England community of Orchard Town, also in the Six Cultures series, there is mention of numerous organized group games and group activities in which the children take part (for example, Little League, Boy Scouts, church choir), as well as a description of the numerous manu-factured toys that all children have in their possession, including blocks, stuffed animals, miniature trucks and cars, tricycles, dolls and accessories, toy guns, soldiers, and board games. There is, however, no mention of any ingenuity or inventiveness displayed by these children in their play or toy creations.

6. Unfortunately, the majority of anthropological descriptions of toys and play and game objects are focused on implements made and used by adults in games (for example, dice, darts, rackets, shinny balls, and sticks). The classic study of this sort is Culin's *Games of the North American Indians* (1907).

7. These are generally lessons learned at a "deutero-learning" level as discussed by Bateson (1972); that is, they concern how and what one learns at a more implicit and abstract level in a learning situation. The Pavlovian dog learns to salivate when he hears a buzzer, but he also learns that he is operating in a fatalistic world where one waits passively for rewards rather than engaging in action.

References

Anderson, R.T., & Mitchell, E. 1978. Play and personality in Denmark. In M.A. Salter (Ed.), *Play: Anthropological perspectives.* Cornwall, N.Y.: Leisure Press.

Bateson, G. 1972. *Steps to an ecology of mind.* New York: Ballantine Books.

Caplan, F., & Caplan, T. 1973. *The power of play.* Garden City, N.Y.: Anchor Press/Doubleday.

Culin, S. 1907. *Games of the North American Indians.* 24th Annual Report, Bureau of American Ethnology. Washington, D.C.: U.S. Government Printing Office. (Republished in 1975, New York: Dover.)

Curtis, H.S. 1915. *Education through play.* New York: Macmillan.

Doyle, P.H. 1976. The differential effects of multiple and single niche play activities on interpersonal relations among preschoolers. In D.F. Lancy and B. Allan Tindall (Eds.), *The anthopological study of play: Problems and prospects.* Cornwall, N.Y.: Leisure Press.

Draper, P. 1975. Cultural pressure on sex differences. *American Ethnologist* 2:602–616.

DuBois, C. 1944. *Peoples of Alor.* Minneapolis: University of Minnesota Press.

Elder, J.L., & Pederson, D.R. 1978. Preschool children's use of objects in symbolic play. *Child Development* 49:500–504.

Fein, G. 1975. A transformational analysis of pretending. *Developmental Psychology* 11:291–296.

Feitelson, D. 1954. Patterns of early education in the Kurdish community. *Megamot* 5:95–109.

———. 1977. Cross-cultural studies of representational play. In B. Tizard & D. Harvey (Eds.), *Biology of play*. Philadelphia: Lippincott.

Feitelson, D., & Ross, G.S. 1973. The neglected factor—play. *Human Development* 16:202–223.

Fischer, J., & Fischer, A. 1963. The New Englanders of Orchard Town, U.S.A. In B. Whiting (Ed.), *Six Cultures: Studies of child rearing*. New York: Wiley.

Garvey, C. 1977. *Play*. Cambridge: Harvard University Press.

Gulick, L.H.. 1920. *A philosophy of play*. New York: Charles Scribner's Sons.

Harkness, S., & Super, C.M. 1983. The cultural structuring of children's play in a rural African community. Paper presented at the annual meeting of the Association for the Anthropological Study of Play, Baton Rouge, La.

Hoebel, E.A. 1966. *Anthropology: The study of man*. 3rd ed. New York: McGraw-Hill.

Jackson, E. 1964. Native Toys of the Guarayu Indians. *American Anthropologist* 66:1153–1155.

Johnson, M.W. 1935. The effect on behavior of variations in the amount of play equipment. *Child Development* 6:56–68.

Kirschenblatt-Gimblett. B. (Ed.) 1976. *Speech play*. Philadelphia: University of Pennsylvania Press.

Kluckhohn, C. 1949. *Mirror for man*. New York: McGraw-Hill.

Konner, M. 1975. Relations among infants and juveniles in comparative perspective. In M. Lewis and L.A. Rosenblum (Eds.), *Friendship and peer relations*. New York: Wiley.

Labov, W. 1972. *Language in the inner city: Studies in the black English vernacular*. Philadelphia: University of Pennsylvania Press.

Leacock, E. 1971. At play in African villages. *Natural History,* Special Supplement on Play, December:60–65.

Levin, H., & Wardwell, E. 1971. The research uses of doll play. In R. Hernon & B. Sutton-Smith (Eds.), *Child's play*. New York: Wiley.

Mann, B.C. 1984. Effects of realistic and unrealistic props on symbolic play. In T.D. Yawkey & A.D. Pellegrini (Eds.), *Child's play: Developmental and applied*. Hillsdale, N.J.: Erlbaum.

Maretzki, T., and Maretzki, H. 1963. Taira: an Okinawan village. In B. Whiting (Ed.), *Six Cultures: Studies of child rearing*. New York: Wiley.

Marshall, L. 1976. *The !Kung of Nyae Nyae*. Cambridge: Harvard University Press.

Mergen, B. 1980. Playgrounds and playground equipment, 1885–1925: Defining play in urban America. In H.B. Schwartzman (Ed.), *Play and culture*. Cornwall, N.Y.: Leisure Press.

Opie, I., and Opie, P. 1959. *The lore and language of school children*. Oxford: Oxford University Press.

———. 1969. *Children's games in street and playground*. Oxford: Oxford University Press.

Parten, M. 1933. Social play among preschool children. *Journal of Abnormal and Social Psychology* 28:136–147. Reprinted 1971 in R. Herron & B. Sutton-Smith (Eds.), *Child's Play.* New York: Wiley.

Piaget, J. 1951. Play, dreams and imitation in childhood. Translated by C. Gattegno & F.M. Hodgson. London: Routledge & Kegan Paul. (Originally published 1945.)

Pulaski, M.A. 1970. Play as a function of toy structure and fantasy predisposition. *Child Development* 41:531–537.

———. 1973. Toys and imaginative play. In J.L. Singer (Ed.), *The child's world of make-believe.* New York: Academic Press.

Rheingold, H.L., & Cook, K. 1975. The contents of boys' and girls' rooms as an index of parents' behavior. *Child Development* 46:459–463.

Saegart, S., & Hart, R. 1978. The development of environmental competence in girls and boys. In M.A. Salter (Ed.), *Play: Anthropological perspectives.* Cornwall, N.Y.: Leisure Press.

Scholtz, G.I.L., & Ellis, M.J. 1975. Repeated exposure to objects and peers in a play setting. *Journal of Experimental Child Psychology* 19:448–455.

Schwartzman, H.B. 1976. Children's play: A sideways glance at make-believe. In D.F. Lancy & B. Allan Tindall (Eds.), *The anthropological study of play: Problems and prospects.* Cornwall, N.Y.: Leisure Press.

———. 1978. *Transformations: The anthropology of children's play.* New York: Plenum Press.

———. 1983. Child-structured play. In F. Manning (Ed.), *The world of play.* Cornwall, N.Y.: Leisure Press.

———. 1984. Imaginative play: Deficit or difference? In T.D. Yawkey & A.D. Pellegrini (Eds.), *Child's play: Developmental and applied.* Hillsdale, N.J.: Erlbaum.

Shoemaker, N. 1964.. Toys of Chama (Eseejja) Indian children. *American Anthropologist* 66:1151–1153.

Singer, J.L. 1973. *The child's world of make-believe: Experimental studies of imaginative play.* New York: Academic Press.

Smilansky, S. 1968. *The effects of sociodramatic play on disadvantaged preschool children.* New York: Wiley.

Sutton-Smith, B. 1981. *A history of children's play.* Philadelphia: University of Pennsylvania Press.

Ungerer, J.A., Zelazo, P.R., Kearsley, R.B., & O'Leary, K. 1981. Developmental changes in the representation of objects in symbolic play from 18 to 34 months of age. *Child Development* 52:186–195.

Updegraff, F., & Herbst, E.K. 1933. An experimental study of the social behavior stimulated in young children by certain play materials. *Journal of Genetic Psychology* 42:372–391.

Van Alstyne, D. 1932. *Play behavior and choice of play materials of preschool children.* Chicago: University of Chicago Press.

Watson, M.W., & Fisher, K.W. 1977. A developmental sequence of agent use in late infancy. *Child Development* 48:828–836.

3
The Affective Psychology of Play

Greta G. Fein

Most of the notable developmental theorists have offered some peripheral observations about pretend play (see Rubin, Fein, & Vandenberg, 1983, for an overview). However, these theorists were primarily preoccupied with other aspects of development—the growth of convergent thought (Piaget), socialization of the mind (Vygotsky), psychosexual development (Freud, Erikson), the origins of schizophrenia (Bateson), mechanisms of arousal (Berlyne, Hutt), or symbolic interactions (Mead). For these theorists, play, in general, and pretend play, in particular, were not of central interest. Rather, a conceptual framework developed in one developmental arena was extended to an arena that the theory had not initially been designed to consider (Sutton-Smith, 1976).

With the exception of Piaget (1962), these theoretical extensions were not based on intensive study of pretend play as it develops in normal children. Theorists identified different aspects of pretense as they related to the theoretical perspective being advanced. A composite of these diverse theories conveys some sense of the multidimensional nature of the pretense and, therefore, a preliminary sense of what a theory of pretense must explain. However, this composite does not convey the force or intricacy of pretend behavior, nor does it provide a coherent or plausible account of the behavior.

Characteristics of Pretend Play

In one study, my students and I examined the pretend play of master players, that is, children who, in the judgment of their teachers and trained observers, engaged frequently in extended pretense with their peers (Fein, 1985; Fein, Kinney, & Lage, in preparation). We identified five characteristics or properties of pretend play that need to be considered in theorizing about the behavior:

1. *Referential freedom* designates the pretending child's relation to the immediate environment; in pretense, the child treats persons, objects,

or other aspects of the immediate setting as if they were otherwise or something else.

2. *Denotative license* refers to the loose and uncertain relation between actual pretend episodes and the child's own past experiences.

3. *Affective relationships* mean that pretend themes are about emotionally consequential aspects of living.

4. *Sequential uncertainty* indicates that pretend episodes often involve repetition with unexpected, moment-to-moment shifts of action, affect, and scene.

5. *Self-mirroring* involves a characteristic similar to recursion, a reflective mirroring of the self in relation to other selves as these are orchestrated and rendered by the players.

Previous theories of pretense have tended to stress one or another of these properties, and no theory has systematically addressed all of them. Nevertheless, an overview of these positions offers some insights regarding general explanatory issues. The purposes of this chapter are, first, to examine previous theoretical accounts of these aspects of pretense and, second, to outline some theoretical notions that might integrate current knowledge and pose questions for future research.

Referential Freedom

A pretending child might treat a stick as a horse, a shell as a cup, a doll as a real baby. In the following monologue, Alan, who is 2½ years old, treats the mop as a fishing pole and then as oars, the carpet as sea water, and a chair as a boat:

> I'm gonna get a fish [He dips the end of the mop to the floor and brings it up.] He got a fish, he got a fish, all by myself. I got me wet . . . in the hair. That's nice sea water. [He gets up and, carrying the mop, goes to the toy shelf where he picks up a toy broom.] I want to row. [He crosses the mop and broom over his head.] I got my boat over here. [He returns to the chair and extends the mop and broom onto the floor on each side of the chair.] Eee, ooh. I'm in my boat! [He now extends the mop and broom over the edge of the table.] I'm gonna get two fish, fish. [Yanking the mop up.] A fish! [He turns toward the caregiver.] This . . . this is your fishing pole. [He gives the broom to the caregiver.] (Fein, 1985)

How can this behavior be explained? One explanation holds that pretense simply reflects the child's confusion about the nature of things in the real world. In this view, the child who treats a stick as if it were a doll or a horse, a fishing pole or oars, is overextending the concepts of doll or horse, which are fuzzy and only partially formed in the child's mind. (Stern [1924] was the first to dismiss pretense as an epiphenomenon, a by-product of the child's hazy categorical boundaries.)

Representational theorists take a different view. Vygotsky (1967), for example, maintained that the child who treats the mop as if it were a fishing pole or an oar, far from being confused, is acquiring the ability to differentiate meaning from object. The action of rowing expresses the child's meaning of an oar as something to move a boat. Initially, the child "sees" a mental image of the actual object; the mop serves as a substitute for the object while referring to it. According to Vygotsky, the mop functions as a pivot separating the meaning of an object from the actual object.

K. Buehler (1930) responded to confusion theory with a provocative question: Would the child be surprised if the stick cried, or in the example above, if a real fish appeared at the end of the mop, or if the carpet was wet? Although Buehler's question has not been examined directly, there are other grounds for dismissing the confusion hypothesis. If pretense represents the child's confusion, substitutional behavior (that is, the tendency to treat one thing as if it were another) should decrease over the second and third years of life as the child's knowledge of objects becomes better differentiated. In contrast, if substitutional behavior reflects the child's emerging representational competence, this behavior would be expected to increase over this period. The extant evidence supports a representational position. Substitutional behavior increases during the second and third years of life (for laboratory studies, see Elder & Pederson, 1978; Jackowitz & Watson, 1980; Pederson, Rook-Green & Elder, 1981; Watson & Fischer, 1977; and for naturalistic studies, see Fein & Robertson, 1975; Kagan, 1981).

The confusion theory also implies that pretense in the early months is haphazard. Because the children are confused, they use whatever objects are available and show little evidence of discrimination or selectivity in their choices. Empirical observations, however, indicate that haphazardness is not a feature of pretense between 12 and 30 months. Studies of spontaneous play indicate that children as young as 18 months of age use dolls, people, and other play materials in a highly differentiated manner (Fein & Apfel, 1979; Fein & Moorin, 1984). Studies of language comprehension indicate that children as young as 13 months of age chose a named object correctly as often from a highly prototypical set as from a less prototypical one (Bretherton, Bates, McNew, Shore, Williamson & Beeghly-Smith, 1981). Further, with age increasingly less prototypical objects can be used in substitutional activities (for example, see Elder & Pederson, 1978; Pederson, et al., 1981; Jackowitz & Watson, 1980).

Other aspects of pretend behavior also conflict with the theory of pretense as confusion. For example, children as young as 12 months of age often communicate by gesture and expression an awareness of pretending (Nicolich,

1977). For another, children use a variety of sophisticated metacommunication procedures for organizing and coordinating the pretend play of their peers (Giffin, 1983). Chaille (1978), in an interview study, found that 5-year-olds had little difficulty discussing the role and object transformations of pretend play. Because this issue is a consequential one for a theory of pretense, other techniques, such as asking children to comment on video recordings of their own play, might be used to map the fine details of what children actually know about this behavior (Fein, 1985).

Referential freedom seems to mark children's representational competence rather than incompetence. One might even describe pretense as an orientation in which the immediate environment is deliberately treated in a divergent manner. Dansky (1980a, 1980b) offers evidence that spontaneous pretense is associated with a transformational set evokable by prior instructions or opportunities to play. Children who engage frequently in pretense respond convergently or divergently in a multiple uses test depending on whether such a set has been previously evoked. Further, children who pretend a great deal tend to be more sophisticated verbally, socially, and intellectually than those who do not (see Fein, 1981, and Rubin et al., 1983, for reviews of these findings). Pretense neither reflects the child's confusion nor leads to confusion.

Denotative License

Referential freedom refers to the pretending child's divergent relation to the immediate environment. By denotative license, I suggest that the playing child also adopts a divergent stance with respect to the actual experience. The pretend events generated by master players are inventions rather than documentaries of real-world occurences, a read-out of what the child feels might be (some of which may have been) rather than an accurate account of the child's knowledge of what is.

About four decades ago, Sears and his colleagues launched an extensive research program based on a correspondence theory of pretense (Sears, 1947). These investigators pursued the notion that because the content of pretense presumably reflected children's real life experiences, one domain could be used to predict the other. It soon became clear, however, that the relation between play content and children's real experience was more complex (Levin & Wardwell, 1962). Children who engaged in aggressive doll play with parental figures had all manner of real parent-child experiences. In some instances, play aggression appeared to reflect actual aggression directed by the parent toward the child: in others, it reflected fantasized experiences; and in still others, play aggression appeared to reveal the child's own inhibited aggressive impulses. When an empirical relationship between observable real world events and the events rendered in play could not be demonstrated, this first version of correspondence theory was abandoned.

A more recent version of correspondence theory holds that pretense represents children's knowledge of everyday events organized as scripts. Several important implications of this idea are discussed by Bretherton (1984). While children's practical declarative knowledge might well be organized in script-like structures similar to those proposed by Schank and Abelson (1977), the question is: Does pretense make use of a system designed to store practical, veridical representations of routine real world experiences? Further, do pretend scenarios necessarily represent events children have actually experienced or can they represent fabricated events?

A script theory approach implies that a pretend statement about a restaurant, for example, would be understood by the players as meaning "This is a restaurant, and everything we know of restaurants applies to the actions we are about to perform." When children pretend about a mother welcoming her child home from school, the episode would be understood to mean, "This is a mother whose daughter has just returned from school, and everything we know of mothers and daughters under these circumstances applies here." According to script theorists, pretend statements can be understood as statements of real-world events based on children's everyday experiencing of these events. Thus pretend scenarios can illuminate children's real-world knowledge.

Consider, however, the relationship between the symbolic signifiers produced in pretend episodes and that which these signifiers might denote. A pretend episode might be about a bad mother who is shot by the police (Giffin, 1983). Or, as in the following episode, it might be about a daughter chasing her dad with a knife, or, even more striking, a daughter chasing her dad with a pretend knife:

SALLY [*to Alison*]: Why don't you go and do your homework? You got any homework? You want to play with your teddy bear?

ELLEN: No, she's being a bad girl today.

ALISON: No, I didn't.

SALLY [*to Ellen*]: What did she do?

ELLEN: She picked up a knife. Was trying to kill her dad.

ALISON [*frowning*]: No, I didn't! I just maked a play one.

ELLEN [*warmly hugs and kisses Alison*]: That's OK, then?

In pretend episodes, children not only portray events they are unlikely to have experienced, but they also portray persons, families, and family relationships that are unlikely to exist. The powerful illusion created by these children rests on highly selective snatches from diverse sources blended into a representational potpourri. As Piaget (1962) noted, his daughter's pretense was "an inextricable medley of scenes from real life and imaginary episodes" (p. 128). Because of the apparent arbitrariness of these relationships, pretend episodes cannot be viewed as literal representations of particular persons, objects, situations, or exchanges. Contrary to expectations of script theory, children appear to exercise considerable denotative license in the meanings expressed in these pretend episodes (Genishi, 1983).

Another question posed by script theory concerns the conceptual status of these pretend scenarios. When children pretend, do they distinguish between scripts of real events and scripts of pretend events? Are pretended events likely to be remembered as if they were real events? If so, children's pretense would be expected to increase the participants' confusion about objects in the real world and about their own real experiences. Recent longitudinal studies of children's play behavior indicate that preschool children high in sociodramatic play are socially and intellectually competent preschoolers and continue to be so three and four years later (see Rubin, in chapter 10 of this book). There is no evidence that in normal children, pretend representations, no matter how counterfactual or counter-experiential, reflect or yield disordered thinking about real events.

Metacommunication theory, which introduces the idea of pretense as framed behavior, offers an interesting alternative to the correspondence theories described above. Bateson (1956), commenting on the denotative peculiarity of pretend play, noted that "The playful nip denotes the bite, but it does not denote what would be denoted by the bite." Consider the statement, "This sentence is false," or the two-part sequence, "The following sentence is false. The preceding sentence is true." Something in these statements jumps out and acts on itself. The meaning keeps recycling: "If true, then false; if false, then true," on and on without stopping. In Bateson's example, the self-referencing statement is placed within a frame: "All statements within this frame are untrue. I love you. I hate you." The first statement seems to point to the second two until one realizes that it also points to itself.

Consider the opening statements of the extended play episode between Ellen, Alison, and Sally:

[*Ellen, Alison, and Sally are on the rug. Charles is hovering nearby.*]
ELLEN [*to Alison*]: My daughter's at school.
SALLY: I'll go check. OK, Mom?
[*Charles takes a beanbag out of a bucket on the shelf.*]
ELLEN: Hey, no, that's for my daughter. She's at school.
[*Alison walks over to Ellen.*]
ELLEN [*cheerfully to Alison*]: Hi, daughter. Oh, you're a good girl. You're home now. [*To Sally*] I think they're having a fire out there.

The exchange among Alison, Ellen, and Sally illustrates the recycling of meaning referred to by Bateson. Remember that these children are really in school. That reality is declared false, except for one daughter for whom it is true yet not true, because school itself is sucked into the pretend frame. The scene and the roles established in this frame are untrue even as the players announce their intention to behave as if they were true, but untrue.

The play frame proposed by Bateson represents a kind of understanding in which "statements about statements of" inform the player that behavior within the frame are statements about behavior not statements of behavior. The engaging paradox is that these metacommunicative "statements about statements of" actually convey the message that play statements are themselves to be understood as "statements about statements of." The difference between psychotic and normal behavior resides in the individual's recognition of the distinction between out-of-frame and in-frame statements.

To illustrate, as the episode unfolds, Alison shifts from a baby to a school-age child to a baby as she is sent to bed, to school, and then to bed; Ellen transforms the beanbags into steaks, which she vigorously pounds as other children join the pounding in the role of mother-helpers. The theme is vaguely a family preparing supper and managing children, but themes and characters are fluid, shifting, changing, and repeating. The important contribution of metacommunication theory is the idea that the events rendered in pretense do not have a straightforward relationships to actual experience, even though they may be about experience.

Affective Relationships

Although divergent thinking is characterized by novel and original associations, most theorists exclude bizarre or inappropriate associations from their definitions of novelty and originality. In pretend play, however, there is often ludicrous distortion, exaggeration, and extravagance, at times bordering on the bizarre, revealing a considerable degree of affective force. Although psychoanalytic theory offers the only extant affective interpretation of pretense (for example, Erikson, 1977; Peller, 1954; Waelder, 1933), research within this perspective has been limited to the notion of catharsis (for example, Gilmore, 1966). In contrast, cognitive theorists have all but ignored the affective side of pretense.

Psychoanalytic theorists generally agree that pretend play is a response to internal or external demands. These demands may come from instinctual desires for gratification, from conflicts with the real world, or from conflicts with societal expectations. However, theorists disagree whether these demands come from specific past experiences and deprivations or reflect more contemporary and generic sources of anxiety. For example, Waelder (1933) is responsible for the traumatic theory of pretense in which "excessive experiences are divided into small quantities, reattempted and assimilated in play" (p. 217). These excessive experiences are specific, disturbing events (such as a painful visit to the dentist) that are repeated and thereby mastered in play. The traumatic theory of play thus offers a special case of correspondence theory in which emotionally distressing events are rendered in play.

Other theorists (Peller, 1954; Erikson, 1977) contend that play expresses the focal anxieties of a particular phase of libidinal development rather than particular life events. In Peller's view, these anxieties change with age. In the earliest years, children's concerns about the body are expressed in play themes that deal with skill and mastery. Alan's scene in which fishing poles yield fish and boats are rowed would be an example of such play. As children age these themes are followed by those dealing with the preoedipal mother; play themes render the all powerful mother who nurtures and restricts, leaves and returns. The children described earlier, who pretended about a daughter returning from school are using a theme drawn from the preoedipal period. The third phase of play reflects the child's oedipal anxieties. The episode in which dad is chased with a knife illustrates the emergence of oedipal themes. Erikson (1977) describes this position:

> The play themes of this age, however, often prove to be dominated by the usurpation and ambitious impersonation of victorious self-images and the killing off of weak and evil "others"; and we nominate for the principle inner estrangement which finds expression, aggravation, or resolution in childhood play the sense of guilt. . . . Thus we experiment with and, in a visionary sense, get ready for a hierarchy of ideal and evil roles which, of course, go beyond that which daily life would permit us to engage in. (p. 100–101)

It may be helpful to note that Ellen's mother and father are divorced and that her mother remarried a few weeks before this scene occurred. Ellen's visits to her father in a distant city are unhappy occasions. Alison and Sally, however, come from intact families. Yet these children readily grasp the import of Ellen's play proposal as Alison skillfully reminds Ellen that these expressions of feeling are only pretense. Whereas an angry encounter with father, or an arbitrary punishment imposed by mother, may have been the real life trauma from which this episode was constructed, the relation between a past event and a pretend episode need not preserve the literal correspondence proposed by Waelder (1933).

Here is an episode taken from the play of 5-year-old Milly that may be more in line with the notion of specific past experience:

[*Linda watches Milly who, decked in jewels and fancy clothes, is dressing the doll. Will, dressed in a man's sport jacket, walks up to them.*]

MILLY [*to Linda*]: That's my boyfriend. He comes in and out of the house sometimes. [*To Will*] Oh, honey! Oh, honey! [*Loudly*] You're gonna be late for dinner. You had enough work.

[*Milly, Linda, and Will chat.*]

MILLY: Telephone . . . [*She picks up phone.*] Hello! Hello! I think he's home. [*She looks at Will, but gets no response.*] I don't think he's home. [*To Will*] Honey, honey, telephone!

WILL: Who is it?

MILLY: I don't know. I don't know your people.

WILL [*takes the phone from Milly*]: Who are you? Oh, it's you again. I knew you were gonna do it. Want me to come over again? Yeah. Yeah.

MILLY [*yelling*]: Tell him you can't come tonight!

[*Will hangs up the phone.*]

While this episode has a feel of specificity about it, it lacks the feel of trauma. On the surface, the scene is about adult-adult relationships. Milly's play tends repetitively to elaborate a few core themes. One theme is body adornment; she spends much time changing from one fancy dress to another in the context of going on a date, shopping, to work, or just generally out. A second theme involves her baby, who she regularly, but anxiously and ambivalently, leaves with a substitute caregiver. The following episode illustrates these manifest themes and suggests the intricate emotional issues embedded in them:

[*Milly goes to the back of the housekeeping area, where she picks up a doll from the crib. She puts on a blue chiffon dress.*]

MILLY [*to Cathy*]: Oh, this is my baby. [*She cuddles the doll.*] Here, you have to put some food in here. [*She points to a lunch box.*] That's my baby [*looking affectionately at the doll in her arms.*]

[*Cathy and Milly sit on chairs in a secluded corner.*]

MILLY: Cathy, please. You're my daughter. He's [the doll] 7. Hear, Cathy? OK?

CATHY: I'm 8 already, and I married my father.

MILLY [*gently stroking Cathy's head*]: You're 8 years old. I've got to change my dress before I go.

[*Milly goes to the dress-up clothes. Jan enters the area.*]

JAN [*to Cathy*]: Where's she going now?

CATHY: She's going shopping.

[*Milly, who had put on a red and white dress, returns.*]

MILLY: I'm a movie star. I'm staying for the weekend and I have to go to work. [*Milly packs the lunch box.*]

MILLY [*to Cathy*]: You're going to the movie?

CATHY: No, I have to stay and take care of the baby.

[*Milly invites Linda, who was watching the play, to join the group.*]

MILLY [*to Linda*]: Want to be my daughter? [*Linda comes forward.*] OK, I have two daughters.

CATHY [*to the doll*]: You have to stay here, honey.

MILLY [*to Cathy*]: No, she's going with me. [*To Linda*] You like me? [*Linda nods. Milly turns to Cathy.*] Want to be our maid? Watch the baby if she poops or peepees.

[*Milly leaves and walks around the room for a few minutes. She returns to the housekeeping area and puts on a pink dress and a red nightgown over it.*]

MILLY [*to Cathy, who is sitting in a chair holding the doll*]: That's my baby.

CATHY: That's my baby. I'm the baby-sitter. I have to baby-sit her.

MILLY: It's still my baby.

CATHY: I'm not getting up [*sic*]. [*Milly walks away.*] OK, I'll get in [*sic*].

Even though vivid life experiences may find their way into pretend episodes, Peller (1954) would argue that these experiences are converted into symbols conveying deeper emotional meanings. These meanings reflect general, age appropriate anxieties that transcend particular life events. Recurring themes deal with physical mastery and appearance, separation and reunion, punishment and retribution, and more generally, with affectional relationships among parents, children, boyfriends, and siblings.

Unfortunately, attempts to examine psychoanalytic views have tended to dwell on the traumatic experience view (Gilmore, 1966). Some of the episodes generated by master players in our sample may have been about specific, obviously unpleasant, traumatic experiences (for example, illness). Others were about happy occasions (for example, weddings, dances, picnics, or family cook-outs). Most of the episodes were thematically fluid. Often these outer, topical forms seemed merely to frame more basic affective issues similar to those discussed by Peller, or perhaps, the visions of good and evil proposed by Erikson. Little systematic attention has been given to the notion that these affective issues reflect children's changing emotional preoccupations or to the possibility that pretense is associated with the regulation of emotion with regard to them (Fein, 1984).

Sequential Uncertainty

Garvey (1977) noted that children seem to have a repertoire of action plans that they use in pretend episodes. An action plan consists of a sequence of events or actions associated with particular roles in characteristic settings. One type of action plan might be "treating-healing" while another might be "averting threat." Once a plan is initiated, a fixed sequence of events unfold. Because this sequence is fixed, other players know what their actions should be. Consider, however, the following episode produced by four 6-year-olds:

[*Rosa, the patient, has received medical attention from Cara, the doctor, and nurses Marla and Terry, for about ten minutes. Quite unexpectedly, Cara makes the following announcement.*]

CARA [*dramatically*]: My patient is dying. Yes, I can see it. Nothing is getting warm in the body, and she's not moving. [*Rosa lies still with eyes closed.*] She's not jerking. She's not breathing. What shall we say to her parents? They're waiting outside.

TERRY: Shhhh. Let's keep quiet and pray to God. [*She clasps her hands and on bended knees whispers.*] Please, please God, save my friend. She's a good friend. Please, God, help us.

[*Terry tells Cara and Marla to close their eyes. She then mouths the numbers one to ten. At ten she looks at the patient with an expression of joy on her face. Jubilantly, she tells the others to open their eyes.*]

TERRY: See, the chest is s-l-o-w-l-y going up, up, down. God helped her to live again because we were all praying hard and we all worked hard. My mommy always says that God loves little children, you know.

Cara is one of the most sophisticated pretend players in our set of fifteen. Her play episodes are among the most orderly in the set. They are lengthy, accompanied by much verbalization and attention to detail. Note that Terry slipped out of the nurse role when praying for her friend. The episode ended with one of the nurses becoming Rosa's mother and the doctor and nurse recommending rest and good food for the patient at home.

In what sense does this episode illustrate an action plan? Having embarked on the theme of illness and treatment, either the patient gets well, dies, or stays the same. After a fairly long stretch of pretense at various treatments (which really dealt with relationships among the players-characters) the patient stayed the same. Cara, without warning or negotiation, introduced the drama of death. Terry's marvelous response to the emergency was also spontaneous, a case of healing considerably beyond the medical situation prevailing until that point. In this example, all possible variations of the action plan occurred: the patient stayed the same, died, and was cured.

Having initiated a particular theme, what outcomes would not satisfy the criteria of an action plan? Was this particular sequence implied by the theme or were other sequences possible? As Garvey notes, in accounting for this behavior, it is necessary to explain how children playing together know what to do next. In this particular episode, the children were skillful and verbal enough to use diverse metacommunicative devices to keep one another informed about what was happening (see Fein, 1985, for a more thorough discussion of sequential uncertainty).

The episode between Milly and Will was also among the most orderly generated by our master players. When one player answers the telephone, one of two things typically happen. Either the conversation establishes a shift in theme (for example, someone coming to the house for a visit or to deal with an emergency), or the telephone conversation itself becomes a focus of the play (for example, another player using a second phone or, as in this case, the call is taken by another player). Which ever the strategy, phone conversations often provide an ideal occasion for the type of metacommunicative devices described by Giffin (1983). In this episode, Will needed to receive the commanding "Honey, honey, telephone" to realize that Milly wanted the play at this point to be about the conversation. But when Will's conversation pointed to a shift away from the larger theme she was orchestrating (boyfriend at the house for dinner), she brilliantly forestalled the shift with a double-layered, in-role, theme-controlling statement.

In an earlier article (Fein, 1985), I argued that in pretense, sequences do not occur in a fixed order and new themes can replace old ones without disturbing the play. Play is joyfully disorderly. Alan did not need to represent his boat and oars before he caught his first fish. He had no qualms about walking on water to claim the oar. Similarly, in the dying patient episode, the sequences cover a variety of states, none essential or unalterable. The Milly-Cathy-Linda episode consisted largely of metacommunicative orchestrations of who was whom, who was coming and who was going. The notion of sequential uncertainty implies a bottom-up processing of pretend scenarios, a view markedly different from the top-down model of action plans proposed by Garvey (1977). Rather than a general action plan such as treating-healing," the previous episode was characterized by moment-to-moment improvisations; one circumstance gave rise to another and the play meandered through loosely connected notions about medical practices and professional relationships between doctors, nurses, patients, and their parents.

Self-mirroring

According to G.H. Mead (1934), the pretending child adopts a special stance toward the self. When children assume play roles, the events that unfold are essentially self-mirroring. In pretense, the individual looks at herself as a transformed self while retaining the core structure of a nontransformed self. At one level, children retain their customary identities, while at another level they respect one another's chosen identities. If Mead is correct, pretend play provides a vehicle in which the self, slipping outside the self, looks at the self. Mead believed that a self-mirroring system of this type implies the beginnings of conscious self awareness. Alan's uncertainty of perspective ("He got a fish, he got a fish, all by myself.") is a poignant reminder of the inherent difficulty of looking at the self without divorcing the observed self from the observing self (Fein, 1983). When mirrors were actually available to our master players, the mirror itself was incorporated into the play, as was the ubiquitous telephone.

Self-mirroring systems tend to produce what Hofstadter (1979) calls "strange loops." Escher, for example, drew a picture of a hand drawing a second hand drawing the first hand, a two-level loop in Hofstadter's system. Alison, pretending to be a child who pretends to attack her father, illustrates a three-level loop in the same system. One-level loops in which children pretend to be themselves (for example, sisters pretending to be sisters) also occur, but rarely. Another example (Mead, 1934) is that of a solitary child alternating in the roles of mother and baby, a relationship in which the child in the role of mother talks to the baby and then responds as the baby to what the mother has said. Even in the simplest loop, a representation of "I" is tied to a representation of "not I" that can only be understood in reference to "I."

The development of pretense as a self-mirroring system is examined in studies of the transition from self-directed pretense to other-directed pretense (see Fein, 1981, for a review of this research). Recently investigators have used Piaget's notion of decentration to describe this transition (Fenson & Ramsay, 1980). When pretense first appears, it is self-directed, for example children feed themselves out of an empty cup or put themselves to sleep. Later they perform these actions with a doll or a human partner. Many children at about this time will successively feed themselves, mother, and other adults in what Nicolich (1977) calls single scheme combinations. Interestingly, the child produces these single scheme combinations when play verbs (such as feed) are used, but not when nonplay verbs (such as give) are used (Fein & Moorin, 1984). If these behaviors mark the beginning of self awareness, then other behaviors thought to reflect this awareness would be expected to emerge, such as self-recognition or the recognition of possession (mine and yours) (Amsterdam, 1972).

A Theoretical Proposal

Let us suppose that the pretending child is aware that the meanings given to objects in the immediate environment are counterconventional and that experiences being rendered may be counterfactual insofar as they might never have happened. Let us also suppose that pretense is essentially an affective, expressive activity, different from other affective, expressive activities because it is about affective states, not a direct expression of these states. These suppositions have implications for the kind of representational system needed to account for pretense and for the way in which this system functions.

Finally, let's endow the playing child with a representational system keyed to detect, pick up, and hold vivid life experiences. These experiences may be real in the sense that they are derived from the circumstances in which appetitive or neural needs are satisfied. These affective experiences may also be imagined or derived from fantasies found on television or in books. Whatever the source or content, such experiences absorbed by the representational system are marked by intense feeling. Within this system, a separate template is reserved as a symbol of the self. This symbol, which mirrors the self as a pretend participant, conveys a consciousness of pretending.

This system is designed to represent affective relationships such as anger at, fear of, love for, approval of, or more subtle feelings about power and helplessness, safety and danger. These affective units record subjective rather than objective information about people, objects, or events in a real or imagined world. They record affective information about the emotionally consequential aspects of living, rather than declarative information about the real world, or procedural information about how to solve problems in the management of encounters with peers or adults. This record will provide clues about the child's inner world, but it will not reveal what the child's actual, observable world is like, what the child knows about this world, or what the child can do in it. Piaget (1962) similarly noted that this symbolism "provides the child with the live, dynamic, individual language indispensible for the expression of his subjective feelings" (p. 167).

Because this affective symbol system represents real or imagined experiences at a fairly general level, it permits the child to construct or reconstruct emotional moments by adding the particulars of persons, things, or occasions. Although play partners may have had little real experience with one set of particulars, they are able to understand general affective meanings and improvise the details as they go along. In fact, the details do not matter so long as they fit reasonably well with the affective meaning being expressed. In pretense, these affective symbolic units are manipulated, interpreted, coordinated, and elaborated in a way that makes affective sense to the players. These affect-binding representational units yield the motivated symbols, according to Piagetian theory, that are always present in pretense, from the infant's rendering of a physiological state in pretending to sleep, to the older child's rendering of intricate emotional overtones in pretending about being sent to bed.

These affective representational templates differ qualitatively and structurally from those associated with declarative and procedural knowledge (Mandler, 1983). The system plays no direct role in the acquisition or application of convergent knowledge. Rather, these affective structures store salient information about especially intriguing, troublesome, or celebrative encounters: gestures, statements, postural adjustments, tonal qualities, facial expressions, and patterned sequences that preserve the vividness of these encounters as they have been personally and even idiosyncratically experienced by an individual child. These templates may become elaborated when children play together. The assimilation rule seems to be: If the affect fits, take it in. Affective templates permit children to think about emotionally important things; pleasant things and nasty things, satisfying things and confusing things. In pretend play, children are thinking out loud and sometimes together about experiences that have emotional meaning for them.

This theory fits Bateson's analysis that the structures reponsible for pretense differ from those that guide children's practical encounters with the world. Pretend behavior reflects an intuitive, suppositional frame within which quasi-real or imagined events are constructed. This system is recursive in the sense that suppositions can be repeated as transformed suppositions preserving kernels of the original experience that in turn preserves crucial kernels of knowledge. As supposition, pretense functions as an interpretive-expressive system designed to manipulate representations without regard for the veridicality or plausibility of the represented outcome. As supposition, it can use exaggeration, absurdity, and distortion of original kernels of truth.

So far, I have suggested that a theory of pretense needs to posit a system able to conserve, manipulate, and reconstitute affective representations separated in some way from those used in practical affairs. In order to make this separation explicit, I will give the affective system a means for detaching pretend behavior from the actual and immediate internal and external environment. The baby who pretends to sleep is not actually tired and has no intention of falling asleep. The neural and physiological mechanisms responsible for sleep are not operating. Rather, the infant simulates a need state that is not being experienced directly. Once the psychological condition that permit such detachment—decontextualization—occurs, affective templates may be mapped onto aspects of the immediate environment, thereby yielding the referential freedom of pretense. The pretending child is able to separate the raw experiencing of affect from pretending about affect.

A somewhat different psychological condition must be posited to separate pretend signifiers from the representational system used to store practical real world knowledge. I use the term *uncoupling* to refer to the ideas that (1) pretense permits denotative license, and (2) children do not believe that their pretend episodes convey life as it is. The episodes children produce in pretense are not, except in pathological cases, mistaken for real life experiences. Decontextualizing alters the playing child's relation to the immediate environment; uncoupling alters the child's relation to actual experience.

In effect, I am proposing a double-layered system of representation, one for practical knowledge and another for affective knowledge. This double-layered system emerges during the third year of life as pretend sequences become increasingly marked by nonstereotyped, personal, counterfactual inventions. Furthermore, this affective system is essential for the individual to become conscious of an inner life and to gain control over its expression.

One developmental implication of this view is that pretense develops in a two-stage sequence. In the second year of life, pretend activities will express deeply felt experiences drawn from real life encounters. Thus the first pretend schemes to appear will express emotionally charged, state-dependent routines such as eating, and sleeping, rather than the more managerial routines such as dressing, bathing, or grooming. This expectation can be readily put to empirical verification. By the third year of life, greater incidence of absurdity and fantastic combinations appears, reflecting more constructive, less veridical themes. At this time the refrains described by psychoanalytic theorists will emerge.

The position I offer suggests other testable hypotheses. Although a system capable of responding selectively to vivid experiences is available to all human children, a dull life or a physical inability to experience life intensely will yield a system that is symbolically impoverished. Infants born with a limited affective range, who are sluggish or apathetic, are candidates for diminished pretense during the second or third years of life. These outcomes might be attenuated, however, if these infants are appropriately stimulated by parents or toys.

For normal children, the best way to diminish pretense is to discourage it. One discouragement is outright criticism. Another is by play interventions aimed at producing declarative or procedural knowledge. A child says, "I am feeding my baby coffee," to which the adult responds, "Babies don't drink coffee." In this exchange, the adult is rejecting the child's departure from real-life experience and, thereby, insisting that play symbols represent real events. Modeling increases the frequency of pretend activities in very young children (Fein, 1975; Fenson & Ramsay, 1980), and pretense increases when children play with their mothers. Further, children who play a great deal with their mothers are not necessarily those who play a great deal on their own (Dunn, chapter 9 of this book). The notions of decontextualizing and uncoupling suggests that the issue is not whether parents (or teachers) play with their children, but how. Social pretense is possible because the players know that the real world is not being represented in the play. They do not make literal demands on the play; they do not quibble about the details. One testable implication of this position is that play will terminate if children insist upon reality criteria, that is, if the suppositional frame is disrupted by the insertion of an external standard for evaluating the appropriateness of pretend enactments. While several investigators have noted that children occasionally negate one another's pretend proposals (Goncu & Kessel, in press), there is no evidence concerning the impact of these negations on the maintenance of play. In the view offered here, play will be disrupted if these negations involve an insistence upon adherence to real world standards.

The affective representational system used in pretense is not necessarily benign. If this system is improperly uncoupled from real world knowledge, affective templates may invade the system of practical representations and lead to misrepresentations of real life experience. If improperly decontextualized, the affective symbol system may disrupt the conduct of practical affairs. Because the affective symbol system may distort real life events or disrupt real world encounters, it needs to be sequestered from practical knowledge and consequential life activities. As children acquire these powerful affective forms, they must also learn how and when to use them. Pretend play may provide a medium for protecting this representational system while children acquire the forms of suppositional or divergent thinking needed to modulate their expression. Children who are skillful pretenders may become reflective responders to real life stress. The notion of sequential uncertainty also lends itself to empirical investigation. Suppose one took a sample of well-formed pretend episodes and presented teachers, parents or children with the first, second, third, or fourth quarters, or, progressively larger segments of an episode. Would these study participants be able to predict what happened next?

Finally, it is necessary to consider why master players find pretend play so appealing and why they sustain it for such lengthy periods. How might we understand pretense as an autotelic activity (Moore & Anderson, 1969)? Pretense provides an unusual opportunity for children to control their own emotional arousal and to maintain a level that is both comfortable and stimulating. In pretense, children are playing with feelings rather than experiencing feelings directly. As Erikson (1977) reminds us, this play is fragile; it cannot tolerate the loss of emotional control or a permeable boundary between the pretended affect and the real affect. The intrinsic motivation of pretense resides partly in the ability of pretending children to convert external sources of arousal into an internal, symbolic form, a variant of the epistemic arousal suggested by Berlyne (1966). Pretense is about emotion, decontextualized from immediate authentic gut responses and, importantly, uncoupled from the actual experiences and settings in which these gut responses are likely to occur.

In effect, the pretend frame contains and disciplines the expression of emotion even as it permits emotional meanings to be explored. According to affective theory, a difference is expected between the expression of emotion in real life situations and its expression in pretense. For example, emotional extremes of longer duration and greater intensity should occur more frequently in realistic play interactions than in pretend play interactions, an expectation readily put to empirical test. This behavior reflects an interpretive-expressive system designed to frame emotionally consequential aspects of living. When children pretend play they are playing with representations, misrepresentations, or rerepresentations of their own affective knowledge.

The theoretical framework described in this chapter and elsewhere (Fein, 1985) integrates several research areas, generates testable hypotheses, and identifies new areas of inquiry. While the particular theoretical fictions proposed here may need to be revised, refined, or abandoned in response to future research, attention to the affective power of pretense is long overdue.

References

Amsterdam, B.K. 1972. Mirror self-image reactions before age two. *Developmental Psychology* 5:297–305.

Bateson, G. The message "This is play." 1956. In B. Schaffner (Ed.), *Group processes: Transactions of the second conference.* New York: Josiah Macy Foundation.

Berlyne, D.E. 1966. Curiosity and Exploration. *Science* 153:25–33.

Bretherton, I. 1983. Event representation in symbolic play: Reality and fantasy. In I. Bretherton (Ed.), *Symbolic play: The representation of social understanding.* New York: Academic Press.

Bretherton, I., Bates, E., McNew, S., Shore, C., Williamson, C., & Beeghly-Smith, M. 1983. Comprehension and production of symbols in infancy: An experimental study. *Developmental Psychology* 17:728–736.

Buehler, K.Z. 1930. *The mental development of the child.* New York: Harcourt Brace.

Chaille, C. 1978. The child's conceptions of play, pretending, and toys; Sequences and structural parallels. *Human Development* 21:201–210.

Dansky, J.L. 1980a. Make believe: A mediator of the relationship between free play and associate fluency. *Child Development* 51:576–579.

———. 1980b. Cognitive consequences of sociodramatic play and exploration training for economically disadvantaged preschoolers. *Journal of Child Psychology and Psychiatry* 20:47–58.

Dunn J. In press. Pretend play in the family. In A. Gottfried (Ed.), *Play interactions: The contribution of play materials and parental involvement to children's development.*

Elder, J.L., & Pederson, D.R. 1978. Preschool children's use of objects in symbolic play. *Child Development* 49:500–504.

Erikson, E.H. 1977. *Toys and reasons.* New York: Norton.

Fein, G.G. 1975. A transformational analysis of pretending. *Developmental Psychology* 11:291–296.

Fein, G.G. 1979. Play and the acquisition of symbols. In L. Katz (Ed.), *Current topics in early childhood education,* Vol. II. Norwood, N.J.: Ablex.

———. 1981. Pretend play in childhood: An integrative review. *Child Development* 52:1095–1118.

———. 1983. The self-building potential of make-believe play: I got a fish, all by myself. In T.D. Yawkey & A.D. Pellegrini (Eds.), *Child's Play: Developmental and Applied.* Hillsdale, N.J.: Erlbaum.

———. 1985. Pretend play: Creativity and consciousness. In D. Gorlitz & J. Wohlwill (Eds.), *Curiosity, imagination, and play: On the development of spontaneous motivational and cognitive processes.* Hillsdale, N.J.: Erlbaum.

Fein, G.G., & Robertson, A.R. 1975. Cognitive and social dimensions of pretending in two-year-olds. ERIC No. ED 119806.

Fein, G.G., & Moorin, E.R. 1984. Confusion, substitution, and mastery. In K. Nelson (Ed.), *Children's Language* (Vol. 5). New York: Gardner Press.

Fein, G.G., & Apfel, N. 1979. Some preliminary observations on knowing and pretending. In M. Smith & M.B. Franklin (Eds.), *Symbolic functioning in childhood.* Hillsdale, N.J.: Erlbaum.

Fenson, L., & Ramsay, D.S. 1980. Decentration and integration of the child's play in the second year. *Child Development* 51:171–178.

Garvey, C. 1977. *Play.* Cambridge: Harvard University Press.

Genishi, C. 1983. Role initiation in the discourse of Mexican-American children's play. Paper presented at the American Educational Research Association, Montreal.

Giffin, H. 1983. The coordination of shared meaning in the creation of a shared make-believe reality. In I. Bretherton (Ed.), *Symbolic play: The representation of social understanding.* New York: Academic Press.

Gilmore, J.B. 1966. The role of anxiety and cognitive factors in children's play behavior. *Child Development* 37:397–416.

Goncu, A., & Kessel, F. In press. Preschoolers' play communications. In F.S. Kessel and A. Goncu (Eds.), Text and context in imaginative play. *New Directions for Child Develoment.* San Francisco: Jossey-Bass.

Hofstadter, D.R. 1979. *Gödel, Escher, Bach: An eternal golden braid.* New York: Basic Books.

Jackowitz, E.R., & Watson, M.W. 1980. The development of object transformation in early pretend play. *Developmental Psychology* 16:543–549.

Kagan, J. 1981. *The second year: The emergence of self-awareness.* Cambridge: Harvard University Press.

Levin, H., & Wardwell, E. 1962. The research uses of doll play. *Psychological Bulletin* 59:27–56.

Mandler, M. 1983. Representation. In J.H. Flavell & E.M. Markman (Eds.), *Cognitive Development,* Vol. 3 of P. Mussen (Ed.), *Manual of child psychology,* 4th ed. New York: Wiley.

Mead, G.H. 1934. *Mind, self, and society.* Chicago: University of Chicago Press.

Nicolich, L.M. 1977. Beyond sensorimotor intelligence: Assessment of symbolic maturity through analysis of pretend play. *Merrill-Palmer Quarterly* 23:89–99.

Moore, O.K., & Anderson, A.R. 1969. Some principles for the design of clarifying education environments. In D.A. Goslin (Ed.), *Handbook of socialization theory and research.* Chicago: Rand-McNally.

Pederson, D.R., Rook-Green, A., & Elder, J.L. 1981. The role of action in the development of pretend play in young children. *Developmental Psychology* 17:756–759.

Peller, L. 1954. Libidinal phases, ego development, and play. *Psychoanalytic study of the child* 9:178–198.

Piaget, J. 1962. *Play, dreams, and imitation in childhood.* New York: Norton. Originally published in 1945, English translation, C. Gattegno & F.M. Hodgson (London: Routledge & Kegan Paul, 1951).

Rubin, K.H. In press. Play, peer interaction, and social development. In A. Gottfried (Ed.), *Play interactions: The contribution of play materials and parental involvement to children's development.*

Rubin, K.H., Fein, G.G., & Vandenberg, B. 1983. Play. In P. Mussen (Ed.), Vol. 4 of *Handbook of child psychology.* New York: Wiley.

Schank, R., & Abelson, R. 1977. Scripts, plans, and knowledge. In P. Johnson-Laird & P. Wason (Eds.), *Thinking: Readings in cognitive science.* New York: Cambridge University Press.

Sears, R.R. 1947. Influence of methodological factors on doll play performance. *Child Development* 18:190–197.

Stern, W. 1924. *Psychology of early childhood.* New York: Holt.

Sutton-Smith, B. 1976. Epilogue: Play as performance. In B. Sutton-Smith (Ed.), *Play and learning.* New York: Gardner Press.

Vygotsky, L.S. 1967. Play and its role in the mental development of the child. *Soviet Psychology* 5:6–18.

Watson, M.W., & Fischer, K.W. 1977. A developmental sequence of agent use in late infancy. *Child Development* 48:828–836.

Waelder, R. 1933. The psychoanlytic theory of play. *Psychoanalytic Quarterly* 2: 208–224.

Part II
Play and Developmental Processes

4
The Developmental Progression of Play

Larry Fenson

Newborn babies enter the world with a range of reflexive behaviors, such as orienting, sucking, and startle responses. But they have no knowledge of the world they encounter. It is primarily through their playful transactions with people and objects that they gain information about physical and social aspects of their environment. At first, these transactions are mainly visual, due to infants' inability to control their hands and fingers. However, by about 5 months of age, infants gain the ability to retrieve objects within their reach. At that point, manipulative investigation begins to combine with visual exploration, vastly enhancing their range of sensorimotor experiences.

By the end of the first year of life, young children have made impressive strides in understanding the nature of the world. At that time, through pretend play, they begin to simulate features of their own experience to further explore the relation between themselves and other people and objects in their environment. The onset of pretend play, however, by no means signals the end of visual exploration and manipulative investigation. Each of these three types of inquiry continues to contribute to children's ever-changing conceptions of their world. To understand how these types of inquiry contribute to child development, researchers have found it convenient to look at each type in relative isolation. I have found it useful to respect these distinctions in this discussion. However, all three generally are linked together in the playing child.

Visual Exploration

Infants are visually responsive to their environment from the moment of birth, and over the course of infancy they acquire a great deal of information

Portions of this paper are adapted from L. Fenson and R.E. Schell, "The origins of exploratory play," to appear in *Early Child Development and Care,* special issue on play, edited by Peter K. Smith, 1985.

about the world solely through visual exploration of their surroundings. Research has produced ample information about changes with age in infants' abilities to visually process and remember information.

Newborn babies spend only a small portion of their waking time looking at the world about them. They are most likely to be visually attracted to stimuli showing high rates of change, for example, moving objects and pulsating lights. Infants' visual interests increase markedly at about 2 months of age, with a corresponding improvement in scanning and tracking abilities. These new skills enable infants to notice and inspect more subtle aspects of visual events, such as the moment of complexity or detail in a pattern.

As experience accumulates and memory ability improves from the rudimentary skills of the 2- to 4-month-old to the better recall capacities of the older infant, infants begin to respond to visual events not only in terms of their perceptual characteristics, but also their meaning. Photographs of human faces, for example, hold special interest for the child by 4 months of age. With further visual experience, infants begin to construct a variety of fundamental schemes or concepts. The increased ability to recall more precisely what has been experienced previously also enables infants to notice and study departures from the normal arrangement of features in a pattern. For example, by 6 to 9 months of age, infants will usually show heightened interest in a drawing of a face in which the features have been rearranged. They also begin to notice departures from a previously experienced sequence of events. For example, Kagan and his colleagues (Kagan, Kearsley, & Zelazo, 1978) had infants watch a series of trials in which a small car rolled down a ramp and knocked over a form made of colored balls. After a set number of these trials, a pin was inserted so that the form would no longer fall over when hit by the car. Children over 12 months of age typically noticed the alteration in the sequence.

In summary, over the course of the first year infants learn a great deal about their environment simply by looking at it. They begin to differentiate among objects in terms of color, size, shape, and other visually-related perceptual attributes. They begin to respond to meaningful properties of objects and subsequently to discrepant visual events.

Manipulative Exploration

Physical contact with objects enables the infant to acquire much more information about objects than by visual inspection alone. This vast new array of properties to which infants now gain access includes texture, weight, flexibility, and temperature, to name just a few. When infants handle objects they are likely to acquire new visual experiences as well. They see objects in motion and in changing positions, both as a result of their *own* actions. This combination of visual and manual exploration makes an inestimable contribution to infants' developing conceptions of the world. Some of the changes that occur in infants' manipulative exploration across successive age periods are described in the following sections.

Birth to 6 months

During the first few months of life, manipulative exploration is quite limited. Babies do watch their own hand movements, but they cannot coordinate their hands and eyes and are unable to reach out and retrieve things. However, from the earliest days of life, infants will grasp objects pressed into their palms and will watch the object as it comes within their field of vision. Long before the sixth month, infants learn to bring the objects within their grasp into their field of vision and to their mouths, generating another mode of exploration—oral investigation.

Although manual skill is quite limited during these first 5 to 6 months of life, infants will use whatever means are available to create or maintain interesting events. For example, infants will kick on a foot pedal (Watson, 1972) or suck at a rapid rate on a specially constructed pacifier (Siqueland & Delucia, 1969) to produce an interesting visual display. As suggested some time ago by Papousek (1967), young infants may produce even relatively uninteresting contingent events simply for the opportunity to exercise control over the environment. Infants' delight in controlling the environment is also reflected in their participation in early social games such as peekaboo (Watson, 1972).

6 to 12 months

From 6 months of age on, with mastery of visually-guided manual activity, manipulative exploration expands rapidly. By 9 months (Rubenstein, 1976) novel objects are selected and explored to a greater extent than familiar ones. Although infants will show more initial and sustained interest in a novel object at 9 months of age, they also may inhibit reaching for a novel object, taking time first to examine the object visually. This newfound inhibition reflected in infants' cautionary behavior at this age suggests the possible emergence of new control mechanisms (Schaffer & Parry, 1972).

What children do with an object, whether familiar or novel, once they have made contact with it also differs in 6- and 9-month-olds. For example, prior to 9 months of age infants tend to treat all similar-sized objects alike (Fenson, Kagan, Kearsley, & Zelazo, 1976). Objects that can be grasped may be banged on surfaces, pushed, twisted or turned, shifted from hand to hand, shaken, visually scrutinized with and without fingering and, whenever possible, brought to the mouth. Between 9 and 12 months, however, infants' manipulative behavior becomes more attuned to the specific features of an object, indicating more efficient extraction of information about the object. For example, Ruff (1984) found that infants of 9 and 12, but not 6 months of age, are more likely to rotate objects varying in shape, finger objects differing in texture, and shift from hand to hand as well as shake those objects varying in weight. There also is a corresponding decline in mouthing as the infant approaches 12 months of age (Belsky & Most, 1981).

Unlike visual exploration, object manipulation offers the possibility of feedback. Infants are most likely to play with objects that are reactive in some way to their manipulation. McCall (1974), for example, found that 8- to 11-month-olds showed the most interest in objects which were responsive to their actions, such as those with plasticity or sound potential. Variations in configural complexity alone, McCall found, exercised little influence on the infants' manipulative interest.

Toward the end of the first year, young children also begin to display interest in how things work, as evidenced by their growing fascination with such devices as light switches, push buttons, and hinged lids on boxes (Piaget, 1952; Fenson et al., 1976). This newfound mechanical interest refers not so much to cause and effect relations (such as the connection between a light switch and a lamp) but to the action of the device itself (the up and down positions of the light switch or the swinging action of a box lid). It is this latter, more focused interest in exploring mechanical devices per se which accounts for the allure of various types of "busy boxes" to young children around 1 year old.

12 to 36 months

There are two new developments near the beginning of the second year of life which alter infants' play in profound ways. First, infants begin to show awareness of the function or meaning of objects; that is, they begin to accommodate their actions to culturally prescribed properties of objects. For example, American infants might push a toy car, insert a key in a lock, and throw a ball. Because of their discovery and growing understanding of the functions of objects 12-month infants find more objects interesting, even those that are no longer novel or unfamiliar at a perceptual level.

Infants also achieve another major milestone near 1 year of age. They develop the capacity to jointly consider two or more objects and/or events (Fenson et al., 1976), which enable them to explore a wide range of interrelations among objects and events: functional relations, spatial relations, causal relations, and categorical relations. Each of these types of interrelations is readily illustrated by the play of 12- to 24-month-old children.

Attention to *functional relations,* for example, may be seen in young children's play with a tea set. They might place a cup on a saucer, a spoon in a cup, or a lid on a pot. Each of these actions not only requires knowledge of the appropriate functions of individual objects, but also the ability to interrelate two objects. Young children's successful experimentation with objects of graded sizes that fit into one another (such as nesting cups) and constructions with building blocks require attention to a variety of *spatial relations* (Foreman, 1982). Understanding of spatial relations develops in a progressive fashion. For example, children are able to duplicate a model formed by stacking one block upon another some time before they can duplicate a horizontal alignment of two adjacent blocks (Johnstone, 1981). Even duplicating the model of one block upon another, however, requires the child to consider the two blocks jointly. Children's developing appreciation of *causal relations* is often seen when they seek their mothers' assistance in various play activities (Piaget, 1952). For example, in asking mother's help in removing the top of a tin containing blocks, the child shows recognition of the relation between a means (mother's help) and a goal (access to the blocks). Finally, when young children in free play physically combine objects that are alike in some way, they demonstrate an ability to attend to *categorical relations* between objects. Typically, the first similarity relationships expressed by infants in free play occur at about 1 year of age or less and are based on perceptual likeness (Fenson et al., 1976; Starkey, 1981). In their second and third years, children show an increasing ability to match objects on the basis of functional and meaningful properties as well (Nelson, 1973; Sugarman, 1981).

Like visual exploration, then, manipulative exploration reflects the steady growth of cognition. As children develop an awareness of the functional-meaningful properties of objects and gain the ability to consider relationships, they become increasingly resourceful, thoughtful, and organized. As a consequence, they progressively learn to control and regulate their play environment rather than behave as a captive of the play setting.

As children move into the preschool years, their manipulative exploration expands into various forms of sensory and motor play. These forms of play include construction activities with blocks and clay, sensory activities with water and sand, and motor activities with vehicles and climbing equipment. These activities give young children an opportunity to explore the properties of materials, to test and develop the capabilities of their own bodies, and to gain an ever-increasing degree of mastery of their world.

Another popular form of sensorimotor play in the preschool years is drawing (and painting). Before age 4 years, children typically show more interest in the process of drawing than in the product. Later, they become increasingly interested in their products and devote much energy to improving their drawing skills. The practice play aspects of drawing and painting are often overlooked, while the clinical aspects are often overemphasized, especially in the preschool years.

Pretend Play

With the cognitive advances reached by the second year of life, children spend much time in mastery play, imposing an increasing degree of order on their world by identifying, comparing, and categorizing objects and events, and accumulating a vast amount of first-time knowledge about the world. At the same time, they begin to show another kind of play behavior that, at first glance, might seem at odds with the goal of mastery play. They begin to pretend, sometimes simulating and sometimes distorting reality. However, these pretend activities are invaluable in helping infants and young children understand physical and especially social features of the world.

In the earliest form of pretense, at about one year, young children simulate some of their own daily routines, such as eating, bathing, and sleeping. Over the course of the next few years, children expand pretend behaviors into the elaborate and whimsical make-believe play activities that seem to capture the very essence of early childhood. The first fleeting signs of whimsical pretense, however, may go entirely unnoticed, not only because they are somewhat ephemeral, but because they co-occur in time with two other major events—walking and talking. Nevertheless, the cognitive skills involved in these early pretend actions and those which follow have far-reaching implications for our understanding of both intellectual and social development. Because of these implications and interest, the developmental course of pretend play has been extensively researched.

Three trends characterize the way pretend play develops in young children. The first trend, termed *decentration* by Piaget (1962), refers to the young child's increasing tendency to incorporate other participants into pretend activities. The second trend, termed *decontextualization* by Werner and Kaplan (1963), refers to the child's increasing ability to symbolically transform objects and other aspects of the environment in the service of pretense. The third trend, which I call *integration,* refers to the child's increasing ability to combine individual actions into coordinated behavior sequences. Each of these trends, as discussed at some length by Bretherton (1984) and by McCune-Nicolich and Fenson (1984), finds its first expression in the pretend play of children during their second year of life. I will trace developments in each of these sets of skills from their onset into the preschool years.

Decentration

The child's earliest pretend acts, at about 12 months of age, are directed toward the self (Piaget, 1962) in the form of familiar schemes like eating and drinking from empty containers. The first decentered acts follow a few months later, in the form of actions directed toward animate and inanimate recipients (Fenson & Ramsay, 1980); for example, a child, might comb a doll's hair or pretend to feed a doll with an empty spoon. In these actions, the doll is treated as a passive, animate-like recipient. Children also begin to incorporate inanimate objects into their pretend play; for example, a child might stir a spoon in a cup or pour pretend tea from a pot to a glass. Earlier, children may direct such actions toward real persons (parents as well as peers), as an intermediate link between self-centered pretend acts and those directed toward animate-like but not truly animate objects (Fein & Apfel, 1979; Shimada, Sano, & Peng, 1979).

In these early instances of decentration, the child serves as the initiator or agent. Around 24 months, however, a new level of decentered actions emerges in children's play in which animate participants (dolls, stuffed toys) are regarded as agents in their own right, rather than as mere passive recipients of the child's actions (Corrigan, 1982; Lowe, 1975). Thus a child might seat a doll in front of a table setting and place a spoon in the doll's hand rather than feed the doll directly. Or the child might in some other manner orchestrate the doll's activities, in recognition of the doll's inferred potential to act independently.

Wolf and her colleagues, in studies examining replica play with dolls and other objects, describe how this form of play changes with age. In one such study, Rubin and Wolf (1979) found that children at first include themselves as actors in pretend skits. Later, in the third year, children become capable of carrying out pretend skits without their own direct participation. Rather, they may serve support roles as narrators or as the voices of animate-like replica participants. (See Wolf, 1982, and Wolf, Rygh, & Altshuler, 1984, for further discussions of these aspects of pretend play.)

Children's growing understanding of agency toward the end of their second year of life is also reflected in their social interactions outside of a pretend frame. Research by Bronson (1981) and Brownell (1982), for example, indicates a shift from physical contact and mutual play with objects during the first half of the second year to vocalization as a mediator of peer interaction during the later half.

The emergence of sociodramatic play, that is, pretend play with other children, in the preschool years both reflects and contributes to the continuing decentering process. In dramatic play with one or more partners, children must learn to take turns, to respond reciprocally to the social initiations of other children, and to assume a variety of roles. They must also learn to communicate about the ongoing play drama (what Bateson, 1972, terms metacommunication); that is, they need to signal when they are moving in and out of the play frame, when they are changing roles, and the like (Bretherton, 1984).

Garvey and Berndt (1977) have explored the richness of sociodramatic play, analyzing videotaped play episodes of pairs of 3- to 5-year-old children. In contrast to some prior studies (for example, Iwanaga, 1973), Garvey and

Berndt found role playing to be quite common even in the youngest children studied, although there were differences in the roles assumed by younger and older preschool children. Younger children usually assumed roles based on everyday reality while playing themselves or another child. Older children were able to assume the roles of other persons, as well as to engage in more diverse activities relevant to the role and to engage in more fantasy role playing.

The reader is referred to the excellent reviews of pretend play by Fein (1981) and Bretherton (1984) and to related chapters in Bretherton (1984) for further discussions of the structure and content of sociodramatic play in the preschool years.

Decontextualization

The first instances of decontextualization occur when the child uses a substitute object. The earliest type of substitution occurs at about 12 months when the child uses realistic replicas (such as a doll-sized baby bottle) in an appropriate manner. At about 18 months of age the child can substitute an object which resembles the intended object (Watson & Fischer, 1977). For example, the child may use a stacking ring as a donut. By the third year of childhood, children also show further advances in their ability to transform the physical environment in the service of pretense. For example, children become capable of using a highly nonprototypic substitute object in their pretend play (Pederson, Rook-Green, & Elder, 1981).

In their third year children also begin to create imaginary objects to support their play activities. Such imaginary objects may be symbolized either through gestures (for example, petting a pretend dog), words ("there's my little dog"), or a combination of gestures and words. Although children under 3 years of age may be able to symbolize imaginary or absent objects via gestures or words in response to verbal requests or modeled demonstrations (Elder & Pederson, 1978; Fenson, 1984; Jackowitz & Watson, 1980), this type of pretense does not become prominent in spontaneous play until well after the third birthday (Overton & Jackson, 1973).

Substitution, invention, and other transformations of reality (for example, adoption of fantasy roles such as Superman) become increasingly common in the preschool years (Matthews, 1977; McLoyd, 1980). It is typically in the child's fourth or fifth year that one of the most dramatic forms of symbolic invention takes place—the creation of an imaginary playmate. In one of the few studies of imaginary companions in the developmental literature, Manosevitz, Prentice, and Wilson (1973) analyzed questionnaires completed by the parents of 212 preschool-age children. The parents of 28 percent of the children reported that their child had at present or in the past one or more imaginary playmates. Firstborns accounted for 73 percent of the imaginary companion group and 49 percent of the nonimaginary companion group, lending support to the commonly held notion that such companions serve, at least in part, as a substitute for real playmates. Among other interesting findings: imaginary companions were reported to appear frequently (57 percent) or almost every day (23 percent), to appear when the child was happy and in high spirits (62 percent), and to provide peaceful companionship (81 percent). (Imaginary playmates had not disappeared by the time the questionnaire was completed for 57 percent of the sample, the disappearance being almost equally split between gradual fading away (50 percent) and abrupt departure (47 percent).

Integration

For most of the first two years of life, exploratory play often has a piecemeal quality about it as the child appears to drift from one object or activity to another, seemingly controlled by rather than in control of the objects or activities in the immediate environment. However, between 18 and 24 months of age, two types of linkage between successive actions appear in the child's play. The simplest type, first seen in spontaneous play at about 18–19 months of age, involve a single linkage theme (Belsky & Most, 1981; Fenson & Ramsay, 1980); for example, a child stirs a spoon in a pot, then in a cup, or feeds two different dolls in succession. These simple pairs, termed "single scheme combinations" by Nicolich (1977), are typically followed within six months (Fenson & Ramsay, 1980, 1981), by the appearance of a more complex type of action sequence. This type, termed "multischeme combinations" by Nicolich (1977), is composed of two or more different, interrelated schemes; for example, a child places a doll in a bed, then covers it with a blanket.

The first multischemes to appear in children's play are usually limited to no more than two acts in succession. Nonetheless, they signify an important new watershed in cognitive development, paralleling in time and perhaps in importance the transition from one- to two-word utterances in the child's speech. There is, in fact, some evidence that the emergence of combinatorial speech and combinatorial play reflect expression in different modes of the same underlying symbolic competency (McCune-Nicolich, 1981; O'Connell & Gerard, 1984; Shore, O'Connell, & Bates, 1983). This competency may involve a developing understanding of temporal relations. Thus, it may be no coincidence that children's first combinations in play and in language occur at about the time that they begin to recognize the various types of relations discussed earlier. Each requires the ability to recognize a link between two or more separate objects and/or events, whether that link be functional, spatial, perceptual, or temporal.

As a result of the expansion of sequential combinations in the third year, the child's play no longer looks like a collage of individual, unrelated actions.

Rather, children are more likely to pursue mini-themes in their play, requiring interconnected actions. Recently, Fenson (1984) studied the appearance of this continuity in play of children 20, 26, and 31 months of age, using three skits (preparing breakfast, bath time, and a visit to the doctor) with a doll as the central figure. The doctor scene, for example, went as follows:

> E feels the baby's forehead, says she is sick and needs to see the doctor. She is put in a wagon, covered with a blanket. E explains that he is "driving the baby to the doctor" as he pulls the wagon. E then says "here we are," takes the baby out of the "car," where she is approached by a teddy bear [the doctor] wearing a stethoscope. The doctor listens to the baby's chest, looks in her eyes and ears with his "light" [a wooden stick], pours imaginary medicine from a bottle to a spoon, and feeds it to the doll, before sending her home in the "car." At home she is put in bed and covered with a blanket.

Children in their third year not only incorporated more elements of the skits into their play than did the younger children, but also exhibited longer strings of interconnected actions reflecting a high level of organization in their pretend play.

Increasing integration also may be seen from the second year on in children's social interactions with their peers. At one year, social behaviors (smiles, gestures, vocalizations) usually occur singly (Hay, Pedersen, & Nash, 1982). By 24 months, children increasingly combine these social behaviors, for example, pointing and vocalizing at the same time (Bronson, 1981).

As children enter the preschool years, they begin to engage in more elaborate and integrated play episodes. These sustained play episodes are often organized around familiar scripts; that is, everyday routines such as mealtime, bedtime, or going shopping (Nelson & Gruendel, 1979). These familiar routines enable children to act on the basis of implicitly shared knowledge, thus facilitating cooperative dramatic play (Nelson & Seidman, 1984), as well as lending more coherence to individual play.

Summary

The lively forms of sociodramatic play in which preschool children delight represent the culmination of a variety of developments in social cognition. Social pretend play requires that children be able to communicate and metacommunicate, that they be able to fantasize, and that they be able to plan, take turns, and respond reciprocally to the actions of other children. The foundations for these abilities are established in the first 2–3 years of life, through children's exploratory activities, through their individual pretend play, and through their social interchanges with others.

References

Bateson, G. 1972. *Steps to an ecology of mind.* New York: Chandler.

Belsky, J., & Most, R.K. 1981. From exploration to play: A cross-sectional study of infant free play behavior. *Developmental Psychology* 17:630–639.

Bretherton, I. 1984. Representing the social world in symbolic play: Reality and fantasy. In I. Bretherton (Ed.), *Symbolic play: The development of social understanding.* New York: Academic Press.

Bretherton, I. (Ed.) 1984. *Symbolic play: The development of social understanding.* New York: Academic Press.

Bronson, W. 1981. Toddlers' behavior with agemates: Issues of interaction, cognition, and affect. In L. Lipsitt (Ed.), *Monographs on Infancy* (Vol. 1). Norwood, N.J.: Ablex.

Brownell, C. 1982. Development of role-taking ability in toddlers. Paper presented at the International Conference on Infancy Studies, Austin, Tex.

Corrigan, R. 1982. The control of animate and inanimate components in pretend play and language. *Child Development* 53:1343–1353.

Elder, J.L., & Pederson, D.R. 1978. Preschool children's use of objects in symbolic play. *Child Development* 49:500–504.

Fein, G.G. 1981. Pretend play in childhood: An integrative review. *Child Development* 52:1095–1118.

Fein, G.G., & Apfel, N. 1979. Some preliminary observations on knowing and pretending. In M. Smith & M.B. Franklin (Eds.), *Symbolic functioning in childhood.* Hillsdale, N.J.: Erlbaum.

Fenson, L. 1984. Developmental trends for action and speech in pretend play. In I. Bretherton (Ed.), *Symbolic play: The development of social understanding.* New York: Academic Press.

Fenson, L., Kagan, J., Kearsley, R.B., & Zelazo, P.R. 1976. The developmental progression of manipulative play in the first two years. *Child Development* 47: 232–236.

Fenson, L., & Ramsay, D.S. 1980. Decentration and integration of play in the second year of life. *Child Development* 51:171–178.

———. 1981. Effects of modeling action sequences on the play of twelve-, fifteen-, and nineteen-month-old children. *Child Development* 52:1028–1036.

Foreman, G.E. 1982. *Action and thought: From sensorimotor schemes to symbolic operations.* New York: Academic Press.

Garvey, C., & Berndt, R. 1977. Organization of pretend play. *JSAS Catalog of Selected Documents in Psychology* 7:Ms. 1589.

Hay, D., Pedersen, J., & Nash, A. 1982. Dyadic interaction in the first year of life. In K.H. Rubin & H.S. Ross (Eds.), *Peer relationships and social skills.* New York: Springer-Verlag.

Iwanaga, M. 1973. Development of interpersonal play structures in 3-, 4-, and 5-year-old children. *Journal of Research and Development in Education* 6:71–82.

Jackowitz, E.R., & Watson, M.W. 1980. The development of object transformations in early pretend play. *Developmental Psychology* 16:543–549.

Johnstone, J. 1981. On location: Thinking and talking about space. *Topics in Language Disorders* 2:17–32.

Kagan, J., Kearsley, R.B., & Zelazo, P.R. 1978. *Infancy: Its place in human development.* Cambridge: Harvard University Press.

Lowe, M. 1975. Trends in the development of representational play in infants from one to three years: An observational study. *Journal of Child Psychology and Psychiatry* 16:33–47.

Manosevitz, M., Prentice, N.M., & Wilson, F. 1973. Individual and family correlates of imaginary companions in preschool children. *Developmental Psychology* 8: 72–79.

Matthews, W.S. 1977. Modes of transformation in the initiation of fantasy play, *Developmental Psychology* 13:211–216.

McCall, R.B. 1974. Exploratory manipulation and play in the human infant. *Monographs of the Society for Research in Child Development* 39, No. 155.

McCune-Nicolich, L. 1981. Toward symbolic functioning: Structure of early pretend games and potential parallels with language. *Child Development* 52:785–797.

McCune-Nicolich, L., & Fenson, L. 1984. Methodological issues in studying early pretend play. In T.D. Yawkey & A.D. Pellegrini (Eds.), *Child's play: Developmental and applied*. Hillsdale, N.J.: Erlbaum.

McLoyd, V.C. 1980. Verbally expressed modes of transformation in the fantasy play of black preschool children. *Child Development* 51:1133–1139.

Nelson, K. 1973. Some evidence for the cognitive primacy of categorization and its functional basis. *Merrill-Palmer Quarterly* 19:21–39.

Nelson, K., & Gruendel, J. 1981. Generalized event representations: Basic building blocks of cognitive development. In A. Brown & M. Lamb (Eds.), *Advances in developmental psychology* (Vol. 1). Hillsdale, N.J.: Earlbaum.

Nelson, K., & Seidman, S. 1984. Playing with scripts. In I. Bretherton (Ed.), *Symbolic play: The development of social understanding*. New York: Academic Press.

Nicolich, L. 1977. Beyond sensorimotor intelligence: Assessment of symbolic maturity through analysis of pretend play. *Merrill-Palmer Quarterly* 23:89–99.

O'Connell, B., & Gerard, A. In press. Scripts and scraps: The development of sequential understanding. *Developmental Psychology*.

Papousek, H. 1967. Conditioning during early postnatal development. In Y. Brackbill & G.G. Thompson (Eds.), *Behavior in infancy and early childhood: A book of readings*. New York: Free Press.

Pederson, D.R., Rook-Green, A., & Elder, J.L. 1981. The role of action in the development of pretend play in young children. *Developmental Psychology* 17: 756–759.

Piaget, J. 1952. *The origins of intelligence in children*. New York: International Universities Press.

———. 1962. *Play, dreams, and imitation in childhood*. New York: Norton. Originally published 1945; English translation, C. Grattegno & F.M. Hodgson (London: Routledge & Kegan Paul, 1951).

Rubenstein, J.L. 1976. Concordance of visual and manipulative responsiveness to novel and familiar stimuli: A function of test procedures or of prior experience? *Child Development* 47:1197–1199.

Rubin, S., & Wolf, D. 1979. The development of maybe: The evolution of social roles into narrative roles. In D. Wolf (Ed.), *New directions for child development* (Vol. 6). San Francisco: Jossey-Bass.

Ruff, H.A. 1984. Infants' manipulative exploration of objects: Effects of age and object characteristics. *Developmental Psychology* 20:9–20.

Schaffer, H.R., & Parry, M.A. 1970. The effect of short-term familiarization on infants' perceptual-motor coordination in a simultaneous discrimination situation. *British Journal of Psychology* 61:559–569.

Shimada, S., Sano, R., & Peng, F. 1979. A longitudinal study of symbolic play in the second year of life. *Bulletin of the Research Institute for the Education of Exceptional Children,* Tokyo Gakugei University, Tokyo, Japan.

Shore, C., O'Connell, B., & Bates, E. 1984. First sentences in language and symbolic play. *Developmental Psychology* 20:872–880.

Siqueland, E., & Delucia, C.A. 1969. Visual reinforcement of non-nutritive sucking in human infants. *Science* 165:1144–1146.

Starkey, D. 1981. The origins of concept formation: Object sorting and object preference in early infancy. *Child Development* 52:489–497.

Sugarman, S. 1981. The cognitive basis of classification in very young children: An analysis of object-sorting trends. *Child Development* 52:1172–1178.

Watson, J.S. 1972. Smiling, cooing, and the game. *Merrill-Palmer Quarterly* 18: 323–339.

Watson, M.W., & Fischer, K.W. 1977. A developmental sequence of agent use in late infancy. *Child Development* 48:828–836.

Werner, H., & Kaplan, B. 1963. *Symbol formation.* New York: Wiley.

Wolf, D., Rygh, J., & Altshuler, J. 1984. Agency and experience: Actions and states in play narratives. In I. Bretherton (Ed.), *Symbolic play: The development of social understanding.* New York: Academic Press.

5
Play-Language Relationships: Implications for a Theory of Symbolic Development

Lorraine McCune

Relationships between symbolic play and language have previously been considered within the broader question concerning thought/language relationships and usually framed in terms of cognitive prerequisites for language. While approaches to this issue during the early 1970s assumed that nonlinguistic measures provided purer assessment of thought than linguistic measures, theoretical analyses (for example, Bates, 1979; Bates, Benvigni, Bretherton, Camaioni, & Volterra, 1977) have suggested that linguistic and nonlinguistic abilities reflect the same underlying cognitive structure. Equal in sophistication, they potentially have the same onset time. Thus, rather than certain cognitive milestones being prerequisite to language milestones, neither ability would necessarily precede the other. Where a given order in timing of development is predicted, this should be based on particular subskills required for the execution of that skill, but not the other (Fischer, 1980).

It is likely that more prerequisite skills and experiences, beyond the shared cognitive base, would be required for language production than for symbolic play. The shared cognitive basis for developments in these two domains is the ability to symbolize. Thus, assessment of play can be used to judge the child's nonlinguistic symbolic ability. But what additional capabilities characterize language skill? A model of language acquisition is needed which will include a number of dimensions, each of which can be assessed separately to yield an overall prediction for the onset of language and various subsequent language transitions. Individual variation on such dimensions should also be useful in accounting for cases where decalage between developments is greater than the moderate level predicted by the shared structure of play and language skills. Theoretically, it should be possible to propose a model for the set of necessary prerequisite skills and experiences which would lead to predictions across several months for particular language skills in

Portions of this chapter were presented to the New York Infancy Group, May 4, 1983, and the American Psychological Association Annual Meeting, Anaheim, Calif., August, 1983. Preparation of this chapter was partially supported by NICHD Grant No. HD 11731.

individual cases. We are actually aided in this by the broad individual differences in the onset of language events which span the age range of 10 to 30 months. Such prediction would be theoretically elegant, and empirically useful, as many babies not speaking by 24 months are now seen by speech/language pathologists, but at present there is no method, for example, to distinguish the 2-year-old who will experience a spurt in the next six months from the one who is in desperate need of intervention of some sort. In this chapter I will suggest an approach to the development of such a multidimensional model for language acquisition.

Theoretical Background

While I posed my original question in Piagetian terms, as Bates and Snyder (1983) noted in a recent review, there is no Piagetian theory of language acquisition. However, a theory harmonious with the cognitive–structuralist point of view has been specified by Werner and Kaplan (1963). In addition to cognitive structuring by the child, Werner and Kaplan emphasized the essential social basis of symbolization in addressor-addressee relationships. They described levels of increasing abstraction for symbols, but failed to articulate either cognitive or social processes to account for these developments.

Symbol Defined

According to Werner and Kaplan, the defining feature of a symbol is reference. They consider four components of symbolic reference: (1) the object "out there," (2) the internal analogue which represents the object, or the internal signified, (3) the internal analogue of the external expression (word or gesture) that is used to refer to the internal signified (that is, the internal signifier), and (4) the external behavior, termed the symbolic vehicle, which articulates this referent. This is diagrammed in figure 5–1. The arrows suggest that with development these components become more distant from one another, while becoming integrated in complex ways. Consideration of Piagetian-type stage transitions accounting for these developments would not be in conflict with the Werner and Kaplan perspective.

The Primordial Sharing Relationship

Similarly, the Werner and Kaplan emphasis on the adult partner in representation is not in conflict with Piaget's views, particularly concerning the decentration from the self and the importance of social transmission in cognitive development. As conceived by Werner and Kaplan, the infant and the adult caregiver share an initial relationship not unlike the positive symbiosis pro-

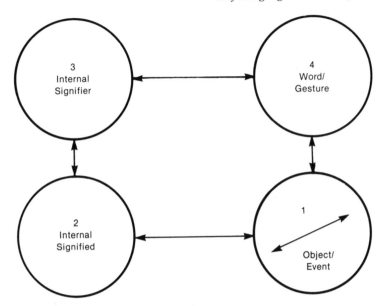

Source: Adapted from Werner & Kaplan, 1963.
Note: Arrows indicate increased distancing with development.

Figure 5–1. Symbolic and Social Aspects of Distancing

posed by Mahler, Pine, and Bergman (1975). As the baby becomes aware that there is an "other" and an object world separate from himself, he initially assumes that the perspective and consciousness of the other are identical with his own. As diagrammed in figure 5–2, with development comes a gradual emergence from this view, and a concomitant desire to continue shared reference which now can be accomplished by various external strategies, such as sharing objects, gesture, and eventually language.

Rationale for Play-Language Correspondences

In contrast with Werner and Kaplan, Piaget (1962) described symbolic development using play rather than language to exemplify successive developments. Furthermore, rather than proposing a continuous process, Piaget emphasized consolidation points yielding a stage-like description of symbolic developments. In addition, the underlying equilibration process involving increasingly complex accommodations and assimilations was invoked by Piaget as the explanatory mechanism for these successive developments, with less emphasis placed on the mother-child relationship as the source of symbolic progress. Despite these differences, a fundamental similarity in the organizing activity attributed to the child and the structural descriptions of

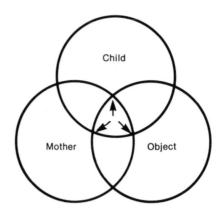

Source: Adapted from Werner and Kaplan, 1963.
Note: Arrows indicate increased distancing with development.

Figure 5–2. Symbolic and Social Aspects of Distancing

language (Werner & Kaplan, 1963) and play (Piaget, 1962) render these approaches complementary rather than conflictual. My (McCune-Nicolich, 1981) predictions concerning play and language correspondences were based on theoretical analyses of these play and language skills, as well as on pilot observations.

On theoretical grounds, I consider the child's expression of pretend action, where the pretend act represents the underlying knowledge of the usual corresponding real-life activity, to be equivalent to the use of a word to refer to internal knowledge of some entity existing in the object world. At this level, both the pretend action and the theoretically equivalent word make reference to a symbolized internal event or entity which is unanalyzed and global in nature. With development, objects and events are more fully analyzed so that in pretend play the child differentiates actions from actors and is able to portray pretend actions using other actors than himself (feed a doll rather than himself). The child should reflect similar differentiation by linguistic reference to parts and attributes of objects, in addition to continuing the more global event reference which characterized initial language. The effect of this development should be a sharp growth in vocabulary.

Once events can be analyzed into components, it is a reasonable step for the child to juxtapose pretend actions to form sequences and combine words to form verbal combinations. Eventually, the child becomes capable of constructing cognitive relationships between symbolic entities, thereby exhibiting planning in play and the regularities of syntactic structure in language. These hypothesized relationships are presented in table 5–1.

Table 5–1
Sequences of Symbolic Development as Expressed in Play and Language

Underlying Development	Play	Language
1. Association of event with habitual action	Recognition of objects	Prelanguage communication
2. Representation of global event as a unit	Self-pretend	Single words, global reference
3. Analysis of represented object/event	Differentiated pretend Pretend with dolls Pretend at others' activities	Reference to broader range Of entities, to parts Of entities, to states
4. Juxtaposition of symbolic elements	Pretend combinations	Simple language combinations
5. Construction of relations among symbolic elements Storage of complete event while component parts are organized	Planning Storage of symbolic goal while intervening steps are accomplished Keeping dual meaning of substitute object (e.g., block = doll) while performing doll-appropriate activities	Development of language rules Storage of complete message while component parts are organized

A Multidimensional Approach to Language Acquisition

Thus far I have described the process of symbol formation in psychological terms following the ideas of Werner and Kaplan (1963) and presented a rationale for expected correspondences between developments in symbolic play and language. A predictive model for language acquisition will have to go well beyond theorizing. The play-language correspondences can be considered a hypothesis subject to evaluation, and the social interactive process of symbolic development a set of assumptions or a working definition which might also be subject to empirical validation at some point. For the moment, however, it is useful to assume a process of cognitive development involving active construction on the part of the child in a manner described by Piaget's theory and a process of symbolic development which encompasses both cognitive processes and social interaction as proposed by Werner and Kaplan. The model therefore includes assumptions concerning cognitive and social processes which would involve both internal consolidation and experience. In addition, biological developments would influence and interact with these dimensions. Thus, biological developments can be considered experiential activities and cognitive construction fundamental dimensions to be evaluated in understanding and eventually predicting essential aspects of language acquisition. The influence of these dimensions can be conceptualized as follows.

Biological Development. With respect to language, brain developments are needed which will allow at least the following functions: (1) representation as described in figure 5–1, (2) articulation of vocal strings recognizable as words and sentences, and (3) maintenance of a relationship between internal representations and external vocal expressions. This could involve significant discrete reorganizations of functions at each language transition, single biological priming(s) allowing each function which may or may not occur together, or a process of relatively continuous biological change. Such reorganization(s) or their basic effects on brain function should be measurable in a manner independent of the linguistic and symbolic functions noted above.

Experiential Influence. Experiential influence affects expressive ability and cognitive construction opportunities in somewhat different but overlapping ways. Thus, some articulation practice via babbling should influence vocal expressive ability. Social experiences involving separation/individuation (Mahler et al., 1975), motivation for interaction, and interaction strategies would influence social participation in language.

Experiences influencing cognitive construction are those which facilitate the cognitive aspects of representation, involving two types of experience: (1) play with objects in both a symbolic play fashion and in a logical or combinatorial manner (for example, doing puzzles, grouping objects by kind, nesting cups); and (2) observation of and participation in events involving people which the child is able to internalize and use as a basis for cognitive consolidation of symbols and social events.

Cognitive Construction. The external manifestations of the Piagetian equilibration process, involving assimilation and accommodation leading to more advanced cognitive structures, can be observed to a degree in the child's behavior. For example, the circular reactions of the first year have their analogue in the second: completing an activity with variations and repetitions. Similarly, the changing role of imitation in language and play suggests such constructions. The cognitive constructive process, whatever its nature, is envisioned as the coordinating function which integrates experiential and biological aspects in a manner leading to qualitative change in language and symbolic function.

Interaction among the Dimensions. To understand how these dimensions interact to effect development, assume that each of the four transitions in symbolic development noted in table 5–1 has biological, experiential, and cognitive (constructive) aspects. Cognitive construction operating through experience requires certain biological readiness. For example, the onset of symbolic behavior at approximately 12 months of age requires the simultaneous observation of first words and first symbolic play acts. At 12 months major changes in behavior occur in a number of additional domains: at stage 6-object permanence, easily measurable attachment; at stage 5 means-ends skills, establishment of a preferred hand for bimanual tasks. If these changes are biologically driven in a necessary but not sufficient manner, it is unclear whether a single biological development in the brain potentiates all these skills, or whether separate biological contributions are needed for different skills. For example, one stream of biological development might lead to symbolization in action which would be sufficient for expression in symbolic play, object permanence, and gesture. Another type of brain development might be needed for control of articulatory skills needed for word formation. Assuming the relationships between hand preference, hemispheric specialization, and language, transitions in hand use might rely on the same biological transition(s) as articulatory control, for example bimanual handedness and variegated syllable use (Ramsay, 1980). Means-ends skills and attachment behaviors might be related to these biological changes but require different experiential components—the former, sufficient action on objects, the latter, sufficient social interaction.

Decalage in development could have its basis in (1) one or more differences in the biological basis of the two skills and potential time lags between these developments, (2) differences in the experiential bases and the extent to which such experiences were available, and (3) time factors for cognitive construction to operate in appropriate experience after the appropriate biological readiness had been achieved. It is also possible that cognitive construction based on experience is necessary to potentiate subsequent levels of biological transition, particularly where neural pathways are implicated.

If different biological transitions (usually closely linked in developmental onset) are required for symbolization onset and control of the articulatory apparatus and appropriate experiences in all relevant areas available so that cognitive construction would operate in a relatively equivalent fashion, both transitions might occur early, leading to correspondence in onset time of the two skills. Differences in timing of biological transition and/or experiential opportunities could lead to decalage. In an extreme case, several symbolic transitions might, over time, be potentiated at the biological level, while articulatory capability remained at a typical pre-12-month level until many months later. In this case a child might show age-appropriate symbolic play but lack appropriate language and display aberrant or absent vocal development. However, there would be nothing to prevent development of strong language comprehension skills leading to a sudden productive spurt when the missing biological transition(s) and sufficient vocal experience to be consolidated through cognitive construction were available, as in the example of children who remain nonverbal until 24 months or even later, then begin speaking in full sentences. A combination of earlier biological development allowing symbolization and hence constructive activity at the comprehension level, with delay in biological priming for articulation, would lead to such a pattern.

Strategies for Evaluating the Model

Ideally, given the assumptions of the present model, it would be useful to specify and measure relevant biological changes, make detailed prospective observations to determine whether and to what extent the appropriate experiences were available, then pinpoint the timing of transitions in the domains hypothesized as related. Lack of synchrony in timing could result because either biological transitions were more complex for one skill than the other (for example, speech requires articulatory control as well as representation, whereas symbolic play, only the latter) or some environmental anomaly occurs (for example, plenty of toy play leading to representation, but inconsistent caregiving leading to a lack of communicative skill with the available partners). For a child with some cognitive deficit, insufficient development of cognitive constructive processes as applied to one or another domain might also lead to delays.

Direct measurement of biological changes in the brain which affect development remain elusive. Therefore, strategies emphasizing behavioral measures provide the first steps for evaluating the proposed model. Such multivariate approaches at PATH analysis would be appropriate for large sample statistical evaluation of behavioral contributions of the model components. My own efforts to date have involved small longitudinal and moderate size cross-sectional samples, a simpler if somewhat less conclusive approach.

First to be examined is the extent to which the proposed correspondences in expressions of symbolic skills are supported. Given statistically reliable support for a correspondence, comparison can be made of discrepant cases where decalage between play and language is observed to cases of correspondence to determine which of the other sources of variation hypothesized in the model might characterize such discrepant cases. Sources of variation differentiating these groups then receive indirect support as necessary but not sufficient contributors to the missing skill. As noted earlier, additional, possibly biologically primed, skills are proposed for productive language beyond those proposed for symbolic play. In such longitudinal samples, play is expected to occur at the same time as or before the corresponding language milestone. In cross-sectional samples, cases of decalage favoring earlier onset of play to earlier onset of language is predicted.

Preliminary Data Supporting the Model

Recent longitudinal and cross-sectional studies offer evidence of the usefulness of this model. These studies, which bear on the development of combinatorial abilities in play and language, suggest how the model might be employed, rather than answer the question at hand.

Longitudinal Study

Five girls were studied longitudinally from early in the single-word period until their language became predominately combinatorial. Two transitions in play and language development were evaluated. All five subjects exhibited combinations in play either at the same time as or prior to using language combinations. Two children first exhibited play and language combinations in the same month, two with a lag between play and language of one and two months respectively, and the fifth child showed a single instance of play and language combinations at the first visit.

The second transition evaluated was that to rule-based combinations in language in relation to hierarchical combinations in play (level 5). As reported in McCune-Nicolich and Bruskin (1981), following the children's development of level 5 play, a number of related developmental shifts were observed in the children's language. Within two months after this transition, positional regularities (Braine, 1976) were first observed in their language combinations. This new combinatorial skill was also reflected in sharp increases in the number of different multiword utterances (types) used, and in mean length of utterance (MLU). In addition, general language capability was facilitated as reflected in large increases in frequency of speaking associated with onset of level 5 play. (See table 5–2.)

The time lag from the play to the language transitions in relation to the children's age and prior language experience illustrates the multidimensional model for language. Subjects 1 and 2, both 20 months old at the time of their level 5 transition, had shown high frequences of speech and some language combinations for two months prior to their level 5 transition. These subjects exhibited positional patterns immediately, as well as showing the other quantitative language changes. Subjects 3 and 4, both 18 months old at the level 5 transition, also exhibited increases in frequency of speech at that time. However, subject 4, a high frequency speaker, exhibited language combinations several months earlier than subject 3. This prior experience with language may account for subject 4's immediate increase in MLU at level 5 attainment, in contrast to subject 3's more gradual increase in MLU. Subject 5 was notable for a low frequency of both symbolic play and language behaviors in the course of the study. At 26 months of age, when her level 5 transition

Table 5–2
Language Changes Associated with Level 5 Play Onset

Months From Onset	Mean Length of Utterances					Total Utterances					Total Multiword Types				
	S1	S2	S3	S4	S5	S1	S2	S3	S4	S5	S1	S2	S3	S4	S5
−3	1.13	1.02	1.00	1.06	1.04	88	120	10	114	74	7	1	0	1	3
−2	1.14	1.07	1.00	1.00	1.11	92	83	71	108	89	5	5	0	4	7
−1	1.19	1.03	1.05	1.09	1.14	93	171	146	333	50	5	3	4	0	5
Onset	1.47	1.17	1.07	1.49	1.19	424	296	417	390	301	103	29	13	18	36
+1	1.89	1.54	1.03	1.72	1.31	317	372	149	439	218	111	97	3	95	38
+2	—	—	1.15	1.74	1.31	—	—	310	460	318	—	—	30	109	67
+3	—	—	1.62	1.84	—	—	—	384	384	—	—	—	104	120	—

Source: Adapted from McCune-Nicolich and Bruskin (1981).
Note: Ages at onset of level 5 play were as follows: S1—21.2 months, S2—19.3 months, S3—18 months, S4—18 months, S5—26 months.

occurred, she had had many more months of opportunity for language experience (although she seldom spoke) and maturation than the other subjects. However, like subject 3 (who was 8 months younger at the transition point), she exhibited immediate increases in frequency of speaking and number of word combinations and slow growth in MLU. The reason for this pattern is unclear. This subject was less interactive with both mother and examiner than the other subjects, suggesting an analysis of her social behavior as one approach to understanding this developmental pattern.

Cross-Sectional Study

Subjects included in this study were twenty-four middle-class children, evenly divided by sex, who ranged in age between 19 and 24 months. Symbolic play assessment was conducted in their homes using materials and procedures described by McCune (Nicolich, 1977). A language sample was obtained from these free play sessions in which each child interacted with the mother and a standard toy set. Assessment of mother-child interaction was conducted independently by a researcher who was unaware of the child's language or play status (as suggested by Adler, 1982). Determination of the child's hand preference was obtained independently using procedures described by Ramsay (1980). Intelligibility was assessed based on the proportion in a given language sample of vocalizations that could be identified as words during the transcription process.

Results revealed that the play levels (1 to 5) formed an ordinal scale (coefficient of reproducibility and scalability both equal to 1.0) when the two lowest levels were pooled (a necessary selection because some of the most advanced subjects failed to exhibit level 1). Results also supported the hypothesis of correspondence. Of the twenty-four subjects, one exhibited only single symbolic acts, eighteen exhibited combinations (level 4), and five exhibited both combinations and the more advanced level of play (level 5) characterized by prior planning of play behaviors. The subject who showed no combinations in play also failed to combine words. Of eighteen children who exhibited combinations in play, twelve showed corresponding combinations in language while six exhibited a decalage between these symbolic domains, a chi-square result significant at the .05 level.

As suggested by the multidimensional model for language acquisition, the eighteen subjects who showed level 4 play combinations as their highest level of play were divided into correspondence (twelve) and decalage (six) groups and compared for intelligibility of speech, quality of mother-child interaction, and hand preference. Separate Fischer exact tests revealed that the decalage group was characterized by a significantly greater number of children exhibiting unintelligibility of speech and one or more extreme features of mother-child interaction than the correspondence group. There was no significant difference between the groups in presence or absence of a hand preference.

These results, although extremely difficult to interpret, show the complexity of the issues involved. The six children who showed combinations in play but not in language differed from the remaining subjects in both intelligibility of speech and a number of social measures most consistently reflecting child behaviors. Thus, four of these subjects showed low frequency of extending objects to their mothers, and a partially overlapping four were low in contingent response to their mothers. Only one of the twelve subjects in the correspondence group showed each of these characteristics. Three of the six decalage subjects' mothers showed two of the following maternal characteristics: mother directive rather than facilitative, mother shows more frequent bids than child, mother shows stronger bids than child. Only one subject in the correspondence group exhibited this mother-directive pattern. Maternal directiveness, which has often been implicated as causal in slowing children's language development, could not have functioned in that manner here, because the five most directive mothers' children were distributed such that two were in the highest play/language group, one in the correspondence group, and two in the decalage group.

Various conclusions could be drawn from these findings. For the children low in intelligibility, biologically based poor articulatory control could be the cause of low frequency of speaking. The more active mothers in the group may be facilitating their children's development, such that without maternal leadership their response would be even less frequent than their present low-contingent output. Alternatively (but not likely), their mothers' intrusiveness deprived the children of vocal practice and led them to try to escape interaction by failing to respond contingently. Other interpretations are certainly equally plausible. Only longitudinal study and more comprehensive measures applied at the case level to a large number of cases will eventually allow prediction of language onset and transitions from other variables, such as interaction with mothers.

In summary, despite considerable work concerning cognition-language relationships in the second year of life, these relationships remain obscure, pending the resolution of at least three major issues. First, there has been an emphasis on cognitive prerequisite models which have been difficult to conceptualize and may prove too narrow to guide research (Bates et al., 1977). Second, in order to test models which go beyond correlation and evaluate structural correspondences across domains, one must be able to specify the sequence of development in both language and nonlanguage abilities, and propose theoretically sound correspondences (Fisher, 1980; McCune-Nicolich, 1981). Third, a realistic model for language acquisition must take account of other noncognitive variables influencing language, both biological and social, thus replacing simple cause-effect predictions with a more multidimensional approach. The model and results presented here suggest one approach to understanding language development which goes beyond the concept of cognitive prerequisites. In attempting to consider cross-domain correspondences in behavior with underlying symbolic developments, as this model suggests, it is essential to consider additional biological and social threads of development which contribute to language development.

References

Adler, L. 1982. Quality of mother-child interaction in relation to play and cognitive development. Unpublished doctoral dissertation, Rutgers University.

Bates, E. 1979. On the evolution and development of symbols. In E. Bates, L. Benvigni, I. Bretherton, L. Camaioni, & V. Volterra (Eds.), *The emergence of symbols: Cognition and communication in infancy.* New York: Academic Press.

Bates, E., Benvigni, L., Bretherton, I., Camaioni, L., & Volterra, V. 1977. From gesture to the first word: On cognitive and social prerequisites. In M. Linus & L. Rosenblum (Eds.), *Interaction, conversation, and the development of language.* New York: Wiley.

Bates, E., & Snyder, L.S. 1983. The cognitive hypothesis in language development. In I. Uzgiris & J.M. Hunt (Eds.), *Research with scales of psychological development in infancy.* Champaign-Urbana: University of Illinois Press.

Braine, M. 1976. Children's first word combinations. *Monographs of the Society for Research in Child Development* 41:(1), no. 164.

Fischer, K. 1980. A theory of cognitive development: The control and construction of hierarchies of skills. *Psychological Review* 87:477–531.

Mahler, M., Pine, F., & Bergman, A. 1975. *The psychological birth of the human infant.* New York: Basic Books.

McCune-Nicolich, L. 1981. Toward symbolic functioning: Structure of early pretend games and potential parallels with language. *Child Development* 52:785–797.

McCune-Nicolich, L., & Bruskin, C. 1981. Combinatorial competency in play and language. In K. Rubin (Ed.), *The play of children: Current theory and research.* Basel, Switzerland: Karger.

Nicolich, L. McCune. 1977. Beyond sensorimotor intelligence: Assessment of symbolic maturity through analysis of pretend play. *Merrill-Palmer Quarterly* 23: 89–101.

Piaget, J. 1962. *Play, dreams and imitation in childhood.* New York: Norton. Originally published 1945; English translation, C. Gattegno & F.M. Hodgson (London: Routledge & Kegan Paul, 1951).

Ramsay, Douglas S. 1980. Beginnings of bimanual handedness and speech in infants. *Infant Behavior and Development* 3:67–77, 1980.

Werner, H., & Kaplan, B. 1963. *Symbol formation.* New York: Wiley.

6
Intrinsic Motivational Aspects of Play Experiences and Materials

Adele Eskeles Gottfried

Intrinsic motivation concerns the performance of activities for their own sake, in which pleasure is inherent in the activity itself (Berlyne, 1965; Deci, 1975). Researchers have considered play to be an intrinsically motivated activity, and intrinsic motivation has often been a defining criterion of play (Neumann, 1971; Rubin, Fein, & Vandenberg, 1983). Yet, advancements in understanding the specific conditions which influence the development, manifestation, and experience of intrinsic motivation in children have important implications for children's experience of play as an intrinsically motivated activity. For example, play researchers attempt to clearly distinguish between play and instrumental activities (Rubin, Fein, & Vandenberg, 1983), yet this distinction may be blurred by the influence of expectations and consequences on play activities (see, for example, Lepper, Greene, & Nisbett, 1973). In this chapter, intrinsic motivation for play experiences and materials will be examined, and implications for the development of intrinsically motivating play experiences and materials will be made. A conceptualization of intrinsic motivation for play will be advanced.

Theories of Intrinsic Motivation

While there have been numerous theories of intrinsic motivation, the theories can be grouped into three emphases: cognitive discrepancy, competence (mastery), and attribution (A.E. Gottfried, 1983).

Cognitive Discrepancy

Cognitive discrepancy theories emphasize intrinsic motivation, which results from children's encountering stimuli that are discrepant from or do not match their existing cognitive structures. Children are motivated to reduce such discrepancies, and they may manifest curiosity, exploration, or play as a result.

Much research and theory about intrinsically motivated play has emanated from this perspective. Berlyne (1960, 1965) has provided a major impetus. According to his theory, stimulus properties such as novelty, surprise, incongruity, or complexity (called collative stimuli) can produce cognitive conflict, thereby increasing arousal above an optimal level. This arousal increase is aversive, and the individual is motivated to reduce the arousal level to the optimal level. These collative stimuli have arousal potential. The individual engages in exploratory behavior to learn more about the collative stimuli and hence reduce this arousal and cognitive conflict. Specific exploration (Berlyne, 1966) occurs in response to encountering a particular collative stimulus, as well as curiosity. Another type of exploration—diversive—occurs in response to levels of arousal potential that are below the optimal. This discrepancy is also aversive (and increases arousal), causing the individual to seek increased exposure to collative stimuli.

Hutt (1981) has identified specific exploration with exploratory behavior and diversive exploration with play. Considerable attention has been given to the distinction between exploration and play. Some researchers believe exploration and play are two distinct categories of behavior (Hughes, 1978; Hutt, 1970, 1981; Nunnally & Lemond, 1973; Wohlwill, 1984), although this distinction has been questioned by others (Weisler & McCall, 1976). Exploration is characterized as more focused, stereotyped, less joyful, and oriented toward learning about the properties of stimuli (Hughes, 1978; Hutt, 1981; Wohlwill, 1984), whereas play, involving children's own transformations of stimuli, is viewed as more variable, more relaxed, and occurring more readily with familiar stimuli (Hutt, 1981; Rubin et al., 1983; Wohlwill, 1984). Nunnally and Lemond (1973) proposed that exploration precedes play. Weisler and McCall (1976) asserted the separation of exploration and play may be difficult or the distinction artificial because (1) the child can alternate between the two, (2) some forms of play may involve unpleasant affect, (3) other forms of play may involve fantasy exploration, and (4) both play and exploration may involve acquisition of information. Wohlwill (1984) suggested that exploration and play exist on a developmental continuum, with exploration characteristic of infancy and play increasing as children cognitively develop.

Overlooked in this debate is the child's subjective experience of an activity as play or exploration, and his or her perception of each type of activity as intrinsically motivating. While this would be difficult to determine in infancy, in the preschool years these perceptions could be determined in response to varying stimulus and arousal inducing conditions. The literature on cognitive discrepancy, exploration, and play has been dominated by an attempt to categorize activities and to investigate specific stimuli that initiate investigatory and ludic behaviors. Yet, these distinctions may have little subjective value to the child. For example, seeking information and reduction of uncertainty (exploration) may be experienced as fun and play, while some forms of play, such as social pretend play, may be founded on affiliative rather than intrinsic motivation. While taxonomies of play have been proposed (Day, 1981; Hutt, 1981), intrinsic motivational value of play from the child's perspective remains undetermined.

Ellis (1984) conceives of play as stimulus seeking behavior to increase arousal. He contends that all collative stimulation can be reduced to novelty, with play representing stimulus-seeking, arousal-increasing behavior. Finally, response-produced variation has been proposed as an intrinsic motivational foundation of play (Rubin et al. 1983).

There is ample evidence that children, from infancy through childhood, attend more to stimuli with collative properties than to familiar stimuli. These stimulus properties include novelty, complexity, and incongruity (A.E. Gottfried, 1983; A.W. Gottfried, Rose & Bridger, 1977; Haywood & Burke, 1977; Nunnally & Lemond, 1973). This finding has been replicated across visual and tactual presentation modes. It has also been found that toys characterized by novelty (Mendel, 1965) and complexity (Ellis, 1984; McCall, 1974) are preferred or played with more by children. McCall (1974) has suggested that in infancy play behavior depends on an inverted U-shaped match between toy properties and developmental abilities (for example, cognitive). However, an inverted U-shaped match has not been substantiated in studies of preferences for stimuli (Wachs, 1977).

The major significance of the cognitive discrepancy view of intrinsic motivation for play behavior is in defining the stimulus conditions of play materials and play experiences which increase arousal and thereby create curiosity, enhance attention, facilitate cognitive processing, and maintain persistence in play. Novelty, incongruity, complexity, and surprise are prime candidates. However, problems emerge in considering the choice of play materials which yield cognitive discrepancy for a specific child. As yet, there are no parameters for matching toy or stimulus properties with specific cognitive abilities. To do this, stimuli would need to be designed to produce discrepancies for each child. Descriptions of developmental changes in play processes (Belsky, Garduque, & Hrncir, 1984; Fenson, Kagan, Kearsley, & Zelazo, 1976) could aid in the selection of play materials that may produce cognitive discrepancies. Taxonomies of play (Day, 1981; Hutt, 1981) could also provide dimensions for matching types of play materials with types of developmental experiences.

In the curiosity and intrinsic motivation literature, multidimensionality has been a major finding. For example, curiosity and exploration are not unitary, global traits, but rather have multidimensional components (Henderson & Moore, 1979; Kreitler, Zigler, & Kreitler, 1974; Vidler, 1977). This indicates that children's curiosity and exploration show low interrelationships across a variety of tasks. My own work on intrinsic motivation has shown multidimensionality in the school context. I have developed an inventory called the Children's Academic Intrinsic Motivation Inventory (CAIMI) which measures children's intrinsic motivation for learning (academic intrinsic motivation) in the subject areas of reading, math, social studies, and science (A.E. Gottfried, 1985). My research reveals that children's intrinsic motivation for school learning is differentiated into these subject area components, which relate specifically to children's perceptions of competence in corresponding subject areas. Overall, intrinsic motivation research is characterized by findings indicative of multidimensionality (A.E. Gottfried, 1983).

Integrating the results of the research on cognitive discrepancy models of intrinsic motivation, the multidimensional nature of intrinsic motivation, and the difficulty of assessing matches between toy properties and children's development, I propose that the most facilitative, cognitively discrepant environment for the play of infants and young children is one characterized by variety of stimulation. This would include toys, stimuli, people, and opportunities for experiencing a variety of play modalities. Variety of stimulation in children's environment has been shown to be positively related to young children's cognitive development (A.W. Gottfried & A.E. Gottfried, 1984; Ulvund, 1980), and play relates to cognitive development in infancy (Belsky et al., 1984). In research on the home environment (A.W. Gottfried & A.E. Gottfried, 1984), variety in home stimulation was found to be a consistently positive and unique predictor of cognitive development from infancy through early preschool years. Hence, in infancy, motivational conditions which facilitate cognitive development may also facilitate play. Children's play activities would be observed for evidence of boredom to provide feedback for changing the environment. Variety of environment and stimulation would maximize the opportunity for cognitive discrepancies to occur and collative stimulus properties to be available. Further, the transitions between exploration and play would be facilitated by variety of stimulation. Variety could also provide familiar experiences which have been proposed as important for pretend play (Fein, 1981) and to initiate diversive exploration in play.

In summary, the cognitive discrepancy approach to intrinsic motivation provides a direction for investigating stimulus conditions influencing play, and for refining objective distinctions between exploration and play. Still unresolved is the concept of multidimensionality of intrinsic motivation in relation to play, and the inability to predict for any individual child which specific experiences are important for play experiences and materials. Provision of variety of stimulation is likely to enhance play activities. Further, children's perceptions of whether an activity is play or exploration, and their perceptions of intrinsic motivation of these activities, would be useful in clarifying the relation between specific stimulus conditions and children's play activities and motivation.

Competence

According to the competence or mastery perspective, children play in order to experience effectance in their environment. A number of theorists have contributed to the view that play provides mastery experiences for children. White (1959) provided a foundation for such theories in proposing that children seek to interact effectively with their environment, which yields feelings of mastery. The motive is intrinsic since there is no external reward which must occur. White specifically exemplified play as a mastery-oriented activity. Bruner (1972, 1973) proposed that play provides an arena whereby new combinations of actions can be tried without concern for consequences. Implicit in his conception is a motive to achieve mastery. Piaget (1962) proposed that in practice play infants repeat their behaviors, not to learn or investigate, but for the joy of mastery and display of power.

A central theme pervading the mastery view of intrinsic motivation is the concept that the child experiences himself or herself as a causal agent of outcomes in the environment (Hunt, 1981; Piaget, 1962; White, 1959). Children who perceive themselves as influencing the environment are more likely to be mastery motivated than those who do not.

Another central theme is that the environment should be responsive to the child's activity in order for him to experience mastery. Hunt (1981) has elaborated on this in his studies of children in an Iranian orphanage, where those whose caretakers responded to their language were more responsive to adults and appeared happier than children for whom this responsiveness did not occur. Hunt concluded that a responsive environment (both animate and inanimate) is important for children's development of intentionality, initiative, and trust. This permits the child to become an active agent in his own development.

Harter (1978a) suggested that mastery is facilitated by optimally challenging experience. While she did not refer to play, the concept of challenge may be important to mastery in play since children may set their own level of challenge for such activities. Differentiation of mastery motivation into components has been proposed by White (1959) and elaborated by Harter (1978a). With development, mastery motivation in play may become differentiated as certain play activities are sought or avoided as a result of differential feedback from the environment. Further, mastery motivation is positively related to feelings of self-efficacy and self-worth. In relation to school tasks, intrinsic motivation has been shown to be positively related to perceptions of competence (A.E. Gottfried, 1985). In my own research, children who were more intrinsically motivated in a school subject area were also more likely to perceive themselves as competent in that subject. In reference to play activities, the experience of mastery in the environment is likely to be related to perceptions of competence about cognitive and social activities which are practiced in play and generalized beyond the play setting.

In the mastery view of intrinsic motivation, stimuli play less of a determining role than the child's interaction with the stimuli. The child may produce novelty or complexity in order to explore their consequences (Bruner, 1972; White, 1959). Hence, motivation derives from the child's activity, which strives toward effectance, rather than from a motive based on arousal reduction. The child's perception of mastery in the environment plays a critical role in his or her play activities; central nervous system arousal reduction is not a component of this form of intrinsic motivation.

Research investigating competence intrinsic motivation has supported the view that children are motivated to master their environment. There has been a great deal of interest in mastery motivation during infancy. One problem with investigating mastery motivation in infancy is that it is difficult to distinguish between motivation and cognitive abilities (Ulvund, 1980). In infancy, mastery motivation is displayed, or inferred, through cognitive or sensorimotor performance.

From infancy through childhood, there is evidence that experiences which facilitate the child's ability to control the environment are related to future learning as well as pleasure with the experience of control. For example, it has been shown that not only were 8-week-old infants able to learn to turn their heads to control a mobile, but they also showed more smiling and cooing compared with infants who could not control the mobile (Watson, 1971). Finkelstein and Ramey (1977) found that 4- to 8-month-old infants who had prior experience with contingent stimulation which they were able to control subsequently more readily learned a discrimination task requiring control of stimulation than infants who received an initial noncontingent stimulation experience. Learning to control the environment may be a process in the development of mastery motivation, and through such contingency experiences children may actually become more competent in controlling the environment.

Pleasure in producing an effect on the environment has also been demonstrated in older children (Nuttin, 1973). Five-year-olds who controlled a machine's onset of lights with a lever preferred this machine to one with programmed lights.

There is evidence that a stimulating and/or responsive early environment is related to mastery motivation in infancy. Yarrow and colleagues have studied mastery motivation through persistence in play behaviors. Responsivity (feedback) of toys at 6 months was significantly related to persistence at 13 months (Yarrow, Morgan, Jennings, Harmon, & Gaiter, 1982) and to production of effects and continuity of play in 12-month-olds (Jennings, Harmon, Morgan, Gaiter, & Yarrow, 1979). In several studies, parental stimulation was related to infants' persistence. Maternal provision of kinesthetic and auditory stimulation at 6 months was related to persistence at 13 months (Yarrow et al., 1982); parental provision of tactile, kinesthetic, and motor stimulation related to persistence problem-solving at 6 months for children of both sexes, and at 12 months for boys (Yarrow, MacTurk, Vietze, McCarthy, Klein, & McQuiston, 1984). Variety of cognitive-oriented caretaker activities was positively related to persistence in infants (Gaiter, Morgan, Jennings, Harmon, & Yarrow, 1982). Belsky et al. (1984) found that home environment, as measured by the HOME inventory, was positively related to 12- to 18-month-old infants' highest spontaneous developmental level of free play, and these correlations were higher than those between the HOME and elicited play, indicating that home environment was related to motivation in self-regulated play activity. Attention focusing by mothers has been found to be causally related to infants' play competence and exploration (Belsky, Goode, & Most, 1980). In an intervention study, Riksen-Walraven (1978) found that infants whose mothers were taught to provide responsive stimulation contingent on their children's activities showed greater exploration of a novel object compared to infants whose mothers were taught to provide stimulation, but not contingently.

Mastery motivation and cognitive measures have been found to be interrelated in infancy. Mastery motivation measures were positively related to the Bayley Mental Development Index both contemporaneously (Yarrow et al., 1982) and longitudinally from 6 to 12 months (Yarrow, McQuiston, MacTurk, McCarthy, Klein, & Vietze, 1983). Jennings et al. (1979) found that cognitively mature play was positively correlated with Bayley scores.

In elementary school children, difficulty level of tasks appears to relate to mastery experiences. Difficulty level of puzzles was related to a greater amount of smiling (Harter, 1977). Humor has been related to cognitive challenge (McGhee, 1984; Zigler, Levine, & Gould, 1966). In my research (A.E. Gottfried, 1985), I found that children's enjoyment of difficult and challenging school tasks, as measured by the CAIMI, was positively related to school achievement and negatively related to anxiety. Challenge has also been recognized as a component of intrinsically motivating educational and computer games (Malone & Lepper, in press).

Generalizing to play, challenge and difficult level may become important ingredients of mastery motivation for play activities. Csikszentmihalyi (1975) views play as the experience of flow in which a balance between challenge and skill occurs in a self-selected activity. Eiferman (1972) has offered a challenge theory of games in which mastery emerges if the participant is able to adjust the degree of challenge to his abilities. Challenge appears to be an important ingredient of intrinsic motivation of play for older children. The extent to which challenge and difficulty are important for the play of infants and younger children needs further investigation.

In summary, mastery, or competence, provides an important aspect of intrinsic motivation for play experiences and materials. Responsivity of play materials appears to be a consistent finding related to mastery motivation in play from infancy through childhood. While environmental stimulation from caretakers appears to relate to mastery motivation, it is unclear as to whether this stimulation needs to be responsive to the young child's actions since research indicates that both contingent and noncontingent caretaker stimulation enhances or relates to mastery motivation. Challenge is a dimension which may be more characteristic of mastery motivation in the play and games of older children but which needs to be investigated as a motivational dimension for young children as well. Overall, play experiences which provide the child with a sense of control and feedback contingent upon the child's activities are likely to be those which enhance mastery motivation. Social, object, and symbolic play would all be included.

What appears to be missing from the literature are studies of specific play activities and environmental responses that produce differential experiences of mastery motivation in children. Persistence and pleasure could be measured in relation to such activities across a wide developmental span. Causal relationships are in need of determination.

Attribution

Research concerned with this aspect of intrinsic motivation has focused on the distinction between intrinsic and extrinsic motivation. Extrinsic motivation is external to the pleasure inherent in task activity. Any activity may be perceived as either intrinsically motivated, or performed for an instrumental reason (such as to receive a reward or other contingency that is not inherent in the activity). Intrinsic motivation is a product of the perception, or attribution, by the individual about the causes of his/her activity. Consequences to the individual as a result of engaging in the activity influence the attribution of the relative degree of intrinsic or extrinsic motivation. Play, therefore, would not immediately be viewed as an intrinsically motivated activity. Rather, whether play is perceived as intrinsically motivating depends on the attributions of the child as to why he/she is playing. Play could be engaged in for instrumental reasons (for example, peer approval, affiliation, competition) whereas nonplay activities may take on play-like qualities when they are experienced as fun or interesting. The attribution perspective on intrinsic motivation has received the least attention in the play literature, yet there are significant implications for play which emerge.

There have been a number of theorists and numerous studies supportive of attribution views of intrinsic motivation. The research has focused predominantly upon the effects of rewards on intrinsic motivation. In general, the research indicates that when children attribute the cause of their behavior to their own efforts, competence, or self-selection of goals, intrinsic motivation is likely to be enhanced. On the other hand, when children attribute the cause of their behavior to external influences such as rewards, or parental or teacher demands, rather than their own efforts, then intrinsic motivation is likely to be diminished. de Charms (1976), Deci (1980), and Lepper (1983) have proposed the existence of this distinction in attribution of causality as related to variations in intrinsic motivation. There have been some exceptions to these findings which merit discussion as well.

Early research indicated that rewards had an undermining effect on intrinsic motivation. Lepper, Greene, and Nisbett (1973) found that nursery school children who expected and received a good player award for engaging in an intrinsically interesting activity (drawing with felt pens) subsequently played less with that activity during free play in their classroom than children who received no award or who unexpectedly received the award. Lepper et al. (1973) termed this negative effect of the expected reward the overjustification effect, meaning that when children are offered an external reward for performing an intrinsically interesting activity, their intrinsic motivation declines because they attribute their interest to the reward rather than to their own behavior. They will engage in the task less on subsequent occasions when the reward is no longer available.

More recent research shows that rewards do not always decrease intrinsic motivation. The effects of rewards depend on such factors as the type and purpose of the reward and the child's initial interest in the activity. In some instances, reward may increase intrinsic motivation. Much of the research investigating the influence of rewards on intrinsic motivation has measured intrinsic motivation as the amount of time spent on an activity in a free choice setting after having been offered an external reward for performing that activity. During the free choice period no reward is available.

In a study of the relative effects of money, symbolic reward (good player award), and verbal praise on 4- and 5-year-olds' intrinsic interest in drawing with felt pens, Anderson, Manoogian, and Reznick (1976) found that verbal praise increased intrinsic motivation and money and the symbolic award decreased intrinsic motivation on the posttest in a free play setting. Dollinger and Thelen (1978) found that different rewards had different effects on intrinsic motivation for maze performance in preschool and young elementary school children. In this study, verbal praise and a good player award given contingently upon competent performance did not decrease intrinsic motivation, whereas a food reward and a self-administered good player award did. The negative effect of self-administration of the reward was interpreted as drawing attention to the reward rather than to the task itself. In other research, children's intrinsic motivation has been found to be negatively affected by rewards made contingent on engaging in a task, but not based on task competence (Swann & Pittman, 1977); visible salient rewards (Ross, 1975); rewards given for activities of initially high intrinsic interest (Loveland & Olley, 1979; McLoyd, 1979); and choice and surveillance of the activity by an adult (Lepper & Greene, 1975; Swann & Pittman, 1977). On the other hand, increased intrinsic motivation has been found when rewards are administered for tasks of initially low intrinsic interest (Loveland & Olley, 1979; McLoyd, 1979).

A few studies have examined the effects of rewards on the complexity or difficulty of the task chosen in a free choice setting. Harter (1978b) found that sixth graders chose significantly easier anagrams to solve when they were given a letter grade for their performance compared to children who were told that the anagrams task was a game. Pittman, Emery, and Boggiano (1982) found that second graders who had received a good player award for playing a shape matching game, played with a simple version of the game significantly more than children who had received no reward. Condry and Koslowski (1979) also reported that rewards may result in children's choice of easier tasks because correct solutions—and reward delivery—are more likely. However, all of these findings need to be viewed with some caution since it is not known how various rewards, such as praise which conveys competence, affect children's engagement in difficult tasks.

These research findings indicate that rewards have complex effects on intrinsic motivation, and whether a given reward increases or decreases intrinsic motivation depends on the meaning it has to the child. Explanations concerning the diverse effects of rewards on intrinsic motivation suggest that it is the influence of the reward on children's perception of competence, or on their self-determination in choosing the activity, that influence subsequent intrinsic motivation (Deci & Ryan, 1980; Lepper, 1983; Pittman, Boggiano, & Ruble, 1983). Rewards that enhance these perceptions tend to facilitate intrinsic motivation. Verbal praise appears to encourage intrinsic motivation because it draws children's attention to their competence. Findings by Boggiano and Ruble (1979) support the view that competence information enhances children's intrinsic motivation. On the other hand, when rewards tend to emphasize the child's perceptions that the reason for his or her task activity is to receive a reward rather than satisfy one's own interest or self-determination of goals, and when this reward imparts little information about competence, then the child's intrinsic motivation for the task declines; and task activity declines when the reward is no longer available. Therefore, the particular type of reward may be less important than the way that reward is used.

It is not clear that preschoolers are able to use the same reasoning as older children to understand the abstract and complex influence of rewards on intrinsic motivation (Kassin, 1981; Lepper & Gilovich, 1981). Morgan (1984) has suggested alternative explanations which may be relevant for younger children, such as cognitive scripts (for example, if somebody promises a reward, the task is uninteresting). Regardless of this developmental difference between younger and older children, the effects of rewards on intrinsic motivation have been found to be similar across the ages.

The age range of subjects for these studies have generally begun with preschoolers. Yet research could be conducted with younger children by observing their persistence in play or choice of play activities subsequent to differential consequences. The generalization of the attribution literature to play activities needs to be empirically determined. Most of the research has focused on play in school settings, or learning tasks. The effects of external consequences on exploratory play, ludic play, or games (Hutt, 1981) needs to be established in nonschool settings. The manner in which various consequences may interact with collative stimuli and mastery opportunities needs to be established. The issue of which consequences would have varying effects, such as those from peers or parents, needs examination.

Developmental level and type of play activity may be moderators of the attribution of play as intrinsically motivating. While it is unlikely that attributions of intrinsic motivation occur in infancy, consequences of play activities may be influential. The development of intentionality in infancy may be related to rudimentary perceptions of play as intrinsically motivating versus play as an instrumental activity due to consequences of infants' play activities. In preschool years and thereafter, rewards and other contingencies would be expected to influence perception of play activities as intrinsically motivating. There may be some types of play which are more vulnerable to extrinsic contingencies than others. For example, using Hutt's (1981) taxonomy, it would be possible to determine the effects of consequence conditions on epistemic and ludic play, or games with rules. Perhaps high arousal collative stimuli or mastery opportunities would interact with consequences and rewards.

Day (1981) has investigated attributional qualities of intrinsic motivation for play and nonplay activities. He has studied the distinction between playfulness and workfulness across a variety of activities (leisure through work) in subjects ranging from the elementary years through adulthood. Day's results indicated that almost all activities have characteristics of both playfulness and workfulness, including leisure activities, and he further proposed that the playfulness and workfulness of activities exist on a continuum. Playfulness is characterized by fun, enjoyment, challenge, self-satisfaction, interest, excitement, and voluntariness, whereas work is perceived as difficult, compulsory, disliked, dull, not interesting, and rewarded. To adults play may become work when engaged in for instrumental reasons, such as business or for professional sports. Work may take on playful characteristics as well, as work activities can be challenging, self-satisfying, and fun. Generalizing this distinction to the play activities of young children has not been established, yet it is possible that social coercion, loss of freedom of choice of play activities, play activities which are not cognitively interesting, and competitiveness, may all modify the child's perception of any play activity as intrinsically motivating. Hence, investigating children's perceptions of varying types of play activities under varying circumstances would be a contribution to knowledge about the attribution of intrinsic motivation of play activities.

The consequences of playing games may influence children's perceptions of games as relatively intrinsic versus extrinsic, or playful versus workful. In games, contingencies may emanate from rules inherent in the game itself (Sutton-Smith, 1971), or from external sources such as rewards from parents or peers. The manner in which these internal and external contingencies interact with the opportunity to experience competence or develop mastery may influence the child's perception of the game as relatively intrinsically or extrinsically motivating.

In conclusion, any play activity may be subject to the child's attribution of intrinsic motivation. The degree to which consequences of play activities enhance the child's perception of competence and self-determination, intrinsic motivation is likely to be enhanced. To the extent that the child perceives that he/she is playing to obtain the consequence, then intrinsic motivation is likely to be decreased. The relationship of consequences of play activities to collative stimulus properties of the play materials, mastery experiences, and developmental skills of the child would be expected to provide a complex and subtle set of factors modifying the child's experience of any play activity as intrinsically motivating.

An Interactive Conceptualizaton of Intrinsic Motivation in Play

Intrinsic motivation has been shown to be differentiated into components, and to be characterized by three different theoretical orientations. Table 6–1

Table 6–1
Implications of Intrinsic Motivation for Play Experiences and Materials: Cognitive Discrepancy, Mastery, and Attribution Perspectives

Intrinsic Motivation Perspective	Play Experiences	Play Materials
Cognitive discrepancy	*Exploration:* Initiated by discrepancy from cognitive level; focused, selective, stereotyped, learning-oriented; motivation inherent in arousal reduction; decreases the novelty of collative stimuli; curiosity	Emphasis is on stimulus conditions which create cognitive discrepancies: novelty, complexity, incongruity, variety, surprisingness.

Table 6–1 continued

Intrinsic Motivation Perspective	Play Experiences	Play Materials
	Play: Variable, relaxed, uses more familiar stimuli, transformations of familiar stimuli; increases exposure to collative stimuli; increases cognitive discrepancies; stimulus-seeking; response produced variation	Emphasis is on stimulus conditions which allow for transformations, such as familiar toys. Opportunity for encountering collative stimuli should be present to allow for diversive exploration.
		For both exploration and play, match stimulus conditions with cognitive level.
Mastery	Effectance in interaction with environment; trial of new behaviors without concern for consequences; experience oneself as a causal agent in environment; self-worth enhanced; experience control over environment; persistence; experience of mastery from task activity itself. Includes object and social play, practice play, symbolic play.	Emphasis is on responsiveness of play materials; feedback provided to child; challenging materials; contingency between action and response; matching developmental abilities with play materials.
	In infancy, parental provision of kinesthetic and auditory stimulation, attention-focusing strategies, and stimulation responsive to child's activities is related to mastery motivation.	
Attribution	Perceptions emphasized. Intrinsic motivation of a play activity dependent on child's interpretation of consequence condition (for example, reward). Intrinsic motivation enhanced when a child attributes play to self-determination of goals, competence, his own efforts. Intrinsic motivation diminished when child attributes play to receipt of rewards, demands of social agents, when rewards are given for an activity of initially high interest, when there is lack of control over choice of activity. Any play activity can be subject to effects of reward.	*Enhancing intrinsic motivation for play:* Provision of outcomes or rewards emphasizing competence, praise for competence *Decreasing intrinsic motivation for play:* Provision of outcomes or rewards which control activity, which are not oriented to competence but to engagement in activity

presents a review of these features as related to play experiences and materials. The cognitive discrepancy perspective emphasizes stimuli and arousal that produce intrinsic motivation to reduce arousal; the mastery perspective emphasizes intrinsic motivation which results from effective interaction with the environment; the attribution perspective emphasizes the child's perception of intrinsic motivation which results from external consequences to the child's behavior. Intrinsic motivation for play is an outcome of the complex interaction and interrelationships between the cognitive discrepancy, mastery, and attributional features of intrinsic motivation. For example, encountering a collative stimulus may produce cognitive discrepancy resulting in exploratory play. Resolution of the cognitive discrepancy may result in the child's experience of mastery for effectively interacting with his or her environment. The consequences which the child receives (for example, verbal praise or disapproval from parents for exploratory play) further influences the child's attribution of play as relatively intrinsically or extrinsically motivated by enhancing or reducing perceptions of competence.

In figure 6–1, I have schematically represented an interaction approach to intrinsic motivation for play. Any play activity may emphasize one or more aspects of intrinsic motivation, and all three aspects of intrinsic motivation may or may not be operative at the same time. Other factors such as developmental cognitive and social abilities, specific available stimuli, environmental responsiveness to play, type, and content of play, complexity and difficulty of play materials, and rewards, may influence the child's experience of play as intrinsically motivating, as well as which aspects of intrinsic motivation are likely to be emphasized. For example, in infancy, it is likely that cognitive discrepancy and mastery aspects of intrinsic motivation are most relevant to play. As social cognitive skills develop, attribution aspects of intrinsic motivation would become more salient for play activities (preschool and later years).

Games provide an example, of interrelatedness of the dimensions of intrinsic motivation in older children. To the degree to which any game provides a challenge appropriate to the skill level of the player (Csikszentmihalyi, 1975), outcomes attributable to personal efficacy, competence, and cognitive discrepancy (such as intellectual or problem-solving games), intrinsic motivation is likely to be enhanced. On the other hand, when the challenge level of the game is too far above or below the skill of the player, perceptions of efficacy and mastery are reduced due to consequences, and when games are boring (do not provide cognitive discrepancy), intrinsic motivation is likely to be reduced.

The bidirectional dotted arrows in figure 6–1 indicate that mutual influences are possible but do not necessarily accompany each play activity. Further, initiation of a play activity could be due to any of the three aspects of intrinsic motivation, and the basis for intrinsic motivation may change within

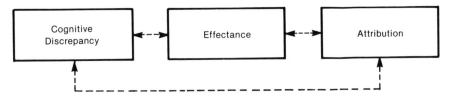

Figure 6–1. Intrinsic Motivation for Play: An Interaction Approach

a sequence. For example, while a novel toy may attract a child's initial interest, intrinsic motivation may move to a mastery emphasis as the toy provides feedback to the child, and as the novel features of the toy are familiarized. Other temporal sequences are possible as well. Effectance motivation for a play activity may generate additional cognitive discrepancies. Rewards for competent play may increase the probability of seeking cognitive discrepancy or mastery experiences.

In conclusion, the conception of intrinsic motivation proposed in this chapter differs in certain respects from prior views of intrinsically motivated play. First, intrinsic motivation in play is viewed as a result of multivariate factors, whereas in prior conceptions a single orientation has been espoused. Second, intrinsic motivation is viewed as a result of the stimuli, mastery, and consequence conditions of play rather than as a criterion of play. Finally, the child's experience of intrinsic motivation in play is an important dimension that needs to be accounted for.

References

Anderson, R., Manoogian, S.T., & Resnick, J.S. 1976. The undermining and enhancing of intrinsic motivation in preschool children. *Journal of Personality and Social Psychology* 34:915–922.

Belsky, J., Garduque, L., & Hrncir, E. 1984. Assessing performance, competence, and executive capacity in infant play: Relations to home environment and security of attachment. *Developmental Psychology* 20:406–417.

Belsky, J., Goode, M., & Most, R. 1980. Maternal stimulation and infant exploratory competence: Cross-sectional, correlational, and experimental analyses. *Child Development* 51:1163–1178.

Berlyne, D.E. 1960. *Conflict, arousal, and curiosity.* New York: McGraw-Hill.

———. 1965. Curiosity and education. In J.D. Krumboltz (Ed.), *Learning and the educational process.* Chicago: Rand McNally.

———. 1966. Curiosity and exploration. *Science* 153:25–33.

Boggiano, A.K., & Ruble, D.N. 1979. Perception of competence and the overjustification effect: A developmental study. *Journal of Personality and Social Psychology* 37:1462–1468.

Bruner, J.S. 1972. The nature and uses of immaturity. *American Psychologist* 27:687–708.

———. 1973. Organization of early skilled action. *Child Development* 44:1–11.

Condry, J., & Koslowski, B. 1979. Can education be made "intrinsically interesting" to children? In L.G. Katz (Ed.), *Current topics in early childhood education,* (Vol. 3). Norwood, N.J.: Ablex.

Csikszentmihalyi, M. 1975. *Beyond boredom and anxiety.* San Francisco: Jossey-Bass.

Day, H.I. 1981. Play: A ludic behavior. In H.I. Day (Ed.), *Advances in intrinsic motivation and aesthetics.* New York: Plenum Press.

de Charms, R. 1976. *Enhancing motivation: Change in the classroom.* New York: Irvington.

Deci, E.L. 1975. *Intrinsic motivation.* New York: Plenum Press.

———. 1980, *The psychology of self-determination.* Lexington, Mass.: Lexington Books.

Deci, E.L., & Ryan, R.M. 1980. The empirical exploration of intrinsic motivational processes. In L. Berkowitz (Ed.), *Advances in experimental social psychology,* (Vol. 13). New York: Academic Press.

Dollinger, S.J., & Thelen, M.H. 1978. Overjustification and children's intrinsic motivation: Comparative effects of four rewards. *Journal of Personality and Social Psychology* 36:1259–1269.

Eiferman, R.R. 1972. It's child's play. In L.M. Shears & E.M. Bower (Eds.), *Games in education and development.* Springfield, Ill.: Charles C. Thomas.

Ellis, M.J. 1984. Play, novelty, and stimulus seeking. In T.D. Yawkey & A.D. Pellegrini (Eds.), *Child's play: Developmental and applied.* Hillsdale, N.J.: Erlbaum.

Fein, G.G. 1981. The physical environment: stimulation or education. In R.M. Lerner & N.A. Busch-Rossnagel (Eds.), *Individuals as producers of their development: A life-span perspective.* New York: Academic Press.

Fenson, L., Kagan, J., Kearsley, R.B., & Zelazo, P.R. 1976. The developmental progression of manipulative play in the first two years. *Child Development* 47:232–236.

Finkelstein, N., & Ramey, C. 1977. Learning to control the environment. *Child Development* 48:806–819.

Gaiter, J.L., Morgan, G.A., Jennings, K.D., Harmon, R.J., & Yarrow, L.J. 1982. Variety of cognitively oriented caregiver activities: Relationships to cognitive and motivational functioning at one and 3½ years of age. *Journal of Genetic Psychology* 141:49–56.

Gottfried, A.E. 1983. Intrinsic motivation in young children. *Young Children* 39:64–73.

———. 1985. Academic intrinsic motivation in elementary and junior high school students. *Journal of Educational Psychology.*

Gottfried, A.W., & Gottfried, A.E. 1984. Home environment and cognitive development in young children of middle-socioeconomic-status families. In A.W. Gottfried (Ed.), *Home environment and early cognitive development: Longitudinal research.* New York: Academic Press.

Gottfried, A.W., Rose, S.A., & Bridger, W.H. 1977. Cross-modal transfer in human infants. *Child Development* 48:118–123.

Harter, S. 1977. The effects of social reinforcement and task difficulty level on the pleasure derived by normal and retarded children from cognitive challenge and mastery. *Journal of Experimental Child Psychology* 24:476–494.

———. 1978a. Effectance motivation reconsidered. Toward a developmental model. *Human Development* 21:34–64.

———. 1978b. Pleasure derived from challenge and the effects of receiving grades on children's difficulty level choices. *Child Development* 49:788–799.

Haywood, H.C., & Burke, W.P. 1977. Development of individual differences in intrinsic motivation. In I.C. Uzgiris & F. Weizmann (Eds.), *The structuring of experience.* New York: Plenum Press.

Henderson, B., & Moore, S. 1979. Measuring exploratory behavior in young children: A factor analytic study. *Developmental Psychology* 15:113–119.

Hughes, M. 1978. Sequential analysis of exploration and play. *International Journal of Behavioral Development* 1:83–97.

Hunt, J.M. 1981. Experimental roots of intention, initiative, and trust. In H.I. Day (Ed.), *Advances in intrinsic motivation and aesthetics.* New York: Plenum Press.

Hutt, C. 1970. Specific and diversive exploration. In H. Reese & L. Lipsett (Eds.), *Advances in child development and behavior* (Vol. 5). New York: Academic Press.

———. 1981. Toward a taxonomy and conceptual model of play. In H.I. Day (Ed.), *Advances in intrinsic motivation and aesthetics.* New York: Plenum Press.

Jennings, K.D., Harmon, R.J., Morgan, G.A., Gaiter, J.L., & Yarrow, L.J. 1979. Exploratory play as an index of mastery motivation: Relationships to persistence, cognitive functioning, and environmental measures. *Developmental Psychology* 15:386–394.

Kassin, S.M. 1981. From laychild to "layman": Developmental causal attribution. In S.S. Brehm, S.M. Kassin & F.X. Gibbons (Eds.), *Developmental social psychology: Theory and research.* New York: Oxford University Press.

Kreitler, S., Zigler, E., & Kreitler, H. 1975. The nature of curiosity in children. *Journal of School Psychology* 13:185–200.

Lepper, M.R. 1983. Extrinsic reward and intrinsic motivation: Implications for the classroom. In J.M. Levine & M.C. Wang (Eds.), *Teacher and student perceptions: Implications for learning.* Hillsdale, N.J.: Erlbaum.

Lepper, M.R., & Gilovich, T.T. 1981. The multiple functions of reward: A social-developmental perspective. In S.S. Brehm, S.M. Kassin & F.X. Gibbons (Eds.), *Developmental Social Psychology: Theory and research.* New York: Oxford University Press.

Lepper, M.R., & Greene, D. 1975. Turning play into work: Effects of adult surveillance and extrinsic rewards on children's intrinsic motivation. *Journal of Personality and Social Psychology* 28:129–137.

Lepper, M.R., Greene, D., & Nisbett, R.E. 1973. Undermining children's intrinsic interest with extrinsic rewards: A test of the "overjustification" hypothesis. *Journal of Personality and Social Psychology* 28:129–137.

Lepper, M.R., & Malone, T.W. In press. Intrinsic motivation and instructional effectiveness in computer-based education. In R.E. Snow & M.J. Farr (Eds.), *Aptitude, learning, and instructing. III. Conative and affective process analyses.* Hillsdale, N.J.: Erlbaum.

Loveland, K.K., & Olley, J.G. 1979. The effect of external reward on interest and quality of task performance in children of high and low intrinsic motivation. *Child Development* 50:1207–1210.

Malone, T.W., & Lepper, M.R. In press. Making learning fun: A taxonomy of intrinsic motivations for learning. In R.E. Snow & M.J. Farr (Eds.), *Aptitude, learning, and instructing. III. Conative and affective process analyses.* Hillsdale, N.J.: Erlbaum.

McCall, R.B. 1974. Exploratory manipulation and play in the human infant. *Monographs of the Society for Research in Child Development* 39:(2), No. 155.

McGhee, P.E. 1984. Play, incongruity, and humor. In T.D. Yawkey & A.D. Pellegrini (Eds.), *Child's play: Developmental and applied.* Hillsdale, N.J.: Erlbaum.

McLoyd, V.C. 1979. The effects of extrinsic rewards of differential value on high and low intrinsic interest. *Child Development* 50:1010–1019.

Mendel, G. 1965. Children's preferences for differing degrees of novelty. *Child Development* 36:453–465.

Morgan, M. 1984. Reward-induced decrements and increments in intrinsic motivation. *Review of Educational Research* 54:5–30.

Neumann, E.A. 1971. *The elements of play.* New York: MSS Information Corporation.

Nunnally, J.C., & Lemond, L.C. 1973. Exploratory behavior and human development. In H. Reese (Ed.), *Advances in child development and behavior,* (Vol. 8). New York: Academic Press.

Nuttin, J.R. 1973. Pleasure and reward in human motivation. In D.E. Berlyne & K.B. Madsen (Eds.), *Pleasure, reward, preferences.* New York: Academic Press.

Piaget, J. 1962. *Play, dreams, and imitation in childhood.* New York: Norton. Originally published 1945; English translation, C. Gattegno & F.M Hodgson (London: Routledge & Kegan Paul, 1951).

Pittman, T.S. Boggiano, A.K., & Ruble, D.N. 1983. Intrinsic and extrinsic motivational orientations: Limiting conditions on the undermining and enhancing effects of reward on intrinsic motivation. In J.M. Levine & M.C. Wang (Eds.), *Teacher and student perceptions: Implications for learning.* Hillsdale, N.J.: Erlbaum.

Pittman, T.S., Emery, J., & Boggiano, A.K. 1982. Intrinsic and extrinsic motivational orientations: Reward-induced changes in preference for complexity. *Journal of Personality and Social Psychology.*

Riksen-Walraven, J.M. 1978. Effects of caregiver behavior on habituation rate and self-efficacy in infants. *International Journal of Behavioral Development* 1:105–130.

Ross, M. 1975. Salience of reward and intrinsic motivation. *Journal of Personality and Social Psychology* 32:245–254.

Rubin, K.H., Fein, G.G., & Vandenberg, B. 1983. Play. In P.H. Mussen (Ed.), *Handbook of child psychology* (Vol. 4). New York: Wiley.

Sutton-Smith, B. 1971. Play, games, and controls. In J.P. Schott & S.F. Scott (Eds.), *Social control and social change.* Chicago: University of Chicago Press.

Swann, W.B., & Pittman, T.S. 1977. Initiating play activity of children: The moderating influence of verbal cues on intrinsic motivation. *Child Development* 48:1128–1132.

Ulvund, S.E. 1980. Cognition and motivation in early infancy: An interactionist approach. *Human Development* 23:17–32.

Vidler, D.C. 1977. Curiosity. In S. Ball (Ed.), *Motivation in education*. New York: Academic Press.

Wachs, T.D. 1977. The optimal stimulation hypothesis and early development: Anybody got a match? In I.C. Uzgiris & F. Weizmann (Eds.), *The structuring of experience*. New York: Plenum Press.

Watson, J.S. 1971. Cognitive-perceptual development in infancy: Setting for the seventies. *Merrill-Palmer Quarterly* 17:139–152.

Weisler, A., & McCall, R. 1976. Exploration and play. *American Psychologist* 31:492–508.

White, R.W. 1959. Motivation reconsidered: The concept of competence. *Psychological Review* 66:297–333.

Wohlwill, J.F. 1984. Relationships between exploration and play. In T.D. Yawkey & A.D. Pellegrini (Eds.), *Child's play: Developmental and applied*. Hillsdale, N.J.: Erlbaum.

Yarrow, L.J., MacTurk, R.H., Vietze, P.M., McCarthy, M.E. Klein, R.P. & McQuiston, S. 1984. Developmental course of parental stimulation and its relationship to mastery motivation during infancy. *Developmental Psychology* 20:492–503.

Yarrow, L.J., McQuiston, S., MacTurk, R.H., McCarthy, M.E., Klein, R.P., & Vietze, P.M. 1983. Assessment of mastery motivation during the first year of life: Contemporaneous and cross-age relationships. *Developmental Psychology* 19:159–171.

Yarrow, L.J., Morgan, G.A., Jennings, K.D., Harmon, R.J., & Gaiter, J. 1982. Infants' persistence at tasks: Relationships to cognitive functioning and early experience. *Infant Behavior and Development* 5:131–141.

Zigler, E., Levine, G., & Gould, L. 1966. Cognitive processes in the development of children's appreciation of humor. *Child Development* 37:507–518.

7
Computer Play

Daniel W. Kee

C omputers pervade our society. These "silent engines" are revolutionizing work and education. Our children's environment and the objects of their attention are being rapidly transformed by computer technology. Already microprocessor-based toys are capturing their interest. These devices play interactive games and offer rich sensory involvement in sight, sound, and touch. Hand-held microelectronic learning aids such as Speak & Spell offer a glimpse of future changes in instructional technology. Furthermore, it is difficult to ignore the fascination children show for video games, nor can we miss the sales promotions of home computer manufacturers which imply that young children will miss important early learning and development opportunities if parents do not provide them with a home computer.

Computer play is an activity often associated with children's use of personal computers and other microprocessor-based devices, including toys and learning aids. Surprisingly, little formal interest has been shown by educators or psychologists in the nature of computer play or how computer play is related to other activities such as computer work or the development of cognitive skills. Thus, I will examine the new phenomenon of children's computer play.

Computer Playthings

A visit to your local toy store will reveal how rapidly computer devices have become commonplace for children. For example, one major chain of toy stores has separate display aisles for computer toys, microelectronic learning aids, video games, home/personal computers, and computer software (pro-

The parent–child research summarized in this chapter was conducted with Patricia E. Worden and supported by grants from Atari's Institute for Educational Action Research and Hughes Faculty Research Program. I thank Pat Worden for her comments and suggestions on this chapter and Annette Gilbert for her efficient word processing.

grams which control the application of small computers). An example of an early computer toy is Merlin. This device resembles a Trimline phone and plays games such as tic-tac-toe and blackjack, and supports other numerical and musical tone activities. Speak & Spell, with its unique synthesized voice, is an exemplar of hand-held learning aids. This book-size device includes a one-line display screen and an A to Z touch-sensitive keyboard. Speak & Spell's synthesized voice guides drill and practice in spelling and the playing of word games. Larger toys include Big Tracks, a tank that can be programmed to traverse a room and fire its cannon in a prearranged sequence. Desktop computer devices include the ubiquitous video game machines, which offer powerful graphics and sound capabilities. Furthermore, by simply changing the program cartridge the nature of the activity supported by the machine can be changed; for example, from Pac Man to a Sesame Street early learning game, such as Cookie Monster Munch.

Finally, an assortment of desktop microcomputers for the home, on display at many toy stores, provide substantial computing power and can be purchased for under two hundred dollars. These home computers are more flexible than video game and hand-held devices because of more versatile input (for example, keyboard, graphics tablet, light pen) and output (television screens and printers) capabilities. Furthermore, they have greater capacity for complex software and programming applications. For example, software can be selected for games, educational activities, word processing, technical tool use, and home/business applications. The computer can also be programmed, by using computer languages such as BASIC, to play word games such as Speak & Spell or to simulate Big Tracks in a fantasy microworld. In addition, a variety of creative computing activities are supported, such as active programming in LOGO (Papert, 1980) and writing, drawing, and music (Levin & Kareev, 1980a).

Although the forenamed computer devices vary in size and function, they share the same microelectronic technology. That is, the "brains" or central processing units of these computer devices are microprocessors located on silicon-based chips less than one centimeter square. These chips contain all the electric logic and circuits which control the computer. This technology has advanced rapidly, allowing more and more circuits to fit on silicon chips. The magnitude of this miniaturization is substantial. For example, a computer as small as a typewriter could be built today with the same number of functional elements as the human brain. Only thirty years ago a computer having the same capabilities would have been the size of New York City (Evans, 1979).

The differences in size and versatility between hand-held and desktop computer devices will be less important in the future. For example, lap-size computers are becoming available with the same computing power offered in desktop machines. Furthermore, given the rapid advances in computer technology, we can look forward to computer devices like Dynabook, suggested in the late 1970s by Allan Kay of Xerox's Palo Alto Research Center (Kay & Goldberg, 1977).

> Imagine having your own self-contained knowledge manipulator in a portable package the size and shape of an ordinary notebook. Suppose it had enough power to outrace your senses of sight and hearing, enough capacity to store for later retrieval thousands of page-equivalents of reference materials, poems, letters, recipes, records, drawings, animations, musical scores, waveforms, dynamic simulations, and anything else you would like to remember and change. (p. 31)

Already children are being exposed to embryonic versions of Dynabook in the form of personal computers. For older children this introduction may occur in schools or computer camps (Shell, 1983). Younger children have opportunities for access in public and private locales such as theme parks (Hakansson, 1983), museums (Kahn, 1977; Markoff, 1984), "computer towns" (Loop, Anton & Zamora, 1983), and store fronts (Watt, 1984a). A significant number of children have video game machines in their homes (Greenfield, 1984; Loftus & Loftus, 1983; Mitchell, 1984). Although these devices are more limited than personal computers, they represent a variant of computer technology which is already commonplace in the home. Personal computers also are becoming more popular in homes. Surveys indicate that the public believes personal computers will become as commonplace as televisions in the near future (Friedrich, 1983). If personal computers follow the same pattern as televisions and electronic calculators, we can expect them to gain virtually universal acceptance in only five years after their initial novelty appeal (Lepper, 1982). Indeed, some computer enthusiasts have predicted that children will have computer friends (D'Ignazio, 1983) and robot teddy bears (D'Ignazio, 1984).

Video game playing is a major activity associated with computer devices, because of the popularity of video arcades and the widespread availability of video game machines in homes. Even though personal computers support more diverse activities, game playing is an introductory activity which precedes other computer uses (Levin & Kareev, 1980a; Kee, 1981). Mitchell's (1984) recent study of home use of video games indicates that family playing time averaged 42 minutes a day during a 4-month period.

Computer Play

Children's computer play is play which depends on computer interaction. It is not directed at the accomplishment of a well-defined external goal. In this section some research themes in children's computer play are identified and briefly reviewed.

Play Environments with Computers

How will children's play be affected when personal computers become a part of their environments? Levin and Kareev (1980a) provide a useful illustration of computer play in the home. Their study involved two boys, ages 7 and 6, observed over a 7-month period. The following vignette provides an illustration of how the computer was assimilated into the more general play activities of the boys.

> They had a drawing displayed on the screen, an assortment of dots scattered about. They huddled in front of the computer and carefully moved the cursor [a dot that can be moved to indicate the current position for drawing] from one dot to another. The boys then ran from the living room into their playroom, where they played for a while. Then they ran back to the computer, carefully moving the cursor over next to yet another dot, and again ran to their playroom. This sequence was repeated several times. Finally, when asked what in the world they were doing, they patiently explained that they were playing "Star Trek." With the computer as "control room panel", they were "warping" from one star to another, then "beaming down" to the planet to explore (in their playroom). (p. 17)

These observations were based on long-term use of a personal computer. In the home, a computer can be a "free" rather than a "scarce" resource. Whether the same kinds of play behaviors emerge in classroom environments depends on such factors as duration of computer use, the ratio of computers to children, whether the computers are a free or scarce resource, and the kinds of software activities supported. Some preliminary evidence concerning computers in preschool classrooms is provided by the Center for Young Children (CYC), University of Maryland. For example, Campbell and Schwartz (1984) observed the influence of the presence versus absence of a personal computer with graphic programs (Scribbler and Creative Crayon) on the free play activities of thirty 4-year-old children over a 4-week period. Other objects in the children's play environment included art materials, blocks, and a housekeeping corner. Results indicate that patterns of neither social nor cognitive play were affected by the presence or absence of the computer. Parenthetically, Wright and Samaras (1984) report that children's play with graphic programs in this CYC project follow Smilansky's (1968) proposed sequence from functional play, to constructive play, to dramatic play.

An important problem for future research will be to evaluate how play in classroom environments changes with long-term computer use and with different kinds of software activities. Furthermore, the effectiveness of software designed to foster group play in classrooms should be evaluated (see Goodman, 1984).

Video Games

Electronic media such as television and radio are known to influence children's behavior (see Greenfield, 1984). Some initial research by Silvern, Williamson, and Countermine (1983; in press) has explored the effects of computer play exposure on children's behavior in a free play situation with toys. For example, Silvern et al. (1983) compared 5-year-old children viewing a Road Runner cartoon on television with 5-year-olds watching older children play a video game, Space Invaders. No differences between the two conditions were observed for level of aggression, fantasy play, or prosocial behavior. In a second study, Silvern et al. (in press) compared children's competitive versus cooperative video game playing. Twenty-eight 6- to 9-year-old children played a one-on-one boxing computer game in the competitive condition, while children in pairs targeted enemy space ships (one child controlled the vertical targeting while the other, the horizontal) in a Star Wars computer game. Their results indicated that the two types of computer play activities did not differentially influence pre/post test changes in different types of play (fantasy, collaborative, or solitary/aggressive) or prosocial behavior.

Although these findings suggest that playing different kinds of video games does not differentially influence subsequent play activities, they should be viewed cautiously. For example, children were given only limited exposure to the computer activity, typically 5 or 6 minutes. Furthermore, appropriate control groups were not included (for example, those without any computer activity), subject exposure to the different conditions was not counterbalanced (for example, Silvern et al., in press), and only a limited range of video game activities were surveyed.

Turning Play into Work

Research indicates that activities high in intrinsic motivation can be undermined by external constraints such as rewards, directions, and surveillance of the activity (Lepper & Green, 1979). For example, preschool-age children's free play interest in drawing with marking pens and the quality of their drawings were impaired by the promise of a good work certificate during an intervention period (see Lepper & Green, 1975). Two recently completed studies (Kee, Beauvais, & Whittaker, 1983; Wood & Kee, in preparation) examined whether the effects of external rewards/constraints have a similar influence on children's interest and/or quality of activity with a microelectronic hand-held learning aid. The highly engaging Speak & Spell device which supports different spelling and word game activities was used. In the first study by Kee, Beauvais, and Whittaker (1983) with sixty third-grade children, subjects were familiarized with Speak & Spell and then given a 15-minute free play session with the device. The factors of reward (none versus the award of a good work certificate) and type of play session (free play versus play with child-selected activity versus play with experimenter-selected activity) were manipulated. Results indicated that neither the children's self-reported interest in Speak & Spell nor their spelling performance were affected by the manipulated variables. A follow-up study by Wood and Kee (1984) with seventy-two sixth-grade children manipulated both the children's spelling interest level (high versus low) and the nature of the reward (none, versus unattractive, versus attractive) (see Condry, 1977). Consistent with our earlier results, pre/post test change scores failed to demonstrate that reward affects either children's interest in spelling activities or their spelling performance. These findings suggest that computer activities which are extremely high in intrinsic motivation may not be subject to negative reward effects.

Although differential reward effects were not observed in the Speak & Spell studies, Kee and Worden (in press) report that a 15-minute free play opportunity with Speak & Spell produced positive changes in children's interest in spelling, reading, word games, and arithmetic games, while no change was observed for their interest ratings of arithmetic or games. Pre- and post-test ratings were also provided by a comparison group that did not play with Speak & Spell. No differences were observed in their rating of the six categories. Thus, a brief play opportunity with Speak & Spell can have a differential impact on children's interests in various educational activities. This finding suggests that Speak & Spell and other similar devices can be used by parents and teachers to catalyze children's interest in different subject areas, thereby increasing opportunities for learning (see A.E. Gottfried, 1983).

Gender Differences in Fantasy Play

Computer games provide excellent opportunities for fantasy involvement. Mitchell's (1984) study of home use of video games indicates that children often report a sense of imaginary participation, and that the extent of fantasy play may depend on both the age of the child and nature of the graphics associated with the game. A recent report by Revelle, Honey, Amsel, Schauble, and Levine (1984) indicates gender differences in the frequency of fantasy involvement. Based on in-depth interviews with twenty-four children (ten girls and fourteen boys) at a computer camp, they found that "boys almost always reported engaging in vivid fantasies while playing computer or video games, and that girls almost never did."

Experimental research by Malone (1980; Malone & Lepper, in press) on what makes computer games fun indicates gender differences in the kinds of fantasy children find appealing. For example, boys appear to prefer intrinsic or endogenous fantasy in which the skill required in the computer game and the fantasy depend on each other. In contrast, girls prefer extrinsic or exogenous fantasies in which the fantasy depends on the skill, but not vice versa. This distinction is illustrated in children's play of the computer game Darts, in which balloons appear at random places on a vertical numbered line which is on the left side of the television screen. The player attempts to guess each balloon's position by typing in whole numbers and/or fractions. After each guess, an arrow shows across the screen from right to left to the specified position. If the guess is correct, the arrow pops the balloon. Malone suggests that in the standard version of this game, the fantasy of arrows popping balloons is intrinsic because the relative sizes of the numbers selected are directly related to the positions of the arrows and balloons in the fantasy. Boys preferred this version of the game. In contrast, girls preferred a version in which the fantasy was extrinsic. That is, children were asked to guess the position of a marker on a line (as opposed to a balloon) on the left side of the screen. If the guess is correct an arrow shoots across the screen from left to right and pops a balloon. In this version of the game the relative sizes of the numbers selected bear no direct relationship to the "positions" of the balloons popped on the right side of the screen when the guesses are correct.

Gender differences also have been reported for other aspects of children's computer activity. For example, boys show greater interest in computer use than girls (for example, Hess & Miura, 1984; Silvern, Countermine, & Williamson, 1982); boys hold more favorable perceptions of computers than girls (for example, Williams, Coulombe, & Lievrouw, 1983); girls are less confident in their computer game playing skills (Mitchell, 1984); and for some kinds of computer activities such as strategy games, girls prefer to know the rules prior to participation, while boys enjoy the process of learning the rules by playing (Revelle et al., 1984). Because of the gender differences suggested for children's computer activities and the "pervasive" differences reported for different kinds of children's play (see Rubin, Fein, & Vandenberg, 1983), analysis of sex dimorphisms in children's computer play should have high priority in future research.

Play and Computer Microworlds

Microworlds are in essence task domains or problem spaces designed for virtual, streamlined experience. These worlds encompass objects and processes that we can get to know and understand. The appropriation of the knowledge embodied in those experiences is made possible because the microworld does not focus on "problems" to be done but on "neat phenomena"— phenomena that are inherently interesting to observe and interact with. (Lawler, 1982, p. 140)

Rich and exciting graphic and text based microworlds can be established for children on personal computers. These microworlds can provide the basis for adventure games (see Greenfield, 1984); simulations of dangerous activities, such as nuclear reactor control (Scram by Atari); and play within different disciplines (Levin & Kareev, 1980a) such as music (Watt, 1984b), art (Bateman, 1984; Watt, 1983; Wright & Samaras, 1984), and logic (Budge's "Rocky's Boots" by The Learning Company).

Computer languages such as LOGO can be used by children to create graphic microworlds for play (see Papert, 1980), or such worlds can be created for them. For example, Lawler (1982) described a beach microworld created for his 3-year-old daughter to facilitate language acquisition skills. This LOGO-based microworld consists of an imaginary beach with objects (bird, boat, dog, sun) which could be manipulated by action commands such as up, down, fly, and walk. The child can select objects for her microworld and control their action by entering correctly spelled object and action words on the computer keyboard. In addition to fostering spelling skills, this beach microworld offers an exciting electronic environment for play.

Campbell and Schwartz (1984) caution, however, that standard observational instruments may not be sufficient to uncover all the features of a child's computer play, particularly the kinds of covert fantasies which might be prompted by the new electronic medium. Verbal protocol techniques may be useful in unlocking some of the spontaneous covert fantasies engaged in by children. Furthermore, the computers can be programmed to record the child's interactions within the microworld. This kind of data can be used to help construct a model of the child's representation of the microworld. Analysis of changes in play activities could then be related to corresponding changes in the child's mental representation. This approach could provide exciting insights into the relationships between play and children's cognitive acquisitions. Indeed, the computer provides a unique laboratory in which play variables can be manipulated and their affect on the nature of play and related behaviors studied. For example, computer worlds offer a fertile means for evaluating the relationship between play and exploration (Wohlwill, 1984), learning (Silva, 1977), problem solving (Vandenberg, 1982), and creativity (Vandenberg, 1980).

Many of the studies reviewed were preliminary in nature and the extant research provides little evidence concerning age-related differences in computer activities. Furthermore, computer play was defined broadly for this review. Thus, distinctions such as exploration versus play and play versus games were not emphasized (see Rubin et al., 1983).

Parent-Child Computer Activity

In this last section, I describe some current work that Patricia E. Worden and I have been engaged in concerning conjoint parent-child computer activities.

We believe that many young children, ages 2 and 3, will become exposed to computers through joint parent-child play or learning event. What might the nature of this parent-child computer activity be like, and how would it compare to other more traditional kinds of parent-child activities? To answer these questions, we videotaped twenty parents (ten mothers and ten fathers) with their 3-year-old sons or daughters. None of the participants had previous computer experience. The computer activity selected was a software program called My First Alphabet, by Atari. This is a rather generic program and representative of the first kind of software parents may select for their young children. In this program, a keyboard entry directs the computer to draw a colorful graphic picture of an appropriate object or animal; the computer draws the letter selected, presents words which begin with the letter, and plays a brief musical tune. Parent-child pairs were videotaped for 12 minutes in this computer activity in which they simply told to push a key and watch what happens. In the videotaped book activity, three alphabet books appropriate for this age range were provided and subjects were instructed to read these books as they would at home. All parent-child dyads participated in both conditions, and order of presentation was counterbalanced.

At this time, only the data from ten mother-child pairs have been thoroughly analyzed. Some of the findings based on this analyses I will highlight. (For a more detailed treatment of these results please see Kee and Worden (in press) or Worden and Kee (1984).)

Our initial analyses focused on general indicators of activity in the two conditions. For example, linguistic complexity measured in terms of mean length of utterance was not observed to differ for children in the computer ($M = 2.80$) and book ($M = 2.67$) conditions, $p > .05$. Major differences, however, were found in the volume of interaction observed. For example, more letters were reviewed in the book condition ($M = 43.40$) than in the computer condition ($M = 18.40$), and the amount of conversation, measured in terms of the number of times a speaker-change occurred on a topic, was also larger in the book ($M = 127.60$) than computer ($M = 92.60$) condition, $p < .05$. These differences are most likely due to the subjects' ability to read the alphabet books at a faster pace than was possible in the computer activity. For example, after a key-press on the computer about 20 seconds was required for the screen to complete its presentation of the display. Generally speaking, parents and children waited for the screen-display to finish. We were surprised that parents did not make better use of this time; for example, by prompting their children to guess the identity of the object the computer was drawing. This kind of parental strategy might develop with more familiarity with the activity or if they were prompted to do so. Also, different alphabet software which either developed the graphic at a faster rate or allowed more user control over the graphics presentation might have an impact on the volume of verbal interaction observed.

Subsequent analyses of verbal activity revealed that different patterns of events were produced by mothers and children in the two conditions. In both, mothers spoke more than their children. These verbal events were categorized into ten groups depicted in table 7–1. To equate for differences in amount of talkativeness, analyses were based on the proportion of the total number of verbal events. For mothers identifications and requests for identifications formed the major verbal activity in the book condition, whereas comments, directives, and negative remarks were more pronounced in the computer task. Thus, the reading was more tutorial (in naming pictures), and the computer activity more controlling and directive. However, the increase in controlling and directive statements was probably due to the need to talk about how to operate the computer keyboard and the necessity to wait for the computer to complete its screen display before entering new letters.

For the children, identifications composed the major verbal activity in both conditions. Comments were also high, particularly in the computer condition. The computer task caused children to lower their identification activity and increase their proportion of comments and, to a lesser extent, questions. Again, this may be due to the requirement to talk about the computer operation. In contrast, all the children were acquainted with how to read a book and thus could concentrate on naming pictures. Recall that the parents and children observed were computer "naive"; the necessity of discussing computer operation would most likely diminish with increased computer experience.

Behavioral analyses were conducted to assess degree of interest and

Table 7–1
Mean Percentages of Verbal Events in Ten Categories for Mothers and Children

Verbal Categories	Mothers' Verbal Events		Children's Verbal Events	
	Book	Computer	Book	Computer
Identifications	26.2 *	17.4	59.4 *	42.8
Requests for identifications	26.2 *	17.8	4.8	3.1
Positive	12.4	16.0	5.9	7.5
Comments	11.2 *	14.0	15.7 *	25.7
Directives	8.3 *	16.3	2.0	4.2
Questions	7.8	9.0	3.9 *	9.0
Negatives	2.5 *	4.7	13.3	13.9
Laughter	1.6	1.9	2.5	1.8
Name	1.9	2.3	1.7	1.4
Extraneous	1.6	0.9	0.6	0.5

Note: An asterisk indicates a significant book versus computer difference, $p < .05$.

involvement by the parents and children in the two media. For example, both tasks were found to be highly engaging with only minimum looking away from either the book or computer. More time was spent looking at books (M = 568.74 sec) than at the computer screen (M = 338.46 sec), p <.05, suggesting that books were more visually attractive. However, time looking at the screen may have been diminished because keyboard entries typically required children to look away from the screen to their finger/key placements (M = 146.67 sec). Analyses of pointing behavior showed that more pointing was observed in the book (M = 142.11 sec) than in the computer (M = 70.50 for keyboard plus screen) condition, p <.05. Furthermore, mothers pointed at the book longer (M = 203.19 sec) than children (M = 81.03 sec), whereas children pointed more at the computer (M = 114.27 sec) than mothers (M = 26.43 sec).

In our study the computer was a novel activity, the 12-minute sessions relatively brief, and the software focused the participants on letter and object identification activities. Children did not have opportunities for nondirected play, and no evidence of play behaviors was observed in analyses of verbal and other behavioral indices. However, I would anticipate that as parents and children became more familiar with the operation and content of the program, play behavior would begin to appear. For example, my 3-year-old son Matthew has played with My First Alphabet for 1½ years. Although he knows most of the letters and objects in the program, he still enjoys calling-up pictures in both story telling and pretend activities. For example, the letter U produces a picture of rain drops falling on an umbrella. Matthew might first observe that it is going to rain, then push the "U" key, and say, "We need a 'brella'." Alternately, he likes to go on pretend walks in the jungle, calling up pictures of the lion or gorilla. My observations also suggest that when young children become more familiar with computer activities, they will often ignore the objective of software programs. For example, Matthew has been playing with a new learning game called Colorasaurus, developed by The Learning Company. One objective of this activity is to place different colored dinosaurs found at the bottom of the screen into rectangles of corresponding colors located in a jungle depicted in the upper portion of the screen. A joystick is used to move the dinosaurs. If a dinosaur is not matched to its color, it falls to the bottom of the screen. After figuring out how to play the game, Matthew started to deliberately missmatch dinosaurs and color rectangles at the top of the screen, whereby missmatched dinosaurs would drop to the bottom of the screen—he was watching/making the "dragons fly" through the jungle.

In summary, our study provides a preliminary sketch of the nature of parent-child interaction with the computers and how it differs from a more traditional activity for parent-child interaction. Results offer implications for the design of software for young children's computer activities and suggestions for effective parental involvement (see Kee & Worden, in press).

Conclusion

New opportunities for children's play and the study of play have been created by advances in computer technology. Microelectronic toys, hand-held devices, and personal computers are becoming commonplace in children's environments. In this chapter an emphasis was placed on personal computer activities because, in contrast to the other computer devices, they promise to have a more profound and lasting impact on child development.

References

Arnold, H.J. 1976. Effects of performance feedback and extrinsic reward upon high intrinsic motivation. *Organizational Behavior and Human Performance* 17: 275–288.

Barnes, B.J., & Hill, S. 1983. Should young children work with microcomputers— Logo before Lego? *The Computing Teacher,* May:11–14.

Bateman, S. 1984. The digital palette: Fundamentals of computer graphics. *Compute,* May:20–32.

Baughman, S.S., & Clagett, P.D. (Eds.). 1983. Video games and human development: A research agenda for the '80s. Cambridge: Gutman Library, Harvard University Graduate School of Education.

Borgh, K., & Dickson, W.P. 1984. Two preschoolers sharing one microcomputer: Creating prosocial behavior with hardware and software. In P.F. Campbell & G.G. Fein (Eds.), *Young children and microcomputers: Conceptualizing the issues.* Reston, Va.: Reston.

Brady, E.H., & Hill, S. 1984. Young children and microcomputers. *Young children,* March:49–61.

Brown, J.S. 1983. Learning by doing revisited for electronic learning environments. In M.A. White (Ed.), *The future of electronic learning.* Hillsdale, N.J.: Erlbaum.

Campbell, P.F., & Schwartz, S.S. 1984. Microcomputers in the preschool: Children, parents and teachers. In P.F. Campbell & G.G. Fein (Eds.), *Young children and microcomputers: Conceptualizing the issues.* Reston, Va.: Reston.

Condry, J. 1977. Enemies of exploration: Self-initiated versus other-initiated learning. *Journal of Personality and Social Psychology* 35:459–477.

D'Ignazio, F. 1983. The computer friend: Getting to know you. *Compute* 5:140–144.

———. 1984. The robot teddy bear. *Compute,* Jan. 6:94–104.

Evans, C. 1979. *The micro millennium.* New York: Viking Press.

Friedrich, O. 1983. The computer moves in. *Time,* Jan. 14–24.

Goodman, F.L. 1984. The computer as plaything. *Simulation and Games* 15:65–73.

Gottfried, A.E. 1983. Intrinsic motivation in young children. *Young Children,* Nov.: 64–73.

Greenfield, P.M. 1984. *Mind and media.* Cambridge: Harvard University Press.

Hakansson, J. 1983. How children learn from electronic sources. In M.A. White (Ed.), *The future of electronic learning.* Hillsdale, N.J.: Erlbaum.

Hawkins, J., Sheingold, K., Gearhart, M., & Berger, C. 1982. Microcomputers in schools: Impact on the social life of elementary classrooms. *Journal of Applied Developmental Psychology* 3:361–373.

Hess, R.D., & Miura, I.T. 1984. Gender and socioeconomic differences in enrollment in computer camps and classes. Unpublished manuscript, Stanford University, Calif.

Kahn, R.A. 1977. Public access to personal computing: A new role for science museums. *Computer Magazine,* April:56–66.

Kay, A., & Goldberg, A. 1977. Personal dynamic media. *Computer Mazagine,* March:31–41.

Kee, D.W. 1981. Implications of hand-held electronic games and microcomputers for informal learning. Paper commissioned by the Home Community and Work Division, National Institute of Education, Washington, D.C.

Kee, D.W., & Worden, P.E. In press. Personal computers in language and reading research: Three vignettes. In B.A. Hutson (Ed.), *Advances in reading/language research.* Greenwich, Conn.: JAI Press.

Kee, D.W., Beauvais, C., & Whittaker, A. 1983. Motivational and learning aspects of a microelectronic learning aid. Paper presented at the annual meeting of the American Psychological Association, Anaheim, Calif.

Lawler, R.W. 1982. Designing computer-based microworlds. *Byte* 7:138–160.

Lepper, M.R. 1982. Microcomputers in education: Motivational and social issues. Paper presented at the annual meeting of the American Psychological Association, Washington, D.C.

Lepper, M.R., & Greene, D. 1975. Turning play into work: Effects of adult surveillance and extrinsic rewards on children's intrinsic motivation. *Journal of Personality and Social Psychology* 31:479–486.

———. 1979. *The hidden costs of reward.* Hillsdale, N.J.: Erlbaum.

Lepper, M.R., & Malone, T.W. In press. Intrinsic motivation and instructional effectiveness in computer-based education. In R.E. Snow & M.J. Farr (Eds.), *Aptitude, learning, and instruction. III. Cognitive and affective process analyses.* Hillsdale, N.J.: Erlbaum.

Lesgold, A.A. In press. Rationale for computer-based reading instruction. In A.C. Wilkinson (Ed.), *Classroom computers in cognitive science.* New York: Academic Press.

Levin, J.A., & Kareev, Y. 1980a. Personal computers and education: The challenge to schools (Technical Report No. 98). La Jolla, Calif.: Center for Human Information Processing, University of California, San Diego.

———. 1980b. Problem solving in everyday situations. *The Quarterly Newsletter of the Laboratory of Comparative Human Cognition* 2:47–52.

Loftus, G.R., & Loftus, E.F. 1983. *Mind at play.* New York: Basic Books.

Loop, L., Anton, J., & Zamora, R. 1983. *Computer town.* Reston, Va.: Reston.

Malone, T.W. 1980. What makes things fun to learn? A study of intrinsically motivating computer games. Xerox, Palo Alto Research Center, Palo Alto, Calif.

Malone, T.W., & Lepper, M.R. In press. Making learning fun: A taxonomy of intrinsic motivation for learning. In R.E. Snow & M.J. Farr (Eds.), *Aptitude, learning, and instruction. III. Cognitive and affective process analyses.* Hillsdale, N.J.: Erlbaum.

Markoff, J. 1984. San Francisco's exploratorium. *Byte* 9:279–286.

Masterson, F.A. 1984. Languages for students. *Byte* 9:233–238.

Mayer, R.E. 1982. Contributions of cognitive science and related research in learning to the design of computer literacy curricula. In R.J. Seidel, R.E. Anderson, & B. Hunter (Eds.), *Computer literacy*. San Francisco: Academic Press.

Mitchell, E. 1984. Home video games: Children and parents learn to play and play to learn. Paper presented at the annual meeting of the American Educational Research Association, New Orleans, La.

Papert, S. 1980. *Mindstorms*. New York: Basic Books.

Piestrup, A. 1984. Game sets and builders. *Byte* 9:215–218.

Quinsaat, M.G. 1981. Implementing computer technology in a classroom setting: An anecdotal report of long-term use. Paper presented at the NIE conference on Issues Related to the Implementation of Computer Technology in Schools, Washington, D.C.

Revelle, G., Honey, M., Ansel, E., Schauble, L., & Levine, G. 1984. Sex differences in the use of computers. Paper presented at the annual meeting of the American Educational Research Association, New Orleans, La.

Richter, P. 1984. This year's computer trends: Higher-priced models, cartoon characters. *Los Angeles Times,* June 10, V:2.

Rubin, K.H., Fein, G.G., & Vandenberg, B. 1983. Play. In P.H. Mussen (Ed.), *Handbook of child psychology* (Vol. 4). New York: Wiley.

Sanders, T.S. 1981. Microcomputer programming in the exploration of children's problem solving skills. Paper presented at the annual meeting of the American Educational Research Association, New York.

Seidel, R.J., Anderson, R.E., & Hunter, B. (Eds.). 1982. *Computer literacy*. San Francisco: Academic Press.

Shell, E.R. 1983. Hack city summer. *Technology Illustrated,* March:63–65.

Silvern, S.B., Countermine, T.M., & Williamson, P.A. 1982. Young children's interaction with a microcomputer. Paper presented at the meeting of the American Educational Research Association, New York.

Silvern, S.B., Williamson, P.A., & Countermine, T.A. 1983. Videogame playing and aggression in young children. Paper presented at the meeting of the American Educational Research Association, Montreal, Canada.

———. In press. Videogame play and social behavior. In J.L. Frost & F. Rhodes (Eds.), *Play and play environments*. Washington, D.C.: Association for Childhood Education.

Smilansky, S. 1968. *The effects of sociodramatic play on disadvantaged preschool children*. New York: Wiley.

Soloway, E., Lockhead, J., & Clement, J. 1982. Does computer programming enhance problem solving ability? Some positive evidence on algebra word problems. In R.J. Seidel, R.E. Anderson & B. Hunter (Eds.), *Computer literacy*. San Francisco: Academic Press.

Sylva, K. 1977. Play and learning. In B. Tizard & D. Harvey (Eds.), *Biology of play*. Philadelphia: Lippincott.

Turkle, S. 1984. *The second self: Computers and the human spirit*. New York: Simon and Schuster.

Vandenberg, B. 1981. The role of play in the development of insightful tool-using strategies. *Merrill-Palmer Quarterly* 27:97–109.

———. 1980. Play, problem-solving and creativity. In K.H. Rubin (Ed.), *Children's play.* San Francisco, Calif.: Jossey-Bass.

Walker, D.F., & Hess, R.D. 1984. *Instructional software.* Belmont, Calif.: Wadsworth.

Watt, D. 1983. Computers and creativity. *Popular Computing,* Nov.:75–78.

———. 1984a. Neighborhood computer centers. *Popular Computing,* May:91–94.

———. 1984b. Musical microworlds. *Popular Computing,* Aug.:91–94.

White, M.A. (Ed.). 1983a. *The future of electronic learning.* Hillsdale, N.J.: Erlbaum.

White, M.A. 1983b. Toward a psychology electronic learning. In M.A. White (Ed.), *The future of electronic learning.* Hillsdale, N.J.: Erlbaum.

Williams, F., Coulombe, J., & Lievrouw, L. 1983. Children's attitudes toward small computers: A preliminary study. *Educational Communication Technology Journal* 31:3–7.

Williams, F., & Williams, V. 1984. *Microcomputers in elementary education.* Belmont, Calif.: Wadsworth.

Wohlwill, J.F. 1984. Relationships between exploration and play. In T.D. Yawkey & A.D. Pellegrini (Eds.), *Child's play: Developmental and applied.* Hillsdale, N.J.: Erlbaum.

Wood, P.F., & Kee, D.W. In preparation. Effects of extrinsic reward on intrinsic interest and task performance in elementary school classrooms.

Worden, P.E., & Kee, D.W. 1984. Parent-child interaction and computer learning: An alphabet game for preschoolers. Paper presented at the meeting of the American Educational Research Association, New Orleans, La.

Wright, J.L., & Samaras, A.S. 1984. Play worlds and microworlds. In P.F. Campbell & G.G. Fein (Eds.), *Young children and microcomputers: Conceptualizing the issues.* Reston, Va.: Reston.

Part III
Social Significance
of Play

8
Representing the Social World in Symbolic Play: Reality and Fantasy

Inge Bretherton

O f all forms of early play, symbolic play or pretense has received the most attention from investigators, because Piaget regarded it—along with language and deferred imitation—as a hallmark of an emerging ability to engage in mental representation (Piaget, 1962). By drawing on detailed observations of his own young children, Piaget was able to illustrate that the development of make-believe play is characterized by a growing distance between the persons and objects that are used as symbols and what the symbols are meant to represent. At first, when a child reenacts everyday activities such as sleeping or eating without feeling tired or hungry, the child's pretend action stands for or symbolizes serious action. At a later period in development, when a child feeds a doll or puts it to bed, the action with the doll becomes a symbol for the child's own acts of going to bed. Later still, when children use blocks as cars and sticks as spoons, the pretend actions on these "placeholder" objects symbolize serious actions with real objects. Thus, in the course of development the child's symbols become more and more dissimilar and distinct from what they are meant to represent. Accordingly, pretense can serve as a gauge of a young child's developing representational ability.

However—and this is crucial—Piaget did not recognize pretense as an actual contributor to cognitive development. The growing abilities that reveal themselves in play do not, he claims, result from play but from serious adaptation to reality in other contexts. For example, when a toddler rocks a pretend baby in her arms because she is not allowed to hold her baby sister, her invention of an alternative reality makes no contribution to cognitive development; it is merely "assimilation of reality to the ego." In Piaget's view, the primary role of pretense in development is affective. As young children

Portions of this chapter were published in a chapter entitled "Representing the Social World in Symbolic Play: Reality and Fantasy," in I. Bretherton (Ed.), *Symbolic play: The development of social understanding* (New York: Academic Press, 1984). During the writing of this chapter I received support from the John C. and Catherine C. MacArthur Network for the Transition from Infancy to Early Childhood.

make dolls relive their own unpleasant past experiences or transform reality in line with their desires, they get a sense of mastery over a world they cannot yet control in reality. In this interpretation, Piaget is very close to psycho-analysts such as Erikson (1963) and Peller (1954).

I take a very different approach to pretend play. My view is not incompatible with Piaget's description of sensorimotor development during the first two years, nor is it incompatible with his views about the affective significance of pretense. However, I differ with his views about the preschool child's egocentric and incoherent thought processes.

For Piaget, representation is mental or interiorized action. Although pretense fits the category of interiorized action (reproduction or transformation of mentally represented action as make-believe), it was not the kind of mental action that interested Piaget. In his view, special types of mental action, the operations (such as classification and seriation) are necessary before thought can become coherent. Figurative thought, or thought about everyday events, becomes organized, coherent, and decentered only at the end of the preschool period when the child has mastered operations (can classify, order, and conserve number and quantity).

Recently, this view has been challenged by a number of cognitive theorists who claim that figurative representation (event representation) may actually provide the bedrock on which operations such as classification and ordering are gradually constructed in the course of the preschool years. According to these theorists, symbolic activity begins with event schemas that represent the temporal, spatial, and causal relations among agents, actions, recipients, and objects (Mandler, 1983; Nelson & Gruendel, 1981). Event schemas are defined as skeletal mental (cognitive and affective) frameworks, created from repeated experience of similar events. Once such schemas are constructed, they serve to guide a person's understanding of reality (assimilation) but continue to develop and differentiate through experience (accommodation). If figurative thinking—use of event schemas—forms the basis for the construction of what Piaget called operative (logical) thought, the study of figurative thinking deserves a much more prominent role in representational development.

Moreover, if the basic building blocks of human thinking are representational schemas of meaningful events, not disembedded symbols, it ought to be possible to demonstrate that infants have the ability to represent an experience in terms of temporal-causal-affective relations among actors, recipients, objects, and locations (Nelson, 1981; Aebli, 1980). However, it is primarily the development of event representation in 3- to 5-year-olds which has received detailed scrutiny (Stein, 1978; Nelson & Gruendel, 1981). For example, Nelson and her colleagues discovered that 3-year-olds can report the correct sequence of events in response to questions such as: What happens when you have a birthday party? When you go to MacDonald's? When you go to the store? While older children add more details to their accounts (Stein, 1978), the reports given by younger children are certainly not chaotic.

In this chapter, I will argue that early pretense can be regarded and studied as a form of event representation which becomes increasingly coherent in the course of infancy and early childhood, and—from the beginning—occurs in social as well as solitary contexts. I will also make the point that even very young children not merely reenact but play with their representations of the social world, which furthers cognitive development.

Because the symbolic medium of pretense (enactment) resembles real-world action, the boundary between here-and-now reality and make-believe must be marked in some way, especially when two or more partners are engaging in joint play (Bateson, 1955; Garvey & Berndt, 1977; Giffin, 1984). I will therefore also discuss evidence showing that children not only reproduce and transform their representations of the social world through play, but that they learn to do so at two conceptual levels—planning (outside the playframe) and acting (within the playframe).

Event Representation in Symbolic Play

In pretending, children simulate and transform routine events of family life, later drawing on other sources as well. Although I discuss the development of early pretense in terms of roles, actions, and props (objects), these three dimensions cannot be regarded as completely independent. Performance of a role always involves actions, and frequently objects as well. However, it is possible to enact a relatively complex role structure (two teddybears engage in interaction) with a simple action structure (the two bears kiss each other). Similarly a complex action structure such as the performance of a lengthy breakfast sequence can be enacted with a simple role structure (the sole actor is the child). Furthermore, enactment of a complex event sequence may or may not involve the use of objects that resemble the objects they stand for. Hence, it is important to look at the development of role structures, action structures, and prop use separately.

Roles

Piaget (1962) outlines a systematic developmental progression from self-representation to the representation of multirole structures. Viewed from the perspective of event representation, the same data illustrate toddlers' developing ability to play roles other than their own and to collaborate in role-play with playmates. Although Piaget made his initial observations on just three children, his findings have since been corroborated by others (e.g. Fenson & Ramsay, 1980; Kagan, 1981; Nicolich, 1977; Wolf, 1982; Watson &

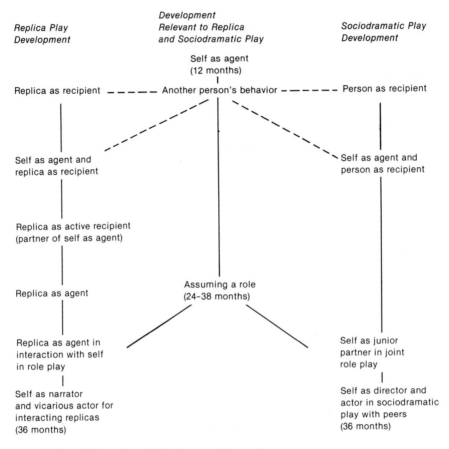

Source: Adapted from the available literature (see text).

Note: Dotted lines refer to the alternative explanation of replica or person as recipient (caregiving, rather than projecting self-behavior onto others).

Figure 8–1. **The Development of Pretend Roles in Replica and Sociodramatic Play**

Fischer, 1977, 1980). There are a few disagreements about the finer distinctions that we ought to make in describing pretense, but the level of agreement among investigators is impressive. Figure 8–1 outlines the development of roles in replica play and sociodramatic play.

Self as Agent. To begin with, babies play at being themselves. They reproduce a behavior such as sleeping without being tired. To call such acts symbolic play requires evidence that the baby is aware of pretending (see Nicolich,

1977; Piaget, 1962). A very clear example is Jacqueline's behavior at the age of 15 months:

> She saw a cloth whose fringed edges vaguely recalled those of her pillow; she seized it, held a fold of it in her right hand, sucked the thumb of the same hand, and lay down on her side, laughing hard. She kept her eyes open, but blinked them from time to time as if she were alluding to closed eyes. Finally, laughing more and more, she cried "nene." (Piaget, 1962, Obs. 64a, p. 96)

In this example, laughing and blinking communicate awareness of make-believe. In other cases, it may be the presence of sound effects (lipsmacking in the course of eating) that signals this awareness.

Another Person's Behavior. Unfortunately, it is not always easy to decide whether a child is reproducing his or her own actions or those of another person. For this reason a number of investigators (Fenson & Ramsay, 1980; Largo & Howard, 1979; Jeffree & McConkey, 1976; Kagan, 1981; Lowe, 1975; Watson & Fischer, 1977) do not attempt to distinguish between pretending at one's own or another person's behavior. For example, when a child lifts a toy telephone receiver to the ear and says "hi," it is not easy to tell whether he or she is pretending at adult behavior, because many children are taught how to use toy telephones. However, Piaget's (1962) description of Lucienne at 19 months is an unambiguous example of a child pretending at an adult's behavior. (Obs. 76a): Lucienne, sitting in an armchair, "reads" the newspaper, pointing and muttering to herself.

Making the distinction between pretending at one's own and other people's actions may be problematic in some cases, but it is important because playful reproduction of another person's behavior can be regarded as the beginning of role taking (or trying out the world from another vantage point).

Persons and Replicas as Recipients of Action. Piaget (1962) and Nicolich (1977) claim that in pretense the use of a doll to simulate one's own behavior is cognitively similar to reproducing another person's behavior. Observations have shown that the two types of pretend behavior occur simultaneously in development. Acts of reading the newspaper and feeding a doll tend to develop in step with one another.

While neither Piaget nor Nicolich distinguishes between play with a live partner and play with a doll, Fein and Apfel (1979) found that feeding a live partner tends to be easier than feeding a doll (a representation of a person). If this finding can be replicated, we have strong grounds for assuming that infants are treating a doll as a human replica when doll-directed behavior does emerge.

A related question concerning early use of a replica as recipient of action is whether the child is merely projecting his own behavior onto a doll or is actually pretending at caregiving. Piaget clearly assumed the former:

> In projecting his own behavior onto others (making dolls cry, eat, drink or sleep) the child himself is imitating the actions they do when they reproduce his own actions. (Piaget, 1962, p. 123)

This statement sounds remarkably like a description of role taking or seeing oneself from the viewpoint of the other (Mead, 1934), doubly remarkable because of Piaget's belief in the profound egocentrism of toddlers.

The distinction between projecting behavior onto a doll and pretending caregiving is difficult to detect because some doll-directed behaviors seem to be unambiguous simulations of caregiving (putting a doll to bed and tucking in its blankets). If the doll is a passive partner rather than a symbolic representation of the self, a higher level of role representation is achieved, the representation of two roles (agent and recipient in interaction). To make the distinction between these two alternative interpretations, when possible, is therefore important.

Parallel Roles (Self as Agent and Other as Recipient). Nicolich (1977) observed that toddlers have a strong tendency to include themselves and the mother or themselves and a doll in the same parallel acts, after each of these behaviors has been mastered separately. This represents a step toward representation of reciprocal interaction with the other person (leading to sociodramatic play) or the doll (leading to more complex replica play). Wolf (1982) also studied parallel play:

> O. presents a bag of toy implements to J. [at 16 months]. Each one that he tries, he tries first on himself, and then on a big doll. He takes out a comb and combs the back and then the front of his hair, then the doll's. He takes toy scissors, clipping at the hair around his and then the doll's ears. (p. 314)

Replica as Active Recipient. I see strong grounds for treating this behavior as a separate category. Mere holding of a bottle to a doll's mouth (the replica as passive recipient) differs from doll feeding accompanied by talking to the doll and/or ascribing feelings and perceptions to the doll (see also Wolf, 1982). Piaget (1962) provides a striking example of this behavior:

> [At 25 months Jacqueline fed her doll] for a long time in the way we used to encourage her to eat her own meals: "a little drop more, to please Jacqueline. Just eat this little bit." (Obs. 81, p. 127)

While the doll is treated as a human figure that has sensations and wishes, the child is not yet vicariously acting *for* a doll. This constitutes the next level.

Replica as Agent. When the child acts for the doll or pretends that a doll can act on its own (feed itself), the child becomes a vicarious actor. This type of behavior has been observed by Fenson and Ramsay (1980), Fenson (1984), Inhelder, Lezine, Sinclair, and Stambak (1972), Lowe (1975) and Watson and Fischer (1980), although it is not always distinguished from use of a replica as active recipient. Curiously, the act of talking for the doll is seldom discussed in this connection, perhaps because of a desire to consider enactive and verbal representation in terms of separate symbol systems. Again, Piaget provides an instructive example:

> J. said "cry, cry" to her dog and herself imitated the sound of crying. On the following day, she made her bear, duck, etc. cry. (Piaget, 1962, Obs. 75a, p. 121)

Assuming a Role. In assuming a role I am conceptually equating the child's acting for the doll with the ability to pretend at being another person (although empirical data to support this hunch are not yet available). Although both activities constitute role play, in the case of animating a doll role play is vicarious, whereas assuming another person's role is direct. Piaget descibes early forms of this identification which he terms "assimilation of the ego to others":

> At 1 J. rubbed the floor with a shell, then with a cardboard lid, saying: "Brush Abebert" (like the charwoman). The same day she pulled her hair back as she looked at herself in the mirror, and said, laughing, "Daddy." (Piaget, 1962, Obs. 76a, p. 122)

As Piaget (1962) notes, such behavior transcends imitation because the child does not merely copy the behavior of others while continuing to be himself; he identifies completely with others. Huttenlocher and Higgins (1978), who draw the same distinction, require that the child make a verbal statement indicating identification with the other. It may, however, be possible to create nonverbal criteria for this level.

Replica as Active Partner. A more complex form of role-representation than either activation of a doll or assumption of another role is engagement in reciprocal interaction with the "active" doll. In doing so, the child has to enact two complementary roles. An example of this type of behavior at 21 months appears in Wolf's (1982) case study:

> J. develops a new pattern of interaction with his jack-in-the-box. If, when he presses down the lid on top of the box, its hand is poking out of the corner of the lid, J. calls out "Ouch, ouch. Boo-boo" (his word for a hurt). He then quickly cranks the lid so that it pops open, rubs down the clown's

hand and kisses it, before careful stuffing it back down into the hole, hand and all. (p. 319)

Miller and Garvey (1984) provide several illustrations of this ability around 30 months (a child mothers a baby doll, but also speaks and cries for it).

Simple Joint Role Play. In joint pretense a child need only enact one role (not two, as is necessary when a doll becomes the active partner). However, joint role play requires the child to coordinate his or her event schemas or action-plans with those of another person, an equivalent ability. Early joint pretense tends to be observed only when a toddler plays with a more experienced partner such as an older sibling or the parent who engages in frequent coaching (see Dunn & Dale, 1984; Miller & Garvey, 1984).

Replica Interaction with Self as Narrator. The development of spontaneous and prompted play with small figures has been extensively studied by Wolf and her colleagues (Rubin & Wolf, 1979; Wolf, 1982; Wolf et al., 1984). (Watson and Fischer (1980) independently investigated some of the same behavior.) Rubin and Wolf emphasize that only in the third year do children learn to animate several small figures without themselves participating in the plot as actor. First attempts at activating two figures often consist of casting them in parallel roles (instead of lion chasing boy, both lion and boy run away). The subsequent mastery of doll play with several interacting figures about whom the child talks as narrator and for whom the child talks as vicarious actor marks a significant step in child development. An example of this simple form of story-telling can be found in Wolf's case study (1982):

> J. has a parent figure and a child figure. O. has also given him some doll furniture. He lays the child in bed, making the parent walk over and kiss the child. Then he makes the child hop out of bed and run off to under the table. He makes the parent figure chase after the child, calling out, "Get you." (p. 320)

Later, the roles assigned to the replicas tend to become more differentiated (a nasty lion may chase a frightened boy, or he may feel lonely; Rubin & Wolf, 1979). Alternatively, each replica can assume more than one social role (a boy can be the doctor's son as well as his patient; Watson & Fischer, 1980).

Joint Play with Interacting Roles. When several players collaborate in socio-dramatic play, each one has to coordinate his role with the others'. Thus, some knowledge of complementary role structures is necessary for collaborative pretense as well as for complex replica play. Miller and Garvey (1984) describe an early instance of this ability: a 30-month-old girl plays "mother" to "baby" and "wife" to "husband," while simultaneously coaching "husband" how to perform the role of "father."

In addition, the role repertoire undergoes development. In analyzing collaborative role play in preschool children between the ages of 3 and 5, Garvey (1977) found it useful to distinguish functional roles from character roles. Garvey's functional roles define the behavior but not the permanent identity of the person in the pretend situation (driver and passenger of a pretend car). Functional roles therefore resemble what Watson and Fischer (1980) call behavioral roles, Rubin and Wolf (1979) call pragmatic roles, and Hutterlocher and Higgins (1978) call role enactments (contrasting it with role play). Even though older children can explicitly identify themselves with another person in play, Garvey's data show that they do not always choose to do so. Hence, functional roles persist after the mastery of character roles.

Diverging somewhat from Garvey's scheme which made a distinction between character roles and family roles, I include in *character roles* family roles (mother, father, baby), occupational roles (doctor, nurse), and fictive roles (Superman, Snow White). Younger children tend to pretend at family roles more than occupational and fictive roles. Moreover, they tend to restrict themselves to those family roles with which they have direct experience (baby or child, father, mother). Older preschoolers continue to enact family roles, but add the roles of husband and wife to their repertoire, as well as occupational and fictive roles.

In summary, it is evident that some forms of role-taking and playing are present as soon as the infant develops beyond self-representation. By 18 to 24 months, these activities include use of replicas as experiencers as well as agents (Wolf, 1982). At the end of the third year a child is capable of much more: in performing a drama including several interacting dolls, he can play an event from several points of view (play and take roles); in joint make-believe a child can coordinate his viewpoint of the make-believe event with that of other children.

Actions

A baby's initial pretend actions consist of single behaviors. Later in the second year toddlers reenact sequences of actions. As with role play, there is major agreement among investigators on the development of pretend actions, but difficulty in defining the activities.

Single Actions. With single pretend behaviors, such as drinking from an empty cup, is the child merely performing the appropriate action with an object, or actually pretending at the function (drinking a pretend liquid)? This is difficult to know because infants' first appropriate acts with meaningful objects are often cursory, as if to indicate "I know what to do with this." However, even when there are indications that the infant is pretending, the meaning of the make-believe action for the child depends on the object with which the infant is playing. The question is easily answered in the case of drinking, since the child presumably notices that the cup holds no liquid. I have observed that many 1-year-olds, given an empty cup, will actually feel its inside before proceeding to drink. However, I am convinced that in pretend telephoning, infants do not realize the function (communication) until much later, even though they know at one year of age to hold the receiver somewhere near the neck-face area. Thus, whether the child pretends at the function as well as the outward action depends on how well he understands the real-world function of particular objects.

Action Sequences. Most investigators (Fenson & Ramsay, 1980; Nicolich, 1977) have reported that children begin to combine acts in pretend play late in the second year. However, in a recent study (Bretherton, Bates, McNew, Shore, Williamson, & Beeghly-Smith, 1981) very simple combinations were observed in 13-month-olds (45 percent of the infants both hugged and/or kissed, and rocked and cooed a teddy-bear or doll; 50 percent lifted a telephone receiver to their neck/face area and said "hi"). While these are simpler combinations than some examples previously described in the literature, they undeniably constitute two separate behaviors. In studying pretense as early event representation, we may therefore have to distinguish finer qualitative levels in the development of scheme combinations. Moreover, the combination of manual and vocal schemes in the representation of actions must be taken into account in the study of early pretense.

The first action sequences described by Nicolich (1977) consisted of applying the same behavior to several objects in turn (stirring in the cup, then stirring in the pitcher). As single-scheme combinations there is no obligatory order in which these two parallel actions must be carried out. In most cases infants acquire the component actions and perform them separately before they combine them into a sequence (Fenson & Ramsay, 1981). It is therefore not paucity of the child's pretend action repertoire that delays the onset of sequences.

Ordered Action Sequences. Ordered action sequences are those in which each action has a meaningful relation to the preceding one. Fenson and Ramsay (1980, 1981) hypothesized that the execution of unordered combinations should precede the reproduction of ordered combinations, but found very few nonordered sequences even at 15 months. Examples of ordered sequences would be pouring "tea" into a cup, then "drinking" from it, or placing a pillow on the doll-bed, then laying the head on the pillow as if to go to sleep. To count as ordered, the scheme sequence has to reflect a logical or ecological order. Most but not all combinations defined as ordered were unidirectional, that is, they were not meaningful when the position of the two component acts was reversed. Such an unordered sequence would be placing the doll in bed, then combing its hair (Fenson & Ramsay, 1980). Fenson and Ramsay's findings are in accord with Nelson and Gruendel's (1981) study in which 3-year-olds reported the component acts of scripts in the correct order. However, the high level of ordering in younger children in the Fenson and Ramsay study may have been partly due to the presentation of the toys in organized sets (personal communication, 1984). Recent studies by Gerard (1984) and O'Connell (O'Connell & Gerard, in press; O'Connell, 1984) contend that ordered sequencing of action, at least in elicitation studies, is mastered only in the course of the third year.

There are few systematic studies describing the development of higher levels of sequencing, yet it is surely necessary to distinguish a mere two-action sequence from the following example provided by Inhelder et al. (1972):

> Thus Pierre, at 22 months, imitates in detail how his mother feeds her baby as he puts the nipple of the bottle to the baby-doll's mouth with a well-coordinated movement, lifts up the baby's head which is resting in the crook of his arm, then holds up the bottle and pulls on the nipple as if it had collapsed, looks at the bottle, shakes it like an adult feeding a baby and "checks" the level of formula in the bottle, then returns the bottle to the baby's mouth, pushing the nipple forcefully against its mouth. (p. 217)

Fenson (personal communication), who studied spontaneous action sequences in 20- to 31-month-olds, found that 50 percent of his sample performed two-act sequences at 20 months. At 26 and 31 months, this percentage had risen to 71 percent. In addition, 33 percent of the 31-month-olds enacted three-act sequences and 17 percent four-act sequences. Rheingold and Emery (in press) observed action sequences somewhat earlier. In their study, all 18-month-olds achieved two-act sequences, and by 30 months all of the children performed meaningful five-act sequences. The cause for this discrepancy may lie in the longer observation period (30 minutes) used by Rheingold and Emery.

Episode Combinations. Some of the longer sequences in these two studies probably consisted of several subepisodes, but there are no empirical studies of episode structure in the pretend play of young children. Inhelder, Lezine, Sinclair, and Stambak (1972) briefly mention the emergence of multiepisode play in the third year, where episodes are linked in a meaningful order (for example, feeding the baby-doll, then giving it a bath). Wolf (1982) describes what I consider to be an early instance of episode combination. In this example, the episodes are accident/treatment:

> J., at 20 months, had a minor accident in which he cut his forehead. For several weeks thereafter he re-enacts the specific details of falling, crying,

being stitched up, wearing a bike helmet to protect the cut using a large doll. (p. 314)

Throughout the toddler period, pretend action sequences are primarily based on everyday experience. Although the 3- to 5-year-olds studied by Garvey (1979) had a considerably larger repertoire of out-of-home and fictional events, much of their sociodramatic play continued to revolve around family life. The older children also incorporated increasingly more out-of-home and fictional material into their joint pretense. A few general themes accounted for the greater proportion of make-believe events: treating/healing, averting threat, packing, taking a trip, going to the store, cooking, having a meal, and repairing were especially popular themes. A theme requires a more abstract framework than a basic-level event schema. For example, to enact the theme "averting threat," a number of very different event schemas or scripts may be instantiated (the threat can be a monster, fire, or getting lost).

Objects

Infants' first efforts at pretending appear to require prototypical objects, such as realistic spoons, telephones, or baby-dolls (Piaget, 1962; Vygotsky, 1966; Nicolich, 1977). Later, such realism becomes less necessary to sustain the make-believe reality, although many children seem to need tangible placeholders to stand for imagined objects. Empty-handed miming is infrequent in spontaneous play until the middle of the third year (Fenson, 1984).

Realistic Objects. The presence of realistic objects provides perceptual/tactile/spatial support for the performance of simple event schemas such as sleeping or eating. Without such support 12-month-olds are unlikely to engage in pretending at all. However, complete realism is *not* required. Abstract (pared down) versions of the real thing also elicit pretend play. Neither Piaget (1962) nor Nicolich (1977) speaks of object substitution when infants use a toy that recognizably resembles a realistic object, even though it is not a "good" prototypical exemplar. This weaker form of substitution is possible even for 13-month-olds. Bretherton, Bates, McNew, Shore, Williamson, and Beeghly-Smith (1981) found that most 13-month-olds performed some pretend behaviors with pared down but recognizable versions of cups, spoons, telephones, dolls, and cars, although they produced significantly fewer symbolic schemes with pared down than with fully realistic objects.

Object Substitution. Later in the second year children begin to use blocks as cars and spoons as telephones. Several explanations for the emergence of such object substitution have been offered. Piaget considered assimilation of one object as another (use of a shell as a cup) to be conceptually equivalent to assimilating another person to the ego (role-play). His interpretation resembles Vygotsky's (1966) notion that substitute objects serve as pivots whose function, in symbolic terms, is to sever the meaning of an object from the real object, making it a true symbol. Not all objects, Vygotsky claims, can function as pivots (a postcard could never serve as a pivot for a horse). Nevertheless, from a Vygotskyan perspective, object substitution implies that meaning has come to dominate over appearances; that the symbol and that which the symbol stands for have come to bear a somewhat arbitrary relation to one another.

Nicolich (1977) took a different approach to object substitution by classifying it under the rubric "planful" behavior. In her study, infant's first object substitutions, late in the second year, coincided with other foresightful acts, such as announcing the script to be enacted or searching for toys relevant to a planned script. The substitution (transformation) resulted from the child's need for an object to fit his plans.

Several recent studies have attempted to identify those features of the substitute object (appearance, function) which interfere most with substitution (Bretherton, O'Connell, Shore & Bates, 1984; Fein, 1975; Jackowitz & Watson, 1980; Kagan, 1981; Killen & Uzgiris, 1981; Largo & Howard, 1979; Watson & Fischer, 1980; Ungerer, Zelazo, Kearsley, & O'Leary, 1981). Others have simply compared play with meaningful and nonmeaningful object sets. Jeffree and McConkey (1976) observed ten children in a playhouse situation at 6-month intervals, beginning at 18 months and ending at 42 months. Two sets of toys, one prototypical and the other consisting of junk materials (cans, boxes, rags) were presented to the children for 5 minutes of spontaneous play. The children played significantly less with the junk materials, but showed their highest level of play with both types of objects. Unfortunately, the findings were not broken down by age and thus they cannot be compared with results obtained by Kagan (1981). Kagan compared spontaneous play with realistic and unrealistic objects in 13- to 25-month-olds. Again, children engaged in more symbolic acts with the realistic toys at all ages, but at 25 months the difference in the proportion of time they spent playing with each type of toy was not significant.

In both of these above studies children played with either a whole set of realistic or a whole set of abstract toys. Only one investigation (Fein 1975) compared the effect of single and multiple substitutions. Children 26-months-old were invited to play with prototypical and abstract versions of a horse and an eggcup. Almost all the children spontaneously fed the prototypical horse with the prototypical cup. Seventy-nine percent of the toddlers fed the prototypical horse with the abstract cup (a clam shell), while 61 percent fed the abstract horse (a shaped piece of metal) with the realistic eggcup. Double substitutions (feeding the abstract horse with the shell) were much more difficult; only 33 percent of the toddlers performed them.

Finally, there is evidence that object substitution is easier when the substitute object is a meaningless placeholder than when it is a familiar object used in a "counterconventional" manner (Bretherton et al., 1984; Ungerer et al., 1981). Perhaps the counterconventional object (a comb to be used as a spoon) already has strong object-associated meanings for the child which interfere with the act of substitution. A placeholder object such as a stick or a block may be imbued more easily with imaginary qualities at the younger ages.

Miming. Investigators generally agree that empty-handed miming, unsupported by perceptual/tactile cues from an object, is uncommon in early pretense (though not in communication; see Acredolo, 1985). Fenson (1984) saw virtually no miming in the spontaneous play of 21- to 31-month-olds, although Piaget (1962) reports an instance of miming at 12 months:

> J. scratched at the wallpaper in the bedroom where there was the design of a bird, then shut her hand as if it held the bird and went to her mother: "Look (she opened her hand and pretended to be giving [her] something).—What have you brought me?—A birdie." (Obs. 74)

Other examples of miming described by Piaget (1962) occurred after the age of two years. At 24 months Jacqueline moved her finger along the edge of a table saying: "finger walking, horse trotting." Note that she actually described the transformation (finger to horse) and that she used a bodypart (the finger) to stand for agent-action (horse-trotting). At 27 months Jacqueline made a circular movement with her fingers, saying "bicycle spoilt," followed by another circular gesture, accompanied by "bicycle mended." Here the gesture appeared to depict the object (the wheel or perhaps the rolling of the wheel as well) whereas the script (breakage/repair) was verbal. At 29 months Jacqueline, in preparation for giving her sister a make-believe bath, mimed an undressing sequence without ever touching Lucienne's clothes. At 30 months she pretended to have a baby in her arms and put it down on an imaginary bed. What is noteworthy about the latter two examples is that they are pure pantomime, in the sense that the child did not depict the object but merely the action on the object. Work by Overton and Jackson (1973) suggests that pure pantomime is more difficult than use of a body part to depict both object and action, although these results are based on a verbal prompting paradigm, not observation of spontaneous instances.

In the course of my own studies I have observed a 13-month-old boy build a tower consisting of several blocks, and then alongside it, construct an imaginary tower of equal height. The same child was also reported to play pebble-tossing games which began with real pebbles but continued with imaginary ones. These examples, taken together with Piaget's observations, suggest that it might be useful to look for instances of spontaneous miming at earlier ages. Finer distinctions in descriptions of miming may be needed. Fenson (1984) points out that "pouring" from an empty pitcher is a form of miming with object support, especially when the child shakes the pitcher to "get out the last drop."

Miming is not the only way in which an imaginary object can be brought into pretense. Sometimes invented substances are merely specified by naming (Fenson, 1984; Bretherton et al., 1984; Matthews, 1977). Verbal invention in the presence of perceptual support is a frequent occurrence during the third year and deserves further study.

Although play with nonveridical objects and miming become more common with age, realistic objects continue to be important. In a study of collaborative pretending, Garvey and Berndt (1977) found that the presence of a realistic prop often led to the instantiation of a related script (their term is action-schema). However, once make-believe was underway, the ongoing script usually determined subsequent object-transformations. In their study of 3- to 5-year-olds, a three-legged stool with a magnifying glass in its center was transformed into a telescope (to spot a fire), a toilet (to take care of baby), a workchair (to perform a household task), a trailer (to pack for a trip) and a milk-carton (to shop for provisions). The last two substitutions did not appear to be inspired by the perceptual properties of the transformed object.

The Integration of Roles, Actions, and Objects

The findings of Nicolich's (1977) longitudinal study of 14- to 19-month-olds, suggest that progress in role representation (making others the recipients of one's action, enacting others' behavior) generally occurs before children begin to enact sequences, and that object substitution is acquired last. However, there may be a trade-off between the three dimensions (roles, actions, and objects). For example, a toddler might be able to represent two interacting roles without sequenced action. Likewise, sequences might first appear in conjunction with self-representation (the lowest level of role performance). Analogous findings have been reported in studies of language acquisition. Children in the two-word stage can specify object-action, agent-object, and agent-action relations, but they cannot combine the components into one agent-action-object relation. If similar trade-offs occur in symbolic play, a child, for example, could use a big bear to kiss a small bear, or use one of the bears to pour juice and then drink it, but he could not make one bear pour juice for the other to drink. The complexity of role and action representation may additionally interact with object substitution. Toddlers may be able to act out a sequence, provided they have access to veridical toys, but revert to single actions with a substitute object. This may be true only in early pretense, however. During the later preschool years nonsuggestive props may help rather than hinder more complex forms of pretense (Phillips, 1945;

Pulaski, 1973, as reviewed in Fein, 1981). The relevant studies in which role-, action-, and object-representations in children's spontaneous play are examined as separate but interacting dimensions still remain to be done.

An additional aspect of event-representation in pretense is acquisition of procedural rules. In sociodramatic play, children not only enact make-believe sequences, but also plan, negotiate, and coordinate their joint enactment. The term *metacommunication* was coined by Bateson (1955, 1956) to refer to messages that inform co-players that "this is play" as opposed to not play.

Metacommunication in pretense becomes very prominent during the fourth and fifth years. Although precursors of this ability can be traced to infancy, systematic studies of metacommunicative signals during the second and third years are still lacking. I suggest that the very same criteria for judging whether a child is engaging in a literal or nonliteral act (Nicolich, 1977) can also be interpreted as metacommunication about play. Several relevant instances are described in Piaget (1962). For example, Jacqueline at 15 months "alluded" to closed eyes by blinking as she put her head on a blanket in pretend sleep (Obs. 64a). At 28 months she announced her transformed identity to her father ("it's mommy"), assuming a third-person bystander role, before requesting that Piaget give "mommy" a kiss (Obs. 79). Yet when she transformed herself into a cat at 32 months (Obs. 79), she merely crawled into the room on all fours saying "meow." Perhaps overt metacommunication is less necessary when the pretend act is not likely to be confused with real-world action. Several further illustrations of metacommunication during the third year can be found in Miller and Garvey (1984) and Dunn and Dale (1984). Very early comprehension, as opposed to production, of metacommunicative signals is suggested by Fein and Moorin's (in press) case study of a 15-month-old girl who responded appropriately to verbal pretend invitations (to "feed" a doll, or adults), but the metacommunicative ability truly comes into its own during the preschool years. Event representation then proceeds on two conceptually distinct levels.

Multiple Conceptual Levels of Event Representation in Pretense

Because acts of pretense can look and sound quite real, it is necessary to identify the make-believe reality as simulation or fiction to avoid misunderstandings. Bateson (1955) first drew attention to the fact that pretense must be framed by the message "this is play." He found such messages logically paradoxical, saying in effect: "These actions in which we now engage do not denote what the actions for which they stand would denote"; or to put it more concretely: "This nip is not a bite."

The management of play at two conceptual levels (communicating outside the playframe about actions to be performed within the playframe) has been examined in three studies, two concerned with the conduct of collaborative make-believe (Garvey & Berndt, 1977; Giffin, 1984) and one with replica play (Scarlett & Wolf, 1979). Each of these studies approached the topic of frame-negotiation from a somewhat different angle.

Garvey and Berndt (1977) go beyond Bateson (1955) in their definition of metacommunication emphasizing that the joint creation of a make-believe reality requires more than the message "this is play." In order to pretend with companions, children need techniques for negotiating about content: what theme or script is to be played, and where as well as how the theme is to be realized. Garvey and Berndt studied forty-eight acquainted dyads, paired by age, with ages ranging from 34 to 67 months. The children were observed during 8 minutes of spontaneous, joint make-believe play in a laboratory playroom. From this material Garvey and Berndt developed a system for categorizing the metacommunicative behaviors (mostly verbal statements) by which children coordinate sociodramatic play:

1.	Mention role	other's	"Are you going to be a bride?"
		own	"I'm a lady at work."
		joint	"We can both be wives."
2.	Mention plan	other's	"Pretend you hated baby fish."
		own	"I gotta drive to the shopping center."
		joint	"We have to eat. Our dinner's ready."
3.	Mention object	transform	"This is the train," putting suitcase on sofa.
		invent	"Now this is cheese," pointing to empty plate.
4.	Mention setting	transform	"This is a cave," pointing to wooden structure.
		invent	"We're there," about imaginary picnic site.

Garvey and Berndt also observed that exits from the pretend world are explicitly negotiated by negating make-believe roles ("I'm not the Dad"), actions ("I'm not dead"), props ("that's not a car"), and settings ("we're not at the beach"). Especially interesting are back-transformations ("it's not a cake anymore"; "please don't push me 'cause I'm not the dragon anymore"). Similar exit statements were analyzed by Matthews (1978).

Giffin's study (1984) focused not so much on the content of metacommunication but on *how* children used a variety of metacommunicative options to coordinate shared meanings. Her analysis of thirty-one play episodes produced by thirty-eight previously acquainted preschool children in groups of two to five players identified a variety of metacommunicative devices on a continuum from explicitly out-of-frame to deeply within-frame. She noted that the children's play seemed to be guided by an unspoken rule not to expose the pretend illusion unnecessarily.

Through the use of exaggerated gestures and postures, children can convey the message "this is play" without explicit metacommunication (Garvey & Berndt, 1977). Not so obvious is how the *content* of play can be coordinated and redirected without stepping outside the playframe. Giffin (1984) discovered that the children in her study were masters at the task. One category of metacommunication, *ulterior conversation,* looked like enactment but was actually a surreptitious way of suggesting a change in the ongoing plot. For example, the question "Is it lunchtime?" when the children were not at that point playing at having lunch was considered ulterior conversation. A somewhat more overt form of metacommunication, but still within-frame, was *underscoring.* This refers to statements such as "I'll pour the milk" spoken as a pitcher was tipped over an empty cup, informing the playmate that the pitcher "contained" milk as opposed to juice. Outside the playframe, at the breakfast table, such statements would sound peculiar (except to someone in another room). Remarks such as "I'm crying" said in a wailing tone of voice disturb the pretend illusion somewhat more obviously, but still remain within the playframe. Similar to underscoring statements, *magicking* refers to statements rhytmically chanted (for example, "wash-wash-wash" accompanied by rubbing clothes; "cooky, cooky, cooky" accompanied by a few stirring motions above a pot). Giffin interprets magicking as a theatrical device, whereby chanting both metacommunicates about and substitutes for an abbreviated make-believe action.

A special sing-song cadence also characterizes *story-telling.* This sophisticated form of verbal make-believe allowed children to develop more elaborate plots without acting them out ". . . and you went to bed right after supper . . . I went to bed later than you . . . I went to bed three hours later than you . . . and the kitty went to bed even before you" (Giffin, 1981). Interestingly, the children tended to couch their storytelling in the past tense. On occasion, a player must metacommunicate outside the playframe. *Prompting* is one such form of metacommunication. The prompter "drops" out of role to whisper: "You didn't talk like that, you say" (modeling in a honeyed voice) "What's the matter, Mother'?" (Giffin, 1984). One of Garvey and Berndt's (1977) protocols illustrates a girl of 39 months prompting a boy of 33 months how to play daddy!

Implicit and formal pretend proposals are another form of metacommunication situated outside the playframe. *Implicit pretend proposals* do not draw attention to the frame, but to designations of roles ("I'm the mommy"), of settings ("this is the kitchen") or transformation of objects ("this is my key" about a stick) constitute communication *about* the play to ensue. *Formal pretend statements* are even more explicit, such as "let's pretend [say, play] we were monsters." In Giffin's study, formal pretend proposals were quite rare and were most likely to occur at the start of play. Once a play episode had begun, players tended to resort to more indirect forms of managing the pretend reality (ulterior conversation, storytelling, magicking). Skilled players, as defined by Giffin, knew when they could afford to metacommunicate within-frame and when it was necessary to step out-of-frame, even though this broke the "illusion conservation rule." An example was the command "pretend that I was dead, but you thought I was alive" (made by a child 45 months old). It is difficult to see how an idea of this complexity could have been conveyed by mere acting (lying still) or by ulterior conversation. Further study is necessary to learn the order in which the various metacommunicative options are acquired and to pinpoint developmental changes in the skill with which they are used.

Independently of the work on collaborative pretense, Wolf and Scarlett (1979) examined how children manage the boundary between make-believe and reality in replica play. Instead of playing the dual role of producer and actor, the child who animates small figures frequently assumes the dual-level roles of narrator (describing to a real or imagined audience what the figures are doing) and vicarious actor (acting and speaking for the figures). Interestingly, many of the metacommunicative devices that are used in sociodramatic play are also found in replica play. Narration, for example, occurs not only in collaborative play where it takes the form of underscoring and storytelling, but also in describing the action of small figures. Out-of-frame formal pretend proposals in sociodramatic play are paralleled by a narrator's proposal to the audience "let's pretend this is cheese" (of a piece of wood). As in sociodramatic play, by the end of the preschool period the bulk of fictive meaning in replica play is carried by what the children say about or for the characters, including their plans and motives (Wolf, 1984).

In sociodramatic and replica play (as well as hybrids thereof) children operate on two levels of event representation (out-of-frame planning and within-frame acting; out-of-frame narration and within-frame vicarious acting). Because they weave from level to level so effortlessly, we have not noticed the presence of conceptually distinct levels in play until recently (caution: I am not talking about developmental levels). Sutton-Smith (1978) has suggested that all play be considered a quadralogue in which an individual player must keep track of four prototypical parties: actor, coactor, director, and audience. Although his position is similar to the one proposed here, his model omits the emphasis on levels of event representation. Conceptually, the relationship of actor and co-actor is situated within the playframe, whereas the relationship of director and co-director is conducted outside the playframe—even if, as in prompting, stepping outside the playframe is brief and intermittent or, as in ulterior conversation or underscoring, only implicit. The audience constitutes a third level that is not analyzed in this chapter.

What is so fascinating about sociodramatic and replica play, is that the logically clear distinction between the acts of planning (or describing) and acting is deliberately blurred, once it has been mastered. Statements that look like acting are really or simultaneously metacommunication about play.

Likewise, real-world action and pretend action are logically distinct. As Bateson has so aptly stated: "The map is not the territory"; yet map and territory (pretense and reality) have a strange way of becoming tangled in pretense. Frightening make-believe themes may become so real that a player feels compelled to step outside the playframe or refuses to enter it, as the following conversation between two preschoolers, taken from Garvey and Berndt's (1977) protocols, illustrates:

Pretend there is a monster coming, OK?

No, let's don't pretend that.

OK, why?

'Cause it's too scary, that's why.

Scarlett and Wolf (1979) also noted that map and territory (fantasy and reality) are sometimes difficult to keep apart. In their study of spontaneous and prompted play with small human and animal figures, 2-year-olds frequently backed away with genuine fear when the observer animated a small toy alligator. Young children were unable to cope with the pretend threat on its own terms (for example by making a lion chase the observer's alligator). At other times the children dropped the narrator role and entered the story scene as deus ex machina to rescue a figure "endangered" by the observer's play. This resembles Garvey and Berndt's (1977) example of the child who refused to play monsters because "it's too scary." Wolf and Scarlett found that the blurring of reality and pretense becomes less frequent with age. However, it never completely disappears and is especially noticeable when the thematic content of pretense is highly emotional. Even adults may weep during dramatic presentations or treat symbolic objects (a flag, a cross) as what they represent (Bateson, 1956). Fictive reality does arouse genuine emotion and participation. It is never completely detached except in the logical sense. Indeed, it would carry little meaning if it were.

Not only does pretense sometimes become too real, real-world concerns intrude into the make-believe world in a number of ways (through the themes which are enacted, in the way roles are distributed, by bits of external reality incorporated into the play). Schwartzman's (1978) study of collaborative play in a day-care center sheds interesting light on this topic. In studying a group of working-class preschoolers over a period of 18 months, she found that the relationship the players had to each other outside the play context (friendships, dominance) affected the content and process of sociodramatic play. For example, high-status children could join ongoing play by imperiously adopting a role or defining an activity. Low-status children had to ask for permission to join the group or play particular roles ("Can I be the witch?"). The roles children played tended to reflect the actual authority structure of the group. Those who frequently played mothers and fathers were the most popular children in the classroom. By contrast, the role of pet (kitty or doggy) was often assumed by one of the less popular children. However, the leading child in the day-care center sometimes paradoxically defined himself or herself in a submissive role even as he or she continued to direct the activities of her co-players. These findings led Schwartzman to claim that play can be regarded as text and context. Play as text is the creation of a make-believe reality within the real-world context of the day care center. Play as context is commentary on the everyday relationships of the players as children in a day care center:

> In order to be a successful player, one must be able to communicate information that simultaneously (and paradoxically) defines one as a player *subject* (e.g., adopting the play role of witch, mother, etc.) and as a person in the defining social context (e.g., the daycare center) and therefore a play *object*. For example, a child (Linda) must be able to communicate to other players that she is both Linda (i.e., a person who leads, dominates, and directs activities, as she is known for this in the general classroom setting) and not-Linda (i.e., a witch or mother) in a play situation. (Schwartzman, 1978, p. 236)

Along similar lines, Garvey and Berndt (1977) found that preschool boys appear far more willing to transform their generational status than their gender. In mixed-sex dyads, boys steadfastly refused the role of mother but accepted the role of father. In single-sex dyads boys did sometimes assume functional roles normally played by females (server of food) but refrained from overtly identifying with a female role. When mixed-sex dyads played "averting threat," the boy—true to stereotype—was usually cast in the role of defender and the girl in the role of victim.

The out-of-frame world also intrudes into the play world in other, less emotionally charged ways. Some of the plot-changes (re-transformations) described by Giffin (1984) were precipitated by the wish to admit new players. When a car to be taken on an imaginary journey became too small to hold all the players who were eager to join, a camper was added to accommodate them. In one case two children created the synthetic role of doctor-mommy which enabled them to play the family and doctor scripts simultaneously, thus satisfying both children's plans. In addition, out-of-frame events (a child falls over) are often taken into the frame by adjusting the plot (the child is taken to a "hospital"). This phenomenon was also noticed by Schwartzman (1978) and by Wolf and Pusch (1982). Such transformations of transformations in response to real-world events or real-world constraints again bring home the paradoxical intertwining of out-of-frame and within-frame content—of map and territory.

A separate aspect of pretense is the transformation rather than recreation of reality through simulation: the roles children play are often not their own, the objects serving as props are frequently not what they purport to be, and the scripts may represent physically impossible worlds. The creation of fictive events in pretense will be discussed next.

The Representation of Subjunctive Events in Symbolic Play

Pretending is hardly ever straight re-production of event schemas. Event schemas and specific memories provide the raw material for make-believe scenes, but most play is not an attempt at faithful reproduction. Rather, make-believe consists of making new maps by transforming old ones (to use the map-territory metaphor yet again).

The term *make-believe* has two meanings. First, it serves to distinguish the level of everyday reality where one actually eats, drinks, and sleeps from the fictive level where one merely simulates these behaviors ("as if" transformations). Second, make-believe refers to "what if" transformations of reality, to the creation of worlds where a spoon can be a telephone, toddlers can be mommy and daddy, animals can speak, and people can fly or become invisible.

Hofstadter (1979) has pointed out that human beings constantly manufacture mental variants on the situations they encounter. These unconsciously manufactured subjunctives represent some of the richest potential sources of insights into how humans organize and categorize their perceptions of reality:

> Think how immeasurably poorer our lives would be if we didn't have this capacity for slipping out of the midst of reality into soft "what if's"! And from the point of view of studying human thought this slippage is very interesting, for most of the time it happens completely without conscious direction, which means that observation of what kind of things slip, versus what kinds don't, affords a good window on the unconscious mind. (p. 643)

Hofstadter proposes a hierarchy of conditions for transforming or "slipping" aspects of reality. The easiest transformations are to transform behaviors (a toddler pretends at adult activities). Higher levels of transformation consists of slipping the context of action, not merely the action (a preschooler plays an adult role vis-à-vis another child who is baby). The highest levels of transformation require slippage of natural laws (the laws of gravity, causality, three-dimensional space). Although this level of transformation may not be activated in thinking about serious alternatives, it is commonly activated in play where gravity is denied, time is contracted and expanded, and causality and values are turned upside down.

Oddly, Piaget (1962) took the ability to engage in counterfactual representation completely for granted. The cognitive implications of the term assimilation to the ego (distorting reality according to one's wishes) are nowhere elaborated. It is something children are simply able to do for the pleasure of mastering reality, liquidating conflicts, compensating for unpleasant experiences, and taking revenge on reality:

> But why is there assimilation of reality to the ego instead of immediate assimilation of the universe to experimental and logical thought? It is simply because in early childhood this thought has not yet been constructed, and during its development it is inadequate to supply the needs of daily life. (p. 166)

But even wishful thinking, it seems to me, requires the cognitive capacity to create alternative worlds, at least in a small way. There is subjunctive thought when pretense serves to correct reality, as illustrated by the following two examples of what Piaget calls "compensatory" symbolic combinations:

> At [28 months], J., not being allowed to play with the water being used for washing, took an empty cup, went and stood by the forbidden tub and went through the actions saying: "I'm pouring out water." At [30 months] she wanted to carry Nonette (i.e., L., who had been born shortly before). Her mother told her she could try later on. J. folded her arms and said: "Nonette's in there. There are two Nonettes." She then talked to the imaginary Nonette, rocked her, etc. (Piaget, 1962, Obs. 84, p. 131)

The same argument can be made when symbolic play is employed to "liquidate" a disagreeable event by "reproducing scenes in which the ego ran the risk of failure, thereby enabling it to assimilate them and emerge victorious" (Piaget, 1962). In the following example Jacqueline alters reality by projecting an unpleasant experience onto another recipient:

> J., at [25 months], was afraid when sitting on a new chair at table. In the afternoon she put her dolls in uncomfortable positions and said to them: "It doesn't matter. It will be all right," repeating what had been said to her. (Piaget, 1962, Obs. 86, p. 133)

The capacity for compensating or liquidating as described by Piaget is important for the affective life of the child. However, distortion of reality—whether for the sake of mastering emotional conflict (Erikson, 1963; Peller, 1954) or for the sake of power-reversal, admiration, and the mere fun of generating paradox (Sutton-Smith, 1979)—must be based on the trasformation of already existing event schemas, for example, substitution of alternative and sometimes paradoxical actors, recipients, objects, or actions to make routine scripts into fantastic ones. Some fanciful events produced in play may merely reflect the child's level of misunderstanding, but most often the distortion seems deliberate. This makes it cognitively as well as affectively interesting.

In this connection it is useful to look at the development of fantastic scripts in pretense. In the second year, much pretense is of the "as if" variety; indeed, it seems to become more realistic and organized. Even if the child plays other roles, these tend to represent familiar people—a fairly low level of "what if." Toddlers do not deliberately toy with the laws of time, space and causality, nor engage in high-level "what if's."

On the other hand, we know from Garvey's (1977) work that fictive roles and actions become increasingly common during the preschool years. Likewise, material from Scarlett and Wolf's (1979) case study supports the notion that impossible worlds with their own natural laws cannot be created by toddlers, but are created by older preschoolers. As these researchers put it, fantasy (not only real-world understanding) undergoes cognitive development.

Conclusion

In considering pretense in terms of tangled levels of reality and subjunctive thought we have moved a long way from the discussion of make-believe in terms of as if or mere simulation. In what way are these phenomena related to the development of social understanding?

I would like to suggest that the ability to engage in serious mental trial and error ("What if I did it this way, rather than that way?") and the ability to engage in make-believe are but two different facets of the same representational function. In other words, organisms that can create mental alternatives prior to action are ipso facto able to play with this ability, just as organisms with great control over motor actions can and do play with their motor skills (Fagen, 1981). Indeed, Piaget (1962) makes much the same claim, noting that *because* representation enables the child to go beyond the perceptual field he can distort reality according to his wishes and subordinate it to the ends he wants to achieve. I differ from him only in claiming that subjunctive skills are of cognitive, not purely affective, signfcance.

Not all children seem willing to play with their representational ability to the same degree (Wolf & Grollman, in press). Beyond infancy the imaginative disposition appears to be more a matter of cognitive style than of cognitive level. Some individuals refuse to contemplate fanciful ideas, or repress them before they become conscious, while others enjoy toying with subjunctive thoughts, however outlandish these might be. Nevertheless, the quality of fantasy which an individual can produce ought to be related to the coherence and sophistication of his real-world social understanding of people, their intentions, motives, feelings, and actions. The ability to create imaginary worlds (even of the low-level "what if" variety) should not, I believe, simply be taken for granted.

A second major component of make-believe is the ability to engage in subjunctive event representation for and with others. This creates both the potential for sharing one's inner world with companions and the potential for deceit or pretense. Bateson (1955) points out that pretense and communication as we know it become possible only when an organism realizes that mood-signs—and I would include all actions—are signals that can be trusted or distrusted, falsified or denied, amplified or corrected. Thus make-believe is linked to the capacity to lie, to "put on a show," to deceive, and, at the other end of the value scale, to engage in sacred ritual. In the case of lying, the communicator hopes that the addressee will not perceive the deception. In the case of make-believe and ritual, the participants jointly agree to create an alternative reality.

It is presumably because of its close association with deceit that children's make-belive play creates both enchantment and unease in adult onlookers. A further reason for unease is the incompleteness of the map/territory distinction. By claiming that "it is only pretend," real-world antagonisms can be surreptitiously acted out. The real can sometimes parade as make-believe. This process can also work in the reverse direction. What started as thrilling make-believe can become frighteningly or distressingly real. Adults, themselves, are not immuned from this effect. Indeed, it is probable that the tendency for map and territory to blend and tangle is an inevitable part of the capacity to simulate reality in order to entertain alternative courses of action.

Mature artists, in their fictive event representations, play much more consciously with potential map/territory confusions and distinctions and with the paradoxes of metacommunication than young children. Many pack as many layers of meaning into a literary work or painting as possible. Others eliminate meaning altogether and play only with the texture of paint or language. Some imagine alternative worlds or utopias, others tease an audience with inappropriate or omitted metacommunication, while yet others explore the paradox of levels by creating plays within plays and pictures within pictures. Preschoolers do not yet exploit these devices with the conscious artfulness of a writer, poet, or painter, but there are occasional glimpses of play with the paradoxes involved in pretense. Giffin's (1981) protocols describe a small boy holding up a match-box car while warning his companion "this is a real fire, this car is burning up." Pretense is intensified by claiming it is real. One of the preschoolers in Garvey and Berndt's (1977) study teased another by claiming she had "stealed" her partner's nonexistent cake. The partner turned the tables on the other child by nonchalantly retorting that it was not cake anymore. Such artful play with pretend devices deserves closer scrutiny.

I want to conclude by proposing that the ability to create symbolic alternatives to reality, and to play with that ability, is as deeply a part of human experience as the ability to construct an adapted model of everyday reality. Indeed, the successful building of accurate models may often involve prior play with a number of alternative possibilities. Conversely, the complexity and quality of subjunctive thought (whether in symbolic play or other contexts) is likely to depend on already existing cognitive structures. This is why creativity, cognitive flexibility, and divergent thinking have frequently been linked to a fantasy predisposition (Sutton-Smith, 1968; Singer, 1973; Lieberman, 1977; Dansky & Silverman, 1975).

As Steiner (1975) says:

> We hypothesize and project thought into the "if-ness," into the free conditionalities of the unknown. Such projection is no logical muddle, no abuse of induction. It is far more than a probabilistic convention. It is the master nerve of human action. . . . Ours is the ability, the need to gainsay or "unsay" the world, to image and speak it otherwise . . . to define the "other than the case," the counterfactual propositions, images, shapes of will and evasion with which we charge our mental being, and by which we build the largely fictive milieu of our somatic and social existence. (pp. 217–218, 222)

I suggest that we ponder why the ability to think of the "other than the case" emerges so early in life—what it means for human development that even a 2-year-old (see Dunn & Dale, 1984) is able and eager to proclaim "I a daddy."

References

Aebli, H. 1980. *Denken: Das Ordnen des Tuns* (Vol. 1). Stuttgart, West Germany: Klett-Cotta.

Acredolo, L. 1985. Symbolic gesturing in language development: A case study. *Human Development.*

Bates, E., Benvigni, L., Bretherton, I., Camaioni, L., & Volterra, V. 1979. *The emergence of symbols: Cognition and communication in infancy.* New York: Academic Press.

Bateson, G. 1956. The message "This is play." In B. Shaffner (Ed.), *Group Processes: Transactions of the second conference.* New York: Josiah Macy, Jr., Foundation. Reprinted 1971 in R.E. Herron and B. Sutton-Smith (Eds.), *Child's play.* New York: Wiley.

Bateson, G. 1955. A theory of play and fantasy. *American Psychiatric Association Research Reports* II: 39–51. Reprinted 1972 in G. Bateson, *Steps to an ecology of mind.* New York: Chandler.

Bloom, L. 1973. *One word at a time: The use of single word utterances before syntax.* The Hague: Mouton.

Bretherton, I., & Beeghly, M. 1982. Talking about internal states: The acquisition of an explicit theory of mind. *Developmental Psychology* 18:906–921.

Bretherton, I., Bates, E., McNew, S., Shore, C., Williamson, C., & Beeghly-Smith, M. 1981. Comprehension and production of symbols in infancy. *Developmental Psychology* 17:728–736.

Bretherton, I., O'Connell, B., Shore, C., & Bates, E. 1984. The effect of contextual variation on symbolic play: Development from 20 to 28 months. In I. Bretherton (Ed.), *Symbolic play: The development of social understanding.* New York: Academic Press.

Brown, R. 1973. *A first language: The early stages.* Cambridge: Harvard University Press.

Dansky, J.L., & Silverman, W.I. 1975. Play: A general facilitation of associative fluency. *Developmental Psychology* 11:104.

Dunn, J., & Dale, N. 1984. I a daddy: 2-year-olds' collaboration in joint pretend with sibling and with mother. In I. Bretherton (Ed.), *Symbolic play: The development of social understanding.* New York: Academic Press.

Elder, J.L., & Pederson, D.R. 1978. Preschool children's use of objects in symbolic play. *Child Development* 49:500–504.

Erikson, E.H. 1963. *Childhood and Society.* New York: Norton.

Fagen, R. 1981. *Animal play behavior.* New York: Oxford University Press.

Fein, G. 1981. Pretend play in childhood: An integrative view. *Child Development* 52:1095–1118.

Fein, G.G. 1978. Play revisited. In M. Lamb (Ed.), *Social and personality development.* New York: Holt, Rinehart and Winston.

Fein, G. 1975. A transformational analysis of pretending. *Developmental Psychology* 11:291–296.

Fein, G.G., & Apfel, N. 1979. Some preliminary observations on knowing and pretending. In M. Smith & M.B. Franklin (Eds.), *Symbolic funtioning in childhood.* Hillsdale, N.J.: Erlbaum.

Fein, G.G., Moorin, E.R. In press. Confusion, substitution, and mastery. In K. Nelson (Ed.), *Children's language* (Vol. 5). New York: Gardner.

Fenson, L. 1984. Developmental trends for action and speech in pretend play. In I. Bretherton (Ed.), *Symbolic play: The development of social understanding.* New York: Academic Press.

Fenson, L. March, 1983. Personal communication.

Fenson, L., & Ramsay, D.S. 1981. Effects of modeling action sequences on the play of twelve-, fifteen-, and nineteen-month-old children. *Child Development* 52: 1028–1036.

———. 1980. Decentration and integration of the child's play in the second year. *Child Development* 51:171–178.

Garvey, C. 1977. *Play.* Cambridge: Harvard University Press.

Garvey, C., & Berndt, R. 1977. Organization of pretend play. *Catalogue of Selected Documents in Psychology* 7:Manuscript 1589.

Geertz, C. 1972. Deep play: Notes on the Balinese cockfight. *Daedalus* 101:1–37. Reprinted 1973 in Geertz, *The interpretation of cultures.* New York: Basic Books.

Gerard, A.B. 1984. *Sequencing and imitation in early childhood.* Unpublished doctoral disseration, University of California, San Diego.

Giffin, H. 1984. The coordination of meaning in the creation of a shared make-believe reality. In I. Bretherton (Ed.), *Symbolic play: The development of social understanding.* New York: Academic Press.

———. 1981. *The metacommunicative process in collective make-believe play.* Unpublished doctoral dissertation, University of Colorado, Boulder.

Greenfield, P.M., & Smith, J. 1976. *The structure of communication in early language development.* New York: Academic Press.

Hofstadter, D.R. 1979. *Gödel, Escher, Bach: An eternal golden braid.* New York: Basic Books.

Huttenlocher, J., & Higgins, E.T. 1978. Issues in the study of symbolic development. In W.A. Collins (Ed.), *Minnesota symposia on child psychology* (Vol 11). Hillsdale, N.J.: Erlbaum.

Inhelder, B., Lezine, I., Sinclair, H., & Stambak, G. 1972. Les débuts de la fonction symbolique. *Archives de Psychologie,* No. 163.

Jackowitz, E.R., & Watson, M.W. 1980. Development of object transformation in early pretend play. *Developmental Psychology* 16:543–549.

Jeffree, D., & McConkey, R. 1976. An observation scheme for recording children's imaginative doll play. *Journal of Child Psychology and Psychiatry* 17:189–197.

Kagan, J. 1981. The second year: *The emergence of selfawareness.* Cambridge, Mass.: Harvard University Press.

Killen, M., & Uzgiris, I. 1981. Imitation of actions with objects. *Journal of Genetic Psychology* 138:219–229.

Kintsch, W. 1974. *The representation of meaning in memory.* Hillsdale, N.J.: Erlbaum.

Kreye, K. 1984. Conceptual organization in the play of preschool children: The effects of meaning, context and mother-child interaction. In I. Bretherton (Ed.), *Symbolic play: The development of social understanding.* New York: Academic Press.

Largo, R., & Howard, J. 1979. Developmental progression in play behavior in children between 9 and 30 months. *Developmental Medicine and Child Neurology* 21:299–310.

Lieberman, J.N. 1977. *Playfulness: Its relationship to imagination and creativity.* New York: Academic Press.

Lowe, H. 1975. Trends in the development of representational play in infants from one to three years: An observational study. *Psychology and Psychiatry* 16:33–47.

Mandler, J.H. 1979. Categorical and schematic organization in memory. In C.K. Puff (Ed.), *Memory organization and structure.* New York: Academic Press.

Mandler, J.M., & DeForest, M. 1978. *Developmental invariance in story recall.* Unpublished manuscript, University of California, San Diego.

Miller, P., & Garvey, K. 1984. Mother-baby role play: Its origin in social support. In I. Bretherton (Ed.), *Symbolic play: The development of social understanding.* New York: Academic Press.

Matthews, W.S. 1977. Modes of transformation in the initiation of fantasy play. *Developmental Psychology* 13:211–216.

―――. 1978. *Breaking the fantasy frame: An analysis of the interruptions and terminations of young children's fantasy play episodes.* Paper presented at the meeting of the Eastern Psychological Association, Washington, D.C.

Mead, G.H. 1934. *Mind, self, and society.* Chicago: University of Chicago Press.

Miller, P., & Garvey, K. 1984. Mother-baby role play: Its origins in social support. In I. Bretherton (Ed.), *Symbolic play: The development of social understanding.* New York: Academic Press.

Nelson, K. 1981. Social cognition in a script framework. In J.H. Flaven & L. Ross (Eds.), *Social cognitive development.* Cambridge: Cambridge University Press.

Nelson, K., & Gruendel, J. 1981. Generalized event representations: Basic building blocks of cognitive development. In A. Brown & M. Lamb (Eds.), *Advances in developmental psychology* (Vol. 1). Hillsdale, N.J.: Erlbaum.

Nelson, K., & Seidman, S. 1984. Playing with scripts. In I. Bretherton (Ed.), *Symbolic Play: The development of social understanding.* New York: Academic Press.

Nicolich, L.M. 1977. Beyond sensorimotor intelligence: Assessment of symbolic maturity through analysis of pretend play. *Merrill-Palmer Quarterly* 2:88–99.

O'Connell, B. 1985. *The development of sequential understanding revisited: The role of meaning and familiarity.* Unpublished doctoral dissertation, University of California, San Diego.

O'Connell, B., & Gerard, R. In press. The development of sequential understanding: Scripts and scraps. *Child Development.*

Overton, W.F., & Jackson, J.P. 1973. The representation of imaged objects in action sequences: A developmental study. *Child Development* 44:309–314.

Peller, L.E. 1954. Libidinal phases, ego development and play. *The Psychoanalytic Study of the Child* 9:178–198.

―――. 1952. Models of children's play. *Mental Hygiene* 36:66–83. Reprinted 1971 in R.E. Herron & B. Sutton-Smith (Eds.), *Child's play.* New York: Wiley.

Phillips, R. 1945. Doll play as a function of the realism of the materials and the length of the experimental session. *Child Development* 16:145–166.

Piaget, J. 1962. *Play, dreams and imitation in childhood.* New York: Norton. Originally published 1945; English translation, C. Gattegno & F.M. Hodgson (London: Routledge & Kegan Paul, 1951).

Pulaski, M.A. 1973. Toys and imaginative play. In J.L. Singer (Ed.), *The child's world of make-believe.* New York: Academic Press.

Rheingold, H.L., & Emery, G.N. In press. The nurturant acts of very young children. In J. Black, D. Olweus, & M. Radke-Yarrow (Eds.), *Aggression and socially valued behavior: Biological and cultural perspectives.* New York: Academic Press.

Rubin, S., & Wolf, D. 1979. The development of maybe: The evolution of social roles into narrative roles. *New Directions for Child Development* 6:15–28.

Scarlett, W.G., & Wolf, D. 1979. When it's only make-believe: The construction of a boundary between fantasy and reality. In D. Wolf (Ed.), *New Directions for Child Development* 3:29–40.

Schank, R.C., & Abelson, R.P. *Scripts, plans, goals and understanding.* Hillsdale, N.J.: Erlbaum.

Schwartzman, H.B. 1978. *Transformations: The anthropology of children's play.* New York: Plenum Press.

Singer, J.L. (Ed.) 1973. *The child's world of make-believe: Experimental studies of imaginative play.* New York: Academic Press.

Shimada, S., Sano, R., & Peng, F. 1979. A longitudinal study of symbolic play in the second year of life. *Bulletin of the Research Institute for the Education of Exceptional Children.* Tokyo Gakugei University, Tokyo, Japan.

Stein, N.L. 1978. The comprehension and appreciation of stories: A developmental analysis. In S. Madeja (Ed.), *The arts and cognition* (Vol. 2). St. Louis: Cemrel.

Stein, N.L., & Nezworski, M.T. 1978. The effect of organization and instruction on story memory. *Discourse Processes* 1:177–191.

Steiner, G. 1975. *After Babel: Aspects of language and translation.* New York: Oxford University Press.

Sutton-Smith, B. 1979. *Play and learning.* New York: Gardner.

———. 1968. Novel responses to toys. *Merrill-Palmer Quarterly* 14:151–158.

———. 1966. Piaget on play: A critique. *Psychological Review* 73:104–110.

Ungerer, J.A., Zelazo, P.R., Kearsley, R.B., & O'Leary, K. 1981. Developmental changes in the representation of objects from 18–34 months of age. *Child Development* 52:186–195.

Volterra, V. 1984. Waiting for the birth of a sibling: The verbal fantasies of a two-year-old boy. In I. Bretherton (Ed.), *Symbolic play: The development of social understanding.* New York: Academic Press.

Volterra, V., Bates, E., Benigni, L, Bretherton, I., & Camaioni, L. 1979. First words in language and action: A qualitative look. In E. Bates et al., *The emergence of symbols: Cognition and communication in infancy.* New York: Academic Press.

Vygotsky, L.S. 1966. Play and its role in the mental development of the child. *Voprosy Psikhologii* 12:62–76.

Watson, M.W., & Fischer, K.W. 1980. Development of social roles in elicited and spontaneous behavior during the preschool years. *Child Development* 18:483–494.

———. 1977. A developmental sequence of agent use in late infancy. *Child Development* 48:828–836.

Wolf, D. 1982. Understanding others: A longitudinal case study of the concept of independent agency. In G. Forman (Ed.), *Action and thought: From sensorimotor schemes to symbol use.* New York: Academic Press.

———. 1981. *How to speak a story: The emergence of narrative language.* Paper presented at the Eleventh Annual Conference of the Jean Piaget Society, Philadelphia.

Wolf, D., & Grollman, S. 1982. Ways of playing: Individual differences in imaginative play. In K. Rubin & D. Pepler (Eds.), *The play of children: Current theory and research.* New York: Karger.

Wolf, D., & Pusch, J. In press. Pretend that didn't happen: Children's responses to interruptions in play. In A. Pellegrini & L. Galda (Eds.), *Play and narrative.* Norwood, N.J.: Ablex.

Wolf, D.P., Rygh, J., & Altshuler, J. 1984. Agency and experience: Actions and states in play narratives. In I. Bretherton (Ed.), *Symbolic play: The development of social understanding.* New York: Academic Press.

9
Pretend Play in the Family

Judy Dunn

T here are striking differences between mothers in the interest and
enthusiasm that they show toward young children's pretend play.
Some join in with alacrity, as the following quotations from mothers
of 4-year-olds in Nottingham show (Newson & Newson, 1978):

> Cowboys . . . I have to hide behind the settee and they come riding round it. .
> . . we all have to get on and go for a ride.

> I'm the patient, or the baby, or the little girl's aunt.

> We have to fight, and I'm the Sheriff of Nottingham and he's Robin Hood.

> We go on a rocket . . . when the spin drier's on for the noise.

Other mothers are simply not interested, and some actively discourage their
children's pretend play (Newson & Newson, 1970):

> He'd make up stories . . . It got so bad that I tried to stop it, because I didn't
> want him to go from an imaginary story to a downright lie—because there's
> not much difference between the two.

> It worries me sometimes—he's got a vivid imagination; and it goes on and on
> and on until he *lives* it; and sometimes, these imaginary people, you have to
> *feed* them with him, do you see what I mean? It worries me.

How important and how widespread are such differences in maternal
interest in children's early symbolic play? What part do mothers, and other
family members, play in the development of children's exploration and enjoyment of the world of fantasy? What are the developmental consequences for a
child who grows up in a family in which the parents are uninterested in or actively discourage his or her make-believe? It is important to recognize that
there are two separate issues here. First is the theoretical argument that interaction with adults plays a crucial role in children's initial ability to play
symbolically (El'konin, 1966; Vygotsky, 1978). This position is extremely
difficult to test: while we can gain suggestive findings from both experimental

observational studies, we cannot establish whether adult modeling is *essential* for the development of early symbolic activity. But we can and should address the second issue—the question of whether differences in the involvement of parents and other family members in children's early symbolic play do have important developmental consequences.

To answer this question we must study children playing at home in their familiar daily routines—to look at naturally occurring family interaction rather than at the behavior of mothers and children in structured 'play' sessions with standardized toys. Studying the behavior of children in their family world is of central importance to those interested in children's play from either a developmental or a clinical perspective. It is important to developmental psychologists for two rather different reasons. First, the findings to date suggest that children's abilities are greatly underestimated when observed solely in more public contexts, such as school, playground, or laboratory. Second, the findings from studies in public settings demonstrate that the importance of *social* pretend in the development of symbolic activities has been misunderstood, that the developmental sequence of solitary to social pretend outlined by Piaget may well be misleading.

For clinicians, studies of children playing in their family world are essential in order to fill the two important gaps in what is known of the implications of parental involvement in children's early pretend play. Studies of mothers' involvement in pretend play have focused almost exclusively upon the significance of this involvement for *cognitive* development. Yet it is often suggested that the developmental importance of pretend play lies in its significance for children's emotional well-being—their exploration of feelings (their own and those of other people), their understanding of social rules and roles, and their communicative skills. The part that parental interaction might play in the link between children's emotional states and their fantasy play remains an important and unexplored issue. Secondly, if pretend play does have a role in children's emotional and social development, it is important that clinicians should understand the significance of individual differences in mothers' involvement in such make-believe. Manuals for parents encourage parents to become involved in children's pretend (White, 1980). But is enough known about the implications of differences in maternal involvement in children's pretend to justify such a point of view? How sensible or realistic is it to suppose that clinicians can in fact alter mothers' practices in this respect?

In this chapter these issues will be discussed in the context of findings from four studies of very young children playing at home with their mothers and siblings. All the studies employed unstructured observations. Study I focused upon firstborn children aged 18 to 24 months (Dunn & Wooding, 1977), study II upon firstborn children followed longitudinally through the infancy of their siblings (Dunn & Kendrick, 1982), study III on secondborn aged 18 and 24 months (Dunn & Dale, 1984; Dunn & Munn, in preparation). I will summarize a few of the findings relevant to the question at issue. The detailed reports of the methodologies and the findings of the studies are given in the references above.

Maternal Participation in Pretend Play

What part do mothers play in the development of children's abilities to pretend? We know from experimental work, such as the study by O'Connell and Bretherton (1984), that mothers can have an important influence on the nature of children's pretend. O'Connell and Bretherton showed that children collaborating with their mothers in structured play sessions demonstrate greater diversity of play than when playing alone, and that this diversity is due to the mothers' explicit guidance of the play. With 28-month-olds, greater diversity was found in symbolic play, rather than in exploratory or combinational play.

> It is important . . . to recognize the role that instruction does play in the child's development, a role Piaget did not emphasize in his work. The child is a part of the social world and this context can provide the child with a wealth of information. . . . Mothers are active and willing teachers of their children but their strategy appears to be the provision of wide-ranging guidance rather than tuning in to the level of their child's ability. Children, in the course of mastering any of a variety of activities, rely simultaneously on their own cognitive skills and constructive processes as well as on any assistance that may come their way from the architects in the social world.

The implication of the findings is that mothers may be important in the development of symbolic play.

How far can these findings be generalized to the real-life world of children and mothers at home? In the O'Connell and Bretherton study the mothers were, in the home session, always in the same room as the children, but were instructed to respond minimally to their child's overtures; in the laboratory session they were instructed to play with the child using the standard set of toys provided. What happens at home, when mothers are busy with household tasks, but are also free to enjoy joining their children's play whenever they wish? What kinds of influence do mothers have on the quality of their children's pretend play?

Frequency of Participation

In our first study (Dunn & Wooding, 1977) of children's play at home we found that the majority of pretend play sequences of firstborn 18- to 24-

month-olds were initiated by the child, but that comparatively few of these were completed by the child without any involvement of the mother (see figure 1 in study). If the mothers did pay attention to the child's play, the time spent by the child in pretend play was significantly greater than the time spent playing alone, suggesting that the child's interest in and motivation for such relatively mature play was affected by the mother's involvement. In Dale's (1983) study of secondborn 24-month-olds, 59 percent of pretend play episodes included some participation by a mother and/or sibling. In our current longitudinal study of secondborn 18- to 24-month-olds, the time spent in joint pretend play with mother or sibling was far greater than the time spent in solitary pretend play. Thus, mothers are involved in many of the very young child's early essays at symbolic play. However, in all these studies there were very wide individual differences in the participation of mothers.

Nature of Participation

The second issue is how interaction with the mother affects the nature of children's pretend play, and what the developmental significance of such maternal involvement might be. The data from the studies suggest that the mothers' involvement was frequently didactic in nature: the mothers used the context of joint pretend play to explore the concepts of size and shape, to encourage classificatory skills, and especially to discuss the function and appropriate use of objects. Concerned with the child's fantasy in terms of its adequacy to reality, mothers' questions and comments frequently focused the child's attention on how things are in the real world. The suggestions and comments that mothers made were very often along domestic lines, or focused upon daily routine experiences (Dunn, 1980) such as:

MOTHER: Are you going to the shops for me?

FRANCES [*3 years old*]: No. I'm going to the shops for Judy first. I got some. They're fish. Now I'm getting some for Mummy. My scooter fall down.

MOTHER: Did it? Never mind. I should go and find somewhere to park it while you are at the shops. Go and find a parking place.

FRANCES: I did.

MOTHER: You did park? Oh.

FRANCES: There wasn't any people.

MOTHER: There wasn't any people? Oh well, you can go and look in the car park and see if you can find a space to park the scooter, then you can go and find me some fish in the market.

FRANCES: I *got* some fish. It's in the cupboard.

MOTHER: Oh. I don't think that that's a very good place for it. Can you put it in the fridge for me?

FRANCES: Oh dear! It's gone! I've eaten it! And Father Christmas eaten it too.

Bretherton (1981) has drawn attention to the interesting distinction between "as if" fantasies and the more exploratory "what if" fantasies. Mothers' suggestions are most commonly of the "as if" kind.

The "conventionality" of the mothers' contributions was evident even when they were joining in the story book fantasies. In the next example the mother was interested in a more everyday theme when her son's make-believe turned toward a fairy story theme, but her suggestions were not taken up (Dunn, 1980):

GARRY: [*playing with a teddy bear*] He's got to have a rest. He feels much better now, Ted does. He's eating it up. He's gone to sleep now. He's got his pillow for his head. Night night.

MOTHER: Have you read him a story?

GARRY: No, he doesn't want a story.

MOTHER: He doesn't want a story? Ooh, you have a story when you go to bed. Why don't you get your caterpillar book and read him that?

GARRY: He doesn't want a story. He's asleep now. . . . Now he's sitting on the chair. 'Cause he's one of the three bears.

MOTHER: One of the three bears? Where's their porridge? Here's Goldilocks. Look.

GARRY: This is . . . Goldilocks. She went for a walk. And sat down there. . . . And Big Father see that [*growls*]. And he went to bed with him. And he went to Goldilocks. And he . . . went in that bed. And it was too little for him so's he could go in it [*growls*]. So Daddy Bear tried Baby Bear's. . . . Baby Bear's tired. Who's this, he says [*growls*]. I'm going to wake her up. And he smacks Little Ted. Waw Waw Waw. Smack smack. . . . He doesn't want to go to bed any more. He wants to go to the toilet. He's doing wee wee on the floor.

MOTHER: He'd better not. Go and sit him on the potty.

GARRY: He's done it. Naughty Bear. . . . He's done weewee in his bed. He's weeing on the floor. . . . He's done it on the sofa. . . . There's Father Bear coming. And Baby wakes up. Smack him! Smacked his father! . . . And Father says "That's my chair!" [*growls*] And smack! Smack! Smack!

Another feature of the clearly social pretend games between mothers and children is the tutoring mothers provide for role play. Miller and Garvey (1984) have traced the important part mothers play in the development of one particular role game—that of mother in "nurturing a baby." Dale's study (using a cross-sectional sample) confirms that such maternal involvement in games focused upon nurturing is common with 24-month-olds. In our ongoing Study IV we find mothers become involved not only in nurturing pretend play sequences but in a range of role games. (See table 9–1).

In these exchanges mothers usually act as spectators in the role play, offering guiding comments as detached observers, rather than joining in as

Table 9–1
Themes of Joint Pretend Games in the Family (Study IV)
(percentages)

	Child with Mother	Child with Sibling
Mealtimes	20	16
Cooking/ironing	9	2
Shopping/going to the park	13	2
Telephoning	4	2
Making a house	4	8
Going to the doctor	4	2
Church	4	2
Bedtime	15	13
Mothers and babies	2	5
Riding horses	2	2
Planes/boats/trains/travel	9	8
Driving cars	3	5
Ambulances/crashes	4	
Shooting/killing people	4	5
Ghosts		2
Monsters		8
Space/moon		8
Desert island		2
Being animals		2

equal partners. This is in marked contrast to the collaboration of siblings in role play.

Finally, a particularly interesting feature of the collaboration of mother and child in joint pretend was frequently explicit discussion of the inner state and feelings of other people. The fantasies frequently concerned incidents involving pain, sadness, cold, warmth, hunger, tiredness, or sleepiness. In communicating about the pretend not only the mothers but also the children as young as 24 months old discussed such feeling states. For twenty-nine 24-month-olds in Study IV, 39 percent of their talk in the course of pretend play referred explicitly to inner states or feelings. The importance of and needs in the social pretend play of such young children not only highlights the interest children have in their inner states, but also suggests that discussion with the mother in joint pretend play provides an opportunity for children to explore the causes and consequences of such states. There was a significant correlation between the mother's use of inner state language at 18 months, and the child's use of inner state language 6 months later ($= .61, N = 21, p < .01$).

Such findings show that joint pretend play between mother and child offers an opportunity for a variety of social learning experiences, as well as a mothers' speech, which is not only specifically didactic but also rich in those features of extension and acknowledgment that studies of language acquisition have emphasized as potentially valuable. It is likely that the active guidance described by O'Connell and Bretherton (1984) in their experimental study takes place during pretend play between mothers and children at home. However, before concluding that mothers' involvement in pretend is developmentally significant, some very important caveats must be taken into account. First, it has not been clearly demonstrated that adult modeling of the kind suggested by El'konin (1966) is *necessary* for the early stages of symbolic play. The theoretical propositions here remain untested. There is, moreover, no clear evidence that children brought up in families in which mothers frequently participate in joint pretend play develop different patterns or skills of make-believe than children whose mothers rarely participate in pretend. Even if there were evidence that children brought up in families in which the mothers participated in joint pretend developed patterns of pretend play that were strikingly mature or elaborate, we could not assume that it was the experience of *joint pretend play* with the mother that was causally important. It could well be that mothers who participate with enthusiasm in joint pretend *differ* in other ways from mothers who are uninterested in such play.

Individual Differences

In the United Kingdom at least, differences between mothers in their involvement in pretend play with young children are marked and widespread. When the children in our current longitudinal study were 24 months old, for instance, the mothers' involvement in joint pretend play with the children ranged from 35 percent to 0 percent (mean = 5.8, S.D. = 9.1). In Dale's (1983) study a similarly wide range of individual differences was observed. Differences in maternal involvement in their children's pretend are apparently relatively stable over time: in our current study the correlation between mothers' involvement in pretend when their secondborn at 18 months and 6 months later was .50.

Differences in maternal involvement in pretend play, however, were not closely related to differences in other forms of joint play with the children. Mothers differed significantly in how frequently they collaborated with their children in nonpretend play (with toys, puzzles, rough-and-tumble, or verbal games): the range was from 29 percent to 0 percent of observation intervals (mean = 8.2, S.D. = 8.2). But no association between the time spent in such play and in joint pretend play. Dale's study also reports no relation between the time mothers spent playing with children and the children playing in other ways. In our first study of siblings and mothers we found no relation between the frequency of mothers' pretend suggestions and the time that they spent playing with their children (Dunn & Kendrick, 1982).

These differences in maternal involvement in pretend play in the study, however, related to differences in the ways in which the mothers conversed with their children. Mothers who made frequent pretend suggestions were more likely to use language for complex cognitive purposes, to discuss motives and intentions of other people, and to justify or rationalize their attempts to control the child (table 9–2). These differences in language use reflect a particular style of relating to a young child, perhaps similar to that described by Light (1979) in his study of the development of social sensitivity in children as reflecting a high degree of symmetry in the relationship between mother and child: "These mothers were not only tuned in to their children's world in the sense that they enjoyed and entered their fantasies, but they were more likely to treat the child formally as an equal in discussing social rules and control issues" (p. 75). They also used language in a more elaborate way to their children, and as table 9–2 shows, their children were more likely themselves to use language in a relatively mature fashion as well as to discuss motives and intentions.

The pattern of these correlations means that we should not look for simple links between any one aspect of the mother's conversational style, such as their interest in making pretend suggestions, and developmental differences between the children. We cannot assume that it is their interest in pretend that is of special developmental significance. However, it is extremely plausible that children brought up in such families will be influenced by the quality of their mothers' style of relating to them, as the correlations in table 9–2 suggest.

It is also evidence of differences in mothers' interest and involvement in pretend that are linked to social class and educational differences. In the Newsons' interview studies of 700 Nottingham families (Newson & Newson, 1970, there were a minority of working-class mothers who disliked and disapproved of their 4-year-olds' fantasy play, and who attempted to "prick the bubble of his illusion." It was strikingly less common for the 4-year-olds from the lowest social class group to communicate their fantasies to their mothers; it was also less common for children from large families to do so. However, the social class effect held, even when family size was allowed for. In their follow-up of these 700 families when the children were 7 years old, the Newsons (1978) found that this concern and anxiety about children's fantasies among this group of mothers was even more pronounced.

We noted earlier that an important gap in what is known about parental involvement in pretend play concerns its significance for children's emotional development. Hetherington's work showed that after divorce—when parents are presumably under stress—there is a notable decrease in children's pre-

Table 9–2
Spearman Rank Correlations between Features of Mothers' and Children's Language
($N = 20$)

Mother	Mother				Child	
	Pretends	*Explores Motives*	*Justification in Control*	*Complex Cognitive Use of Language*	*Pretends*	*Explores Motives*
Complex cognitive use of language	0.55*	0.75*	0.43	0.69*	0.50*	0.44
Pretends		0.51*	0.57*	0.60*	0.91*	0.43
Explores motives of others			0.41	0.51*	0.26	0.62*
Justification in control				0.30	0.51*	0.37
C's complex cognitive use of language					0.54*	0.43*
C pretends						0.19

tend play (Hetherington, Cox, & Cox, 1979). But we do not know how this decrease, which presumably reflects disturbance in children's emotional security, is linked to parents' actual involvement in pretend play. Rubin, Fein, and Vandenberg (1983) speculate about the processes underlying such findings.

> Perhaps, more importantly, parents may influence exploratory, functional, constructive, and pretense play indirectly by providing their children with responsive, sensitive, and secure bases that reduce stress and anxiety in unfamiliar settings.

However, we do not have grounds as yet for assuming that mothers' interest in joint pretend with children is closely linked to the emotional quality of the relationship between them.

Implications of Individual Differences

To summarize the implications of these individual differences:

1. If differences are found in children's behavior that are related to parental participation in joint pretend, it cannot be inferred that there is a causal link between this parental interest in pretend and the child outcome measures.

2. It is therefore not clear that strategies for intervention at a level of teaching or encouraging mothers to participate in children's play will be practical or effective.

3. More research is needed to understand whether maternal involvement in joint pretend is an index of the warmth or security of the relationship or primarily an interest by mothers in children's intellectual and symbolic pursuits.

The Family Context of Early Pretend Play

The home observation studies highlight one important and hitherto neglected point. It is not only mothers—or even *primarily* mothers—who are involved in very young children's pretend play. In each of the studies of two-child families in Cambridge we find that for some children siblings are extremely important partners in early pretend play. Children's experiences with different family partners differ widely. There is no systematic relationship between the amount of joint play with mothers and with siblings. In some families there is frequent pretend play with both mother and sibling, in others, only with the mother, or the sibling. The children who engaged in pretend play with their siblings enjoyed very close and affectionate relationships with these siblings (Dunn & Dale, 1984). While such sibling-child pretend play was common in only a third of the samples in Studies III and IV, there are some special features of this sibling-child pretend play that suggest it may be of quite special developmental interest.

First, the nature of the collaboration in joint pretend differs markedly from that of mother and child. Mothers, as we have noted, usually act as spectators to children's fantasies. They make pretend suggestions and offer comments, but rarely enter the game as full partners. In play between child and sibling, however, both child and sibling collaborate as partners in the shared pretend. Siblings take complementary roles to one another. Their play involves close meshing of the actions and themes of the two partners.

Second, in play with a sibling, children as young as 24 months old take part in joint role enactment and joint role play. They can make explicit a transformation of their own identity and can share a framework of pretend play with the other child. This remarkably mature behavior for such young children has not been observed in children primarily involved in joint pretend with mothers or fathers. In pretend play with a sibling, children under 3 can communicate about play roles. The Cambridge studies show that such communication and effective collaboration in role play occurs in about a quarter of the 2-year-olds observed, sufficiently frequent to refute the following claim:

> Although negotiations and communications about play roles have been reported to exist (and to play a causal accommodative role in development; Matthews, 1978a) in the interactions of children 4, 5, and 6 (Fein, 1979b, Matthews, 1978a; Sutton-Smith, 1971a), they do not appear in toddler and young 3-year-old conversations. Perhaps, then, one reason for the lack of spontaneous sociodramatic or group fantasy interactions in 2- and 3-year-olds results from the inability to produce and comprehend the message, "This is play" (Garvey & Berndt, 1977). Children of these young ages may simply not have grasped the notion that pretend play can be a social endeavor with shared rules about the production and communication of symbolic representations (Rubin, Fein, & Vandenberg, 1983, p. 725).

These arguments show just how seriously we may underestimate children's abilities by failing to study them in their entire family world.

Dunn and Dale (1984) observed other ways in which the distinctive features of the sibling relationship make possible such collaboration: the familiarity of the social world of child and sibling, the affection and support of the sibling, and the older child's proficiency in world of pretend, as well as his saliency as a model for the child.

Third, there are important differences in the nature of the themes of shared pretend with mother and with siblings (see table 9–1). With their siblings, children engage in pretend games concerning much less mundane experiences than the domestic and routine scripts of bedtime and eating, shopping and cooking that are most common with mothers. Fantasy play with a sibling takes the child into space, into a world of monsters, into combat, to the bottom of the sea, to desert islands, or to the moon.

This evidence for distinctive differences in the nature of shared pretend with sibling and with mother implies that the significance of children's early social play within the family is very different for those children with highly participant mothers from those with highly participant siblings. The findings suggest, too, that growing up in a family with a mother who is uninterested in and unsupportive of pretend play will not necessarily be a disadvantage, if the family includes a friendly and affectionate sibling. Indeed, siblings may well be a more important influence on developing children's interest in pretend than mothers. While Dale (1983) found no relation between the amount of pretend children engaged in on their own, and mothers' involvement in pretend, there was a significant correlation between the time children spent in pretend play alone, and their experience of pretend play with their siblings.

Developmental Implications

What are the most significant implications of the results of these observational studies of children playing at home with their mothers and siblings? Four points stand out as worth emphasis.

1. The first concerns the relative significance of solitary and social pretend play in development. To understand the early development of symbolic play, it is necessary to study social play, not simply solitary play. It is not an original point. Valentine pointed out nearly fifty years ago that daily observation of children at home allows make-believe play to be discovered "at a much earlier age in the intimate life of the family than has been reported in the observations made of children in groups" (Valentine, 1937). He stresses that a factor of great importance in development is the degree of familiarity children have with the other individuals.

    The widely accepted view that "solitary leads to social" must at least be reconsidered.

2. When we do study children in the family world in which their ability to pretend develops, we see that to suggest that children under 3 cannot negotiate or communicate about the rules and roles of a shared pretend game is to considerably underestimate these capabilities of children.

3. Studies of family patterns of joint participation in pretend highlight the

variety of developmental paths by which children may achieve the social understanding and communication skills on which joint pretend play, especially role play, depends. The quality of particular family relationships, with mother or with siblings, is likely to influence the particular pattern of development. Individual differences in mothers' interest in pretend are extremely marked, and linked to differences in conversational style and in social class that are likely to be associated with differences in children's verbal and representational skills. However, even in a family in which the mother is uninterested in and discouraging of early pretend, if a child has a warm and affectionate relationship with an older sibling it is likely that he or she will enjoy a rich, exciting and very early initiation into the world of pretend, with all the possibilities of exploring social roles and social rules that this implies.

4. The significance for emotional development of individual differences in children's early experience in the world of pretend, especially in the support and participation of their parents, urgently need our attention. Until we know more of the possible links between a child's emotional well-being, the nature of his early pretend play, the interest of his parents and siblings in that play, and other aspects of his relationship with these family members, we are not in a position to pronounce on the importance of encouraging parents to become involved in this early pretend.

References

Bretherton, I. 1984. Representing the social world. In I. Bretherton (Ed.), *Symbolic play: The development of social understanding*. New York: Academic Press.

Dale, N., 1983. Early pretend play within the family. Unpublished doctoral dissertation, University of Cambridge, Cambridge, England.

Dunn, J. 1980. Playing in speech. In C. Ricks & L. Michaels (Eds.), *The state of the language*. Berkeley: University of California Press.

Dunn, J., & Dale, N. 1984. I a Daddy: 2-year-olds' collaboration in joint pretend with sibling and with mother. In I. Bretherton (Ed.), *Symbolic play: The development of social understanding*. New York: Academic Press.

Dunn, J., & Kendrick, C. 1982. *Siblings: Love, envy and understanding*. Cambridge: Harvard University Press.

Dunn, J., & Wooding, C. 1977. Play in the home and its implications for learning. In B. Tizard & D. Harvey (Eds.), *The biology of play*. London: S.I.M.P./ Heinemann Medical Books.

El'konin, D. 1966. Symbolics and its functions in the play of children. *Soviet Education* 8(7):35.

Hetherington, E.M., Cox, M., & Cox, R. 1979. Play and social interaction in children following divorce. *Journal of Social Issues* 35:26–49.

Light, P. 1979. *The development of social sensitivity.* Cambridge: Cambridge University Press.

Miller, P., & Garvey, C. 1984. Mother-baby role play: Its origins in social support. In I. Bretherton (Ed.), *Symbolic play: The development of social understanding.* New York: Academic Press.

Newson, J., & Newson, E. 1970. *Four year olds in an urban community.* Harmondsworth, England: Pelican Books.

———. 1978. *Seven year olds in the home environment.* Harmondsworth, England: Pelican Books.

O'Connell, B., & Bretherton, I. 1984). Toddlers' play, alone and with mother. In I. Bretherton (Ed.), *Symbolic play: The development of social understanding.* New York: Academic Press.

Rubin, K.H., Fein, G.G., & Vandenberg, B. 1983. Play. In P.M. Mussen (Ed.), *Manual of child psychology* (Vol. 4).

Valentine, C.W. 1937. A study of the beginnings and significance of play in infancy. II. *British Journal of Educational Psychology* 8:285.

Vygotsky, L.S. 1978. *Mind in society.* Cambridge: Harvard University Press.

White, B.L. 1980. *A parent's guide to the first three years.* Englewood Cliffs, N.J.: Prentice-Hall.

10
Play, Peer Interaction, and Social Development

Kenneth H. Rubin

T here has not been much attention in the available play literature to the use of play observations to identify children who may deviate from normality in some way. In this chapter, I propose that observations of children's play may be useful in the identification of children at risk for socioemotional problems. In so doing, I suggest that not all forms of children's play are adaptive; indeed, I suggest that the very frequent display of certain forms of play *at certain ages* may be a useful warning signal for psychologists and educators that something may not be quite right.

A number of years ago I developed a play scale for studying child behavior in play. This scale has helped me and other researchers to understand what children do in their "spare time" and to discover what appear to be maladaptive play styles in children. The scale is now proving helpful in identifying young children as potentially at risk for later problems.

The Play Observation Scale

Approximately ten years ago, the first Waterloo observational studies of preschoolers' free play were conducted (for example, Rubin & Maioni, 1975; Rubin, Maioni, & Hornung, 1976). Smilansky's (1968) volume concerning the production of sociodramatic play of children living in different Israeli socioeconomic strata provided useful insight. The categories defined by Smilansky were borrowed from Piaget's *Play, Dreams and Imitation in Childhood* (1962),

1. *Functional play:* Children simply repeat the same movements with or without objects. There is no purpose to construct anything. Instead children repeat actions, imitate themselves, try new actions and then imitate them, and so on. Simple manipulation and exploration of toys is representative of functional play. This form of "play qua exploration" allows the young child to gain some firsthand feedback from his environment

(for example, messing around with fingerpaint). Piaget referred to this type of play, which develops during infancy, as sensorimotor play.

2. *Constructive play:* The second category involves the construction or creation of something. Play is sustained by constructive goals ("I won't quit until this road is built"). From the sporadic handling of sand or blocks during functional play, the young child as a preschooler, moves to building something from these materials that remains even after he has finished playing.

3. *Dramatic play:* Dramatic or pretend play involves some aspect of non-literality—symbolic transformations and the production of decontextualized behaviors. Pretend play allows the child to be many things at once; he can be himself, actor, observer, and participator in a symbolic exercise.

4. *Games-with-rules:* The final category involves spontaneous acceptance of a division of labour, prearranged rules, and the adjustment to these rules. Although rarely evident during the preschool and kindergarten years, this is one ludic activity that accompanies us into our adult lives.

These four types of play were thought to develop in a relatively fixed sequence, with functional play appearing first in infancy, and games-with-rules last at about 6 or 7 years of age. Both dramatic or pretend play and constructive play actually appear to emerge at about the same time. The sequence from functional to dramatic and constructive play, may be the result of the infant's or toddler's quiet responses to the late Corrine Hutt's two important questions about objects; that is, opportunities to manipulate objects, in a functional-sensorimotor fashion, and to explore these objects, may well provide the young child with the answer to the question "What do these things do?" Once the object-derived question has been answered, the youngster poses the self-derived question, "What can *I* do with these things?" The answers come in the forms of construction and pretense.

In our early studies, my colleagues and I went beyond the standard use of the Piagetian-derived cognitive play categories. A principal interest concerned the social contexts within which the various cognitive play forms took place. Thus, in a rather simple move, the cognitive play forms just described were nested within Parten's (1932) three social participation categories of solitary, parallel, and group activities. My colleagues and I added to the scale the incidence of onlooker, unoccupied, reading, conversational, transitional, and rough-and-tumble activities, and a place for the names of the focal child's playmates and the affective quality of the interaction (positive, negative, neutral) when "group play" or conversations were coded. The resulting Play Observation Scale is illustrated in figure 10–1.

The methodology basically consisted of taking six 10-second time samples of free play per child per day over an extended period (such as one or two months). Thus, across 30 minutes of observation we would have 180 data points.

Child's Name: _____		Sex: _____				
School Name: _____		Date: _____				

	Time Sample Number (10 seconds)					
Category	*1*	*2*	*3*	*4*	*5*	*6*
Unoccupied						
Onlooker						
Reading						
Conversation						
Transitional activity						
Rough-and-tumble activity						
Exploration						
Solitary						
Functional						
Constructive						
Dramatic						
Games						
Parallel						
Functional						
Constructive						
Dramatic						
Games						
Group						
Functional						
Constructive						
Dramatic						
Games						

1. names of playmates; affective quality of interaction
2. _____
3. _____
4. _____
5. _____
6. _____

Figure 10–1. The Play Observation Scale

The Development of Play in Childhood

The Play Observation Scale has been used to derive developmental data in various venues. Thus far researchers have reported developmental data on children ranging in age from 2 to 7 years, described the play behaviors of children from lower- and middle-class socioeconomic milieus, and examined the play of children living in two-parent versus one-parent homes. Rather than describe all of these data, I refer you to the chapter on *Play* in Rubin, Fein, and Vandenberg's *Handbook of Child Psychology* (1983).

In a nutshell, the developmental data can be described as follows:

1. From 3 to 5 years of age, the frequency of parallel play decreases and group play increases. The frequencies of unoccupied and onlooker behaviors decrease, whereas conversations with peers increase.
2. From 3 to 5 years of age, the frequency of functional play decreases, while dramatic play and games-with-rules increase.
3. From 3 to 5 years, the frequencies of solitary-functional, solitary-dramatic parallel-functional, and parallel-dramatic play decrease. Group-constructive play, group-dramatic play, and group games increase.

Correlates of Children's Play

Can observations of children's free play provide us with the necessary clues about their social, emotional, and cognitive development? In our large-scale research program we have examined whether particular play forms correlate differentially with a variety of developmental measures. The results of these studies indicate quite clearly that observations of free play can be reliable indicators of social, social-cognitive, and cognitive competence in 4-, 5-, and 6-year-olds. For example, our data reveal the following:

1. In preschool, kindergarten, and grade 1, children who produce a high frequency of *solitary-functional* play (the least mature form of play) perform more poorly on social and impersonal problem-solving tasks and on measures of verbal IQ (PPVT, receptive vocabulary). Furthermore, their teachers rate them as socially incompetent and their peers dislike them. This finding with regard to peer rejection stems from two sources: when we administer a sociometric battery test to children and ask them who it is they like and/or dislike in their class, children who produce a high frequency of solitary-functional play receive many dislike ratings from their peers. In addition, solitary-functional players, when they interact with others, are observed to engage in more negative encounters and receive fewer social initiations from others than their more maturely playing age-mates (for example, Rubin, 1982a; Rubin & Clark, 1983).
2. Children in preschool, kindergarten and grade 1, who engage frequently in *solitary-dramatic* play, fare similarly to the solitary-functional players. That is, they are rejected by peers, rated by teachers as socially maladroit, and perform poorly on measures of perspective-taking and social problem solving (for example, Rubin, 1982a; Rubin & Clark, 1983).

3. Identical results are reported for children who engage in high frequencies of both *parallel-functional* and *parallel-dramatic* play.

    Why is it that these relations occur? In the case of functional play, the answer is quite simple. Functional or sensorimotor activity is a rather immature form of behavior, especially for 4-, 5-, and 6-year-olds. Consequently, it is not surprising that immature or non-normative behaviors correlate negatively with indices of peer popularity, social-cognitive development, and teacher ratings of social competence.

    The dramatic play data, on the other hand, may be of surprise to those psychologists and educators who believe that all forms of pretense are good for young children. Quite clearly this is not the case. When dramatic play is evinced in early childhood, it occurs most often in group settings; in preschoolers, approximately two-thirds of pretend play occurs in interactive groups (Rubin, 1982b; Rubin, Fein & Vandenberg, 1983). This means that nonsocial pretense is a non-normative form of behavior when produced frequently in group (such as classroom) settings. Non-normative behaviors (such as immaturity, and aggression) have been associated with peer rejection and social-cognitive deficits in numerous other reports (Coie & Kupersmidt, 1983; Dodge, 1983).

4. Some forms of play in childhood are associated with indices of developmental maturity and adaptation. *Parallel-constructive* play (for example, drawing and puzzle activities) is related positively with peer popularity, teacher ratings of social competence, and both impersonal and social problem solving in early childhood (that is, in preschool and kindergarten). Furthermore, high frequencies of *group-dramatic* play in preschool and kindergarten are associated positively with popularity, social competence, perspective-taking, and social problem-solving skills.

5. The category of play in kindergarten and grade 1 that correlates most positively and significantly with measures of peer popularity, social competence, and social-cognitive development is *group games-with-rules*. This category is, of course, the theoretically most mature form of social and cognitive play in the Play Observation Scale hierarchy.

6. Finally, in another series of longitudinal analyses, my colleagues and I have found that high frequencies of *solitary-* and *parallel-functional* and *dramatic* play in kindergarten predict peer rejection, social behavioral problems, and poor performance on social problem-solving measures in both grades 1 and 2. Alternately, high frequencies of sociodramatic play and social games in kindergarten predict popularity and good social problem-solving skills in grades 1 and 2 (Rubin, 1984).

    These particular correlations appear to be somewhat unidirectional. Thus, the kindergarten measures of social competence and social-cognition do not predict the aforementioned play forms in grades 1 and 2.

The Waterloo Longitudinal Project

My own interests in children's play derived from an initial concern whether and how peers can play an active role as socialization agents. Therefore, I am less concerned with the connection between play and the development of symbolic representation than with the social benefits of play. My long-standing interests, led me to use the Play Observation Scale to target small numbers of children who deviate, to some extent, from the normal play patterns of their peers. The particular group of children that has attracted my attention in the Waterloo Longitudinal Project are those who interact very infrequently with their peers during free play periods.

The impetus for the project stems from a variety of theoretical and empirical sources. First, Piaget (1932) and Sullivan (1953), among others, have suggested that peer interaction allows children to experience role and rule negotiations and conflicts within an egalitarian social context. Such experiences have been thought to provide children with a pathway toward becoming sociocentered, empathic, responsive, and responsible young citizens. Neo-Piagetians have advanced sociodramatic play and game-with-rules as particularly advantageous for social and social-cognitive growth and development (for example, Saltz & Brodie, 1982).

Learning and social-learning theorists and researchers have also indicated that children can be taught social and cognitive skills directly (through tutelage) and indirectly (through observation) by their peers. Peers also provide each other with emotional support in threatening or novel situations (Schwarz, 1972).

Finally, there is now accumulating a body of data suggesting that the quantity and quality of early peer interaction is predictive of later school performance and mental health status. Children who have been identified as isolated from and/or rejected by their peer group appear to be at risk for school drop-out, antisocial behavior, and psychopathology in adolescence and in the early years of adulthood (Cowen, Pederson, Babigian, Izzo & Trost, 1973; John, Mednick & Schulsinger, 1982; Roff, Sells & Golden, 1972).

These perspectives suggest that peer interaction is a significant force in the development of social, social-cognitive, and cognitive skills. Unfortunately, however, not all children are equally likely to engage others in social discourse. The long-term prognosis for these children may not be good. Yet, until we began the Waterloo Longitudinal Project, we knew very little about the correlates and consequences of social withdrawal in early childhood. Furthermore, procedures for identifying severely withdrawn children were not well developed. Now, four years into the project, my colleagues and I feel that we have found an adequate targeting device, the Play Observation Scale. We are also garnering some interesting data suggesting that severely withdrawn young children could very well be at risk for particular psychosocial problems.

The Targeting Procedure

Basically, I am interested in children who deviate in some extreme fashion from their age-group and classroom social play norms. My first research efforts included children attending a large number of preschools and kindergartens in Southwest Ontario. All children fell within the normal range of intelligence. Through the use of the Play Observation Scale over a 1-month period, I devised the targeting scheme described in table 10–1. Three groups were identified by degree of sociability: *isolate, average,* and *sociable* children. The isolate and sociable groups each represented approximately 15 percent of the population.

Initial Findings

Given the targeting procedure just described, my colleagues and I examined some of the concomitants of extreme isolate status. Consequently we gathered data on perspective taking, social problem solving, communicative competence, peer popularity, and teacher ratings of social competence. The results of this early work have been described at length in several recent journal articles and chapters. Let me summarize some of the findings:

1. In both preschool and kindergarten, isolate children produce more transitional, "off-task" activity than their more sociable age-mates. They are also less boisterous in their play; for example, withdrawn children are less likely to engage in rough-and-tumble play encounters (Rubin, 1982b).

2. The quality of solitary play varies between isolate and nonisolate young children. Withdrawn preschoolers engage in more solitary-functional and solitary-dramatic play, but in an equal amount of solitary-construc-

Table 10–1
The Sociability Targeting Procedure

Isolate:	Σ solitary play & Σ onlooker behavior & Σ unoccupied = 1 SD above age group M and 10 percent above class M
	&
	Σ group play & Σ conversations = 1 SD below age group M and 10 percent below class M
Sociable:	Σ solitary play & Σ onlooker behavior & Σ unoccupied = 1 SD below age group M and 10 percent below class M
	&
	Σ group play & Σ conversations = SD above age group M and 10 percent above class M

Source: Adapted from Rubin (1982b).

tive play when compared with their more sociable counterparts (Rubin, 1982b). Given our earlier findings that solitary-functional and solitary-dramatic play are associated positively with indices of peer rejection and social maladjustment, these play data seem rather significant.

3. The quality of group play varies between isolate and nonisolate children. When preschoolers and kindergarteners were observed to play with others, the sociable children were more likely than isolates to participate in dramatic and games oriented activities (Rubin, 1982b). Given the significance that many developmental psychologists attach to sociodramatic play and social games, these findings could be expected ultimately to predict lags in social-cognitive and social development.

4. In preschool and kindergarten, extremely withdrawn children do not receive significantly more negative sociometric ratings than the other groups (Rubin, 1982b).

5. Teachers rated preschool isolates as more fearful/anxious than the other two groups (Rubin, 1982b).

6. On a social problem-solving measure, children were required to suggest how cartoon characters could best go about solving problems in which one character desired an object in the possession of a second character (see Rubin & Krasnor, in press, for full descriptions). Isolate children produced fewer different alternatives and were more likely to suggest adult intervention strategies than were their more sociable age-mates (Rubin, Daniels-Beirness, & Bream, 1984; Rubin & Krasnor, in press).

7. We filmed two 15-minute free play sessions of isolate or sociable children paired with same-age, same-sex, average dyadic partners. Isolate children were more likely than either of the other groups to emit nonsocial, egocentric utterances. Many of these utterances were directed toward nonpresent or imaginary others (Rubin, 1982b).

8. When isolate children directed requests to their dyadic partners, they tended to be of a low-cost genre (attention-getting goals). The more sociable children were more likely to direct "high cost" requests (object acquisition, other action goals) to their play partners (Rubin & Borwick, 1984).

Despite the production of lower cost requests, isolates experienced less compliance to their directives than did the other children. Furthermore, when their requests failed, isolate children were less likely to modify their original strategies (that failed) than were their more sociable partners (Rubin & Borwick, 1984).

To summarize, our data portray the young isolate child as identified by the Play Observation Scale to be somewhat anxious, deferent to her/his peers, less mature and boisterous in her/his play, and perhaps more dependent on adults than more sociable age-mates to solve social problems. They are not disliked by their peers; consequently a good many psychologists such as Asher, Markell, and Hymel (1981) and Gottman (1977) have suggested that these children are not at risk for later problems, and that attention should be focused on rejected children because they demonstrate more psychological and academic problems in adolescence and young adulthood. With this note of caution (actually, admonition) in mind, our initial data cannot allow us to conclude that young, severely withdrawn children are at risk for later problems, in part, because of a lack of knowledge concerning the stability and the long-term correlates of early isolate (nonsocial) behaviors.

Recent Findings

Many of the kindergarteners who participated in the first year of the Project were followed subsequently into grades 1 and 2. The children were observed during naturalistic free play in these grades, as were all other age-mates who may have entered the project for the first time in a given year.

Through the use of the Play Observation Scale, children were identified as isolate, average, and sociable targets in grades 1 and 2. Initial analyses reveal that over 60 percent of those isolate kindergarten children who remained in the study into grade 2 were similarly targeted in the latter grade. Interestingly, over 80 percent of the sociable kindergarten children maintained that stable status.

The longitudinal data indicate also that children targeted as continuously isolated from kindergarten to grade 2 are actually similar to their average and sociable counterparts in several ways. For example, they are as popular among their peers (sociometrically) and they can think about solutions to social dilemmas involving object acquisition and friendship initiation as well as their more sociable age-mates (Rubin, in press; Rubin & Krasnor, in press). These data alone would support the conclusions by Asher et al. (1981) and Gottman (1977) that withdrawn children or continuously isolated children are not at risk for later difficulties.

However further examination of our full corpus of data suggests otherwise. Despite being reasonably liked by their peers, and despite having a normal social-cognitive problem-solving repertoire, isolate children do not believe that they, themselves, are socially competent. They also differ from their more sociable counterparts in that they perceive themselves to be less skilled in the arenas of academic and physical-motor competence as well. Thus, despite non-negative, objective indicators of social competence, there appears to be a breakdown in the self-system.

What could be happening to produce such significant negative self-perceptions in this group? Some recent data concerning children's role relationships during play provide some possible clues. When isolate children engage in dyadic free-play with a non-isolate partner, they are more likely to take on deferent, submissive roles. Furthermore, when they attempt to play dominant roles (such as managerial, teacher), they are more likely to be rebuffed than their more sociable counterparts. Finally, they are "easy marks"; their more sociable play partners are extremely successful in gaining compliance from them (Rubin, in press). This combination of social deference and social failure could be the reason isolate children have poor self-perceptions of their own competencies.

The Play Observation Scale is extremely useful in identifying a small group of children who, throughout the early years of childhood, fail to interact with peers at a normal rate. By grade 2, some of the costs of continuous social withdrawal become apparent. Continuously withdrawn youngsters are socially anxious and submissive, and they seem to recognize that something just isn't right; their self-perceptions are far from flattering. Given this perspective, I believe that extremely withdrawn children *do* represent an at risk population. I would further suggest that they are at risk for internalizing problems such as depression. They are not at risk for the same reasons as rejected children. This latter group is characterized by aggressive acts and poor social-cognitive, problem-solving skills; they appear to be at risk for externalizing problems. Continuously targeted isolate children are quite different from rejected-aggressive children.

Conclusion

In this chapter I have attempted to describe how observations of children's naturalistic free play can aid in identifying forms of social and cognitive play that may be maladaptive in early childhood. The Play Observation Scale developed in this research has also allowed the identification of a small group of children who may be at risk for later socio-emotional problems. It may well be that observations of children at play can provide us with a looking-glass not only into the cognitive content of children's minds, but also into the affects which often guide the performance of cognitive and social skills.

Future research efforts will center on (1) why it is that some young 3- and 4-year-olds become severely withdrawn from their age-group, and (2) what it is that psychologists and educators can do to prevent or ameliorate the problems associated with social isolation in childhood.

References

Asher, S.R., Markell, R.A., & Hymel, S. 1981. Identifying children at risk in peer relations: A critique of the rate-of-interaction approach to assessment. *Child Development* 54:1427–1434.

Coie, J.D., & Kupersmidt, J.B. 1983. A behavioral analysis of emerging social status in boys' groups. *Child Development* 54:1400–1416.

Cowen, E.L., Pederson, A., Babigian, H., Izzo, L.D., & Trost, M.A. 1973. Long-term follow-up of early detected vulnerable children. *Journal of Consulting and Clinical Psychology* 41:438–446.

Dodge, K.A. 1983. Behavioral antecedents of peer social status. *Child Development* 54:1386–1399.

Gottman, J.M. 1977. Toward a definition of social isolation in children. *Child Development* 48:513–517.

John, R., Mednick, S., & Schulsinger, F. 1982. Teacher reports as a predictor of schizophrenia and borderline schizophrenia: A Bayesian decision analysis. *Journal of Abnormal Psychology* 91:399–413.

Parten, M.B. 1932. Social participation among preschool children. *Journal of Abnormal and Social Psychology* 27:243–269.

Piaget, J. 1932. *The moral judgment of the child.* Glencoe: Free Press.

Piaget, J. 1962. *Play, dreams and imitation in childhood.* New York: Norton. Originally published 1945; English translation, C. Gattegno & F.M. Hodgson (London: Routledge & Kegan Paul, 1951).

Roff, M., Sells, S.B., & Golden, M.M. 1972. *Social adjustment and personality development in children.* Minneapolis: University of Minnesota Press.

Rubin, K.H. 1982a. Non-social play in preschoolers: Necessarily evil? *Child Development* 53:651–657.

———. 1982b. Social and social-cognitive developmental characteristics of young isolate, normal, and sociable children. In K.H. Rubin & H.S. Ross (Eds.), *Peer relationships and social skills in childhood.* New York: Springer-Verlag.

———. In press. Socially withdrawn children: An "at risk" population? In B. Schneider, K.H. Rubin, & J. Ledingham (Eds.), *Peer relationships and social skills in childhood* (Vol. 2), *Issues in assessment and training.* New York: Springer-Verlag.

Rubin, K.H., & Borwick, D. 1984. The communicative skills of children who vary with regard to sociability. In H. Sypher & J. Applegate (Eds.). *Social cognition and communication.* Hillsdale, N.J.: Erlbaum.

Rubin, K.H., & Clark, L. 1983. Preschool teacher's ratings of behavioral problems. *Journal of Abnormal Child Psychology* 11:273–285.

Rubin, K.H., Daniels-Beirness, T., & Bream, L. 1984. Social isolation and social problem-solving: A longitudinal study. *Journal of Consulting and Clinical Psychology* 52:17–25.

Rubin, K.H., Fein, G.G., & Vandenberg, B. 1983. Play. In P. Mussen (Ed.). *Manual of child psychology* (Vol. 4). New York: Wiley.

Rubin, K.H., & Krasnor, R. In press. Social-cognitive and social behavioral perspectives on problem solving. In M. Perlmutter (Ed.), *Minnesota Symposia on child psychology* (Vol. 18). Hillsdale, N.J.: Erlbaum.

Rubin, K.H., & Maioni, T.L. 1975. Play preference and its relationship to egocentrism, popularity, and classification skills in preschoolers. *Merrill-Palmer Quarterly* 21:171–179.

Rubin, K.H., Maioni, T.L., & Hornung, M. 1976. Free play behaviors in middle and lower class preschoolers: Parten and Piaget revisited. *Child Development* 47:414–419.

Schwarz, J.C. 1972. Effects of peer familiarity on the behavior of preschoolers in a novel situation. *Journal of Personality and Social Psychology* 24:276–284.

Saltz, E., & Brodie, J. 1982. Pretend-play training in childhood: A review and critique. In D.J. Pepler & K.H. Rubin (Eds.), *The play of children: Current theory and research*. Basel, Switzerland: S. Karger.

Smilansky, S. 1968. *The effects of sociodramatic play on disadvantaged preschool children*. New York: Wiley.

Sullivan, H.S. 1953. *The interpersonal theory of psychiatry*. New York: Norton.

11
Social Class and Pretend Play

Vonnie C. McLoyd

I n *The Effects of Sociodramatic Play on Disadvantaged Children,* Smilansky (1968) compellingly set forth an issue with which scores of researchers have since wrestled, namely, the ways in which position in the class structure of society affects the imaginative play of children. The book describes a stunningly ambitious program of research involving children in thirty-six kindergarten and nursery-school classes in Israel and a subset of their parents. As the title of the book suggests, Smilansky's research focused on sociodramatic play, a subcategory of pretend play in which two or more children assume different pretend roles and enact an imaginary situation in a cooperative and interdependent fashion.

Smilansky's work led her to three major conclusions: (1) that lower-class children from certain cultural backgrounds (for example, the children of parents from Middle Eastern and North African countries) engage in less and poorer-quality sociodramatic play compared to their middle-class counterparts (children of parents from European countries); (2) that deficits in children's sociodramatic play develop because parents, first, give little if any direct training and encouragement in the basic techniques of sociodramatic play, and, second, inhibit through their childrearing attitudes and practices the child's development of verbal, cognitive, and social abilities essential for well-developed sociodramatic play; and (3) training by adults in the techniques of sociodramatic play can ameliorate these deficits and positively affect verbal, cognitive, and social skills.

With almost palpable excitement, some scholars in the United States set out to test empirically the validity and generalizability of these conclusions while others uncritically seized them to affirm their suspicions that economic privation truncated imagination and related skills. This suspicion was not altogether unwarranted, for empirical researchers had consistently reported that lower- and working-class parents valued obedience, neatness, and cleanliness more highly than middle-class parents, who tended to value curiosity and self-control more highly (Duvall, 1946; Kohn, 1959, 1963). On the

This chapter is a modified and expanded version of an earlier publication (McLoyd, 1982).

assumption that social structure exerts a major influence on values which, in turn, affect behavior, Kohn (1963) speculated that these differences stem in large measure from differences in the occupational conditions which different social classes experience. A similar thesis was advanced by Rubin (1976) in her impressively insightful and sensitive study of the lives of working-class adults. As she explained:

> Past experience combines with present reality to create future expectations, because parents, after all, do not raise their children in a vacuum—without some idea of what the future holds for them, some sense of what they will need to survive the adult world for which they are destined. In fact, it is out of just such understandings that parental attitudes and values about child-raising are born. Thus, professional middle-class parents, assuming that their children are destined to do work like theirs, . . . call for an educational system that fosters those qualities. . . . In most working-class jobs, creativity, innovation, initiative, flexibility [required for professional or executive work] are considered by superiors a hindrance. . . . Those who must work at such jobs may need nothing so much as a kind of iron-willed discipline to get them to work every day and to keep them going back year after year. No surprise, then, that such parents look suspiciously at spontaneity whether at home or at school . . . [and] that early childhood training tends to focus on . . . discipline. (pp. 127–128)

In addition to the fact that Smilansky's (1968) conclusions appeared to dovetail so nicely with reported class differences in parental values, the timing of her book could not have been more auspicious. America had just recently awakened to discover the extent of poverty in its populace and begun to appropriate vast sums of money to assist researchers in ascertaining and finding ways to negate the potential adverse effects of poverty on children. It was also a time when the concept of cultural deprivation held sway in the social science literature as an explanation for the distinctive behavior of lower-class and ethnic minority children (Baratz & Baratz, 1970; Tulkin, 1972). No doubt these secular trends had some influence on the direction of Smilansky's work and, in turn, increased the chances that her work would be greeted favorably by the American research audience.

Prior to the release of Smilansky's book, some scholars characterized the pretend play of lower-class children as defective and changeworthy (Sigel & McBane, 1967) and demonstrated the positive effects of training on dramatic play in middle-class children (Marshall & Hahn, 1967). However, it was Smilansky who emerged as the standard-bearer, first, because both assessment and prescription were components of her intervention model and, second, because her analysis of the qualitative nature of sociodramatic play and its role in intellectual development and educational achievement was clear, insightful, and extensive. For example, she delineated the essential components of well-developed sociodramatic play (for example, imitative make-believe role play, use of verbalizations or movements as substitutes for real objects, use of verbal descriptions as substitutes for action and situations, cooperation between at least two children, enactment lasting at least 10 minutes, and verbal interaction related to the play episode). Several researchers adopted these components, in some cases with slight modifications (such as required duration of enactment) (Fein & Stork, 1981; Griffing, 1980; Griffing, Stewart, McKendry & Anderson, 1983), while others based their definitions of different kinds of play on those provided by Smilansky (Rosen, 1974; Rubin, Maioni, & Hornung, 1976).

With the precipitous increase in empirical findings indicating that play facilitates or is linked to behaviors which we value highly such as divergent thinking (Dansky & Silverman, 1976; Johnson, 1976; Lieberman, 1965), problem solving (Bruner, 1976; Klinger, 1969; Sylva, 1977, Sylva, Bruner & Genova, 1976), social role and physical conservation (Fink, 1976; Golomb & Cornelius, 1977), perspective and role taking (Burns & Brainerd, 1979), and spatial relations and classification skills (Rubin & Maioni, 1975), the urgency increased, first, to ascertain if indeed there were deficiencies in the play of lower-class children, and, second, to correct identified or putative deficiencies since they may have deleterious consequences for critical domains of social and, particularly, intellectual development. That is, researchers reasoned that if pretend play enhances development, then conversely, its attenuation may impede development to a similar degree. What, then, do almost twenty years of research tell us about the pretend and sociodramatic play of children from different socioeconomic backgrounds?

Studies of Social Class Differences in Pretend and Sociodramatic Play

Amount of Pretend and Sociodramatic Play

We begin with a brief overview of Smilansky's (1968) research. Smilansky's interest in sociocultural differences in sociodramatic play was piqued when she attempted to use sociodramatic play as a means to further the intellectual development of lower-class Israeli children of parents from Middle Eastern and North African countries. She aborted this plan when she observed that these children "play very little and most of them do not participate in sociodramatic play at all" (p. 4) and sought instead to verify sociocultural differences in sociodramatic play and identify the sources of these differences. Five field workers observed thirty-six kindergarten and nursery-school classes in Israel, half of which were attended by lower-class children of Middle-Eastern and African descent and half by middle-class children of European descent

(Study 1). Relying principally on qualitative and descriptive analyses, she reported that the middle-class children engaged in more sociodramatic play, enacted richer episodes and a larger variety of roles, produced more verbalizations, and used symbolic play objects more often and realistic play objects less often than the lower-class children.

Subsequent to this comparative study, Smilansky introduced an extensive intervention program to increase the frequency and quality of sociodramatic play among the lower-class children (Study 2). To establish different baselines with which to contrast the effects of intervention, two control groups were studied, one composed of lower-class Israeli children of Middle Eastern or African descent and one comprised of Israeli children of European descent. To constitute the latter control group, Smilansky *combined groups of lower- and middle-class children* because, as Smilansky (1968) noted, *"We did not find significant differences in their sociodramatic play"* (p. 109). Smilansky explained that lower-class Israeli children of European descent, unlike those of Middle Eastern and African descent, suffered no play deficits because of environmental stimulation (such as television) and differences in the ways of growth and development which served to mitigate the potentially deleterious effects of economic privation.

Like those reported by Smilansky, the findings of more recent studies of the effects of social class on the tendency to engage in sociodramatic play are not in full agreement. Most, but not all, of these studies report that middle-class preschoolers engage in sociodramatic play more frequently than do lower-class preschoolers (Fein & Stork, 1981; Griffing, 1980; Rosen, 1974; Udwin & Shmukler, 1981; White, 1978). A minority of studies reports no differences (Golomb, 1979; Stern, Bragdon, & Gordon, 1976) or a more complex pattern of findings, such as that reported by Rubin et al. (1976). These researchers found that middle-class children engaged in more sociodramatic play but did not differ from lower-class children in the amount of solitary-, parallel-, or associative-dramatic play or total dramatic play. One study of the amount of time children spend in sociodramatic play actually reported differences in favor of lower-class children. Eiferman (1971), in her study of almost 14,000 children from Jewish and Arab cultures, found that lower-class first- and second-graders engaged in more sociodramatic play (termed *collective symbolic play*) than middle-class children.

Two studies have focused on differences between working-class and middle-class children in pretend play rather than sociodramatic play. Tizard, Philips, and Plewis (1976) regarded as pretend play any instance in which children treated either objects or themselves as other than they were, even if the child did not speak. Using these criteria, they found that middle-class preschoolers engaged in more pretend play, but were no more likely than working-class preschoolers to perform dramatic impersonations or engage in a higher level of social play (ranging from solitary play to cooperative play with role differentiation). Unfortunately, symbolic and nonsymbolic play were not distinguished within level of social play, making it impossible to determine whether differences existed between the two groups in amount of sociodramatic play.

Smith and Dodsworth (1978) regarded as pretense any nonliteral or make-believe use of verbalizations, actions, or objects. They found that among English middle-class preschoolers, compared to working-class preschoolers, more time was spent in pretend play and more children participated in a single pretense episode (2.60 versus 2.03, respectively). However, the two groups were similar in the amount of time they spent in associative and cooperative play.

Quality of Sociodramatic Play

While some researchers have found that middle-class children enact longer episodes of sociodramatic play than lower-class children (Griffing, 1980; Smilansky, 1968, Study 1), others have found neither length of sociodramatic episode (Fein & Stork, 1981; Smilansky, 1968, Study 2), length of pretend play episode (Smith & Dodsworth, 1978), nor complexity of pretend play (Golomb, 1979) to be related to social class. Fein and Stork (1981) found the overall quality of sociodramatic play among middle-class children to be higher than that among lower-class children, but only one (frequency of verbalization) of eleven measures (such as complexity of language, originality and diversity of object, role, and scene transformation) that composed the overall quality score was significantly related to social class.

Stern et al. (1976) reported no social class effects on approximately 75 percent of the 30-plus indices of pretend play, and large differences (defined as a difference of 15 percent or more in occurrence) on 25 percent of them. The only large difference found positive for middle-class children at both age levels (3 and 4 years) was a tendency for the latter to enact highly specific roles and persons (for example, mother as opposed to parent or human being). The remaining large differences were found either at both ages but positive for lower-class children, or for one age and not the other.

Object Use during Pretend Play

The findings regarding social class differences in the use of objects during pretend play are mixed. This lack of consistency does not appear to be due to differences in the ages of the samples. Some studies report that economically advantaged children show greater imaginary and elaborated use of objects, an increased tendency to invent imaginary objects, and less use of objects as their form intended (replica use) (Griffing, 1980; Smilansky, 1968, Study 1; Smith & Dodsworth, 1978). However, other studies report no relationship between social class and the frequency with which preschoolers use objects as though they possess imaginary properties, use representative and nonrepresentative objects as referents, or invent imaginary objects for which concrete referents are absent (Fein & Stork, 1981; Smilansky, 1968, Study 2; Stern et al., 1976).

Social Class × Age Interactions

Eiferman (1971) found that low-income first and second graders, but not third through eighth graders, residing in Israel engaged in sociodramatic play more frequently than their economically advantaged counterparts. This pattern of results prompted Eiferman (1971) to conclude that disadvantaged children are not less disposed toward and less facile in the collective enactment of pretense during childhood as suggested by Smilansky (1968), but rather reach the peak of their symbolic play activity later than middle-income children, and specifically after the age period observed by Smilansky. At best, Eiferman's findings provided only modest support for this conclusion since no data were presented for preschool-aged children.

Only two other studies in the literature lend any degree of support to Eiferman's hypothesis. Griffing et al. (1983) conducted a follow-up study of imagination, self-concept, and school achievement among 10- and 11-year-old lower-class and middle-class Afro-American children whose sociodramatic play had been studied when they were in kindergarten. When asked about their current and past (when they were younger) pretend play with friends, lower-class girls reported that they still played house and with dolls with their friends, whereas middle-class girls reported that they had engaged in these imaginative activities only when they were younger. Middle-class girls were more likely than lower-class girls to report that they were involved in reality-oriented activities such as Girl Scouts or choir and had little time to play. The findings led Griffing et al. to suggest that lower-class and middle-class children may have different timetables with regard to the development of sociodramatic play.

Stern et al. (1976) found evidence that middle- and low-income preschoolers peak at different ages on certain components of pretend play, but the direction of these differences was not consistently in line with what would be predicted on the basis of Eiferman's hypothesis. At age 3, middle-class children surpassed lower-class children in verbalizations, use of accessories, and use of three or more signifiers, whereas at 4, lower-class children surpassed middle-class children on these variables. However, lower-class children surpassed middle-class children at age 3 in the degree to which their play was understood on the basis of verbalizations made about the play, whereas at age 4, middle-class children surpassed lower-class children.

Other observational studies of the interaction effects of social class and age on pretend and sociodramatic play do not support Eiferman's hypothesis. Neither Fein and Stork (3- to 4.5-year-olds versus 5- to 6.5-year-olds), Golomb (3.4- to 6.1-year-olds), nor Smith and Dodsworth (3- versus 4-year-olds) reported significant age × social class effects. Moreover, in the only study which found both significant age differences and significant social class differences, the pattern of the latter was not similar to that of the former, further discounting the developmental lag hypothesis (Fein & Stork, 1981).

In any case, Eiferman's hypothesis remains a provocative one which we believe has not been tested adequately. What is clearly needed is observational and, ideally, longitudinal study of children representing a wider range of ages, encompassing both the preschool and grade school years.

Perhaps because of the relative paucity of data, there appears to be less controversy about the onset and very early development of pretend play in children from different socioeconomic backgrounds. What little data are available suggest that there may be no social class differences during these early stages. White (1978), for example, found no significant correlation between pretend play and social class for 1½- or 2-year-olds, but reported a significant positive correlation for 3-year-olds. Comparative studies by Kagan, Kearsley, and Zelazo (1978) of American infants and Guatemalan infants living in a "modern" versus impoverished village also suggest that their early pretense may be unaffected by socioeconomic status.

Summary of Findings

Taken as a whole, studies of social class differences in pretend and socio-dramatic play are inconclusive. Substantial disagreement with respect to the major dependent variables is apparent. There is far less evidence of lower quality than depressed frequency of sociodramatic play among economically disadvantaged children, though findings with respect to the latter have not been univocal or particularly robust.

Irrespective of the findings themselves, this body of research is inconclusive because of problematic data gathering and processing procedures, confounding classroom and school variable, and insufficient consideration of how the primary medium of sociodramatic play, namely verbal behavior, may be affected by ecological variables. Perhaps some or all of these factors are implicated in the disagreements among studies. The discussion of these issues which follows is not predicated on the assumption that there are or are not real social class differences. Consideration of confounding variables, for example, should not be interpreted necessarily as an argument for the null hypothesis. There may well be reliable social class differences, but existing information is inadequate to make such a determination. As noted in the following discussion, studies which report no significant social class effects themselves are characterized by a number of problems which undermine their validity and generalizability. Consideration of each of these issues does concede, however, that future research should make vigorous attempts to eliminate potentially confounding variables and methodological biases so that systematic variation between children from different social classes, if found, can be confidently attributed to social class rather than a host of contaminating factors. When social class differences are found, researchers need to press even harder to understand their source. As Smith (1983) has reminded us, social class is an umbrella variable which should serve only as a conceptual way station on the road to identifying more proximate variables which cause or underlie the observed differences.

Methodological Problems and Issues

Problematic Data Gathering and Processing Procedures. It is unclear whether variation in previous findings is due to differences in how social class groups were operationally defined. Higgins (1976) aptly noted that the use of social class as an independent variable requires, at the very least, specification of both the indices used to determine social class and the exact nature of the social class samples that were actually compared. In most studies, the designation of social class was based on parents' occupation and/or education level (Eiferman, 1971; Fein & Stork, 1981; Griffing, 1980; Rubin et al., 1976; Smith & Dodsworth, 1978; Tizard et al., 1976; White, 1978; Stern et al., 1976), though only two of these studies actually used standardized indices of social class (Griffing, 1980; White, 1978). In some studies, supplemental information was provided about whether the family was a welfare recipient or at the poverty level (Griffing, 1980; Rosen, 1974; Stern et al., 1976).

Comparability of samples across studies, though more difficult to ascertain when nonstandardized measures of social class are used, is virtually impossible to determine when the exact nature of the social class sample eventually formed (Rosen, 1974; Smith & Dodsworth, 1978) and the criteria for social class differentiation are unspecified (Golomb, 1979; Smilansky, 1968, Studies 1 and 2). Mueller and Parcel (1981) recently criticized the imprecise, often impressionistic, criteria psychologists use to identify social class levels, and the use of outdated measures (for example, Hollingshead) when they are used at all. Their suggestions regarding specific alternative measures of social class which take into account recent societal changes (such as increase in the number of single parent families) and specific changes in the labor force (increase in the number of families with multiple wage earners) merit careful attention if social class research is to be both valid and cumulative.

Rosen's (1974) research makes clear the hazards of indexing social class on bases other than detailed demographic information. The pretest-posttest design called for a group of culturally advantaged children (all Caucasian), contrasted with a group of culturally deprived children (all Afro-American). Demographic data gathered after pretest observations revealed that a substantial number of the Afro-American children were actually from middle-class-oriented families. Only because of these unexpected characteristics of the sample was Rosen able to circumvent the confounding of social class and race built into the original research design.

Future research should also make greater differentiation among social class groups, especially within the lower-income stratum. The life circumstances and conditions of the underclass are different from those of the more stable, upper-lower and working-class segments of society (Billingsley, 1968; Higgins, 1976), factors which may well impact on children's pretend play. Previous research tentatively suggests that children from middle-class backgrounds may be the most different from children whose parents are members of the nonworking underclass (Griffing, 1980; Rosen, 1974), and somewhat less different from children whose parents are manual, semiskilled or unskilled workers (Fein & Stork, 1981; Tizard et al., 1976).

Previous studies are plagued by a number of other methodological flaws and ambiguities. In the Griffing (1980) study, groups of four children, two boys and two girls, were asked to play mommies and daddies (also house), despite the fact that 83 percent of the lower-class children were from single parent families, while 83 percent of the middle-class children were from two-parent families. Lower-class children, then, were essentially requested to enact interdependent behavior to which they had probably received less real-life exposure.

Efforts to synthesize and reconcile findings are further hampered by failure to perform or report statistical tests of significance (Golomb, 1979; Smilansky, 1968; Stern et al., 1976; Tizard et al., 1976, Study 2) and delineate research methods (Golomb, 1979). It is, of course, unnecessary to belabor the interpretational ambiguity posed by studies which confound social class and culture (Smilansky, 1968, Study 1; Stern, 1976).

Lack of Systematic Efforts to Control Classroom and School Variables. One of the most troublesome aspects of the majority of studies is the confounding of social class and classroom factors such as curriculum, materials, space, and affective environment. With one exception (White, 1978), children in all of the reviewed studies were observed in school or day-care settings, typically, though not always, during the free play period. In a majority of studies, children from different social classes were drawn from different and socially homogeneous classrooms (Eiferman, 1971; Griffing, 1980; Rosen, 1974; Smilansky, 1968, Studies 1 and 2; Smith & Dodsworth, 1978; Tizard et al., 1976, Study 1; Stern et al., 1976). Therefore, differences between the children may reflect classroom effects rather than social class differences in symbolic competence. For example, in the Smith and Dodsworth (1978) study, one of the two working-class classrooms was situated in a high-rise development and the other was staffed by nurses rather than trained teachers (and both may have operated to depress the frequency of pretend play among the working-class children). Neither condition existed in the middle-class classrooms.

In some studies, children from the same socioeconomic background also came from different and socially homogeneous classrooms (Eiferman, 1971; Griffing, 1980; Rosen, 1974; Smith and Dodsworth, 1978; Tizard et et., 1976, Study 1; Stern et al., 1976). This sampling procedure, however, does not necessarily neutralize or randomize classroom effects if the lower- versus middle-class sample was drawn from an unequal number of classrooms (Griffing, 1980; Rosen, 1974) or if lower- and middle-class classrooms differed systematically on variables affecting pretend play.

Indeed, recent research indicating systematic variation in children's pretend play as a function of school and situational factors makes reevaluation of those studies which ignore these variables obligatory. Greater teacher-directness (Huston-Stein, Friedrich-Cofer, & Susman, 1977) decreased emphasis on classroom language instruction (Tizard et al., 1976, Study 1), a discovery-based versus structured curriculum (Johnson, Ershler, & Bell, 1980), certain types of teacher training (Tizard et al., 1976, Study 1) and toys with ambiguous functions (McLoyd, 1983b) are all factors that have been observed to produce lower levels of certain types of symbolic play among preschool children. Inhibitory factors may actually be more prominent in homogeneous lower-class classrooms. Gouldner (1978), for example, found that teachers of lower-class, inner-city, Afro-American kindergarteners, compared to teachers of white, middle-class suburban kindergarteners, were more demanding of silence, order, and obedience, and more likely to be judged by their colleagues on the basis of their effectiveness as disciplinarians. Stern et al. (1976) reported that the length of the free-play period at lower-class kindergartens was substantially shorter than at the middle-class kindergartens. The indoor classroom itself, in contrast to outdoor settings, appears to inhibit symbolic play among working-class preschoolers, while facilitating it among middle-class preschoolers (Tizard et al., 1976, Study 1). There is also limited evidence that children's symbolic play across different settings may not be significantly correlated, raising questions about the generalizability of individual differences found in one physical context (Singer, 1973).

A few researchers have eliminated the confounding of social class and classroom factors by observing lower- and middle-class children within social heterogeneous classrooms (Fein & Stork, 1981; Rubin et al., 1976; Tizard et al., 1976, Study 2). Their findings indicate higher frequencies of sociodramatic play (Fein & Stork, 1981; Rubin et al., 1976) and pretend play (Tizard et al., 1976, Study 2) among middle-income children. However, as noted previously, these differences were tempered by nonsignificant social class effects on other types (Rubin et al., 1976) and components (such as object transformations) of pretend play (Fein & Stork, 1981), and were only marginally significant (Rubin et al., 1976) or untested for their statistical signifiance (Tizard et al., 1976, Study 2).

Observation of lower- and middle-class children in socially heterogeneous classrooms does not necessarily ensure elimination of possible confounding factors such as unfamiliarity with play materials and feelings of apprehension (Rubin, Fein, & Vandenberg, 1983; Schwartzman, 1978), both of which are known inhibitors of pretend play (Fein, 1981; Hutt, 1970). It has been suggested that lower-class children may be more unfamiliar with play materials in the preschool setting because they are less likely to have in their home the variety of play materials found in middle-class homes or preschool classrooms (Fein & Stork, 1981; Rubin et al., 1976). Further, they may be more apprehensive toward the teacher as an authority figure if they had received more threats and negative directives from their parents (Fein & Stork, 1981; Wooton, 1974). In keeping with these hypotheses, it has been recommended that social class differences in pretend play be assessed only after systematic attempts have been made by the researcher to familiarize lower-class children with play materials, their teachers, and the school environment in general (Fein & Stork, 1981). Ideally, the success of these attempts should be empirically verified.

Smith (1983) suggested that if researchers familiarize lower-class children with a variety of play materials, on the assumption that they are less familiar than middle-class children with these materials, and later found no social class differences, such a finding would not discount social class differences in the "real world," if lower-class children tend to have fewer play materials in most settings they encounter. As I indicated elsewhere (McLoyd, 1983a), such a finding would, indeed, suggest the absence of social class differences in pretend play competence, even though we might expect performance differences in the absence of this familiarization process. After all, it is highly improbable that mere elimination of environmental factors which inhibit symbolic expression also modifies the child's basic symbolic capacity.

If we assume that familiarity increases and apprehension decreases automatically as a function of time, another possibility is to simply chart the pretend play of lower- and middle-class children over the school year so that changes in each group relative to the other can be examined. This strategy, however, does not decisively eliminate the possibility that failure of the two groups to converge over time is due to factors other than deficiencies in symbolic competence. More specifically, whether lower-class children are generally less comfortable in the classroom setting may have less to do with how much time they have spent there and more to do with stable home versus school discontinuities in acceptable verbal and social behaviors (Riessman, 1964), and valued cognitive styles (Boykins, 1978; Cohen, 1971). Stable classroom dynamics such as hierarchical social relations and cleavages, and differential student-teacher interaction (Gouldner, 1980; Rist, 1970) may also be important determinants. For a multiplicity of reasons, then, the classroom or school may be a less appropriate context to assess social class differences in symbolic competence.

Some of the casual observations of scholars not necessarily interested in children pretend play suggest that we may gain much insight into the imaginative lives of poor children when we study them in home settings. For example, in the course of his fieldwork with poor families and children in eastern Kentucky, Looff (1971), a clinical child psychiatrist, encountered a thirteen-member family living in a three-room shanty. Despite an existence that was so bleak that the crew of a Walter Cronkite television program chose them in the winter of 1963–64 to portray to the nation some aspects of Appalachian life, the children in this family appeared to have a rich fantasy life. As Looff explained:

> Wayne [6-years-old] and his younger brother and sisters took delight in showing me their toys—tin cans, old spoons, boards—with which they had scratched out part of the hillside behind the cabin. Their wild delight in mastering at least this much of their environment was matched by elaborate fantasies of playing that they were miners, earth-movers, or hunters. Following their lead, Danny [an 11-year-old who was withdrawn, apathetic, and doing poorly in school] slowly, tentatively began to relate with me and to talk. He asked me to sit with him in his playhouse. A shy pride was revealed in a faint grin that creased his face as he showed me how he had built it from sticks, car fenders, old toilet seats, burlap bags, and scraps of tarpaper. . . . He spoke of the imaginary playmates who shared his playhouse. He played dolls with them, feeding them, he said, on red beans, water, gravy, and oatmeal. (pp. 98–99)

Notwithstanding the apparent advantage of conducting observations in home settings, it is unlikely that school settings will be replaced as the primary venue for research on children's play. When research is conducted in the school, strategies are especially needed to eliminate motivational and affective inhibitors of pretend play. A playroom might be set up at the school but away from the classroom. (A two-room mobile laboratory is ideal.) Lower- and middle-class children could be familiarized with the setting and encouraged to think of it as a "safe and fun place" where they, ostensibly alone with their peers, can do whatever they wish without adult observation and supervision. Subsequent to familiarization, dyads or triads could be brought to the playroom for covertly observed play sessions. Under these conditions, preschool children display richer sociodramatic play and more risqué pretend behavior and language in their adult role enactments (for example, simulating intimacy, profanity) than preschool children observed in the presence of a familiar adult (McLoyd, Morrison, & Toler, 1979).

One other strategy merits serious consideration. Rather than attempting to control motivational and affective differences within one setting, a different setting might be chosen for each respective group precisely because of its facilitory effect on pretend play (Fein & Stork, 1981). For one, the highest level of symbolic competence may be expressed in a home or neighborhood setting, and for the other, a school setting. Alternatively, both groups of children might be observed in the same two settings, one chosen to be optimal for each group. Implementation of this research strategy, of course, requires more knowledge than is currently available about the ecological determinants of pretend play within lower- and middle-class children. It has also been suggested that observations of lower- and middle-class children be conducted in a variety of settings. This method would not only inform researchers about where pretense is most likely to occur for each group, thereby allowing designation of optimal settings, but it would also permit distinction between "typical" and "best" display of pretense within the two groups (Fein & Stork, 1981).

Verbal Behavior As an Indicator of Symbolic Processes. Verbalizations and, to a lesser extent, vocalizations (such as onomatopoeia) elucidate the symbolic content of play. Though some research on pretend play has been based entirely on spontaneous nonverbal behavior (for example, Lowe, 1975), Huttenlocher and Higgins (1978) have argued that without verbal evidence that play behavior (such as imitation of adult behavior, play with representative and nonrepresentative toys) is meant to designate an absent model or object ("Pretend I am the mother"), symbolic processes need not be involved. The child's behavior may reflect nothing more than exemplification or practice of social skills, the toys' limited potential or functional substitutability, or what the child has learned about the appropriate use of toys. The importance of their argument is their call for a more rigorous and unifying definition of symbolic behavior.

Though Huttenlocher and Higgins (1978) were concerned with overestimation of symbolic competence as a result of inadequate operational definitions, there is also reason to be concerned about the converse, that is, underestimation of symbolic competence. For example, there is evidence that older preschoolers display lower levels of understanding of social roles in solitary free play than in a modeling procedure which elicits role-related behavior (Watson & Fischer, 1980). A certain amount of verbal communication is necessary in sociodramatic play to create, plan, and negotiate the episode, but the possibility remains that some designations may not be verbally referenced (such as object or action substitutions). In a number of previous studies of social class differences in sociodramatic and pretend play, lower-class and working-class children made fewer verbalizations than middle-class children (Smilansky, 1968, Study 1; Smith & Dodsworth, 1978; Stern et al., 1976). In the Griffing (1980) study, the largest difference between the two groups was the extent to which verbal behavior was used as a substitute for situations ("Let's pretend that this is a supermarket and we're shopping"), while in the Fein and Stork (1981) research, frequency of pretend verbalizations was the only sociodramatic component for which a significant social class difference was found.

Lower-class children's behavior varies substantially as a function of the situation (Cazden, 1970) and may be mediated by sociolinguistic factors including suspicion that their behavior will have adverse consequences (Labov, 1972). Because they are more likely to speak nonstandard English and less likely to code switch from the latter to standard English (Gouldner, 1978), lower-class children are more likely to be admonished about their speech patterns in the classroom. The potential inhibition of spontaneous verbal behavior (Labov, 1972; Riessman, 1964) which supports and externalizes pretense, then, constitutes another reason why the classroom may be less optimal as a setting to study pretense in lower-class and working-class children.

Addressing this issue in a practical sense requires identification of procedures which encourage or provoke verbal expression, or which reduce the observer's reliance on verbal expression. In addition to observing children in settings which facilitate uninhibited, spontaneous behavior, children can simply be probed about the meaning of ambiguous free play behaviors (Fein & Stork, 1981; Pulaski, 1973). This procedure may yield information beyond that already available to the observer, and as such provide a better estimate of the child's symbolic competence, but it may also inhibit display of pretense because of the necessary disruption and adult presence. Verification of these outcomes seems worthwhile.

It is surprising that experimental research on social class differences has not been done. It may be especially instrumental in reducing, though not eliminating, the observer's reliance on verbal behavior as an indicator of pretense. At the very least, certain components of sociodramatic play, such as make-believe with objects, can be studied in experimental settings. Children might be elicited to model pretense with signifiers which vary in their prototypicality (Elder & Pederson, 1978; Fein, 1975). Very early role-playing competence can be assessed by modeling role-playing behavior of varying complexity and examining how the modeled demonstration is integrated in the child's subsequent free play (Watson & Fischer, 1977). These procedures can be grounded in a game to discourage defensive behavior. To satisfy Huttenlocher and Higgins's (1978) criterion, it may be possible to generate questions which provoke explanations from children about why an object or their behavior can be used to designate another object or person ("Is this really, really a horse?" "Then why did you or how can you treat it like a horse?"). Such experimental procedures can be used with very young children (under 3 years) who have limited verbal skills and have not entered nursery or preschool, making it possible then, to assess the onset and very early development of pretense unaffected by school or curriculum factors.

There is considerable lack of conceptual clarity about the extent to which symbolic processes are implicated in play which is "make-believe," "imaginative," "representational," or "imitative." The claim that disadvantaged children's play is imitative (child imitatively feeds and bathes doll, puts doll to bed), but not imaginative ("Let's pretend that I already fed and bathed the baby and now I'm putting her to bed," when only the last activity is actually imitated) seems to imply that their play is primarily nonsymbolic (Smilansky, 1968; Sutton-Smith, 1972). This need not be the case if we assume, as did Piaget (1962), that even deferred imitation involves the "symbolic evocation of absent realities" (p. 67) based on storage and retrieval of mental or memory images. Furthermore, the term "imitative" belies the information processing and generative capacities inherent in the observed action schema. As Garvey and Berndt (1975) argued,

> Performance of an action format of the schema . . . is not imitative but involves processes of active reconstruction of a unit of adult daily activity. . . . It seems unlikely that the event sequences . . . were directly copied from any singly adult model. Rather, bits and pieces of experience may have been grasped and conjoined in the process of the child's construction of the schema. Once the schema is formed, it is productive, [that is,] it generates specific variants of the schema which control the performance. (pp. 11–13)

Assessment of the components of sociodramatic play is necessary in future comparative research if social class differences are to be linked to specific symbolic processes (Fein & Stork, 1981), a task which few researchers have undertaken (Fein & Stork, 1981; Griffing, 1980; Stern et al., 1976). Such information enhances our understanding of the nature of sociodramatic play in children from different socioeconomic and cultural backgrounds and is particularly instructive to intervention efforts where strategies are presumably based on some understanding of those components most lacking.

In addition to measuring the quantity of sociodramatic play, three dimensions, each having its own components, might be identified within each bout of sociodramatic play. The first dimension might relate to the role itself and have as its components specificity of role (is child pretending to be a human being, an adult, or a nonhuman creature with a name who descended from space?), and type of role (remote versus within the realm of the child's personal experiences and concrete reality, the basis of Saltz, Dixon, & Johnson's (1977) distinction between thematic-fantasy and sociodramatic play).

A second, more complex dimension might be involvement or depth of role play, constituted by components such as change of voice to represent signified expressions of feelings, emotions, or psychological states, as opposed to concrete behavior, distinctive and meaningful role-related gestures (patting or rocking doll, jumping from chair to simulate superhero) and diversity of role characteristics (mother is nurturant, metes out punishment, teaches, performs instrumental acts; superhero is noble, daring). This dimension may capture some of the communication patterns of lower-class children ignored in previous research. In a number of these studies, some or all of the lower-class children were Afro-American (Griffing, 1980; Rosen, 1974; Stern et al., 1976) or members of an ethnic minority (Smilansky, 1968). Among Afro-Americans, especially lower-class groups, verbal communication is laced with distinctive nonverbal expressions and frequent displays of affect (Hannerz, 1969; Kochman, 1972; Akbar, 1974). Though it is not clear how early this style of communication emerges, first- and second-grade Afro-American girls have been found to make prominent use of nonverbal behavior (hands on hips, point and shaking fingers at "naughty" child) in their pretend enactments of the maternal role (Brady, 1975).

A third dimension might focus specifically on language and object use. Components might include language used to plan play, substitute for action, invoke, clarify, or negotiate rules, or perform other functions (Smilansky, 1968; Stern et al., 1976). Object use might be differentiated on the basis of whether a concrete signifier was similar or dissimilar to the signified, or nonexistent altogether (Elder & Pederson, 1978; Stern et al., 1976).

Further inquiry into differences in children's *style* of pretense is needed. Sutton-Smith and Heath's (1981) ethnographic work led them to distinguish two styles of imaginative behavior, which they term oral and literary. They suggest that in cultures in which the oral style predominates, imagination is typically of a rhetorical kind which is embedded in verbal exchanges between the central performer and the group. In cultures in which the literate style predominates, imagination is often in a solitary context and emphasizes distancing from the everyday world and representation of things not present. They contend that these cultural styles can be discerned in the elicited stories of children as young as 2 years of age. Those of Afro-American, working-class children, according to these researchers, tended to be relatively personal in character, drawn from but embellished beyond real experiences, while those of white, middle-class children tended to be relatively impersonal and fantastic in character. There is need for both empirical verification of Sutton-Smith and Heath's conclusions and additional ethnographic work which penetrates the unique qualitative styles of pretense among children from different socioeconomic and cultural backgrounds.

Social Class Differences in Maternal Practices and Attitudes Regarding Pretend Play

El'konin (1971) asserted that an understanding of the normative use of objects is a precondition for the emergence of dramatic play, and that this knowledge is formulated only in the joint activity of the child with adults. He claimed that, at the very least, it is necessary for adults to suggest the possibility of play utilization and the renaming of objects. The role of parents is one of the issues to which these hypotheses speak and is an issue which has received only minor scholarly attention. Available research indicates that pretense occurs relatively infrequently among young children (24 months and below) in the home and when it does occur, it is more likely to be initiated by the child than the mother (White, 1978; White & Watts, 1973; Dunn & Wooding, 1977). Mother's attention to the child's play apparently serves to lengthen the play bout (Dunn & Wooding, 1977), though high levels of maternal directives during interactive pretense actually appear to discourage imaginativeness in the preschool child (Shmukler, 1981).

Because it is both scanty and conflicting, existing research does not provide a firm basis to judge whether the attitudes and practices of lower- and working-class parents regarding pretend play differ reliably from those of middle-class parents. Smilansky (1968) visited the homes of 120 lower-class and middle-class children to determine the antecedents of infrequent and poor quality sociodramatic play. She reported that lower-class parents were less likely than middle-class parents to join in the games of their children, teach them how to play, provide toys suited to dramatic play, encourage them to abandon the "real" world when playing, or praise them when they succeeded in sustaining a game. The validity of these conclusions is unclear because Smilansky provided no information about the conduct of the observations, the measurement of specific variables, or the magnitude of the reported differences.

Studies of working-class and middle-class families in England lend some, but not unqualified, support for Smilansky's conclusions. In his visit to the homes of 4-year-olds, Wooton (1974) observed less discussion of play objects and play themes among working-class families than middle-class families. Along similar lines, Dunn and Wooding (1977) found that working-class mothers were less likely than middle-class mothers to jointly attend to and play with objects and initiate bouts of object play with their 18- to 24-month-olds. Collard (1971) indicated that lower-class mothers were less likely than middle-class mothers to report playing imitative games with their 9- to 13-month-old infants.

Other findings appear contrary to this pattern of results. Dunn and Wooding (1977) reported no signficant relationship between social class and maternal involvement in the child's pretense at home. White and Watts (1973) indicated that the mothers of 2-year-olds predicted to develop poorly (most of whom were lower-class) initiated more pretend play activity with their children than the mothers of those predicted to show superior development (most of whom were middle-class). It has been speculated that middle-class parents are more tolerant of imaginary playmates and less likely to regard imaginative behavior as lying and to punish it when observed (Freyberg, 1973), but empirical support for this claim is lacking. Manosevitz, Prentice, and Wilson (1973) found no relationship between social class (Hollingshead's class I versus classes II–V) and parents' attitudes toward their preschooler's imaginary companions, or whether children had an imaginary companion. Only a small proportion of parents discouraged imaginary companion pretense or believed that it was harmful (less than 10 percent). We can regard Manosevitz et al.'s findings as suggestive, at best, because of the heterogeneous nature of the group to which class I was compared.

Clearly, more effort should be devoted to understanding the role of parents in the onset and development of pretense in children. Future research should also give attention to the contribution of siblings and other members of the household, especially in lower-class families where household membership tends to be larger. Even if the mother spends only a modest amount of time in playful exchanges with her child, this does not necessarily indicate that the child has a dearth of playful interaction with adults or older children. For example, Young (1971) found that while Afro-American infants living in a small southern town often were discouraged from exploring the inanimate environment, they were seldom without human companionship and often engaged in teasing games and playful social exchanges with numerous household members other than the mother.

References

Akbar, N. 1974. *Racial differences and the black child.* Paper presented at the American Psychological Association Headstart Regional Consultants Meeting, Atlanta, Georgia.

Baratz, S., & Baratz, J.C. 1970. Early childhood intervention: The social science base of institutional racism. *Harvard Educational Review* 40:29–50.

Billingsley, A. 1968. *Black families in white America.* Englewood Cliffs, N.J.: Prentice-Hall.

Boykins, A.W. 1978. Psychological/behavior verve as a differentiating factor in the task-academic performance of Afro-Americans and whites: Pre-theoretical considerations. *Journal of Negro Education* 4:343–354.

Brady, M.K. 1975. This little lady's gonna "boogaloo": Elements of socialization in the play of black girls. In R. Bauman (Ed.), *Black girls at play: Folkloric perspective on child development.* Austin, Tex.: Southwest Educational Development Corp.

Bruner, J.S. 1976. Nature and uses of immaturity. In J.S. Bruner, A. Jolly, & K. Sylva (Eds.), *Play: Its role in development and evolution.* New York: Basic Books.

Burns, S.M., & Brainerd, C.J. 1979. Effects of constructive and dramatic perspective taking in very young children. *Developmental Psychology* 15:512–521.

Cazden, C.B. 1970. The situation: A neglected source of social class differences in language use. *Journal of Social Issues* 26:35–60.

Cohen, R. 1971. The influence of conceptual rule-sets on measures of learning ability. In C. Brace, G. Gamble, & J. Bond (Eds.), *Race and Intelligence.* Washington, D.C.: American Anthropological Association.

Dansky, J.L., & Silverman, I.W. 1976. Effects of play on associative fluency in pre-school children. In J. Bruner, A. Jolly, & K. Sylva (Eds.), *Play: Its role in development and evolution.* New York: Basic Books.

Dunn, J., & Wooding, C. 1977. Play in the home and its implications for learning. In B. Tizard & D. Harvey (Eds.), *The biology of play.* Philadelphia: Lippincott.

Duvall, E.M. 1946. Conceptions of parenthood. *American Journal of Sociology* 52:193–203.

Eiferman, R.R. 1971. Social play in childhood. In R.E. Herron & B. Sutton-Smith (Eds.), *Child's play.* New York: Wiley.

Elder, J.L., & Pederson, D.R. 1978. Preschool children's use of objects in symbolic play. *Child Development* 49:500–504.

El'konin, D. 1971. Symbolics and its functions in the play of children. In R.E. Herron & B. Sutton-Smith (Eds.), *Child's play.* New York: Wiley.

Fein, G. 1975. A transformational analysis of pretending. *Developmental Psychology* 11:291–296.

———. 1981. Pretend play in childhood: An integrative review. *Child Development* 52:1095–1118.

Fein, G., & Stork, L. 1981. Sociodramatic play in a socially integrated setting. *Journal of Applied Developmental Psychology* 2:267–279.

Fink, R. 1976. The role of imaginative play in cognitive development. *Psychological Reports* 39:895–906.

Freyberg, J. 1973. Increasing the imaginative play of urban disadvantaged kindergarten children through systematic training. In J.L. Singer (Ed.), *The child's world of make-believe.* New York: Academic Press.

Garvey, C., & Berndt, R. 1975. *The organization of pretend play.* Paper presented at American Psychological Association, Chicago.

Golomb, C. 1979. Pretense play: A cognitive perspective. In N. Smith & M. Franklin (Eds.), *Symbolic functioning in childhood.* New York: Wiley.

Golomb, C., & Cornelius, C.B. 1977. Symbolic play and its cognitive signficance. *Developmental Psychology* 13:246–252.

Gouldner, H. 1978. *Teacher's pets, troublemakers, and nobodies.* Westport, Conn.: Greenwood Press.

Griffing, P. 1980. The relationship between socioeconomic status and sociodramatic play among black kindergarten children. *Genetic Psychology Monographs* 101:3–34.

Griffing, P., Stewart, L.W., McKendry, M., & Anderson, R. 1983. Sociodramatic play: A follow-up study of imagination, self-concept, and school achievement among black school-age children representing two social-class groups. *Genetic Psychology Monographs* 107:249–301.

Hannerz, U. 1969. *Soulside: Inquiries into ghetto culture and community.* New York: Columbia University Press.

Higgins, E.T. 1976. Social class differences in verbal communication accuracy. A question of "which question?" *Psychological Bulletin* 83:695–714.

Huston-Stein, A., Friedrich-Cofer, L., & Susman, E.J. 1977. The relation of class-room structure to social behavior, imaginative play, and self-regulation of economically disadvantaged children. *Child Development* 48:908–916.

Hutt, C. 1970. Specific and diverse exploration. In H. Reese & L. Lipsett (Eds.), *Advances in child development and behavior.* New York: Academic Press.

Huttenlocher, J., & Higgins, E.T. 1978. Issues in the study of symbolic development. In W.A. Collins (Ed.), *Minnesota symposia on child psychology* (Vol. 11). Hillsdale, N.J.: Erlbaum.

Johnson, J.E. 1976. Relations of divergent thinking and intelligence test scores with social and nonsocial make-believe play of preschool children. *Child Development* 47:1200–1203.

Johnson, J.E., Ershler, J., & Bell, C. 1980. Play behavior in a discovery-based and a formal education preschool program. *Childhood Development* 51:271–274.

Kagan, J., Kearsley, R.B., & Zelazo, P.R. 1978. *Infancy: Its place in human development.* Cambridge: Harvard University Press.

Klinger, E. 1969. Development of imaginative behavior: Implications of play for a theory of fantasy. *Psychological Bulletin* 72:277–298.

Kochman, T. 1972. *Rappin' and stylin' out: Communication in urban black America.* Chicago: University of Illinois Press.

Kohn, M.L. 1963. Social class and parent-child relationships: An interpretation. *American Journal of Sociology* 68:471–480.

———. 1959. Social class and parental values. *American Journal of Sociology* 64: 337–351.

Labov, W. 1972. *Language in the inner city: Studies in the black English vernacular.* Philadelphia: University of Pennsylvania Press.

Lieberman, J.N. 1965. Playfulness and divergent thinking: An investigation of their relationship at the kindergarten level. *Journal of Genetic Psychology* 107:219–224.

Looff, D.H. 1971. *Appalachia's children.* Lexington: University Press of Kentucky.

Lowe, M. 1975. Trends in the development of representative play in infants from 1 to 3 years: An observational study. *Journal of Child Psychology and Psychiatry* 16: 33–47.

Manosevitz, M., Prentice, N.M., & Wilson, F. 1973. Individual and family correlates of imaginary companions in preschool children. *Developmental Psychology* 8:72–79.

Marshall, H., & Hahn, S.C. 1967. Experimental modifications of dramatic play. *Journal of Personality and Social Psychology* 5:119–122.

McLoyd, V.C. 1982. Social class differences in sociodramatic play. A critical review. *Developmental Review* 2:1–30.

———. 1983. Class, culture, and pretend play: A reply to Sutton-Smith and Smith. *Developmental Review* 3:11–17.

———. 1983. The effects of the structure of play objects on the pretend play of low-income preschool children. *Child Development* 54:626–635.

McLoyd, V.C., Morrison, B., & Toler, B. 1979. *The effects of adult presence versus absence on children's pretend play.* Paper presented at Hampton-Michigan Research Exchange, Hampton Institute, Hampton.

Mueller, C.W., & Parcel, T.L. 1981. Measures of socioeconomic status: Alternatives and recommendations. *Child Development* 52:13–30.

Piaget, J. 1962. *Play, dreams, and imitation in childhood.* New York: Norton. Originally published 1945; English translation, C. Gattegno & F.M. Hodgson. (London: Routledge & Kegan Paul, 1951).

Pulaski, M.A. 1973. Play as a function of toy structure and fantasy predisposition. In J.L. Singer (Ed.), *The child's world of make-believe: Experimental studies of imaginative play.* New York: Academic Press.

Riessman, F. 1964. The overlooked positives of disadvantaged groups. *Journal of Negro Education* 33:225–231.

Rist, R.C. 1970. Student social class and teacher expectations: The self-fulfilling prophecy in ghetto education. *Harvard Educational Review* 40:411–451.

Rosen, C.E. 1974. The effects of sociodramatic play on problem-solving behavior among culturally disadvantaged preschool children. *Child Development* 45: 920–927.

Rubin, K.H., Fein, G., & Vandenberg, B. 1983. Play. In P.M. Mussen (Ed.), *Manual of child psychology* (Vol. 4). New York: Wiley.

Rubin, K.H., & Maioni, T.L. 1975. Play preference and its relationship to egocentrism, popularity, and classification skills in preschoolers. *Merrill-Palmer Quarterly* 21:171–179.

Rubin, K.H., Maioni, T.L., & Hornung, M. 1976. Free play behaviors in middle and lower class preschoolers: Parten and Piaget revisited. *Child Development* 47:414–419.

Rubin, L.B. 1976. *Worlds of pain: Life in the working-class family.* New York: Basic Books.

Saltz, E., Dixon, D., & Johnson, J. 1977. Training disadvantaged preschoolers on various fantasy activities: Effects on cognitive functioning and impulse control. *Child Development* 48:367–380.

Schwartzman, H.B. 1978. *Transformations: The anthropology of children's play.* New York: Plenum Press.

Shmukler, D. 1981. Mother-child interaction and its relationship to the predisposition of imaginative play. *Genetic Psychology Monographs* 104:215–235.

Sigel, I., & McBane, B. 1967. Cognitive competence and level of symbolization among 5-year-old children. In J. Hellmuth (Ed.), *The disadvantaged child* (Vol. 1). New York: Brunner/Mazel.

Singer, J. 1973. Observing imaginative play: Approaches to recording, rating, and categorizing. In J. Singer (Ed.), *The child's world of make-believe: Experimental studies of imaginative play.* New York: Academic Press.

Smilansky, S. 1968. *The effects of sociodramatic play on disadvantaged preschool children.* New York: Wiley.

Smith, P.K. 1983. Differences or deficits? The significance of pretend and sociodramatic play. *Developmental Review* 3:6–10.

Smith, P.K., & Dodsworth, C. 1978. Social class differences in the fantasy play of preschool children. *Journal of Genetic Psychology* 133:183–190.

Stern, V., Bragdon, N., & Gordon, A. 1976. *Cognitive aspects of young children's symbolic play.* Unpublished paper, Bank Street College of Education, New York.

Sutton-Smith, B. 1972. *The folkgames of children.* Austin: University of Texas Press.

Sutton-Smith, B., & Heath, S.B. 1981. Paradigms of pretense. *Quarterly Newsletter of the Laboratory of Comparative Human Cognition* 3:41–45.

Sylva, K. 1977. Play and learning. In B. Tizard & D. Harvey (Eds.), *Biology of play.* Philadelphia: Lippincott.

Sylva, K., Bruner, J., & Genova, P. 1976. The role of play in the problem-solving of children 3–5 years old. In J. Bruner, A. Jolly, & K. Sylva (Eds.), *Play: Its role in development and evolution.* New York: Basic Books.

Tizard, B., Philips, J., & Plewis, I. 1976. Play in pre-school centres-II. Effects on play of the child's social class and of the educational orientation of the centre. *Journal of Child Psychology and Psychiatry* 17:265–274.

Tulkin, S.R. 1972. Analysis of the concept of cultural deprivation. *Developmental Psychology* 6:326–339.

Udwin, O., & Shmukler, D. 1981. The influence of sociocultural, economic and home background factors on children's ability to engage in imaginative play. *Developmental Psychology* 17:66–72.

Watson, M.W., & Fischer, K.W. 1977. A developmental sequence of agent use in late infancy. *Child Development* 48:828–836.

———. 1980. Development of social roles in elicited and spontaneous behavior during the preschool years. *Developmental Psychology* 16:483–494.

White, B. 1978. *Experience and environment* (Vol. 2). Englewood Cliffs, N.J.: Prentice-Hall.

White, B., & Watts, J.C. 1973. *Experience and environment* (Vol. 1). Englewood Cliffs, N.J.: Prentice-Hall.

Young, V.H. 1971. Family and childhood in a southern Negro community. In J. Bracey, A. Meier, & E. Rudwick (Eds.), *Black matriarchy: Myth or reality?* Belmont, Calif.: Wadsworth.

Part IV
Parent-Child Interaction in Different Populations

12
The Development of Caregiver-Infant Interaction: Illustration from the Study of Maltreated Infants

Dante Cicchetti

Research on maltreated children and their families has a particular urgency given the number of individuals who suffer the consequences of this major disorder. Recent estimates indicate that over 1 million children are maltreated each year (National Center on Child Abuse and Neglect, 1981). While interest, efforts, and funding in the area of child maltreatment research have grown rapidly in the past two decades, our information and knowledge have not kept pace in providing accurate understanding of the etiology, transmission, and consequences of child maltreatment. Child maltreatment research initially was focused on physical abuse. An important contribution has been made to this field by Giovannoni and Becerra (1979), who through extensive case reviews and interviews with professionals dealing with maltreatment on a daily basis (police, protective service social workers, lawyers, and pediatricians) have documented the diversity and perceived severity of eight major subtypes of maltreatment. Attention to the diversity of types of abuse and neglect is crucial to an accurate understanding of the causes and consequences of child maltreatment. Giovannoni and Becerra (1979) have documented through case review that most children experience more than one type of maltreatment, so, if we ignore interacting effects of the multiple types of maltreatment, we will emerge with a clouded picture of the sequelae of maltreatment, and we will not know the factors that lead up to the various maltreatment acts and conditions perpetrated by the caretakers. Child maltreatment must be addressed in its complexity if we are to generate theories and empirical findings that can guide treatment and prevention efforts to reduce the occurrence and the consequences of child abuse and neglect.

A major focus of recent research in the area of child maltreatment has been on the etiology of the phenomenon (Belsky, 1980; Cicchetti & Rizley,

The writing of this chapter as well as the research reported herein were supported by Grant # 90–C–1929 from the National Center on Child Abuse and Neglect and by Grant # 1–R01–MH37960–01 from the National Institute of Mental Health. I would like to thank Kathy McPherson and Russell Riopelle for typing assistance.

1981; Cicchetti, Taraldson, & Egeland, 1978; Parke & Collmer, 1975). While research on etiology is important in order to develop parent treatment programs and major preventive techniques, it is equally important to document the ways in which maltreated children may be impaired by their experiences.

The Study of Maltreated Infants

Within a broader conceptualization of infant psychopathology, the study of infants who have been maltreated is particularly useful. Maltreatment per se does not constitute an emotional disorder; however, the experience of being maltreated places the infant at high risk for both current and future developmental dysfunction (Aber & Cicchetti, 1984). Maltreatment is a phenomenon in which a multiplicity of factors, including parental psychopathology, environmental stress, child characteristics, and social isolation are involved (Belsky, 1980; Cicchetti, et al. 1978). Since maltreatment is specifically *not* a "within the child" disorder, a transactional model of development that emphasizes the mutual, ongoing, dynamic nature of the transaction among the infant, his/her caregivers, and the environment must be used (Cicchetti & Rizley, 1981).

In addition to the entre that the issue provides for the investigation of emotional disorders in infancy, child maltreatment is an important phenomenon to study for other reasons as well. First, the investigation of atypical populations of children can contribute significantly to a theory of normal development, primarily by affirming it, challenging it, and requiring a more fully integrated theory that can account for both normal and psychopathological processes. Second, the chaotic, disorganized home setting in which many maltreated infants are reared, the stressful life circumstances that characterize these settings, and the inconsistent or abusive patterns of care often experienced by maltreated infants represents an extreme on the continuum of caretaking environments. Maltreated infants are therefore at high risk for the negative consequences of "caretaking casualty" (Sameroff & Chandler, 1975) and their study of maltreated infants, can illuminate the role and influence of environmental factors on the organization of emotional development.

Socioemotional Competence in Maltreated Infants

An important but unresolved task for developmental researchers in recent years, has been to develop an integrative theory of development that incorporates both the simultaneous advances in the social, emotional, and cognitive domains and the mutual ongoing transaction between the child and the environment. To accomplish this, it is useful to adopt the organizational perspective of development as proposed by Werner and Kaplan (1963) and elaborated by Sroufe (1977). According to this perspective, the early years of life can be segmented into developmental periods, each of which is characterized by a pivotal task that must be resolved by the child before progressing to the next period. While each task remains important over the life span, it is most salient during one particular developmental period (see Cicchetti & Schneider-Rosen, in press). Each salient task embraces elements from the social, emotional and cognitive domains, as well as their complex interrelationship.

The organizational perspective is particularly useful when considering the construct of competence. This construct has had a long history and a multitude of uses, from White's (1959) discussions of motivation to Waters and Sroufe's (1983) recent elaboration of social competence. According to both Waters and Sroufe, the competent child is one who is able to utilize external and internal resources to achieve a favorable developmental outcome. *External resources* refer to environmental influences that promote the ability to coordinate cognition, affect, and behavior in an adaptive manner (for example, social relations, stimulating play objects). *Internal resources* refer to specific skills and individual characteristics that enable the child to capitalize on external resources. Thus, competence or adaptation is defined as the child's successful resolution of one developmental task most salient for his or her age period. Conversely, incompetence or maladaptation occurs when the child does not successfully negotiate the relevant task. In recent years, a number of developmentalists have proposed and agreed upon a delineation of salient issues spanning the early years of childhood (see Cicchetti & Schneider-Rosen, in press; Greenspan, 1979). Arousal modulation, differentiation of affect, the formation of a secure attachment relationship, the development of individuation and autonomy, and enthusiasm for problem solving are considered to be among the most salient developmental issues of the infancy period. In addition, each developmental period poses a concomitant task for the competent caregiver (Sander, 1962). Through the use of the organizational framework, investigators can seek to uncover lawful relationships between the child, family, and environmental characteristics that influence a child's behavior at a given point in time.

Differentiation of Affect

As Aber and Cicchetti (1984) noted, very few investigators have focused on theoretically meaningful, stage-salient tasks of socioemotional development of maltreated children during infancy and early childhood. Abnormalities in the development of affective communication between infants and caretakers have been studied by Gaensbauer and his colleagues. Gaensbauer and Sands

(1979) identified six patterns of distorted affective communications from infant to caretaker, including affective withdrawal, lack of pleasure, inconsistency/unpredictability, shallowness, ambivalence/ambiguity, and negative affective communications (for example, distress, anger, sadness). In a subsequent study, Gaensbauer, Mrazek, and Harmon (1980) delineated four relatively consistent affective patterns that could represent the predominant communicative pattern of a mother-infant dyad. These four groups were labeled (1) *developmentally and affectively retarded* (characterized by lack of social responsiveness, emotional blunting and inattentiveness to the environment), (2) *depressed* (exhibiting inhibition, withdrawal, aimless quality of play, and sad facial expressions), (3) *ambivalent/affectively labile* (showing sudden shifts from engagement and pleasure to withdrawal and anger), and (4) *angry* (characterized by active, disorganized play and low frustration tolerance, with frequent angry outbursts). While the direction of causality of these atypical communication patterns remains ambiguous, it is apparent that deviant styles of affective displays, decreased responsivity and reciprocal interactions, aberrations in the patterns of initiating, maintaining, or terminating interaction, and deviations in the capacity to express emotional states, tend to characterize the mother-child dyad. The work of Frodi and Lamb (1980) indicates that maltreating parents have different psychophysiological responses to the cries of infants, thereby suggesting that these parents are less effective than nonmaltreating parents in responding to the affective expressions of their infants. However, the mutually-reinforcing nature of the inadequacies in the infant's communicative system, and differential impact of emotional displays upon the contingent, sensitive responsiveness of the caregiver, may serve to perpetuate the deviant patterns of interaction in this dyad and result in atypical developmental outcomes in the emotional and behavioral repertoire of the maltreating infant. Thus, it is essential that research be directed toward illuminating the transactional nature of maltreatment (Cicchetti & Rizley, 1981), focusing on the developmentally-salient emergence, expression, mediation, and control of affective states. The contribution of both the caregiver and the infant to the maintenance or remediation of early developmental deviations must be considered.

The Development of Attachment

Since the advent of Bowlby's (1969) seminal exposition on attachment theory, there has been general assent among developmental psychologists that the establishment of a secure attachment relationship between an infant and his/her caregiver is one of the primary tasks during the first year of life. Bowlby's ethological perspective has been greatly influenced by psychoanalytic principles (Bretherton, in press). According to his formulation, the attachment relationship has both a physical and a psychological function. It possesses evolutionary survival value, as the caregiver serves to protect the infant from potential physical harm. A number of diverse infant behaviors, such as smiling, vocalizing, and clinging promote physical proximity to and contact with the attachment figure. In addition, the relationship has the psychological set-goal of "felt security" that will enable the infant to explore both the social and inanimate worlds (Sroufe & Waters, 1977).

Contemporary attachment theory has emphasized this function of the attachment relationship, stressing the enduring affective tie between infant and caregiver (for example, Ainsworth, 1973; Sroufe & Waters, 1977), rather than focusing on individual behaviors emitted by the infant. According to this theory, the quality of the relationship is dependent upon the quality of interaction between the mother-child dyad during the first year of life. The widely employed "Strange Situation" procedure was developed by Ainsworth and Wittig (1969) for assessing the quality of the attachment relationship. This procedure consists of a standard series of seven three-minute episodes, during which the infant is exposed to a series of increasingly stressful events. The infant's responses to a new room and an unfamiliar female stranger, both in the presence and the absence of the caregiver, are appraised (see Ainsworth, Blehar, Waters, & Wall, 1978, for a detailed elaboration of this technique). In particular, the infant's response to the caregiver in the two reunion episodes is especially important for evaluating the quality of the attachment relationship.

Based upon the organization of infant behaviors during the Strange Situation, infants are classified into one of three categories. Infants in Groups *A* and *C* are considered to be insecurely attached to the caregiver and will either avoid her (Group *A*), or manifest angry, resistant behavior alternating with proximity-seeking or passive behavior (Group *C*) upon reunion. In contrast, the securely attached infant (Group *B*) will use the caregiver as a secure base from which to explore the environment. If distressed, he/she will first approach the caregiver to seek comfort and then return to play. If not distressed, the infant will greet the caregiver positively and will actively initiate contact. Ainsworth et al. (1978) concluded that approximately 70 percent of all nonclinical samples of infants are securely attached, while 30 percent (20 percent *A*, 10 percent *C*) are insecurely attached to their primary caregiver.

Several recent empirical studies have examined the relationship between maltreatment and quality of attachment. Two of these studies are cross-sectional in design (Crittenden, in press; Schneider-Rosen & Cicchetti, 1984), and three are longitudinal (Egeland & Sroufe, 1981a, 1981b; Schneider-Rosen, Braunwald, Carlson, & Cicchetti, in press). All five studies adhere to a theoretically derived focus on this stage-salient developmental task of infancy and employ the Strange Situation procedure as a means of assessing attachment. These uniformities permit increased confidence in the consistent finding by all five studies that maltreated infants are significantly more likely to be insecurely attached to their caregivers than comparison infants. Schneider-Rosen and Cicchetti (1984), as a typical example, found that in a sample of 18 19-month-old maltreated infants, 12 (67 percent) were classified as insecure (Group A = 7, Group C = 5), while 6 (33 percent) were classified as secure (Group B). In contrast, 5 (26 percent) of the 19 matched comparison infants were classified as insecure (Group A = 2, Group C = 3), while 14 (74 percent) were classified as secure. This marked group difference clearly demonstrates the deleterious impact that maltreatment may have upon this developmental task of infancy.

Crittenden's (in press) investigation addresses the somewhat surprising finding of the other investigations that some maltreated infants appear to be securely attached to the caregiver. Crittenden pays particular attention to the function and interpretation of the behavior of maltreated infants in the context of their unique relationship with the caregiver, and points out that the Strange Situation procedure and attachment classifications were derived from a sample of white, middle-class infants and their caregivers. In an effort to validate the use of this assessment technique for other populations of infants, particularly those who have been maltreated, Crittenden has gathered extensive data on the ordinary, daily interactions of a sample of maltreated infants and their caregivers. Of the forty-six infants in the sample (range = 11–24 months) ten were abused, eleven were neglected, sixteen had been marginally maltreated, and nine were lower-class comparison infants.

When Ainsworth's $A/B/C$ system was used to classify the infants' behavior in the Strange Situation, it appeared that a number of maltreated infants were securely attached to their caregivers (Group B). However, Crittenden derived a new classification (A/C) characterized by anxious behavior combined with moderate to high proximity-seeking, avoidance, and resistance. When this additional classification was used, *none* of the neglected or abused infants were classified as secure, while 50 percent of the problematic infants and 88 percent of the comparison infants were so classified. These classifications of caregiver-infant attachment were associated with distinct patterns of behavior on the part of both members of the dyad; for example, the maltreating mothers were less sensitive and responsive, or more hostile and/or inconsistent with their infants, while the maltreated infants were more difficult or passive than the comparison infants.

This study vividly illustrates the mutual nature of the attachment relationship and highlights the contributions made by each member of the dyad (cf. Gaensbauer et al., 1981). Crittenden suggests that some maltreated infants may receive a secure classification by appearing pseudo-cooperative, and their caregivers may appear pseudo-sensitive, but in such cases the dyad is fearful of really challenging the relationship. Since the actual relationship is not captured by a forced classification as A, B, or C, Crittenden argues, the addition of the A/C group permits a clearer characterization of the infants' behavior. As in the Schneider-Rosen and Cicchetti (1984) study described earlier, Crittenden demonstrated that maltreatment potently disrupts the development of the optimal attachment relationship.

Longitudinal studies by Egeland and Sroufe (1981a, 1981b) and Schneider-Rosen et al. (in press) have demonstrated the instability of attachment classifications of maltreated infants, particularly those who were classified as secure upon the initial assessment. For example, in Schneider-Rosen et al.'s study, of the four maltreated infants who had a secure attachment at 12 months of age, three developed insecure attachments by 18 months (two *A*'s, one *C*). Likewise, three of the four securely attached 18-month-old infants developed insecure attachment relationships by 24 months (two *A*'s, one *C*). The results suggest that the early secure relationships of maltreated infants are potentially transient in nature. These changes in quality of attachment may occur when the ongoing transaction between the infant and the caregiver is disrupted in any way. The durability of the relationship may be unable to withstand the stress of factors either external to the dyad (such as, poverty, family illness) or within it (the experience of maltreatment).

Egeland and Sroufe (1981b) also found that the attachment classifications of maltreated infants were less stable than comparison infants over a period of six months. The attachment classification changes that occurred were more likely to be from secure to insecure, or insecure to insecure, than from insecure to secure. Egeland and Sroufe placed 87 maltreated infants into four groups, defined by maternal behavior and attitude toward their infants: psychologically unavailable (N = 19), physically abusive (N = 24), hostile/verbally abusive (N = 19), and neglectful (N = 25). A substantial number of these infants had also been physically abused. A control group of 85 infants who had received adequate care was used. The investigators used Ainsworth's classifications, adding a group *D* to characterize those infants who were not easily categorized into one of Ainsworth's three groups, namely, anxious infants who were apathetic or manifested disorganized behavior not markedly avoidant or resistant.

The comparisons made between the four groups of maltreated infants and the comparison group demonstrate that the maltreated infants were significantly less likely to be securely attached to their caregivers, and more likely to shift attachment classifications over time. For example, among the infants of the psychologically unavailable mothers who were not physically abused, the number of securely attached infants fell from 57 percent at 12 months to 0 percent at 18 months, while the number of insecure/avoidant (Group *A*) attachments rose from 43 percent to 86 percent, and 14 percent shifted to Group *D*. In comparison, there was a slight increase in the number of secure attachments (67 percent to 71 percent) and slight reductions in the number of insecure/avoidant (18 percent to 16 percent) and insecure/resistant (15 percent to 13 percent) attachments among the control infants between 12 and 18 months. These results support those of Schneider/Rosen et al. (1984) and highlight the stability of the attachment classifications of the nonmaltreated comparison infants. This investigation is also important because the results differentiate among the effects of various forms of maltreatment on infant emotional development.

Schneider-Rosen et al. (in press) have extended Cicchetti and Rizley's (1981) model of the etiology, transmission, and sequelae of child maltreatment in order to account for the processes leading to the formation and current state of the attachment relationship. This model highlights an ongoing transaction between a variety of factors which may serve to support or inhibit competent behavior at any point in time (see figure 12–1). Within this model, there are two broad categories that influence competence: (1) *potentiating factors* which increase the probability of manifesting incompetence and (2) *compensatory factors* which increase the likelihood of manifesting competent behavior. Potentiating factors include the enduring influence of vulnerability factors (longstanding psychological, environmental, sociocultural, or biological factors that may inhibit competence) and the transient influence of challengers such as stressful life events. Similarly, compensatory factors include enduring protective factors and transient buffers.

Accordingly, this model provides a way of conceptualizing stability or change in attachment not only in a population of infants at risk (maltreated infants) but in all caregiver-infant dyads. It is assumed that the current quality of attachment represents neither enduring nor transient factors alone, but a variety of factors that must be considered in combination with one another in order to account for a specific developmental outcome. It then becomes possible to explain the finding that some maltreated infants achieve secure attachment relationships. Rather than assuming that this is impossible, as Crittenden does, this transactional model illustrates the multiplicity of influences on the infant's quality of adaptation and allows for the identification of factors (such as, severity and duration of maltreatment, quality of social support network, and life stress) that support or inhibit the successful resolution of the task of attachment at any point in time.

The Relation between Quality of Attachment and Cognitive, Social, and Personality Development

Currently, a number of researchers in the area of child maltreatment have demonstrated interest in questions of how individual differences in the quality of the attachment relationship relate to variations in cognitive, social, and personality development. For example, Schneider-Rosen and Cicchetti (1984) studied the relation between quality of attachment and early emergence of visual self-recognition, an early marker of self-awareness (Lewis &

		Impact on the Attachment System	
		Potentiating Factors	Compensatory Factors
Temporal Dimension	Enduring Factors	*Vulnerability Factors* Enduring conditions that promote harmonious interaction between the infant and the caregiver and maintain responsive, sensitive, and continuous care.	*Protective Factors* Enduring conditions in the caregiving environment that decrease the harmony of interaction and the quality of care.
	Transient Factors	*Challengers* Transient but significant conditions that increase the probability of inconsistent or inadequate care being provided for the infant.	*Buffers* Transient but significant conditions that protect the infant against negative consequences of temporary disruptions in the quality of care.
	Outcome	Insecure Attachment	Secure Attachment

Figure 12–1. Factors Associated with Qualitative Differences in the Attachment Relationship

Brooks-Gunn, 1979). They found a powerful association between a secure attachment relationship and the presence of visual self-recognition in non-maltreated youngsters: 90 percent of a group of nonmaltreated 19-month-olds who showed self-awareness assessed by Lewis and Brooks-Gunn's (1979) mirror and rouge procedure evinced a concomitant secure attachment relationship with their mothers. This finding nicely corroborates the theoretical work of Ainsworth (1973), Bowlby (1969), and Mahler, Pine, and Bergman (1975), among others, that a secure attachment should foster the emergence of autonomy and individuation. Schneider-Rosen and Cicchetti (1984) uncovered a different underlying structural relation between quality of attachment and self-awareness in maltreated toddlers. Some maltreated youngsters who were securely attached did not demonstrate visual self-recognition, while others who were insecurely attached did recognize themselves. Thus, even at an early age maltreated youngsters reveal an early problem in self-development.

In another interesting observation, Schneider-Rosen and Cicchetti (1984) found that the maltreated youngsters showed different affective reactions to their rouge-marked mirror images than did their nonmaltreated counterparts. When observing their rouge-marked faces, most toddlers show an increase in positive affect. Mans, Cicchetti, & Sroufe (1978) likewise have shown that mental-age matched youngsters with Down's syndrome evince this same accompanying increase in positive affect. While the lower-class nonmaltreated toddlers were no different from Lewis and Brooks-Gunn's (1979) middle-class children in their affective displays to their mirror-images, the maltreated youngsters revealed marked deviations with the vast majority showing negative or neutral affect. These findings, in concert with the earlier results of more insecure attachments and a different relation between attachment status and early self-awareness in maltreated children, point to a different underlying organization in the relation between affective and cognitive development in these toddlers.

Similarly, Egeland and Sroufe (1981b) have reported that the cognitive development of infants of psychologically unavailable mothers underwent a dramatic decline of approximately 40 points in developmental quotient, from their initial Bayley (1969) assessment at 9 months to their second Bayley (1969) assessment at 24 months. Concomitantly, the attachment relationships of these babies changed in a similar fashion. At 12 months, 50 percent of these infants had developed a secure attachment relationship with their mother; by 18 months none of them had retained that secure attachment.

Aber (1982) demonstrated that a likely analogue to the issue of the attachment/exploration balance (Ainsworth, 1973; Bowlby, 1969) during the infant period was the dependency/effectance balance during the preschool and school-age years. Aber's study supported the conclusion that a history of maltreatment has a negative impact on a broadly defined and measured concept of "affectance motivation" (Harter, 1978; White, 1959), as measured by variability seeking and preference for novelty. This finding is an important theoretical link to the research on the development of maltreated infants and toddlers. Children who as infants have not been able to develop a secure attachment with their primary caregiver, as toddlers cannot use the attachment to the caregiver as a base of security from which to explore the external world (Egeland & Sroufe, 1981a, b; Schneider-Rosen & Cicchetti, 1984). Aber's findings with older children suggest that maltreated preschool and early school-age children also experience conflicts between developing a secure relationship with important adults on the one hand, and moving beyond those concerns of security to a masterful, independent, and generally optimistic engagement in the world at large on the other hand. Aber's findings of an increase in dependent and avoidant behaviors directed toward novel adults and a decrease in affectance motivation among maltreated and school-age children resemble the findings of Egeland, Sroufe and their colleagues of an increase in the proportion of insecure attachments and a decrease in environmental exploration and independent mastery attempts among maltreated infants and toddlers (Egeland and Sroufe, 1981b; see also

Sroufe, 1983, for similar findings among samples of nonmaltreated infants and toddlers). The conflict between security issues and mastery motivation, while organized differently at each developmental stage, may prove to be a persistent theme in the socioemotional development of maltreated children.

The Role of Infant Competence in Later Adaptation

The organizational approach to development conceptualizes competence as the child's successful resolution of the stage-salient developmental tasks of his/her age. Accordingly, we must ascertain the relationship between competence/incompetence on these stage-salient developmental tasks and future adaptation/maladaptation.

While there has been no research on the relationship between incompetence on stage-salient developmental issues and the later development of psychopathology in maltreated infants, several recent prospective studies with nonclinical populations of infants suggest that emotional incompetence in infancy may be predictive of later maladaption. For example, Sroufe, Fox, and Pancake (1983) found that infants who had been classified as insecurely attached to their caregivers at 12 and 18 months of age were rated as being more dependent during the preschool years. In addition, the preschool children who had been securely attached were found to have higher self-esteem and were rated by teachers as being more emotionally healthy (Sroufe, 1983). Likewise, Lewis, Feiring, McGuffog, and Jaskir (1984) found that for boys, insecure attachment classifications at age 1 were significantly related to later psychopathology, as assessed by higher symptom ratings on Achenbach's (1978) Child Behavior Profile (CBP). However, the results of these studies show that not all insecurely attached children inevitably develop later problems. Thus, psychopathology cannot be viewed as a linear, main-effects model, but rather as a dynamic transactional one (Sameroff & Chandler, 1975).

As depicted in figure 12–2, early maltreatment may lead to either later competence or incompetence. However, while competence at one stage in life may be predictive of competence at a later stage, this is not necessarily the case. There are many factors that mediate between early and later adaptation or maladaptation that may allow alternative outcomes to occur. For example, early successful resolution of developmental tasks may be interfered with by environmental factors that inhibit competence at a later stage. Conversely, early problems or deviations in the successful resolution of a development task may be countered by major changes in the child's experience that could result in the successful negotiation of subsequent developmental tasks.

In light of our broader conceptualization of infant emotional disorders, it is possible to conceive of such dysfunction in terms of an insecure attachment

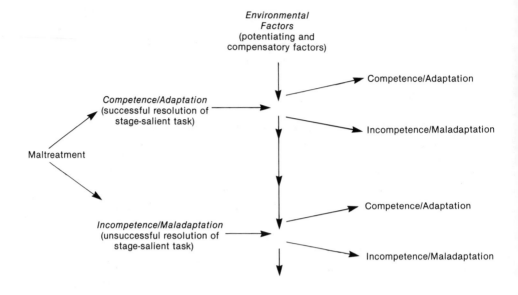

Figure 12–2. A Schematic Model of the Relationship between Early Maltreatment and Later Developmental Outcome

relationship that exists between the infant and the caregiver. Thus emotional dysfunction is not a static syndrome that is present or absent within the infant, but rather a transactional process that is influenced and modified by environmental factors. Clearly, not all insecurely attached infants become or continue to remain emotionally maladjusted; however, it is conceivable that insecure attachment relationships are a way to identify emotional maladjustment in infancy.

Even though infants may not manifest overt pathological symptoms, they may nonetheless be emotionally maladjusted. Early treatment, in the form of caregiver-infant intervention, and remediation/alleviation of significant environmental stresses, when possible, would be an important step in improving the infant's emotional well-being.

References

Aber, J.L. 1982. *The socioemotional development of maltreated children.* Unpublished doctoral dissertation, Yale University.

Aber, J.L., & Cicchetti, D. 1984. The socio-emotional development of maltreated children: An empirical and theoretical analysis. In H. Fitzgerald, B. Lester & M. Yogman (Eds.), *Theory and research in behavioral pediatrics.* New York: Plenum Press.

Achenbach, T.M. 1978. The child behavior profile: Boys aged 6–11. *Journal of Consulting and Clinical Psychology,* 1978 46:478–488.

Ainsworth, M. 1973. The development of infant-mother attachment. In B. Caldwell & H. Ricciutti (Eds.), *Review of child development research* (Vol. 3). Chicago: University of Chicago Press.

Ainsworth, M.D.S., & Wittig, B.A. 1969. Attachment and exploratory behavior of one-year-olds in a strange situation. In B.M. Foss (Ed.), *Determinants of infant behavior* (Vol. 4). New York: Wiley.

Ainsworth, M.D.S., Blehar, M.C., Waters, E., & Wall, S. 1978. *Patterns of attachment: A psychological study of the strange situation.* Hillsdale, N.J.: Erlbaum.

Bayley, N. 1969. *The Bayley scales of infant development.* New York: Psychological Corporation.

Belsky, J. 1980. Child maltreatment: An ecological integration. *American Psychologist* 35:320–335.

Bowlby, J. 1969. *Attachment and loss* (Vol. 1). New York: Basic Books.

Bretherton, I. In press. Attachment theory: Retrospect and prospect. In I. Bretherton & E. Waters (Eds.), Growing points in attachment theory and research. *Monographs of the Society for Research in Child Development.*

Cicchetti, D., & Rizley, R. 1981. Developmental perspectives on the etiology, intergenerational transmission, and sequelae of child maltreatment. *New Directions for Child Development* 11:31–55.

Cicchetti, D., & Schneider-Rosen, K. In press. An organizational approach to childhood depression. In M. Rutter, C. Izard, & P. Read (Eds.), *Depression in children: Developmental perspectives. New York: Guilford.*

Cicchetti, D., Taraldson, G., & Egeland, B. 1978. Perspectives in the treatment and understanding of child abuse. In A. Goldstein (Ed.), Prescriptions for Child Mental Health and Education. Elmsford, N.Y.: Pergamon Press.

Crittenden, P.M. In press. Relationships at risk. In J. Belsky & T. Nezworski (Eds.), *Clinical implications of attachment theory.* New York: Plenum Press.

Egeland, B., & Sroufe, L.A. 1981a. Attachment and early maltreatment. *Child Development* 52:44–52.

———. 1981b. Developmental sequelae of maltreatment in infancy. *New Directions for Child Development* 11:77–92.

Frodi, A., & Lamb, M. 1980. Child abuser's responses to infant smiles and cries. *Child Development* 51:238–241.

Gaensbauer, T.J., & Sands, K. 1979. Distorted affective communication in abused/neglected infants and their potential impact on caretakers. *American Journal of Child Psychiatry* 18:236–250.

Gaensbauer, T., Mrazek, D., & Harmon, R. 1980. Affective behavior patterns in abused and/or neglected infants. In N. Frude (Ed.), *The understanding and prevention of child abuse: Psychological approaches.* London: Concord Press.

Giovannoni, J., & Becerra, R. 1979. *Defining child abuse.* New York: Free Press.

Greenspan, S. 1979. *Intelligence and adaptation.* New York: International Universities Press.

Harter, S. 1978. Effectance motivation reconsidered: Toward a developmental model. *Human Development* 21:34–64.

Lewis, M., & Brooks-Gunn, J. 1979. *Social cognition and the acquisition of self*. New York: Plenum Press.

Lewis, M., Feiring, C., McGuffog, C., & Jaskir, J. 1984. Predicting psychopathology in six-year-olds from early social relations. *Child Development* 55:123–136.

Mahler, M., Pine, F., & Bergman, A. 1978. *The psychological birth of the human infant*. New York: Basic Books.

Mans, L., Cicchetti, D., & Sroufe, L.A. 1978. Mirror reactions in Down's syndrome infants and toddlers: Cognitive underpinnings of self-recognition. *Child Development* 49:1257–1260.

National Center on Child Abuse and Neglect. 1981. *Study findings: National study of incidence and severity of child abuse and neglect*. Washington, D.C.: DHHS Publication No. (OHDS) 81–3125, September.

Parke, R.D., & Collmer, C.W. 1975. *Child abuse: Review of child development research* (Vol. 5). Chicago: University of Chicago Press.

Sander, L. 1962. Issues on early mother-child interaction. *Journal of the American Academy of Child Psychiatry* 1:141–166.

Sameroff, A., & Chandler, M. 1975. Reproductive risk and the continuum of caretaking casualty. In F. Horowitz (Ed.), *Review of child development research* (Vol. 4). Chicago: University of Chicago Press.

Schneider-Rosen, K., & Cicchetti, D. 1984. The relationship between affect and cognition in maltreated infants: Quality of attachment and the development of visual self-recognition. *Child Development* 55:648–658.

Schneider-Rosen, K., Braunwald, K.G., Carlson, V., & Cicchetti, D. In press. Current perspectives in attachment theory: Illustration from the study of maltreated infants. In I. Bretherton & E. Waters (Eds.), Growing points in attachment theory and research. *Monographs of the Society for Research in Child Development*.

Sroufe, L.A. 1979. Socioemotional development. In J. Osofsky (Ed.), *Handbook of infant development*. New York: Wiley.

———. 1983. Infant-caregiver attachment and patterns of adaptation in preschool: The roots of maladaptation and competence. In M. Perlmutter (Ed.), *Minnesota symposium in child psychology* (Vol. 16).

Sroufe, L.A., & Waters, E. 1977. Attachment as an organizational construct. *Child Development* 48:1184–1199.

Sroufe, L.A., Fox, N.E., & Pancake, V.R. 1983. Attachment and dependency in developmental perspective. *Child Development* 54:1615–1627.

Waters, E., & Sroufe, L.A. 1983. Competence as a developmental construct. *Developmental Review* 3:79–97.

Werner, H., & Kaplan, B. 1963. *Symbol formation: An organismic-developmental approach to language and the expression of thought*. New York: Wiley.

White, R. 1959. Motivation reconsidered: The concept of competence. *Psychological Review* 66:297–333.

13
Parent-Child Play Interaction in Hospital Settings

Jerriann M. Wilson

Hospitalization can be traumatizing to a child. It can affect his or her growth and development and lead to problems even after the hospital stay. Pediatric settings are changing now. They concentrate not only on the primary physical needs of the child but also on his or her secondary or psychosocial needs. Because a child who is hospitalized is still a child, it becomes particularly important to include a familiar activity like play in the strange and frightening world of the hospital.

Children's Reactions to Hospitalization

Research over the past four decades has shown that (1) during a hospital stay children suffer emotionally from separation from their parents, (2) hospitals traditionally have provided stimulation that is less than desirable as well as different from the familiar, and (3) the unfamiliarity of the hospital setting and procedures is upsetting to children (Mason, 1965; Vernon, Foley, Sipowicz, & Schulman, 1965). Children's growth and development can be adversely affected by such experiences (Crocker, 1974; Gellert, 1958; Langford, 1948; and Thompson & Sanford, 1981). Children find their normal activities, as well as opportunities for intellectual stimulation, limited during hospital stays. Peer interaction and other relationships can be compromised by the separation of friends and family members. The plethora of treatments can force a dependency on the staff just when a child was exercising independence at home. Regression in habits and skills may occur as a response to or a defense against the anxieties that are aroused. The lack of privacy afforded a patient and the intrusive procedures he or she endures affect the child's sense of body image and self-esteem. The fears children bring with them of needles, bodily harm, anesthesia, disfigurement, lack of control, and dying, and the phenomenon of hospitalization being viewed as a punishment for misdeeds, are all affirmed and validated by the hospital experience.

Children's reactions to hospitalization have been categorized as responses to pain, stress, and physical discomfort by Gellert (1958). Common behaviors noted in the hospital include crying, fear, withdrawal, destructiveness, regressive behaviors, and sleeping poorly. These seem to be psychological in nature. Vernon et al. (1965) formulated several causes of this psychological upset. Three of the major causes are: (1) separation from parents, (2) age of child at admission, and (3) unfamiliarity of hospital setting. The impact of these factors can be ameliorated somewhat by the hospital with some special planning.

The landmark work of Robertson (1958) and Bowlby (1960) examined separation issues, their impact on the settling in process, and the three stages (protest, despair, and denial/detachment) that hospitalized children can experience. The separation of parents and children is easily corrected and has been acted upon by a number of institutions. In many hospitals, parents are accorded 24-hour visiting as well as live-in accommodations. Parents are incorporated into some of the care of their children.

It is difficult to control the second determinant, age at which a child will be hospitalized, although Mason (1965) suggests postponing elective procedures until after the critical ages of the preschool years. Different age groups have different areas of vulnerability and sources of stress. Evidence indicates that children from 6 months of age to 4 or 5 years generally deal least well with the hospital experience. Hospitals continue to find ways to help children of all ages cope with the experience. The presence of parents makes a significant difference for younger children. Play is also a common denominator, taking forms appropriate to different ages.

The third determinant of psychological upset is unfamiliarity of the hospital setting. Gellert (1958) made an apt observation: "To a child, a hospital is like a foreign country to whose customs, language, and schedules he must learn to adapt" (p. 125). Pediatric settings must do what they can to create a greater sense of normalcy for children and their families, recognizing the need to look at the people, equipment, and routines that pediatric patients typically experience. A child can encounter over fifty staff in the first twenty-four hours; that number should be reduced. Unfamiliar equipment should be kept in storage areas. Most routines of the hospital are not like those at home but can be made more familiar through orientation. The most familiar routines like play, school, and group meal times must be planned for in a pediatric setting. Having a routine helps children adjust to their day.

Not every child has a negative experience (Azarnoff & Flegal, 1975). It is a period of positive growth for some children as they learn to cope successfully with the new environment, separation from family members, and the other consequences of being in a hospital.

Rationale for Play

Because the hospital is so unlike home and carries with it a magnitude of stress-producers that make it difficult for a child to cope with the resulting trauma, children need the vehicle that play provides to help deal with that stress. Play should be an integral part of a pediatric setting because it contributes to quality patient care in a number of ways.

Children encounter many people in the hospital and find some of the contacts fleeting. Golden (1983) discusses the importance of forming therapeutic relationships which are based on the development of trust. Play and particularly play programs offer the opportunity to build the trust relationship. Because the facilitator of the play activities is often the most constant person on the unit, he or she can become a trusted individual.

For children, play continues the learning/growing process and provides an outlet for self expression and a sense of mastery. In the hospital the emphasis is on sickness, but play can capitalize on the wellness part of a child's being.

Parents benefit from play. They appreciate the involvement of their children in play activities and seem to relax physically when they sense the normalcy brought back into their child's life by play. It is crucial that parents be encouraged to take an active role in play with their child because it will help continue the normal parenting tasks. As they observe others involved with their child, parents may discover new ways of engaging their child in play. The approach of some hospitals has been to help parents learn more about play—both its meaning and its direct application to their children. "Emphasis is on the developmental and interactional value of play, and their hope is to help bring above a more mutually helpful and rewarding relationship between the mother and the child which will carry over when the child leaves the hospital" (Hardgrove & Dawson, 1972, p. 195).

Staff, too, can appreciate what play does for their patients, as well as what it tells them about their patients. Jolly (1969) offers advice to his colleagues, "If play is essential in ordinary life, it is all the more important in hospital life . . . . Doctors and nurses throughout the world must be made aware that play hastens the recovery of the sick child" (p. 487–488). Some studies have shown that it is easier to work with patients who are made more content by play (Wolfer & Visintainer, 1979). Research is now looking at the hypothesis that participation in play activities by hospitalized children speeds up their recovery and thus decreases their length of stay. Proof of this would make an important contribution to cutting the cost of hospitalization.

How Play Is Provided

Play has always existed in hospitals, but organized hospital play is relatively new. Some of the earliest hospital play programs were founded in the 1920s through the 1940s, but the greatest period of growth was in the late 1960s and early 1970s. Their names varied—play therapy, children's activities, recreation therapy—but their objective was singular. In the 1960s, some programs began using the name "child life" to represent their play program, connoting that more than just play was provided (educational activities, work with parents, interpretation of procedures), although play was still the main focus.

The Association for the Care of Children's Health (ACCH) has made important contributions in defining and supporting the role of play and child life programs in hospitals. Current figures indicate there are 309 child life and related programs in the USA and 33 in Canada (ACCH, 1984). The child life role as described by ACCH is carried out by an individual focusing on the emotional and developmental needs of children. Through the use of play and other forms of communication, the child life specialist seeks to reduce the stress of health care and enable children and families to cope with these experiences positively. This member of the health care team typically has a background in education, child development, or psychology, has had an internship experience in a child life setting, and has well grounded skills in working with a wide variety of children and families. There are now several colleges offering bachelor and master degrees in "the hospitalized child," and there is a professional organization within ACCH called the Child Life Council (Child Life: Career Information).

Certain conditions must be satisfied in order to create a setting in which good play can occur (Chance, 1979). First, the atmosphere must be geared to children, offering a child-welcoming climate in the decor and especially the presence of a playroom. Accessibility within the playroom such as space for wheelchairs and intravenous poles to move also encourages play (Piserchia, Bragg & Alvarez, 1982). Second, play materials and creative media that are familiar to children need to be present. They should offer a variety of use, structure, and level of complexity for the differing needs of children. Medical play equipment, although not necessarily familiar, is essential. Third, a supportive, consistent adult must be present. This individual, who should be responsive and interactive, can enhance play by participating in it (Pearson, Cataldo, Tureman, Bessman & Rogers, 1980). Ideally the supportive adult should be a parent, particularly the mother. As this is often not possible, a mother substitute could be considered, such as a nurse, a volunteer, or a child life specialist (Bolig, 1984). Branstetter (1969) showed that a mother substitute, if a constant person, could provide a similar degree of comfort as the mother. With this supportive person present the children cried less, interacted with others more, and played more than those whose mothers were not available.

Play can happen anywhere—on a treatment table during a dressing change, on the elevator on the way to x-ray, or in the child's bed as he creates "caves" in his bed sheets—but the playroom offers a special setting. The playroom is a safe place for children where no painful treatments occur and where there is the opportunity for a variety of choices to be made (one of the few places where a child can choose). The playroom becomes a link between the home and hospital where play, visiting with family, group meals times, and other familiar activities occur.

Generally, the playroom is open to patients and their parents and usually offers a variety of programming options in addition to free play. Play sessions can be one-to-one, group oriented, or a combination. Toys and games appropriate to the children's developmental levels and physical conditions are available and special activities are programmed during the day. Supervised play is an important component as expressed by Bolig 1984:

> The more time children spent in a supervised play/activities program, the more internal . . . they became. This finding suggests that play, activities and/or relationships established through play can contribute to an increased perception of control of events and reinforcements. Theoretically, children who became more internal may be able to cope more effectively with subsequent events by being more active, inquiring, and demanding of the environment than previously. (p. 327)

The presence of a child life specialist as a facilitator tends to make the play more constructive and positive (Williams & Powell, 1980) and it gives some assurance that adult help is available if questions or concerns arise. Adult supervision guarantees a sense of order and routine in the daily play events. Children who come from chaotic home settings with limited opportunities for enrichment can thrive and grow in the richness of a well developed play program (Rae, 1981).

Limiting Factors

There are several factors that inhibit successful play in a pediatric setting. Crocker (1981) categorizes these factors as (1) immobility because of physical restraints, (2) dull environment such as the kind caused by isolation, (3) overstimulating environment due to the mechanical and human complexities of care on the high technology units, and (4) fear because of separation and unfamiliarity. The fear element must be dealt with constantly in all facets of hospitalization while the other three occur in special circumstances.

Bed rest is a confining circumstance dictated by a need for traction or for very limited movement to facilitate healing. Such confined children can be cut off physically from participation within a group activity or even from the playroom as a whole, although some orthopedic surgeons allow and encourage their traction patients to be moved to a playroom. The immobilizing features of a body cast also inhibit participation. Belson and Nash describe such children who, when left on their own, will choose not to play actively or will play with little enthusiasm, joy, or concentration. These children must be wheeled into a playroom area and involved in a group with help from parents, volunteers, staff, or other children. Adaptations of equipment (prism glasses, vertical lap boards with clips to hold drawing paper, horizontal mirrors suspended amidst traction lines, and long tongs to allow for reaching) enable a child to participate. Two children who cannot be moved to a playroom can be placed together in one patient's room so they can play side by side; or occasional playroom activities can be held in the patient's room with the mobile children joining in.

Intravenous apparatus (IVs), catheters, drainage tubes, or bandaging are encumbrances that inhibit hospital play. Activities that require the dominant hand could be difficult if that hand holds the IV. These restrictions must be anticipated. Connection to a monitoring or suction device limits an ambulatory child's play. Children's activities must be in a small radius, or they must be reminded to move the IV pole as they move from one activity to another or to other sections of the room. Activity planning for these patients requires special creativity. For example, one badly burned child with heavily bandaged hands chose to fingerpaint the only way she could—with her feet.

Isolation restrictions severely limit play because the group experience is impossible, the environment is dull, and routines are repetitive. Sensory deprivation can be extreme in this setting, caused by the need to separate a child for his or her own protection or for the protection of others. O'Connell (1984) discusses the situation of the Laminar Air Flow Room and the role of play. A child life specialist visits these special isolation rooms several times a day. Because the routine varies so little from day to day for the children, they enjoy the choice of activities offered by the play program. Both short- and long-term play projects are useful for the immediate reward value and the benefit of looking forward to the next day. Parents who spend many hours in these isolation rooms also benefit from the play, which helps to alleviate their tedium.

Intensive care typifies the other extreme—an overstimulating setting with a myriad of medical activities occurring simultaneously to several patients in the same room. A lack of curtains or the urgency of medical interventions exposes a patient to a terrifying array of events. Typically a patient may withdraw and is thus not easily involved in play. Research (Pearson et al., 1980) shows that toys are not enough to encourage play in an intensive care unit and that a play facilitator can help a child be more interactive with his or her play materials. Play helps children become more distracted from the trauma around them, and may even help the healing process. Strother (1982) describes the role of play as part of the recuperative process which allows a child to reenact a traumatic event, such as an accident or ambulance ride. Using play materials, a child experiences a sense of mastery and a change "in her role from victim to the person in charge, thereby gaining reassurance and comfort" (p. 3). The author recalls a recent case of a very withdrawn child who arrived via helicopter after an automobile accident and played ceaselessly with a toy helicopter landing again and again on his traction-encased bed. It was only after this play that he began to talk about his concerns.

Unique Areas

When implementing play in the hospital two areas deserve special mention—infant units and outpatient areas. The infant's experience can be particularly passive, especially if a child life program has limited resources and does not include play coverage for this age group. An appropriate program to encourage and maximize emerging developmental capabilities of infants will encourage and reinforce parents' natural instincts. Stranger anxiety makes unfamiliar environments, unknown caregivers, and uncomfortable procedures an overwhelming emotional challenge. This is especially true if parents are not present. Furthermore, the child's need for exploration and stimulation is a powerful motivating force in healthy development. These needs should be responded to both with familiar caregivers well-experienced in the age group's psychosocial needs and with the provision of play materials such as plastic mirrors at eye level, activity boards attached to crib rails, and mobiles containing interesting items that can be touched and manipulated. When providing such play materials, consideration must be given to the primary care of the child. Placement of toys should permit quick medical access such as lowering of bed rails (Goldberger, 1979).

For preterm infants, the subject of "infant stimulation" is topical and controversial as researchers and developmental pediatricians determine how much extra stimulation should be presented to preterm infants who are trying to adapt to an already overstimulating life. With very young, very ill preterm infants, effort must be made to *reduce* handling and to keep stimulation to a minimum, and only to build in increased stimulation with routine care as the infant matures. Placing stuffed animals and other toys in isolettes as well as stimulation programs for preemies may be more in response to adults' needs that in the infant's best interest. They are useful in helping parents and other caregivers feel that they are adding to the quality of the infant's life and, consequently, are important to the infant. Care must be taken that such interventions do not cause stress or consume energy that overtaxes the infant, or that the placement of toys does not endanger tubes and other medical equipment, air flow through isolettes' air circulation system, visual access to infants, and compromise infection control (Goldberger, 1984).

The second unique area, outpatient services, includes several different settings, all of which can benefit from play programs. The outpatient and emergency areas are often the first view of the hospital to a child and his family, and it should present a positive impression. Day surgery units, some private doctor's offices, and health maintenance organizations (HMOs) are utilizing child life personnel. These services focus on the child life specialist's ability to plan constructive play opportunities, communicate with families on play and child development issues, and offer information on the developmental status of the patients. Play activities can be the same as those offered in inpatient areas. Williams and Powell (1980) reported that supervised play activities increased the children's positive responses in the outpatient play area and decreased the negative ones. For instance, the activity in the play/waiting area was less chaotic. The benefit extends beyond children. Parents' attitudes were examined by Zilliacus and Enberg (1980) who found that parents watching or participating with their children in play learned new play activities and felt more relaxed.

Play Activities

Many different kinds of play are offered to hospitalized children, and most are similar to those in any good preschool or school setting. The hospital play program should be well balanced and include:

messy activities, which children find comforting, like finger painting; pudding painting; clay, sand, and water play; and bubble blowing

creative art, for the satisfaction it gives and its therapeutic value in coping with body image issues (Cameron, Juszczack & Wallace, 1984)

crafts, to complete and share with family members

games, for the social and therapeutic aspects (Azarnoff & Flegal, 1975)

construction with building and block sets, as well as woodworking and building with junk for older teens

books and story records, for active and passive listening, in a group or in isolation (Plank, 1971)

field trips within the hospital, from the kitchen to the telephone paging room, to further understanding of the institution

music, for its therapeutic and relaxing qualities, particularly for infants (Lindsay, 1981)

films, for entertainment as well as therapeutic/educational value in dealing with hospitalization (Melamed & Siegel, 1975)

dramatic play with home and hospital garb, as a chance to focus on the familiar and experiment with the unfamiliar (Belson & Nash)

tape recorder, for parent-recorded stories and conversations, to be played in absence of families (McCain, 1982) *animals,* for the comfort a child can receive from taking care of a pet in the playroom (Wilson, 1979a)

outdoor play, whether a child is ambulatory enough to swing and slide or tend a raised garden from a stretcher (Wilson, 1979a)

closed circuit television, which offers entertainment, a chance to be on television, and an interactive opportunity between playroom and isolation room to play call-in BINGO (Guttentag & Kettner, 1983)

video games, which offer interactive opportunities and provide a distraction from treatment, resulting in reduced anxiety and a decrease in unpleasant physical symptoms (Kee, 1981; Pediatric News, 1982)

education as part of play, to help a child with his sense of mastery and increase his knowledge while in the hospital (Wilson, 1979b, Rae, 1981)

A particularly valuable form of dramatic play for hospitalized children is medical play. It can successfully bring together child, staff, and parent in a venture that will heighten a child's awareness of his hospital encounter, offer new information, help his expression of feelings, and bring to the forefront the child's misinformation so that it can be corrected. Typically, a medical play corner is established in a playroom with many of the tools of medical care, including plastic syringes (without needles), anesthesia masks, x-ray viewing boxes, stethoscopes, and IV arm boards and tubing. Hard and soft dolls, family and medical puppets, and doll hospitals provide the "patients" for the children. Fein (1979) suggests providing play equipment with varying degrees of definition and realism, ranging from real medical equipment to replicas of medical tools, which allow children a choice. The play concentrates on sensory and concrete experiences to inform and educate the child, for example, using a syringe to simulate giving injections, looking at x-rays to discover that the machines only take photographs and do not read minds, applying a cast to a doll to duplicate one the patient will receive the next day, using a doctor puppet to pretend to draw blood as a basis for discussing how much is actually taken, or holding an anesthesia mask to a doll's face to draw out fears of being put to sleep permanently.

Medical play can be offered in groups or on a one-to-one basis (Clatworthy, 1981; Golden, 1983), with careful thought for the needs and ages of those involved. The degree of structure for the medical play setting varies with the anxiety level of the child. A less anxious child more readily utilizes the play materials, while a child experiencing conflict may need more guidance and direction from the adult. Children need to be reminded that there is a reason for each medical procedure and for the hospital stay too. If misconceptions arise, the child life specialist can explore the areas of confusion and correct the information (Chan, 1980).

Medical play is presented differently to the various age groups. Toddlers and older infants understand the placement of a stethoscope or anesthesia mask on a doll. Preschoolers benefit from being able to handle safe medical equipment. Young school-age children are often vigorous participants in detailed medical dramatic play with gowns, masks, and lots of paraphernalia. Older school-age patients are comfortable creating a drama with a "visible man" and a miniature operating room table, while teenagers may enjoy making video or audio tapes to "help other kids" get ready for surgery. Adaptions of medical play make it meaningful to a wide age range of pediatric patients.

Parents can be vital participants in their children's medical play whether in initial preparation for a procedure or review of what happened previously. Parent participation is particularly for the preschooler who is still dependent on the parent to help allay important fears. Research shows that as parents feel more comfortable in the hospital setting, they experience a greater sense of well being which they pass on to their children (Skipper & Leonard, 1968). These children appear to recover faster, as demonstrated by their physiological signs (temperature, blood pressure, and pulse rate). The playroom presents a relaxed, nonthreatening atmosphere. In this setting the parent also may learn new information about the child's care which allows for reinforcement of the teaching to a child later. A parent thus becomes an ally in the process and the treatment.

Conclusion

"Play intervention for children in hospital settings is an unqualified necessity . . . in helping a child leave the hospital healthier than when he or she arrived" (Golden, 1983, p. 213). A child's opportunity for play could easily be thwarted by the events and the environment of the hospital. It is crucial to recognize and facilitate the need that hospitalized children have for play. Play focuses on one of the healthy aspects of children's lives, and can be used to reassure and help them retain a sense of normalcy in the hospital. Medical play further focuses on preparing children for procedures or aiding them to cope with the hospitalization experience. For the hospitalized child the absence of some activities may be inconsequential, but play is a necessary ingredient for continuing growth and development.

References

Association for the Care of Children's Health (ACCH). 1984. *Directory of child life programs in North America.* Washington, D.C.: Association for the Care of Children's Health.

Azarnoff, P., & Flegal, S. 1975. *A Pediatric Play Program.* Springfield, Ill.: Charles C. Thomas.

Belson, P., & Nash, S. Play and children in hospital. In *Play in hospital* (flyer), London: National Association for the Welfare of Children in Hospital.

Bolig, R. 1984. Play in hospital settings. In T.D. Yawkey & A.D. Pellegrini, (Eds:), *Child's play: Developmental and applied.* Hillsdale, N.J.: Erlbaum.

Bowlby, J. 1960. Separation Anxiety. *International Journal of Psychoanalysis.* 41: 89–113.

Branstetter, E. 1969. The young child's response to hospitalization: Separation anxiety of lack of mothering care. *American Journal of Public Health* 59:92–97.

Cameron, C.O., Juszczack, L., & Wallace, N. 1984. Using creative arts to help children cope with altered body image. *Children's Health Care* 12:108–112.

Chan, J.M. 1980. Preparation for procedures and surgery through play. *Paediatrician* 9:210–219.

Chance, P. 1979. *Learning through play.* Piscataway, N.J.: Johnson & Johnson.

Child Life: Career Information (flyer). Washington, D.C.: Association for the Care of Children's Health.

Clatworthy, S. 1981. Therapeutic Play: Effects on hospitalized children. *Children's Health Care* 9:108–113.

Crocker, E. 1974. A review of the literature concerning the effects of hospitalization and illness on children. *Journal of the Association for the Care of Children in Hospitals* 3:3–9.

———. 1981. Play programs in pediatric settings. In E. Gellert (Ed.), *Psychosocial aspects of pediatric care.* New York: Grune & Stratton.

Fein, G.G. 1979. In P. Chance (Ed.), *Learning through play.* Piscataway, N.J.: Jonnson & Johnson.

Gellert, E. 1958. Reducing the emotional stresses of hospitalization for children. *American Journal of Occupational Therapy* 12:125–129, 155.

Goldberger, J. 1979. Infant play materials for the hospital setting. *Australasian Nurses Journal* 8:9–10.

———. June 1984. Personal communication.

Golden, D.B. 1983. Play therapy for hospitalized children. In C.E. Schaeffer & K.J. O'Conner (Eds.), *Handbook of play therapy.* New York: Wiley.

Guttentag, D.N., & Kettner, R.B. 1983. Closed circuit television: A unique tool. *Children's Health Care* 12:25–28.

Hardgrove, C.B., & Dawson, R.B. 1972. *Parents and children in the hospital.* Boston: Little, Brown.

Harvey, S. 1980. The value of play therapy in hospital. *Paediatrician* 9:191–197.

Jolly, H. 1969. Play is work. *Lancet* 2:487–488.

Kee, D.W. 1981. Implications of hand-held electronic games and microcomputers for informal learning. Paper presented at the National Institute of Education Conference, Washington D.C.

Langford, W.S. 1948. Psychologic aspects of pediatrics. *Journal of Pediatrics* 33: 242–250.

Lindsay, K.E. 1981. The value of music for hospitalized infants. *Children's Health Care* 9:104–107.

Mason, E.A. 1965. The hospitalized child—His emotional needs. *New England Journal of Medicine* 272:406–414.

McCain, G.C. 1982. Parent-created recordings for hospitalized children. *Children's Health Care* 10:104–105.

Melamed, B.G., & Siegel, L.J. 1975. Reduction of anxiety in children facing hospitalization and surgery by use of filmed modeling. *Journal of Consulting and Clinical Psychology* 43:511–521.

O'Connell, S.R. 1984. Recreation therapy: Reducing the effects of isolation for the patient in a protected environment. *Children's Health Care* 12:118–121.

Pearson, J.E.R., Cataldo, M., Tureman, A., Bessman, C., & Rogers, M.C. 1980. Pediatric intensive care unit patients—Effects of play intervention on behavior. *Critical Care Medicine* 8:64–67.

Pediatric News. 1982. Video games may ease chemotherapy sessions in young. *Pediatric News*. October 1982.

Piserchia, E.A., Bragg, C.F., & Alvarez, M.M. 1982. Play and play areas for hospitalized children. *Children's Health Care* 10:135–138.

Plank, E.N. 1971. *Working with children in hospitals*. Cleveland: Press of Case Western Reserve University.

Rae, W.A. 1981. Hospitalized latency-age children: Implications for psychosocial care. *Children's Health Care* 9:59–63.

Robertson, J. 1958. *Young children in hospitals*. New York: Basic Books.

Skipper, J.K., & Leonard, R.C. 1968. Children, stress, and hospitalization: A field experiment. *Journal of Health and Social Behavior* 9:275–287.

Strother, D.B. 1982. Play. In *Practical applications of research*. Bloomington, Ind.: Phi Beta Kappa's Center on Evaluation, Development, and Research.

Thompson, R.H., & Stanford, G. 1981. *Child life in hospitals*. Springfield, Ill.: Charles C. Thomas.

Vernon, D.T.A., Foley, J.M., Sipowicz, R.R., & Schulman, J.L. 1965. *The psychological responses of children to hospitalization and illness*. Springfield, Ill.: Charles C. Thomas.

Williams, Y.B., & Powell, M. 1980. Documenting the value of supervised play in a pediatric ambulatory care clinic. *Journal of the Association for the Care of Children's Health* 9:15–22.

Wilson, J.M. 1979(a). Child life. In P.J. Valletutti & F. Christopolos (Eds.), *Preventing physical and mental disabilities—Multidisciplinary Approaches*. Baltimore: University Park Press.

———. 1979b. School as part of a child life program. *Australasian Nurses Journal* 8:4–8.

Wolfer, J.A., & Visintainer, M.A. 1979. Prehospital psychological preparation for tonsillectomy patients: Effects on children's and parents' adjustment. *Pediatrics* 64:646–655.

Zilliacus, K., & Enberg, S. 1980. Play therapy in the pediatric out-patient department. *Paediatrician* 9:224–230.

Part V
Consequences of Play Materials and Parent-Child Interaction

14
Play Materials and Intellectual Development

Robert H. Bradley

The importance of the social environment for children's development is widely acknowledged. A rich literature exists describing the relation between cognitive, social, and emotional functioning and various aspects of the social environment. Much less is known about the relation between attributes of the physical environment and children's development. Some important work in this area is being done (see, for example, chapter 15 of this book), but overall the literature is not rich with either empirical findings or theoretical propositions.

In this chapter, I will focus on one aspect of the relation between the physical environment and development in children, that between play materials and intellectual development. The chapter consists of three parts: first, a summary of the literature that demonstrates the association between play materials and intellectual development during childhood; second, an examination of Mueller's (1976) cross-systems model as applied to toddler play; and, third, a discussion of Vygotsky's concept of the "zone of proximal development." Rather than focus on a critical analysis of available information, this chapter identifies features of these three bodies of literature that might serve to guide more detailed research.

Review of Empirical Findings

In his theory of cognitive development Piaget postulated that much of children's early learning occurs as a result of direct encounters with the physical environment. Because of Piaget's great impact on cognitive psychology, child development researchers became interested in the significance of toys, games, and materials as contexts for intellectual development during childhood. In this section, I review findings from observational research done in the homes of young children that addresses the relationship between the availability of toys and other materials in the home and children's intellectual development.

General Findings

Perhaps the most intensive home observational studies of the relation between the presence of toys and materials during the first two years of life and children's intellectual development have been those done by Wachs (Wachs, Uzgiris, & Hunt, 1971; Wachs, 1976, 1978). His first study, of 102 predominantly lower-class children, revealed that the availability of books and toys during the second year of life was significantly correlated with several scales from the Infant Psychological Development Scale at 22 months, but not at 15 or 18 months. Research done on a second sample of thirty-nine children showed a substantial relationship between the number of audiovisually responsive toys and children's performance on object permanence and the development of schemes throughout the second year of life. After they were 18 months old, children's scores on the use of objects as means scale were also related to the number of audiovisually responsive toys available to them. In a follow-up study, Wachs (1978) reported that the presence of audiovisually responsive toys in the second year of life was correlated .60 with IQ at age 30 months.

Clarke-Stewart (1973) found evidence that even during the first year of life the availability of toys was related to subsequent intellectual development. Her study involved repeated observations of thirty-six predominantly low SES children and their mothers in home and laboratory settings and assessments of infants competence from ages 9 to 18 months. The observations revealed that the child's dependency on the mother diminished over that period while his interest in aspects of the physical environment increased. By age 17 months, children spent an average of 34 percent of their time interacting with their mothers and about 50 percent of their time playing with, looking at, and investigating objects (about 20 percent with toys and 30 percent with other household objects). Clarke-Stewart observed a correlation of .39 between the number of toys available to the child in the home and conglomerate measure of competence derived through factor analysis. Variety of toys was correlated .34 with the competence measure, while the child's actual use of toys and objects was correlated .46. Variety of toys was correlated .47 with Bayley MDI at 17 months; and the use of toys and objects was correlated .36.

There is also some evidence that the availability of toys during infancy is related to later competence. For example, Tulkin and Covitz (1975) found that the number of environmental objects available at 2 years of age was correlated .40 with middle-class girls' performance on the Illinois Test of Psycholinguistic Abilities (ITPA) at age 6 but not to their Peabody Picture Vocabulary Test (PPVT). For working-class girls, the correlations were .55 with ITPA and .40 with PPVT. In a longitudinal study of sixty-one representative London children, Moore (1968) found that the toys, books, and experiences present in the children's homes at age 30 months was correlated .40 with IQ at age three for boys, and .30 for girls. Even with social class partialled out, the correlations remained .36 for boys and .14 for girls. However, the correlation between the 30-month home environment scores and IQ at age 8 was .60 for both sexes (about .45 with social class partialled out). Correlations with reading achievement scores at age 7 were .50 for boys, .70 for girls.

One of the most comprehensive studies of the relation between the availability of play materials early in life and later intellectual development, Barnard, Bee, and Hammond (1984), involved 163 working-class and middle-class families from the Seattle area. The Play Materials subscale of the Home Observation for Measurement of the Environment (HOME) Inventory was administered children at 4-, 8-, 12- and 24-months-old. Bayley Scales were administered to these children at ages 1 and 2 years, and the Stanford-Binet at age 4. Correlations between the Play Materials scores and measures of intellectual competence were low but significant (.20 to .40). Correlations for a subgroup of well-educated mothers were low (.20 to .30). They were slightly higher (.30 to .40) for mothers with less than a high school education. Correlations were clearly higher for boys (.30 to .50) than for girls (.20 to .30). When maternal education and SES were partialled out of the correlation between Play Materials and intellectual competence, some attenuation was noted, but the partial correlations remained significant (.20 to .30).

In Siegel's (1984) longitudinal study of preterm and full-term infants from working-class backgrounds in Hamilton, Ontario, Canada, negligible correlations were observed between 12-month scores on Play Materials and concurrent scores on the Bayley and the Uzgiris-Hunt Scales. However, 3-year scores on Play Materials showed low to moderate correlations (.30 to .50) with 3-year Stanford-Binet and Reynell Language scores for both preterm and full-term samples. Similarly, 5-year scores on Play Materials were correlated .50 with concurrent scores on the McCarthy General Cognitive Index. Infants' 12-month Play Materials scores were also correlated with 3-year IQ scores but only for preterm children.

While most studies of normal children have reported significant correlations between the availability of toys and objects during the first three years of life and children's cognitive development, there have been exceptions. A good example of such exceptions can be found in the research of Gottfried and Gottfried (1984). Their study of predominantly middle-class white families in California showed few instances of significant correlations between Play Materials and children's intellectual development. In one of the few studies of children at developmental risk, Allen, Affleck, McGrady, and McQueeny (1983) found a correlation of .53 between Play Materials and children's scores on the Comprehensive Developmental Evaluation Chart (CDEC) at age 9 months. The correlation between scores at 9-month scores on the CDEC and scores at 18-month on Play Materials was .66, suggestive of a child effect on the provision of play materials. Interestingly, in this same study of children with severe perinatal complications and genetic disorders, there was no signficiant correlation between Play Materials and any SES measure.

Even fewer studies of the availability and use of play materials during the preschool period and their relationship to intellectual development have been reported. However, as the research by Siegel (1984) demonstrated, the same general pattern of relationships appears to hold. For example, Ware and Garber (1972) studied the relationship of 4-year-old Mexican-Americans and black Americans, and found that the availability of materials for learning in the home correlated .30 with children's scores on the Preschool Inventory. A study comparing language-impaired (Down's syndrome) children, language-delayed (no apparent organic basis for the developmental problem) children, and children with normal language skills, conducted by Wulbert, Inglis, Kriegsman, and Mills (1975), showed that the amount and appropriateness of toys during the preschool years significantly differentiated the homes of language delayed and normal groups.

A longitudinal study of older (ages 8 to 14) handicapped children was conducted by Nihira, Meyers, and Mink (1980; 1981; 1983), involving 114 TMR children (mean IQ = 42.4, SD = 9.9) from southern California who were living at home. The home environments of the children were assessed with the HOME Inventory (Caldwell & Bradley, 1979), the Family Environment Scale (Moos & Moos, 1974), the Home Quality Rating Scale (Meyers, Mink, & Nihira, 1977), various indices of family adjustment, and various demographic and structural descriptions of the home. The child was assessed using the Adaptive Behavior Scale and parental ratings of social and psychological adjustment. Three canonical analyses were performed on the data: (1) home environment versus child characteristics; (2) home environment versus family adjustment; (3) family adjustment versus child characteristics. In analysis I, the first canonical variate was between the overall "harmony and quality of parenting" and the "social adjustment of the child." Highly loaded on this factor was stimulation through toys and equipment. In analysis II, the first canonical variate was between overall "harmony and quality of parenting" and "observed coping level." Again, stimulation through toys and equipment was highly loaded (.60) on the first factor. In a follow-up 3 years later, Nihira, Meyers, and Mink (1983) attempted to further delineate the relation between home environment, family adjustment and child competence by looking for direction of effects among the environmental and developmental variables. Improvements in Personal Maladaptation over the 3 year period were significantly related to the stimulation through Toys, Games, and Reading Materials subscale, with the effects of initial maladaptation and all other environmental variables partialled out

(– .35). Children whose initial cognitive status was highest had parents who provided more stimulation through toys, games, and materials three years later. In essence, there appears to be a reverberating circuit with the provision of cognitively stimulating experiences through toys, equipment, and materials leading to higher levels of social and personal adjustment. Simultaneously, children with better cognitive and social skills elicit from their parents greater cognitive stimulation (including the provision of more advanced toys and materials), in sum, the maintenance of a more nearly optimal environment. The degree of optimality appears positively related to maternal education and negatively related to the number of children present in the home.

Findings from the Little Rock Longitudinal and Consortium Studies

During the past two decades we have been involved in two research studies that have particular relevance for this discussion: (1) the Longitudinal Observation and Intervention Study (Caldwell, Elardo, & Elardo, 1972); and (2) the Consortium study on home environments and child development.

The Longitudinal Observation and Intervention Study (LOIS) was designed to explore the question of exactly when the decline in development so often observed in economically disadvantaged circumstances begins. Recruitment of subjects for this study commenced in 1970. Some 130 children were involved in the observational (nonintervention) groups for the project. Approximately 60 percent of the participants were black, the remainder white. Both racial groups were heterogeneous with respect to SES. However, the black sample were from mostly lower-class and working-class backgrounds, whereas the white sample were from predominantly working-class and middle-class backgrounds. Participants entered the study at about age 6 months. They were periodically assessed with developmental measures through age 54 months, then with achievement tests after school entry. Their home environments were also periodically assessed using the HOME Inventory. The infant version of HOME was used on children up to age 3. This forty-five-item combination observation/interview procedure is done in the infant's home environment with both the infant and primary caregiver present. The items are clustered into six subscales: (1) maternal responsivity, (2) acceptance of child, (3) organization of the environment, (4) play materials, (5) maternal involvement, and (6) variety in daily stimulation. Of the six subscales, play materials has shown one of the most consistent relationships with intellectual development. As table 14–1 shows, scores on the Play Materials subscale taken when the child was 6 months old correlated .41 with 36-month IQ and .45 with 54-month IQ; 12-month scores on Play Materials correlated .56 with 36-month IQ and .52 with 54-month IQ;

Table 14–1
Correlations between 6-, 12-, and 24-month HOME Scores and Mental Test Scores Gathered at 1, 3, and 4½ Years

| | Time of HOME Assessment | | | | | | | |
| | 6 Months | | | 12 Months | | | 24 Months | |
HOME Subscales	1-Year MDI[b]	3-Year IQ	4½-Year IQ	1-Year MDI	3-Year IQ	4½-Year IQ	3-Year IQ	4½-Year IQ
Responsivity	.09	.25*	.27	.15	.39*	.34*	.49*	.50*
Restriction	.13	.24*	.10	.01	.24*	.21	.41*	.28*
Organization	.20	.40*	.31*	.20	.39*	.34*	.41*	.33*
Play materials	.05	.41*	.44*	.28*	.56*	.52*	.64*	.56*
Involvement	.08	.33*	.28*	.28*	.47*	.36*	.55*	.55*
Variety	.27*	.31*	.30*	.05	.28*	.32	.50*	.39*
Total score	.16	.50*	.44*	.30*	.58*	.53*	.71*	.57*
Multiple correlation[a]	.30	.54*	.50*	.40	.59*	.57*	.72*	.63*

*$p < .05$.
[a]This represents the multiple correlation of all six HOME subscales.
[b]MDI = Mental Development Index from Bayley Scales.

24-month scores on Play Materials were correlated .64 with 36-month IQ and .56 with 54-month IQ. A follow-up study involving thirty-seven of the LOIS children found correlations of around .50 between 12-month scores on play materials and first grade achievement test scores (Bradley & Caldwell, 1984). Similar correlations were observed for 24-month Play Materials scores.

Beginning at age 3, the fifty-five item preschool version of the HOME Inventory was administered. The items are clustered into eight subscales: (1) toys and materials, (2) language stimulation, (3) physical environment, (4) pride and affection, (5) stimulation of academic behavior, (6) modeling of social maturity, (7) variety of stimulation, and (8) physical punishment. Scores on the Toys and Materials subscale at 36 months correlated .47 with 3-year IQ and .48 with 54-month IQ. Scores on the Toys and Materials subscale at age 54 months were correlated .55 with concurrent IQ scores. Correlations with first grade achievement test scores were between .40 and .50.

After reviewing sets of simple correlations between HOME subscales and subsequent mental test performance in our sample, we became interested in further delineating the nature of the relationship. We first examined gender and race differences in the relationship, which provided some interesting results. Separating the sample into male and female groups produced higher correlations than the combined sample (median correlations between scores on the Play Materials subscale of HOME and 3-year-old's IQ were in the .60s). Also, correlations between Play and Materials and IQ for boys were consistently high (.62 at 6 months, .74 at 12 months, and .72 at 24 months). For girls, the correlations started lower but attained the same level at 24 months (.49 at 6 months and .74 at 24 months). When the sample was separated by race, the correlations between Play and Materials and 3-year IQ for whites, were essentially constant from 6 months (.46 at 6 months, .45 at 12 months, and .47 at 24 months). For blacks, the correlations started lower but gradually rose to a slightly higher level at 24 months (.28 at 6 months, .45 at 12 months, and .51 at 24 months). Thus, while there was some evidence for specificity of effect along gender and race lines, the association between Play and Materials and intelligence was significant for all subgroups in our sample.

A second concern was whether the observed relation between the availability of play materials early in life and later intelligence occurs because of the correlation between early environment opportunities and later environmental opportunities or because of the particular salience of toys during the first year of life. To examine this issue, we performed a series of partial correlation analyses using Play Materials scores and 3-year IQ. Specifically, children's 6-month Play Materials scores were correlated with 3-year IQ controlling for 12-month Play Materials scores; then 12-month Play Materials scores were correlated with IQ controlling for 6-month Play Materials scores. A similar set of partial correlations was done using 12-month and 24-month Play Materials scores. Separate analyses were done by gender and race.

For girls, the partial correlation between 6-month Play Materials and 3-year IQ, controlling for 12-month Play Materials, was not significant. Similarly, the partial correlation between 12-month Play Materials and 3-year IQ, controlling for 24-month Play Materials, was not significant. By contrast, for these girls the opposite set of partials was highly significant (.53 between 12-month Play Materials and 3-year IQ controlling for 6-month scores on Play Materials; .53 between 24-month Play Materials and 3-year IQ controlling for 12-month scores on Play Materials). This evidence suggests that the observed correlation between Play Materials and IQ results from a stable pattern of environmental opportunities for girls.

The pattern for boys was somewhat different. There is evidence that Play Materials available during the first year or so of life may have some unique value. The partial correlation between 6-month Play Materials scores and 3-year IQ, controlling for 12-month scores on Play Materials, was significant ($r = .46$), as was the partial correlation between 12-month Play Materials and IQ, controlling for 24-month Play Materials ($r = .38$). Indeed, the partial correlation between 24-month Play Materials scores and later IQ, controlling for earlier Play Materials scores, was no higher ($r = .32$).

For whites, the set of partial correlations indicated that scores on Play Materials at all three time points contribute about the same to 3-year IQ (.20 to .30). For blacks, on the other hand, later scores on Play Materials were more predictive than earlier scores.

A third concern of the relation between play materials and intellectual development is the extent to which the observed relation between the availability of toys in the first year of life and later IQ might be mediated through more specific cognitive processes. To examine this issue, we rescored children's performance on the Bayley Scales according to the three item clusters identified by Yarrow, Rubenstein, and Pederson (1975): (1) goal-directedness, (2) social responsiveness, and (3) language use. Using scores on these differentiated clusters at 6 and 12 months, we performed a series of simple path analyses. Results from these analyses indicated that the three behavioral clusters assessed at 6 months do not appear to mediate the relationship between 6-month Play Materials scores and later IQ. The path coefficients indicate that most of the relation between that HOME subscale and later IQ could be considered a direct effect. However, the path coefficients between 6-month scores on Play Materials and later IQ indicate a measurable indirect effect for 12-month scores on both goal-directedness and language use.

A related study attempted to find a set of predictors among environmental processes and cognitive processes measured during the first year of life that would provide the most efficient prediction of later IQ. Stepwise multiple regression analyses were done using 6-month and 12-month HOME subscale scores and 12-month Bayley cluster scores to predict 3-year IQ.

Separate analyses were done for females and males. For boys, the most efficient set of predictors included 12-month Play Materials scores, 6-month Play Materials scores, and 12-month language use scores (adjusted $R = .78$). For girls, 12-month Play Materials and maternal responsivity scores (adjusted $R = .70$).

Despite the fact that the stepwise regression analysis showed that Play Materials for boys and Play Materials plus Maternal Responsivity for girls provided efficient prediction of 3-year IQ, other findings within the data suggested that the mere availability of toys may not be sufficient for facilitating intellectual development; specifically, Play Materials was significantly correlated with Maternal Involvement (.61 to .75). Thus, availability of appropriate play materials in conjunction with consistent encouragement may be useful for development. To further elucidate the relation between environment and development, a simple regression procedure was employed using 6-month Play Materials, 12-month Play Materials and 12-month Maternal Involvement scores for boys. For girls, 12-month Maternal Responsivity, 12-month Play Materials, and 12-month Maternal Involvement scores were used. The procedure used was like the one described by McCall, Appelbaum, and Hogarty (1973):

> One strategy in attempting to substantiate the selection of particular variables as major contributors to a multivariate result is to demonstrate that (a) the selected subset of variables will produce significant differentiation between groups when considered separately from the remaining variables, and (b) the remaining variables do not differentiate between groups if the subset is covaried. If, in addition, the subset differentiates the groups after the remaining variables have been covaried, the remaining variables apparently contribute little in addition to the special set. (p. 54)

Results of the simple regression procedures (see table 14–2) for boys were as follows: (1) the multiple correlation using 6-month Play Materials, 12-month Play Materials and 12-month Maternal Involvement scores to predict IQ was $R = .77$, and the multiple R using all 6 subscales at both 6 and 12 months was .80; (2) a significant residual correlation was observed between the three selected environmental variables and 3-year IQ with the nine remaining environmental variables covaried ($R = .58$); and (3) the residual correlation between the nine remaining variables and IQ was not significant when the three selected environmental variables were covaried ($R = .18$). For girls, the same basic pattern emerged: (1) the multiple correlation using 12-month scores on Maternal Responsivity, Play Materials, and Maternal Involvement to predict 3-year IQ was $R = .73$; (2) the residual correlation for the selected environmental set was significant ($R = .73$); and the residual for the remaining nine environmental variables was nonsignificant ($R = .22$).

Table 14–2
Regression Models Using Early Environment and Early Developmental Scores to Predict IQ at Age 3

Predictor Variables[a]	Multiple R^2	Adjusted Multiple R^2
Males[b]		
1. Play materials (12 months), play materials (6 months), language competence (12 months)	.63	.60
2. Play materials (12 months), play materials (6 months), MDI (12 months)	.62	.58
Females[b]		
1. Play materials (12 months), responsivity of mothers (12 months)	.52	.49
2. Play materials (12 months), responsivity of mothers (12 months)	.52	.49

[a]Predictor variables listed in order of their importance in the regression model.
[b]The first regression model used vocal competence and goal directedness, and the second regression model used MDI scores, as cognitive measures.

A fourth area of focus for our studies of the relation between environmental processes and intellectual development was on bidirectionality of effect. Cross-lagged panel analyses were done using Bayley Mental Development Index scores at 6, 12, and 24 months as measures of intellectual development and HOME subscale scores at the same time points as measures of environmental processes. Separate analyses were done for three HOME subscales: Play Materials, Maternal Responsivity, and Maternal Involvement. The results in the case of Play Materials indicate that the primary direction of effect in the period from 6 to 12 months may be from child to environment (that is, more capable children elicit more appropriate play materials from their parents). However, in the period from 12 to 24 month, the effects seem about equal in both directions. The pattern of coefficients for Maternal Involvement seemed similar to that for play materials in the 6- to 12-month period; but seemed to reverse itself in the 12- to 24-month period (that is, the more encouragement from mother at age 12 months, the higher the MDI score at 2 years). No discernible pattern for direction of effect emerged for Maternal Responsivity. Despite skepticism expressed about doing panel analyses on developmental data, these findings offer some tentative clarification about the nature of the relationships between environmental processes and intellectual development during infancy.

A final study utilizing the Little Rock longitudinal sample that has implications for the relation between play materials and intellectual development in children was reported earlier this year by Bradley and Caldwell (1984).

They examined the relation between HOME subscale scores and family demographics when infants were 1- and 2-years-old. This study was done to determine the extent to which the environmental processes tapped by the HOME might be attributable to common socioeconomic, family structure, and racial characteristics, using the demographic variables of race, sex, SES, degree of crowding in the home, and birth order.

Multivariate analyses of covariance were done with demographic variables entered in the following order: degree of crowding, birth order, social status, sex, race, sex × social status, race × social status, and sex × race. Criterion variables were the six HOME subscales. Separate analyses were done for 12-month and 24-month HOME scores. For 12-month HOME scores, overall multivariate effects were noted for birth order and crowding. Significant univariate effects for Play Materials were obtained for crowding, and birth order (R-square = .35). For 24-month scores, significant multivariate effects were noted for birth order, race × social status, and race × sex. Significant univariate effects for Play Materials were noted for crowding, birth order, social status, and race (R-square = .52). For both time points, scores on Play Materials were strongest for family structure as compared to social status characteristics. Thus, while part of the relation between Play Materials and intellectual development may be attributable to the relation between HOME scores and social status, most of the relationship does not seem attributable to such associations. The relationship between family structure characteristics and scores on Play Materials is significant.

In addition to the Little Rock longitudinal study, we are involved in a research consortium study to examine the relation between early environmental processes and children's development over the first 5 years of life. This study pools data from six sites in North America. Site I is Little Rock (lower- to lower-middle-class blacks, plus lower-middle to upper-middle-class whites). Site II is Houston (lower-class to working-class Mexican-American). Site III is Chapel Hill, North Carolina (middle-class whites, lower-class blacks). Site IV is Los Angeles (middle-class whites). Site V is Seattle (working-class and middle-class whites). Site VI is Hamilton, Ontario (working-class whites). The data from these six sites were combined for joint analyses because of the large amount of overlap in both measures used in the individual studies and the ages at which major measures were administered. The total sample included more than 1500 children and their families, although complete data sets were available for only a few hundred cases.

Among the more interesting analyses done on the consortium data set were path analyses involving environmental and developmental data at 12, 24, and 36 months, with Stanford-Binet IQs the outcome measure of focus. Variables included in these analyses were SES, Bayley MDI scores at 12 and 24 months, Maternal Responsivity and Play Materials scores at 12 and 24 months, Toys and Materials and Pride, Affection, and Warmth scores at 36 months, and IQ scores at 36 months. Since full data sets were not available on all participants, a total of three path analyses were done. For the first analysis, Maternal Responsivity and Play Materials scores at 24 months were not available. As figure 14–1 shows, there are significant paths running from 12-month scores on the Play Materials subscale to Bayley scores at both 12 and 24 months, a strong path from Play Materials scores at 12 months to Toys and Materials scores at 36 months, a significant path from Bayley MDI score at 24 months to Toys and Materials at 36 months and to IQ scores at 3 years, and a significant path from 36-month Toys and Materials scores to 3-year IQ. In the second path analysis, 36-month scores on HOME subscales were not available (see figure 14–2). Path coefficients were similar to those shown in figure 14–1, except that the path from 24-month Play Materials to 3-year IQ was weaker than that from 36-month Toys and Materials to 36-month IQ; and the path from 24-month MDI to 3-year IQ was stronger. Figure 14–3 displays the most complete path model. It shows a continuing influence of SES on the provision of toys and play materials (in the .20 to .30 range), significant paths from Play Materials to mental test scores at all three time points (.20 to .36), and diminishing paths from the quality of the socioemotional environment to mental test scores (.23 to .06). A generally stable path is shown between Play Materials scores across the three time points (around .40), and increasing paths among mental test scores (.29 to .47).

Overall, the path analyses indicate that socioeconomic status influences the kinds of experiences (socioemotional support and objects) that a child has. The greatest impact is noted during the first year of life, much of which is sustained through the first 3 years. New influence on the socioemotional environment declines each year so that the path from SES to Pride, Affection, and Warmth at age three is nonsignificant (.07). However, SES appears to have significant new impact on the provision of appropriate toys and materials each year (.19 with Play Materials at age 2 and .23 with Toys and Materials at age 3). The impact of SES on mental test scores is sustained by the socioemotional support and cognitive stimulation provided in the homes of children. The effect of these particular environmental processes shows up as early as the first year of life and increases thereafter. While the additional influences in the socioemotional environment diminish each year the availability of appropriate toys and materials provides additional impetus for cognitive growth throughout the three year period (for example, the paths from Play Materials to Bayley MDI at 24 months is .36, the path from Toys and Materials at 36 months and 3-year IQ is .35). In essence, a kind of reverberating circuit between intelligence and the provision of play materials is begun as early as the second year of life. Having more appropriate toys and materials leads to more advanced cognitive functioning, which in turn leads to the provision of more appropriate toys and materials. Throughout this period, the stronger path of influence leads from play materials to mental development.

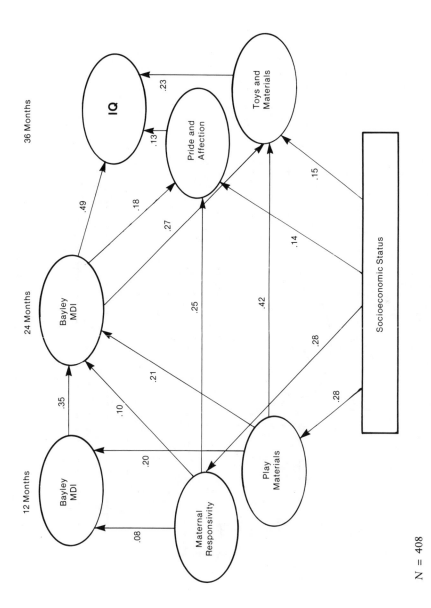

Figure 14–1. Path Analysis without 24-Month HOME

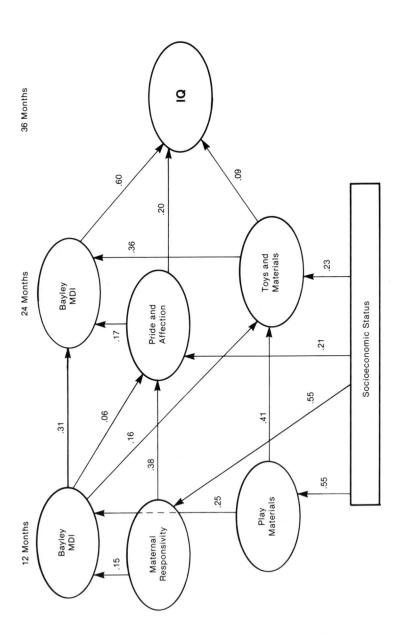

36 Months

24 Months

12 Months

Figure 14–2. Path Analysis without 36-Month HOME

$N = 295$

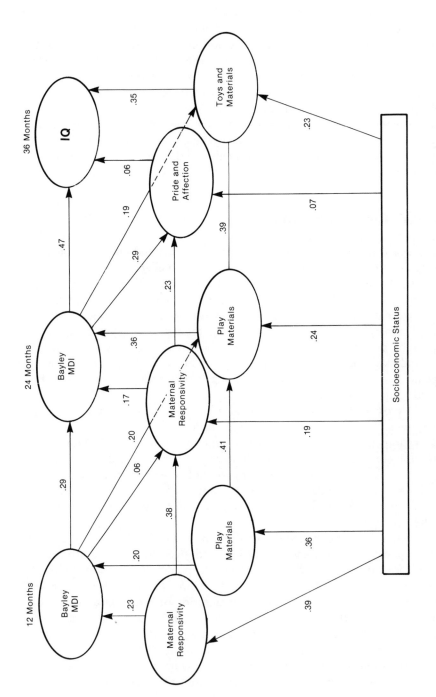

Figure 14–3. Path Model for Home Environment and Intellectual Development at 12, 24, and 36 Months

An interesting finding from these analyses is that higher intelligence may lead to obtaining more socioemotional support. Indeed, the impact of brightness seems to be as great for the socioemotional environment as it is for the provision of appropriate toys and materials after the first year of life. The gap between the highs and lows gets wider in terms of both measured intellectual performance and the quality of cognitive and socioemotional support available to the child. However, after age three, most of the increase in mental test scores comes from the provision of greater cognitive stimulation (in this instance measured by the provision of toys and materials but probably also from direct encouragement of achievement and the provision of other educationally enriching experiences).

Mueller's Cross-Systems Model

With regard to the relation between play materials and children's development, the cross-systems model articulated by Mueller (1979) and his colleagues (Mueller & Vandell, 1979; Mueller & Rich, 1976; Mueller & Brenner, 1977; DeStafano & Mueller, 1983) serves as a useful complement to the observational research done in home environments. According to Mueller (1979), emerging social structure among toddler peer groups "does not depend on peer-related skills; instead it relies on the toddler's attachment to toys and skill with toys. From the start, toddler's find themselves coming together because they share skills for things like opening the jack-in-the-box or sliding down the slide (p. 174)."

The cross-systems model evolved in conjunction with research on toddler playgroups. Specifically, the design of the cross-sectional study involved observations of two groups of boys (Playgroup I boys were 12 months old when the study began, Playgroup II were 16½ months old). Both groups were observed in play settings over a period of seven months. Two teachers were present in the room at all times. The boys were observed in three behavioral contexts: peer-peer dyads, peer-peer group situations, and parent-toddler situations.

A major finding of the study was that peer social interaction and social skills in playgroups showed significant growth over the seven month period. Nonetheless, activity with things remained the predominant mode of play. At 16 months, all six boys in Playgroup I spent more of their time watching toys than peers and teachers combined. The duration of watching toys was also much greater than that for watching people (70 percent to 30 percent). Moreover, much of the children's time in contact with other children was a time-of-object focused play with a common toy. Mueller (1979) concluded from his investigation that the overwhelming impression one got from looking at the play sessions of boy toddlers was the "toddler's passion for things."

The research of Mueller and his colleagues revealed that play materials function as a contextual basis of toddler social interaction; up to the age of 2, 83 percent of all social interactions involved physical objects.

> Unlike the ever-accommodative mother, infants and toddlers don't see peer adjustment as their central developmental task. Nevertheless, they are drawn into contact by the reciprocal interest in physical things. They initiate each other's toy play and gradually learn to control each other and not only the toy. (Mueller, 1979, p. 188).

Observations of the toddlers in playgrounds indicates not only that toddlers engage in social interactions because of common interest in toys and objects, but also that the purposive nature of peer contacts creates an autonomous social system for peer relations, one which ultimately affects mother-child interactions. Using cross-lagged panel techniques to examine directions of influence between peer-peer interactions and mother-child interactions over the seven-month study period, Mueller (1979) found that improvements in the quality of peer interaction served more as a source of improvement for infant-parent interaction than improved mother-child interaction facilitated improved peer-peer interaction. It's as if toddlers learned the game of social interaction in a purposive peer interaction.

Mueller (1979) summarized his research by reference to the cross-systems model of early social development. The model identifies both a cognitive structure and a social structure as operative in social development. Cognitive growth evolves from structured social interactions.

> The interactions change the child, and after several children have changed in similar ways, new forms of social structure are created; these in turn foster further cognitive change. Both brain and social system are organized and each reorganizes the other over again across development. For example, object-centered contacts (a social structure) are a consequence of object skills (a cognitive structure). Yet, coordinated SDBs (a cognitive structure) are products of social interactions of playgroup (a social structure). The results of the playgroup study appear consonant with the function for play described by Bruner, Jolly, and Sylva (1976), "What appears to be at stake in play is the opportunity for assembling and reassembling behavior sequences for skilled action." (p. 15)

In summary, part of the connection between play materials and intellectual development may be their joint relation to social interaction and social development (with both peers and adults). Playthings and other physical objects form the basis for purposive encounters which themselves involve learning, but which also lead to further development in both cognitive and social domains. Within the context of play, toys may lead to the development of physical and social skills together with imaginative reconstruction of ideas and social interactions. "Play is imagination in the service of mastery."

Lev Vygotsky's "Zone of Proximal Development"

Lev Vygotsky remains one of the most brilliant, yet underutilized, theorists in the field of child development. Prior to the translations of his work by Cole, John Steiner, Scribner, and Souberman (1978), few Americans knew anything about Vygotsky's ideas other than those dealing with the relationship between thought and language. Working within a Marxist tradition, he focused on the relation of humans to their environments. Unlike many of his academic contemporaries, Vygotsky constantly grappled with notions of human development in terms of their applicability to human pursuits. He was founder of the Institute of Defectology in Moscow, where he dealt with problems of educational practice especially as it applied to the physically and mentally handicapped. Vygotsky's ideas on the relationship of learning and development are pertinent to our understanding of play materials and intelligence.

I will examine Vygotsky's theory as it relates to three issues: (1) the relation of tool and symbol in early child development; (2) the relation of learning and development in children; and (3) the relation of objects and actions to meaning. The latter two issues have special relevance to the relation of play materials and intellectual growth evolving from play settings.

Tools and Symbols in Early Childhood

Following the research of the Buhlers, Vygotsky (1978) became interested in the practical intelligence of infants. His observations suggested that practical intelligence early in life developed independently of speech. Intellectual development was determined "both by the child's degree of organic development and by his or her degree of mastery in the use of tools" (p. 21). In essence, play materials and other physical objects that children can act upon become stimulus materials needed for early cognitive development.

According to Vygotsky, a dialectical unity of tool and symbol systems evolves in children, beginning in the second year of life. Speech joins forces with eye and hand in the solution of practical problems. "Children not only speak about what they're doing; their speech and action are part of one and the same complex psychological function, directed toward the solution of the problem at hand" (p. 25). The two systems, although separable, become highly integrated. Vygotsky argues that the convergence of these two systems in early childhood is the single most signficant event in the history of intellectual development.

Children's early attempts at marrying speech to practical intelligence to solve a problem may be characterized as clumsy, often comical. Speech merely accompanies hand and eyes; its contribution is primarily emotional, reflecting the success of failure of the activity and aimed at garnering external support in helping to solve the problem. However, as language develops and as the number of problem solving experiences increases, the union of tool and speech systems becomes more efficient. Rather than having to take direct action in solving every problem, a child can use speech to plan and direct the action. Two things must be present for the marriage of tool and symbol systems to become productive: (1) normal opportunities for the language system itself to develop, and (2) a varied, responsive, and manipulable object environment. To reiterate, in early infancy intellectual development is dependent on the mastery of tools (objects) per se. Later in infancy, as speech and tool systems join, children seek not only continual opportunities for tool mastery but also repeated experiences in a responsive physical environment which allows the speech system itself to become a tool in problem solving.

For Vygotsky, intellectual development in humans is closely tied to improvements in how the various systems (such as tool and symbol) mediate activity (use indirect ways to solve problems). While tool and symbol systems work together to solve problems, they differ in the ways they mediate activity.

> A most essential difference between sign and tool, and the basis for the real divergence of the two lines, is the different ways that they orient human behavior. The tool's function is to serve as the conductor of human influence on the object of activity; it is externally oriented; it must lead to changes in objects. It is . . . aimed at mastering . . . nature. The sign, on the other hand, changes nothing in the object of a psychological operation. It is . . . aimed at mastering oneself; the sign is internally oriented. (p. 55)

In this context, Vygotsky does not use the word *tool* synonymously with the word *object* (or obviously the words *play materials*). *Tool* refers to the indirect function as mediator of an object to accomplish some activity. As mediators of activity tools are linked to higher intellectual functioning. Vygotsky expresses the relation of both tools and symbols to higher intellectual functioning.

> The use of artificial means, the transition to mediated activity, fundamentally changes all psychological operations just as the use of tools limitlessly broadens the range of activities within which new psychological functions may operate. In this context, we can use the term higher psychological function, or higher behavior, as referring to the combination of tool and sign in psychological activity. (p. 55)

Thus, during the first three years of life, play materials and other responsive physical objects provide an arena of opportunities for intellectual development. During earliest infancy, they provide opportunities for the development of perceptual and manual skills as well as the mastery of tools. In later infancy, play materials and tools also provide opportunities for problem solving experiences as speech system become increasingly more efficient in guiding solutions to tasks.

During the preschool years, play materials provide yet another avenue for intellectual development. This additional avenue is best understood in reference to Vygotsky's discussion of the "zone of proximal development."

The Zone of Proximal Development

Key to understanding the relevance of Vygotsky's theory to the relation of play materials and intellectual development among preschool children is his concept of the "zone of proximal development." Vygotsky proposed a different relationship between learning and development than the ones espoused by his behaviorist, gestaltist, and cognitivist contemporaries. He stated that a dynamic, interdependent relationship exists between learning and development in humans. To explain this relationship he introduced the concept of the zone of proximal development. According to Vygotsky, there are at least two developmental levels. Level 1, the "actual development level," represents mental functions that have been established as a result of certain already completed developmental cycles. This level can be determined by giving a child a standard measure of intellectual functioning. Level 2, the "potential development level," involves those things a child can accomplish with the assistance of an adult or more capable peer but cannot yet do independently. Learning can be through instruction or imitation, but it "awakens a variety of internal processes that are able to operate only when the child is interacting with people in his environment and in cooperation with his peers. Once these processes are internalized, they become part of the child's developmental achievement (p. 90)." Thus two children with the same actual development level (test scores) might well differ in terms of problems they can successfully solve because of social influences. The "distance between the actual developmental level as determined by independent problem solving and the level of potential development as determined through problem solving under adult guidance or in collaboration with more capable peers" (p. 86), is what Vygotsky calls the zone of proximal development.

In summary, learning and development are complementary, dynamically interacting processes. An individual's level of intellectual development sets boundaries on the kinds of learning that can take place. Within these boundaries specific kinds of learnings help to shape the course of future intellectual development. Thus, the zones of proximal development established incidentally through instruction or by imitation play a central role in intellectual development.

With respect to preschool children, Vygotsky felt that play settings afforded a particularly rich environment for the creation of zones of proximal development. The potential value of play settings (and play materials used in play settings) in establishing zones of proximal development can perhaps best be understood in terms of Vygotsky's ideas on the relationship of actions and objects to meaning.

Objects, Actions, and Meaning

Using the research of Lewin as a basis for drawing conclusions, Vygotsky (1978) states that "things dictate to a child what he must do" (p. 97). Places, objects, and other real events exert a powerful motivational force on a child's behavior. In infancy, motivation is married to perception; perception a stimulus to activity. Things possess an inherent motivational capacity—stairs are to be climbed, doors opened, wheels turned. Only as a child's cognitive capability increases is he able to act independently of what he sees, hears, and feels. Motivation then becomes divorced from perception. The meaning of a situation is not wholly determined by inherent features of the situation.

Vygotsky discusses the gradual evolution of children's thinking during the early childhood years in terms of two ratios: (1) the object/meaning ratio and (2) the action/meaning ratio. Early in life objects dominate meaning and action. Children's behavior is impelled by things and their understanding of those things determined by their inherent features. With advances in cognitive capability, the field of meaning is separated from the field of perception. Then children can use things imaginatively in the service of their motives, as the play setting determines the meaning of the object (the tree branch becomes the magic wand). In play, toys and other objects become pivots detaching the meaning of words from the real objects they designate (in pretending that a stickhorse is a horse, the word *horse* is no longer isomorphic with the real animal it designates). The word is no longer the property of the thing itself. At this point in development, play materials, and other objects become vehicles for transporting meaning from real objects. Objects no longer dominate meaning but can be a way of transferring meaning from a real to an imaginary situation. This stage of intellectual development is a transitional one between the object-dominated thinking of the infant and adult thought that it totally free from situational constraints. Thus, in the play of preschool children toys are important in a different way than they are to infants. Rather than dominate they assist in the development of new meaning. The object/meaning ratio is one in which meaning has a larger share.

The transition in the action/meaning ratio is similar to the transition in the object/meaning ratio. Early in life actions dominate. A child can do more than he understands. Later, in the play of preschool children, actions (pretending to fly like Superman, swirl like a ballerina) become pivots for real events (that is, actions assist meaning). In imagination, internal and external actions are inseparable (slashing through the air with a Star Wars laserssword places the child beside Luke Skywalker, locked in fateful combat with Darth Vader).

In play, actions and objects do not determine the meaning of the situation, although they often operate as catalysts. Rather, they help to carry out the wishes, intentions, and motivations of the child as they operate in imagination. Play materials and actions provide a channel through which meaning is realized and motivations fulfilled.

For Vygotsky (1978), play among preschool children establishes a zone of proximal development. "In play a child . . . behaves beyond his average years, above his daily behavior (p. 102)." Play is seen as the "highest level of preschool development." It begins in an imaginary situation quite similar to a real one. Gradually imagination forges a set of rules within which the objects and actions in play operate to the "conscious realization of its purpose." The rules that arise naturally from the imagined situation place strong constraints on the child's activity as play continues. The child's actions "are in fact subordinated to the meaning of things and he acts accordingly. . . . From the point of view of development, creating an imaginary situation can be regarded as a means of developing abstract thought" (p. 103).

In considering the potential significance of play materials for intellectual development during the preschool years, it is important to bear in mind that play situations are often powerful environments, engendering numerous cognitive, social, and emotional motives. Attention to the activity within play is frequently intense. Therefore, the likelihood of learning (both incidentally and through instruction) is great. The freedom to use imagination in the service of the rules of play provides a fertile ground for new linkages of ideas that transfer to real world contexts. In Vygotsky's terms, the zone of proximal development can be substantially broadened in play.

Summarizing Vygotsky's ideas, toys and other objects may serve to enhance learning, and thus to create a zone of proximal development, in several ways: (1) as an initiator of action, that is, the simple availability of materials often enduces a child into play or attempts at tool mastery while indirectly learning accrues through those activities; (2) as a catalyst for incidental learning through use of the toy; (3) as a focus of social learning (imitation) of peers and adults; (4) as a focus for instruction from peers and adults; (5) as the subject of instructions and demonstrations provided to others and (6) as props in imaginative or pretend play as the child becomes teacher, the child himself learns.

Conclusion

Several tentative conclusions are offered regarding the relationship between play materials and intelligence:

1. Young children spend a considerable amount of time viewing and interacting with toys and other objects.
2. There is a moderate correlation between the availability and use of toys and children's mental test scores beginning as early as the second year of life.
3. The relation between play materials and intelligence is a reciprocal one, with brighter children eliciting more appropriate play materials.
4. Part of the observed correlation between toys and intellectual development may reflect their joint relation to family social status and parental encouragement of development, but the total relationship does not seem attributable solely to these factors.
5. Toys and other objects frequently serve as the focus of social encounters (more fully social as the child matures). Such encounters afford numerous opportunities for direct and incidental learning.
6. Toys and other physical objects appear to have an inherent attractiveness for young children. They draw children into action and serve as a source of skill development and tool mastery.
7. Toys can serve as a catalyst for imaginative play and can serve to carry the meaning of the play situation to full realization. They may also help to provide a link between learnings derived from the imaginative world of play and the more concrete settings of the real world.

Many theories about the relation between play materials and intellectual development remain speculative. Much of the apparent strength of that relationship may derive from the fact that play materials frequently enlist three major intrinsic motives: curiosity, mastery, and affiliation (Yarrow, Rubenstein, & Pederson, 1975). As the child matures, they are likely to enlish a number of secondary motives as well. The heightened attention and persistence that eminate from these motives increase substantially the likelihood of greater learning, and in turn helps drive development. As Caldwell (1968) cogently argued nearly 2 decades ago, the optimal environment for young children is one that should include a wide variety of responsive objects and play materials. As fuel for the imagination of young children, such materials may also provide impetus to what Vygotsky calls the development of higher psychological processes.

References

Allen, D., Affleck, G., McGrade, B., & McQueeny, M. 1983. Characteristics of home observation for measurement of the environment inventory in a sample of high-risk/developmentally disabled infants. *Infant Behavior and Development* 6: 53–60.

Barnard, K., Bee, N., & Hammond, M. 1984. Home environment and cognitive development in a healthy, low-risk sample: the Seattle study. In A.W. Gottfried (Ed.), *Home environment and early cognitive development: Longitudinal research*. New York: Academic Press.

Bradley, R., & Caldwell, B. 1984. The relation of infants' home environments to achievement test performance in first grade: A follow-up study. *Child Development* 55:803–809.

———. 1984. The HOME inventory and family demographics. *Development Psychology* 20:315–320.

Caldwell, B., Elardo, P., & Elardo, R. 1972. The longitudinal observation and intervention study. Paper presented at the Southeastern Conference on Human Development. Williamsburg, Virginia.

Clarke-Stewart, K.A. 1973. Interactions between mothers and their young children: Characteristics and consequences. *Monographs of the Society for Research in Child Development,* 38, Nos. 6 & 7.

DeStafano, C. 1976. *Environmental determinants of peer social behavior and interaction in a toddler play group*. Unpublished doctoral dissertation. Boston University.

Gottfried, A.W., & Gottfried, A.E. 1984. Home environment and cognitive development in young children of middle-socioeconomic-status families. In A.W. Gottfried (Ed.), *Home environment and early cognitive development: Longitudinal research*. New York: Academic Press.

McCall, R., Appelbaum, M., & Hogarty, P. 1973. Developmental changes in mental performance. *Monographs of the Society for Research in Child Development* 38, No. 3,

Meyers, E., Mink, I., & Nihira, K. 1977. *Home quality rating scale*. Pomona, Calif.: Neuropsychiatric Institute—Pacific State Hospital Research Group.

Moore, T. 1968. Language and intelligence: A longitudinal study of the first eight years. Part II. Environmental correlates of mental growth. *Human Development* 11:1–24.

Moos, R., & Moos, B. 1981. *Family Environment Scale Manual*. Palo Alto, Calif.: Consulting Psychologist Press.

Mueller, E. 1979. Toddlers + toys = An autonomous social system. In M. Lewis & L. Rosenblum (Eds.), *The child and its family*. New York: Plenum Press.

Mueller, E., & Brenner, J. 1977. The origins of social skills and interaction among play group toddlers. *Child Development* 48:854–861.

Mueller, E., & Rich, A. 1976. Clustering and socially directed behaviors in a play group of 1-year-olds. *Journal of Child Psychology and Psychiatry* 17:315–322.

Mueller, E., & Vandell, D. 1979. Infant-infant interaction: A review. In J. Osofsky (Ed.), *Handbook of infant development.* New York: Wiley-Interscience.

Nihira, K., Meyers, E., & Mink, I. 1983. Reciprocal relationship between home environment and development of TMR adolescents. *American Journal of Mental Deficiency* 88:139–149.

———. 1980. Home environment, family adjustment and development of mentally retarded children. *Applied Research in Mental Retardation* 1:5–24.

Siegel, L. 1984. Home environmental influences on cognitive development in pre-term and full-term children during the first 5 years. In A.W. Gottfried (Ed.), *Home environment and early cognitive development: Longitudinal research.* New York: Academic Press.

Tulbin, S., & Covitz, F. 1975. Mother-infant interaction and intellectual functioning at age six. Paper presented at the biennial meeting of the Society for Research in Child Development, Denver.

Vygotsky, L. 1978. Mind in society: The development of higher psychological processes. In M. Cole, V. John-Steiner, S. Scribner & E. Souberman (Eds.), Cambridge: Harvard University Press.

Wachs, T. 1976. Utilization of a Piagetian approach in the investigation of early experience effects: A research strategy and some illustrative data. *Merrill-Palmer Quarterly* 22:11–29.

Wachs, T., Uzgiris, I., & Hunt, J. 1971. Cognitive development in infants from different age levels and different environmental backgrounds: An explanatory investigation. *Merrill-Palmer Quarterly* 17:283–317.

Ware, W., & Garber, M. 1972. The home environment as a predictor of school achievement. *Theory into Practice* 11:190–195.

Wulbert, M., Inglis, S., Kriegsman, E., & Mills, B. 1975. Language delay and associated mother-child interactions. *Development Psychology* 11:61–70.

Yarrow, L., Rubenstein, J., & Pederson, F. 1975. *Infant and environment.* New York: Wiley.

15
Models of Physical Environmental Action: Implications for the Study of Play Materials and Parent-Child Interaction

Theodore D. Wachs

Recent theoretical reviews (Bronfenbrenner, 1977; Wohlwill, 1983) clearly indicate that the environment is not unitary but rather is highly differentiated, containing a variety of specific subunits or levels. In this chapter I will focus on the most molecular of these levels, corresponding to what Bronfenbrenner has called the microsystem. Until very recently, most research and theory has focused on only one aspect of the microsystem, namely, the social environment, such as interactions between children and caregivers (Wachs & Gruen, 1982; Wohlwill, 1983). There has been a relative neglect of the other major component of the microsystem, the physical environment, which is the stage or setting upon which social transactions take place. Using play as an example, research on the effect of play upon development has focused primarily on what caregivers do with children during play (Clarke-Stewart, 1973; Belsky, Good, & Most, 1980; Carew, 1980), with relatively little interest in the relationship of play-setting or objects used in play to subsequent development.

This one-sided emphasis on the social environment has been justified by the contention that the physical environment can have little impact upon development unless it is mediated by social variables (Provence & Lipton, 1962; Clarke-Stewart, 1973; Parke, 1978). This contention appears to have worked its way into general acceptance in spite of the fact, as noted by Mac-Phee, Ramey, and Yates (1984) that the data to support this contention "are sparse and somewhat contradictory" (pp. 346–347).

Our neglect of the physical environment may also be because until recently there has been little theoretical dissection of the nature of the physical environment. However, development of a taxonomy of the dimensions of the physical environment (Wachs & Gruen, 1982), coupled with theoretical

The author gratefully acknowledges the comments and caveats of Professors Allen Gottfried and Joachim Wohlwill on a preliminary version of this chapter.

advances in perceptual psychology, now allows us to make specific predictions about which aspects of the physical environment are relevant to children's development, regardless of the nature of the child's social environment. Of particular interest are extensions of Gibson's (J. Gibson, 1979; E.J. Gibson, 1982) concept of affordances to the study of physical environment, as seen in the recent work of Wohlwill (1983) and Heft (in press).

This chapter consists of three sections. First, I briefly discuss available evidence on the relationship of specific physical environment parameters to subsequent cognitive development. Second, I present models defining relationships between the social and physical microenvironments, and I present some data which offers a test of these competing models. Finally, and perhaps most critically, I demonstrate how my study of the physical environment led to specific models of environmental action, which illustrate the process by which both physical and social environments can influence cognitive development.

Relationship between Physical Environment and Cognitive Development

Much of the available evidence of the relationship of specific dimensions of the physical environment to cognitive development for the first five years of life has been summarized by Wachs and Gruen (1982). As can be seen in table 15–1, seven dimensions of the physical environment have been shown to be

Table 15–1
Summary of Physical Environment Factors Showing Consistent Relationships to Cognitive Development over the First Five Years of Life

Parameter	Direction of Relationship to Cognitive Performance	Comment
Availability of stimulus material	Positive	Primarily relevant in first nine months of life
Variety of stimulus material	Positive	As child gets older, changes in available objects may be more critical than number of different objects available
Responsivity of the physical environment	Positive	
Ambient background noise	Negative	Particularly salient for males and at-risk infants
Overcrowding	Negative	
Regularity of scheduling	Positive	May be mediated by age and by ability under study
Physical restraints on exploration	Negative	

consistently related to various aspects of cognitive development, across a variety of studies, during the first five years of life. These include: (1) *availability of stimulus material,* which is positively related to development and relevant primarily for the first nine months of life; (2) *variety of stimulus material,* which is positively related to development and involves both numbers of different stimuli available (short-term variety) and changes in stimulus material over time (long-term variety); (3) *responsivity of the physical environment,* which is positively related to development at most ages and for most developmental parameters; (4) *ambient background noise,* which is negatively related to development, particularly for boys and at-risk infants; (5) *overcrowding,* which appears to be negatively related to development at most ages and for most developmental parameters; (6) *regularity of scheduling,* which is positively related to development, but may be mediated both by the age of the chld and by the developmental parameters under study; and (7) *physical restraints upon exploration,* which is negatively related to development at most ages and for most developmental parameters. Evidence appearing since the Wachs and Gruen book generally supports these conclusions (Wachs, in press), except for the possibility that availability of stimulus material may be relevant after the first year of life as well (Gottfried, 1984). Little evidence is available on the role of physical microenvironmental parameters past 5 years of age, although both variety of intellectually stimulating material in the home (Kelleghan, 1977) and family configuration (Zajonc, 1983) have been consistently related to a variety of cognitive parameters in older children (Wachs, in press).

The above results not only show the relevance of the physical environment to various aspects of cognitive performance, but also indicate which dimensions of the physical environment appear to be most salient. However, this research does not answer the critical question of the relationship between physical environment and development. Are the above results due to an independent impact of the physical environment, or are they due primarily to adults mediating the physical environment for the child?

Relationship between Physical Environment and Social Environment

Figure 15–1 represents a series of simplified path models indicating different interrelationships between the physical and social environments as these affect cognitive development. Model I illustrates the independent impact of the physical and social environments upon development. Model 2 hypothesizes that the physical and social environments covary, and that it is this covariance which accounts for variability in subsequent development. Model 3 is a stronger form of model 2, going beyond covariance and suggesting that the impact of the physical environment is due primarily to the social environment

1. Independent effects

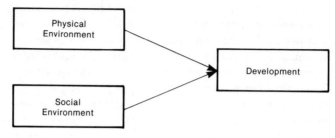

2. Covariance

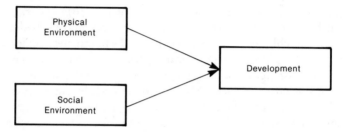

3. Social mediates physical

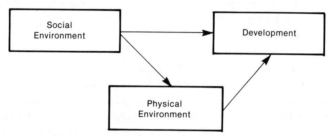

4. Physical mediates social

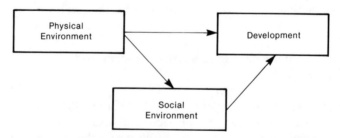

Figure 15–1. Models of the Relationship between the Physical and Social Environments

mediating the physical. Model 4 suggests that the physical environment mediates the social environment, a position which is rarely seen in developmental psychology, but is more common in cross-cultural studies (for example, McSwain, 1981; Woodson & da-Costa-Woodson, 1984).

Virtually no evidence (McPhee et al., 1984) is available to test the validity of these models. To approach this question of validity, I present data from two recent studies. In the first study (Wachs & Gandour, 1983) both physical and social environmental parameters were repeatedly measured on a substantial sample ($n = 100$) of 6-month-old infants. Our measure of the physical environment was sections I–III of the Purdue Home Stimulation Inventory (PHSI) (Wachs, Francis & McQuiston, 1979); our measure of the social environment was the Yarrow Scale (Yarrow, Rubenstein & Pedersen, 1975). PHSI sections I–III consist of thirty-three item codes measuring various physical aspects of the infant's environment. These thirty-three items reduce to twelve factors, nine of which address the physical dimensions of the infant's environment. The Yarrow scale includes sixteen observational categories, from which are computed eleven summary scores describing various aspects of the infants' social environment.

In testing the interrelationship between the physical and social environments, we selected five of the nine physical environment factors. The factors chosen were those which are most consistently related to cognitive performance, as shown in table 15–1. Since the physical environment may have an impact upon development independent of social influences, it is necessary to study those aspects of the physical environment which have been shown to be consistently related to development. The five factors chosen were defined by seven PHSI codes which most clearly measured these factors, and which could be divided most easily into those physical environment parameters providing either high affordance (category 1) or limited affordance (category 2) for the child. Gibson (1979) defines affordance as the degree of fit between stimulus properties and behaviors which are naturally associated with these stimulus properties. For example, blocks are objects which afford the child the opportunity to place two physical surfaces together, as in stacking blocks or hitting them together. Examining the physical environment in terms of affordances allows a distinction to be made between those aspects of the physical environment which provide multiple affordances to the child and those which provide few. Based on the theories of Wohlwill (1983), category 1 items contained stimulus properties which afforded the child specific uses of stimuli. The codes chosen measured the availability, variety, and responsivity of physical objects in the 6-month-old's environment. Category 2 items contained only limited stimulus properties; and the codes chosen measured background noise and overcrowding.[1]

To test the available models we correlated the eleven Yarrow scale scores with the codes defining our two classes of physical environment factors. These data are shown in table 15–2.

Table 15–2
Correlations between Physical and Social Environments at 6 Months

Physical Environment—Category 1 (High-Affordance with Social Environment)

Yarrow Scale Codes	PHSI Codes
Visual stimulation	Availability of stimulus material—(number of small objects;
Auditory stimulation	number of papers and magazines)
Contingent vocalization	Variety of stimulus material—(new toys)
Tactile stimulation	Responsivity of stimulus material—(number of audiovisu-
Kinesthetic stimulation	ally responsive toys)
Smiling to baby	
Playing with baby	
Adult social mediation with reinforcement	
Adult social mediation without reinforcement	
Expression of affection	
Response to distress	

Of the forty-four correlations for category 1, none was significant.

Physical Environment—Category 2 (Low-Affordance with Social Environment)

	PHSI Codes		
Yarrow Scale Codes	Noise Rating	Number of Siblings (Crowding)	Number of Rooms in Home/Number of People at Home (Crowding)
Visual stimulation			
Auditory stimulation	− .19*	− .24**	.17*
Contingent vocalization	− .18*	− .25**	.19*
Tactile stimulation			
Kinesthetic stimulation			.16*
Smiling to baby		− .19*	
Playing with baby			− .27**
Adult social mediation with reinforcement	− .20*	− .24**	
Adult social mediation without reinforcement			− .29**
Expression of affection			
Response to distress			

*p > .05.
**p > .01.

For category 1 correlations, the data show no relationship between adult interactions and physical environment parameters which provide affordances. Since the physical environment parameters chosen are those most consistently related to development, these results clearly did not support model 2 (covariance). Neither did the results support model 3 (social factors mediate the physical environment) since there was not even a moderate degree of association between specific physical and social environmental paramaters. Rather, these results support model 1 (independent effects), suggesting that those aspects of the physical environment which have affordances are independent of social mediation, at least at 6 months of age.

In contrast, there is a high proportion of significant correlations in the second set of physical environment categories, *low-affordance stimuli.* Twelve out of the thirty-three correlations are significant, with the overwhelming majority of these (ten out of twelve) negative. The relation of these low-affordance items to development is also primarily negative, as noted earlier.[2] On the surface these results do not support either models 1 (independent effects) or 2 (covariance). However the results show that higher levels of ambient background noise are significantly and negatively related to amount of auditory stimulation, contingent parental vocalization, and reinforcement of the child's play activities. Similar findings are also seen for the number of siblings (a measure of crowding). Logically, I find it difficult to understand how low levels of contingency or auditory stimulation by adults can produce higher levels of background noise or crowding in the home. Rather, I view these findings as suggesting that the presence of noise or crowding *interferes* with parental reinforcement or auditory stimulation of the infant. Thus, these data offer little support for model 3 (social mediates physical), but can support either model 2 (covariance) or model 4, (physical mediates social).

In the second study used to test the validity of the models (Wachs & Chan, 1984), both physical and social environmental parameters were measured on a sample of 12-month-old infants ($n = 48$), with the physical environment parameters again being derived from the PHSI. The same physical environment factors are examined as those described previously for the 6-month-olds. The social environment measures consisted of ten dimensions drawn from the social environment section of the PHSI. The majority of the social environment dimensions assessed various aspect of the infants language environment. The intercorrelations are shown in table 15–3. There are approximately the same percent of significant intercorrelations for the low-affordance parameters at 12 months of age as was shown at 6 months. Given the similarity in the relationships, these results again do not support model 3 (social mediates physical) for the low-affordance dimensions of the physical environment, but can support the validity of either model 2 (covariance) or model 4 (physical mediates social).

In contrast to the age 6 months results, the data for the age 12 months

Table 15–3
Correlation between Physical and Social Environments at 12 Months

	PHSI I–III Codes						
	High-Affordance (25%)				Noise	Low-Affordance (30%)	
	Availability		Variety	Responsivity		Crowding	
PHSI IV Codes	Objects	Papers	Toys	Number of AV Toys	Rating	Number of Siblings	Number of Rooms/Number of People
Parental involvement			.32*			-.28*	
No adult present						.54**	
Number of adult vocalizations			.34**			-.49**	
Number of objects named			.34**	.28*			
Number of no response to vocalizations			-.36**			.52**	
Number of nonverbal responses to vocalization							
Number of words repeated	.25*				-.25*		
Number of verbal responses to vocalization			.30*			-.38**	
Physical contact	.31*				.31*		
Use of coercion			.44**	.26*	.36**	-.40**	

*p < .05.
**p < .01.

sample indicate a much higher proportion of significant relationships between high-affordance physical dimensions and social interactions at 12 months. Since the two data sets are not longitudinal, it is impossible to tell whether this discrepancy represents a genuine developmental shift in the infants' environment or a variation in the sample. Because of the similarity in the results for the low-affordance dimensions at 6 and 12 months, I favor the former interpretation. In any event, the results at 12 months suggest that parents who provide their infants with a variety of toys and objects are also more likely to be highly involved with their infants (either positively, or negatively as in the case of coercion) and are more likely to vocalize to and respond to their infants' vocalizations. Given this relationship it is unlikely that the availability of varied objects in the home leads to greater responsivity and involvement (model 4, physical mediates social), but the results could support either model 2 (covariance) or model 3 (social mediates physical).

Fortunately, it is possible to do a direct test of the validity of these competing models. We collapsed the significant social and physical environment predictors into data sets and entered them into a hierarchical multiple regression in the following order:

1. Maternal Verbal Level (WAIS-R)
2. Social Environment Data Set
3. Physical Environment Data Set
4. SES Level

When data sets are entered hierarchically, the unique contribution of each data set is assessed only after variance associated with the earlier predictors has been partialed out. Using this analytic strategy we were able to determine whether the physical environment data set made a unique contribution to the prediction of our criterion variable (two measures of 12 months language performance) after variance due to the social environment had been accounted for. If model 3 (social mediates physical) is valid, we would expect no unique contribution to be associated with the physical environment data set in this situation. These results are shown in table 15–4. As can be seen in both analyses, the results do not support the contention that the physical environment must be mediated by the social environment in order to have an impact upon language development (model 3). Rather, in both cases the physical environment data set adds unique predictive variance.

Summarizing across these two independent studies leads to the following conclusions. In neither study was the contention supported that the impact of the physical environment must be mediated by the social environment for cognitive development. Rather, the nature of the impact of the physical environment depends upon what aspect of the physical environment is being considered. In the case of physical environment parameters which are low-

Table 15–4

Maternal Verbal IQ, Social Environment, Physical Environment, SES, and Language Performance at 12 Months for the Total Sample: Significant Multiple Correlation and Squared Multiple Semipartial Correlation Coefficients

Step Variable	First Words[a]		Declarative Performance Level[b]	
	sR^2	F	sR^2	F
1 MIQ (maternal verbal IQ)	.01	.55 (df = 1/35)	.05	2.38 (df = 1/32)
2 Social environment data set	.24	2.88* (df = 5/32)	.43	3.91** (df = 8/32)
3 Physical environment data set	.32	5.51** (df = 5/32)	.15	2.69* (df = 5/32)
4 SES	.09	10.23** (df = 1/35)	.01	.35 (df = 1/32)

*$p < .05$.
**$p < .01$.
[a]$R = .82; F = 6.08$ (df = 12/35); $p < .01$.
[b]$R = .79; F = 3.68$ (df = 15/32); $p < .01$.

affordance, the results suggest *either a covariance process (model 2) or a process where the impact of the social environment is mediated by the physical environment (model 4).* For those aspects of the physical environment which are high-affordance, the results suggest an interaction with age. At 6 months the results suggest independent effects of the physical and social environments upon development (model 1). At 12 months the data suggest a covariance between the two dimensions of the environment, with *variation in development occurring not because of the contributions of the physical or social environments per se, but rather as a function of certain types of parents structuring the infant's environment in certain ways* (for example, parents who provide their infants with a variety of new play objects are also more likely to repeatedly name these objects for their infants).

The data thus far presented have first shown that specific dimensions of the infant's physical environment are related to various aspects of early development. These data have also shown that the physical environment is not necessarily dependent upon social environment for producing variability in children's performance. Given this, I present my final point, namely, that models of environmental action derived from studies of the physical environment may also be useful in explaining the nature of the relationship between the social environment and development.

Models of Environmental Action

Until very recently the predominant model of environmental action was what I have called the "Guinness" model. This title arrives from the old advertising slogan for Guinness Stout "Guinness is good for you." Note that in this slogan there are not qualifications. The makers of Guinness do not say, for example, that Guinness is good for your cardiovascular system but not good for your colon; they do not suggest that Guinness is good for you if you are 18 years but not good for you if you are only 18 months of age; they do not say that Guinness is good for you, only if you do not have a history of alcoholism in your family. Until recently a similar conceptual scheme occurred whenever researchers or clinicians talked about environmental impact. Good environments were good for all aspects of development for all children at all ages; similarly, bad environments were bad for all aspects of development for all children at all ages. The historical basis for this conceptualization of global environmental impacts has been traced by Hunt (1977) to the influence of the psychoanalytic and Gestalt theories.

In contrast to the above global model, data emerging from our research on the physical environment suggests two things. First there is a tremendous amount of specificity in environment-development relationships, with specific aspects of the physical environment predicting only specific aspects of development at specific ages for specific individuals. Secondly, the most appropriate model of environmental action is not the global model or a pure specificity model, but rather what we call the Bifactor Environmental Action Model (BEAM). BEAM postulates that a small subset of environmental parameters behave in global fashion in their influence upon development, while the majority of environmental parameters are highly specific in nature. One aspect of this model is shown in figure 15–2.

As an example of results from the study of the physical environment which led to these conclusions, table 15–5 summarizes relationships between specific physical environment parameters and specific aspects of Piagetian sensorimotor development across the second year of life (Wachs, 1979).[3] Physical environment parameters are shown on the vertical axis while the sensorimotor indices are shown on the horizontal axis. The numbers below refer to age periods, during which the particular environment-development correlations were statistically significant. These data support neither a global nor a purely specific model but rather illustrate the existence of a bifactor pattern of environmental action. Specifically, only the presence of auditory-visually responsive toys and ambient background noise are consistently related to most aspects of sensorimotor development across the second year of life. The majority of the physical environment dimensions are related only to specific aspects of development, or only to development at specific age periods.

It could be argued that such a pattern is unique to the physical environment. However data shown in table 15–6 dispells this notion. Table 15–6 presents a summary of results for specific aspects of the social environment and specific aspects of sensorimotor development across the second year of life (Wachs, 1984a). Congruent with the BEAM model, only vocal contin-

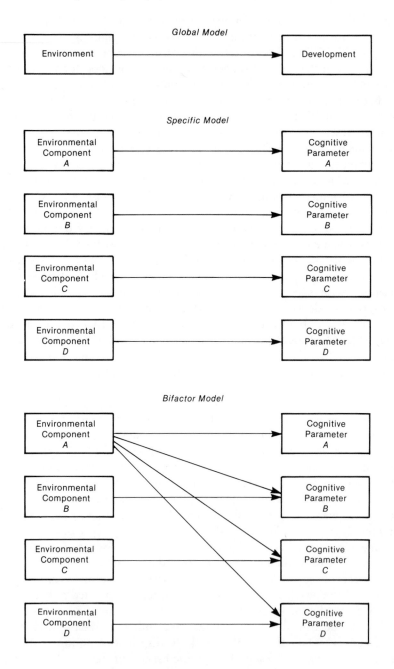

Figure 15–2. Models of Environmental Action

Table 15–5
Physical Environment Parameters and 12- to 24-Month Sensorimotor Development Summary of Cutting Score Analysis

Code	Sign	of	F	S	C	OIS	VI	GI
Number of audiovisually responsive toys	+	12–23	12–23	12–23	15–20	12–23		18–23
Noise rating	–	12–20	12–17		15–23	15–23	12–23	12–23
Rooms/people	+	12–17	12–17	12–23		12–23		
No physical restrictions on exploration	+	15–20	15–20		18–20			
Floor freedom	+	18–23	18–23				15–23	
Regularity—meals	+	12–17		12–20				
Stimulus shelter	+		18–23	12–23			12–23	15–20
Number of stimulus sources on	–		12–17					
Access to papers and books	–		12–17					
Number of strangers in home	–		15–17					
New toys	+			12–20				
Number of room decorations	+				12–20			
Toys in one place	–				12–17			
Number of people in home	+					12–23	12–17	
Mobile	–							

Note: Nine codes unrelated to development.

Table 15-6
Social Environment Parameters and 12- to 24-Month Sensorimotor Development Summary of Cutting Score Analysis

Code	Sign	of	F	S	C	OIS	VI	GI
Number of contingent verbal responses	+	12-20	15-20	12-23		12-23	12-23	11-20
Number of nonverbal contingent responses	-	12-23	12-17		15-17		12-23	15-23
Number of spontaneous sibling vocalizations	+		12-17	12-23	12-17	12-20		15-20
Amount time adult watching	-	12-17	12-17		12-17	12-23	15-20	12-17
Number of contingent vocal expansions	+		12-17	15-20	12-17			15-20
Interactions characterized by questions	+	12-20		12-23		12-23	12-20	
Affect characterized as neutral	+	12-20	12-20	12-23	18-20			15-20
Number of times known object referred to	+		12-20	15-20		12-23		
Number of contingent vocal comments	+		15-20	12-23			12-20	
Number of times food/drink given to child	-	15-23	15-23		15-17			
Interactions characterized by teaching	+			12-23		12-23	12-20	
Interactions characterized by praise	+			12-17	12-20		12-17	
Exploration encouraged	+C -GI			12-14				12-17
Number of spontaneous adult vocalizations	+		12-20	12-17				
Number of object names	+		12-20			12-20		

Variable	Sign							
Number of contingent vocal repetitions	+	12–17					12–23	12–23
Number of contingent questions	+						12–23	15–20
Amount of time child interacted with	+			15–23				
Adult ignores child initiation	−			12–20				
Adult rejects child reactions	−	12–14					18–23	
Slow response to distress	−	12–14						
Interactions characterized by coercion	+					12–20		12–20
Interactions characterized by nurturance	1		12–23			12–20		
Training stimuli not distinctive	−		18–23			18–23		
Affect characterized as negative	−	12–20	15–20					
Investment characterized as low	1			12–23		12–23		12–20
Vocalizing while active	+		12–27					
Interactions characterized by comments	+		12–14					
Interactions characterized as nonverbal	−		15–23					
Duration of physical contact	−				12–20			
Adult responds positively to child initiations	+				12–14			
Number of times objects demonstrated/explained	−						12–23	
Adult responds positively to child reactions	+						18–20	
Verbal "garbage"	+							15–20
Interaction characterized by denial	+							12–20
Adult not available	−							15–20

Note: Seventeen unrelated to development.

gencies are significantly related to most aspects of sensorimotor development across all age periods. Again, the majority of relationships are either age specific, development specific, or both age and development specific. While the data in table 15–6 come from my own research, reviews of data from other researchers clearly support the existence of both specificity in environment-development relationships and the validity of the BEAM model rather than the pure global or pure specificity models of environmental action (Wachs & Gruen, 1982; Wachs, in press).

Another aspect of the bifactor model which emerged initially from our research on the physical environment is the possibility of individual differences in responsivity to the environment (organism-environment interaction). In spite of evidence to the contrary, especially from intervention studies, most theories have assumed a global model of environmental action, namely, that the same environmental stimulation will have the same impact upon all individuals exposed to the stimulation (Wachs & Gruen, 1982). In contrast, the BEAM model hypothesizes that while there is a small subset of environmental parameters which influence all individuals in the same way, the impact of the great majority of environmental parameters will be mediated by the characteristics of the individual upon whom the environment impacts. This is shown in figure 15–3.

An introduction of the concept of individual differences in reactivity may seem incongruent with the main theme of this book, namely, the contribution of play materials and parent involvement to child development. This theme suggests a global model. However, if the bifactor model is correct, then focusing *solely* on play material and parent involvement without considering the child may lead to highly misleading conclusions about the contributions of play materials and parent involvement.

What evidence do we have that the impact of the physical and social environment will be mediated by the individual characteristics of the child? Unfortunately it is not easy to answer this question because earlier environmental studies were not designed to consider individual differences in reactivity. Further, with certain exceptions (Murphy & Moriarty, 1974; Wachs, 1977) there has been little consideration as to which individual difference parameters serve to mediate the impact of the environment upon development. For this reason much of my recent research has involved identification of individual difference parameters which may mediate the impact of the environment, rather than model testing per se. However, it was the study of sex differences in reactivity to the physical environment which first defined the individual differences component of the bifactor model.

Ample evidence for differential male-female environment-development correlations can be found in the literature. However, the value of most of these studies for illustrating differential reactivity is minimal because no provision was made to test whether the different male-female environment-

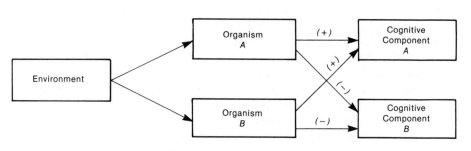

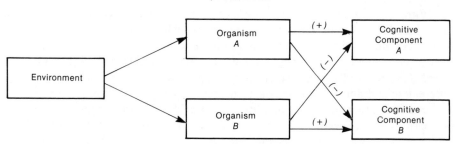

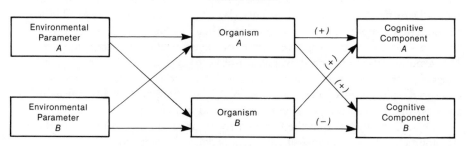

Figure 15–3. Models of Organism–Environment Interaction

development correlations were due to differential reactivity or to the possibility of different environments being provided to male and female infants (for example, Honzik, 1967a, 1967b). We have made this distinction in our own research, however, initially with the physical environment (Wachs, 1979), and later with the social environment (Wachs, 1984a). Our results suggest the existence of differential reactivity by males and females to similar environmental circumstances. For example, our results for the physical environment indicate that male infants are more sensitive to the impact of ambient noise, whereas females are more sensitive to long-term variety in the environment. Our social environment data suggest that males may be more sensitive to a lack of social interactions, whereas females may be more sensitive to interactions that inhibit the development of a sense of autonomy. Reviews of other research studies of environmental influences support the hypothesis that certain environmental parameters will have differential impact upon males and females, both with infants and toddlers (Wachs & Gruen, 1982), and with older children (Wachs, in press).

Within the framework of the bifactor model, my most recent research on individual differences in reactivity has moved away from the parameter of sex differences, and in the direction of more theoretically relevant individual difference parameters, such as temperament. Thomas and Chess (1976) hypothesized that the child's temperament may act as a mediator, with children of different temperaments processing environmental input in different ways. Unfortunately, there has been very little empirical follow-up on their hypothesis until recently. Several of my recent studies bear on this topic. One of our studies illustrates an interesting convergence between our results on temperament as a mediator and other research data with high-risk infants. This convergence is shown in figure 15–4.

The left side of figure 15–4 reports data from Field (1981), comparing full-term with preterm infants. Field suggests that preterm infants have a narrower arousal range than full-term infants, as exemplified by a raised attentional threshold and a lowered aversion threshold. Our data, presented on the right side of figure 15–4 compare temperamentally easy with temperamentally difficult 6-month-old infants (Wachs & Gandour, 1983). These results show a similar pattern, with more difficult infants being *more reactive* than easy infants to the negative aspects of the environment such as ambient background noise (a lowered aversion threshold) and *less reactive* to positive aspects of the environment such as social interactions (a raised attentional threshold). These differences occur even though there are no differences in the environments of temperamentally easy and difficult babies.

These data suggest that there is a narrower arousal range common to the development of risk infants (whether risk is defined either biomedically as in the case of prematurity, or in terms of biobehavioral characteristics such as difficult temperament. This narrow arousal range implies that the same stim-

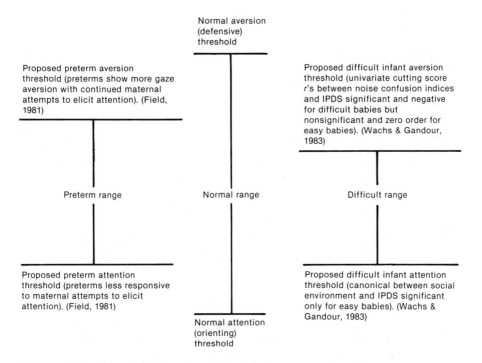

Normal aversion
(defensive)
threshold

Proposed preterm aversion
threshold (preterms show more gaze
aversion with continued maternal
attempts to elicit attention). (Field,
1981)

Proposed difficult infant aversion
threshold (univariate cutting score
r's between noise confusion indices
and IPDS significant and negative
for difficult babies but
nonsignificant and zero order for
easy babies). (Wachs & Gandour,
1983)

Preterm range   Normal range   Difficult range

Proposed preterm attention
threshold (preterms less responsive
to maternal attempts to elicit
attention). (Field, 1981)

Proposed difficult infant attention
threshold (canonical between social
environment and IPDS significant
only for easy babies). (Wachs &
Gandour, 1983)

Normal attention
(orienting)
threshold

**Figure 15–4. Attention-Aversion Thresholds in At-Risk and
Nonrisk Infants**

ulation may have different effects on risk and nonrisk populations. These
results also suggest that appropriate intervention might be used with risk
infants to compensate for this narrow arousal range. For example, in a just
completed dissertation by a graduate student of mine (Peters-Martin, 1984),
mothers of premature infants were trained not only to emphasize positive
social interactions, but also to limit stimulation when the infant was showing
aversive reactions. Preterm infants receiving this procedure showed more
optimal development than did preterms whose mothers were trained in intervention strategies which were not specifically tailored to the infants' individual characteristics.

Providing further support for the theory that temperament may act as a
mediator of environmental influences are the results from recently completed
studies indicating that temperamentally difficult infants react differently than
do temperamentally easy infants when exposed to standard laboratory procedures (Wachs & Smitherman, in press), and that the impact of the physical
and temporal organization of the home environment upon cognitive performance is mediated by the activity level of the infant (Peters-Martin & Wachs,

1984). Our data from this latter study are congruent with earlier results by Schaffer (1966), indicating that active infants are better able to tolerate prolonged hospitalization than are inactive babies, in terms of the impact of the hospitalization upon cognitive function.

Another potential individual differences parameter, relates to the distinction between children who are primarily object-oriented and those who are primarily socially-oriented. This distinction has appeared in several studies. Nelson's (1981) work on early language development distinguishes between referential and expressive children. The work of Shotwell, Wolf, and Gardner (1980) on the development of symbolization in toddlers and preschoolers distinguishes between patterners and dramatists. Nakamura and Finck (1980) distinguish between social- and task-oriented children in classroom situations. All of these studies center around the common theme that there are two distinct clusters of children, one whose development is characterized primarily by interest in and interaction with objects, the other whose development is characterized primarily by interest in and interaction with persons.

My own interest in this potential individual difference parameter came from Yarrow's initial work on the development of mastery (competence) motivation in toddlers. Intrigued by inconsistencies in the relationship between environment and mastery behavior (Wachs, 1984b), it became apparent that most available studies in the area (Gaiter et al., 1981; Jennings, et al., 1979; Yarrow et al., 1982, 1984) were attempting to predict *object mastery* from parent-child *social interactions*. Such an approach is valid only if we assume that parent-child social interactions operate in a global fashion, in terms of promoting the child's desire to master objects regardless of the child's own orientation. However, if some children are motivated primarily by interaction with objects, while other children are motivated primarily by interaction with persons, variability in mastery behavior as a function of social interactions (using the bifactor model) should occur only for the latter group of children.

As a first test of the validity of this hypothesis it would be necessary to make the same object-social distinction for mastery behavior as has been made in other domains. To do this we coded the object and social mastery behaviors of 12-month-olds in both a free and structured play session. Our results (Wachs, 1984b) support the generalizability of the object-social dichotomy to mastery motivation; specifically, the correlations between object and social mastery behavior within or across play situations were either zero order or negative, as shown in figure 15–5. Encouraged by the generalizability of this dichotomy, we are currently designing a study involving the inter-relationship between infants' physical and social environments and their object/social mastery motivation behavior. Our prediction is that children who are object-oriented will be primarily reactive to the physical

Object Codes: 3 = object premastery behavior

                        4 = object mastery behavior

Social Codes: 6 = social mastery behaviors

                        7 = social orientation behaviors

Structured Play

	3	4	6	7
7	−.20	−.17	.26	
6	−.01	.14	—	
4	.72	—		
3	—			

Free Play

	3	4	6	7
7	−.60	−.37	.60	
6	−.67	−.19	—	
4	.62	—		
3	—			

Structured Play

Free Play	6	7
4	.12	−.23
3	−.05	−.13

Free Play

Structured Play	6	7
4	−.44	−.21
3	−.47	−.44

Figure 15–5. Interrelationship of Infants' Object and Social Mastery Behaviors in Structured and Free Play Activities

aspects of the environment, whereas children who are socially-oriented will be primarily reactive to the social aspects of the environment.

Conclusion

To paraphrase the old Homeric saying: whom the gods would destroy they first let speculate on incomplete data sets. At the risk of destruction let me attempt to tie this object/social orientation dichotomy to both the theme of this volume and to the larger issue of environmental action.

The theme of this book is the contribution of play materials and parental involvement to children's development. However, as research is increasingly showing, this main effects question of how play or interaction per se influence development is an inadequate approach to the problem. Rather than examine the global relationship of the environment to child development I propose that it is more productive to ask, *what components of the environment for which children?* Using the social-object dichotomy as an example, if a child is primarily object oriented, optimal development should occur for this child primarily when the child encounters a physically rich environment, encompassing a variety of age appropriate responsive objects. In contrast, if this child is forced into an environment characterized primarily by social interactions, a mismatch between organism and environment would occur which could hinder the child's development. Similarly, emphasizing toys to a socially oriented child would increase the probability of mismatch between child and environment, whereas emphasizing social interactions would more likely facilitate development. Such speculation is congruent with what we now know about environmental action.

Looking at the question of environmental influences more broadly the evidence I have presented on the physical environment and the bifactor model calls for changes in orientation at both theory and public policy levels. In terms of theory, we have for the most part reified the law of parsimony in canonizing main effect models of environmental action. However, properly interpreted, the law of parsimony does not refer to the simplest explanation per se, but rather the simplest explanation given the nature of the phenomena. As McCall and McGhee (1977) have noted, there is no a priori reason to assume that nature is necessarily parsimonious when it comes to human development. Given the available evidence supporting the concepts of environmental specificity and nonuniform responses to the environment at both the infrahuman (Globus, 1975; Greenough & Juraska, 1979; Sackett, Rubenthal, Fahrenbruch, Holm, & Greenough, 1981) and human levels (Wachs, 1984c; in press), environmental models which stress only main effects (as seen in the use of global terms like "maternal deprivation" or "optimal maternal care") at best greatly oversimplify the role of environment upon development. It is important to move away from global main effect theories to more interactive theories that consider the joint contribution of both the organism and the environment (Wachs, 1983).

A similar statement can be made of environmental intervention programs for children with various types of cognitive or social deficits. The prevalent intervention approaches have been main effect, wherein all children in a given program are exposed to a heterogeneous mass of so-called enriched experiences. The literature uniformly shows that the most frequent outcome of this "enrichment" is small mean group gains and major variability within groups (Wachs & Gruen, 1982; Wachs, in press). Ignoring the possibility of different outcomes with different types of stimulation or of individual differences in response to intervention risks not only the program (loss of funding based on disappointing results) but also the children, some of whom may be receiving in appropriate environmental experiences.

In closing, it may seem that I have muddied what some have thought was a fairly simple and clear-cut question: the relation or environment to development. If that is correct then I have accomplished my purpose. Hopefully, future theories and interventions will consider simultaneously both the physical and social aspects of the child's environment. Hopefully, future theories and interventions will also consider the possibility of differential impact of the environment upon cognitive development as a function of the age of the child, the environmental conditions under study, and the individual characteristics of the child.

Notes

1. To readers the distinction between low and high affordance stimuli may seem speculative and unnecessary, given the more obvious distinction between foreground and background stimuli. However, the potential importance of the construct of affordances makes it important to at least attempt to apply this model to our data.

2. Although, as Wohlwill (personal communication) has noted, theoretically within a Hebbian framework low-affordance background stimulation items need not be negatively related to development.

3. The patterns of environment-development correlations shown in tables 15–5 and 15–6 emerged after we had eliminated those correlations which appeared to be random in nature, via use of a "cutting score" procedure (Wachs, 1979).

References

Belsky, J., Goode, M., & Most, R. 1980. Maternal stimulation and infant exploratory competence. *Child Development* 51:1163–1170.

Bronfenbrenner, U. 1977. Toward an experimental ecology of human development. *American Psychologist* 72:513–521.

Carew, J. 1980. Experience and the development of intelligence in young children at home and in daycare. *Monographs of the Society for Research in Child Development, 45,* no. 186.

Clarke-Stewart, K. 1973. Interactions between mothers and their young children: Characteristics and consequences. *Monographs of the Society for Research in Child Development,* 38, Nos. 6 and 7.

Field, T. 1981. Infant arousal, attention and affect during early interaction. In L. Lipsitt (Ed.), *Advances in infant behavior and development,* Norwood, N.J.: Ablex.

Gaiter, J., Morgan, G., Jennings, K., Harmon, R., & Yarrow, L. 1982. Variety of cognitively oriented caregiver activities: Relationship to cognitive and motivational functioning at 1 and 3½ years of age. *Journal of Genetic Psychology* 141: 49–56.

Gibson, E.J. 1982. The concept of affordance in development. In W. Collins (Ed.), *Minnesota Symposium on Child Psychology,* (Vol. 15). Hillsdale, N.J.: Erlbaum.

Gibson, J. 1979. *The ecological approach to visual perception.* Boston: Houghton Mifflin.

Globus, A. 1975. Brain morphology as a function of presynaptic morphology and activity. In A. Reisen (Ed.), *The developmental neuropsychology of sensory deprivation.* New York: Academic Press.

Gottfried, A.W. 1984. Home environment and early cognitive development: Integration, meta-analysis and conclusions. In A.W. Gottfried (Ed.) *Home environment and early cognitive development: Longitudinal research.* New York: Academic Press.

Greenough, W., & Juraska, J. 1979. Experience-induced changes in brain size and structure. In M. Hahn, C. Jensen & B. Dudek (Eds.), *Development and evolution of brain size,* New York: Academic Press.

Heft, H. In press. High residential density and perceptual cognitive development. In J. Wohlwill & W. VanVliet (Eds.), *Habitats for children: The impact of density,* Hillsdale, N.J.: Erlbaum.

Honzik, M. 1967a. Environmental correlates of mental growth: Prediction from the family setting at 21 months. *Child Development* 38:337–364.

———. 1967b. Prediction of differential abilities at age 18 from the early family environment. *Proceedings of the American Psychological Association* 2:151–152.

Hunt, J.M. 1977. Specificity in early development and experience. O'Neill invited lecturer. Myer Children's Rehabilitation Institute. University of Nebraska Medical Center.

Jennings, K., Harmon, R., Morgan, G., Gaiter, J., & Yarrow, L. 1979. Exploratory play as an index of mastery motivation. *Developmental Psychology* 15:36–375.

Kellegan, T. 1977. Relationship between home environment and scholastic behavior in a disadvantaged population. *Journal of Educational Psychology* 69:754–760.

McCall, R., & McGhee, P. 1977. The discrepancy hypothesis of attention and affect in infants. In I. Uzgiris & F. Weizman (Eds.), *The structuring of experience,* New York: Plenum Press.

MacPhee, D., Ramey, C., & Yeates, K. 1984. The home environment and early mental development. In P.W. Gottfried, (Ed.) *Home environment and early cognitive development: Longitudinal research.* New York: Academic Press.

McSwain, R. 1981. Care and conflict in infant development. *Infant Behavior and Development* 4:225–246.

Murphy, L., & Moriarty, A. 1974. *Vulnerability, coping and growth.* New Haven: Yale University Press.

Nakamura, C., & Finck, D. 1980. Relative effectiveness of socially oriented and task-oriented children and predictability of their behaviors. *Monographs for the Society for Research in Child Development.* Vol. 45.

Nelson, K. 1981. Individual differences in language development. *Developmental Psychology* 17:170–187.

Parke, R. 1978. Children's home environment: Social and cognitive affects. In I. Altman, & J. Wohlwill (Ed.), *Children and the environment.* New York: Plenum Press.

Peters-Martin, P. 1984. *Effects of hospital-based intervention with mothers of preterm infants on mother-infant interaction and maternal self-confidence.* Unpublished doctoral dissertation, Purdue University.

Peters-Martin, T., & Wachs, T.D. 1984. A longitudinal study of temperament and its correlates in the first 12 months. *Infant Behavior and Development* 285–298.

Provence, S., & Lipton, R. 1962. *Infants in institutions.* New York: International Universities Press.

Sackett, G., Rubenthal, G. Fahrenbruch, C., Holm, R., & Greenough, W. 1981. Social isolation rearing effects in monkeys vary with genotype. *Developmental Psychology* 17:313–318.

Schaffer, H. 1966. Activity level as a constitutional determinant of infantile reaction to deprivation. *Child Development* 37:595–602.

Shotwell, J., Wolf, D., & Gardner, H. 1980. Styles of achievement in early symbol use. In M. Foster, & S. Brandes (Ed.), *Symbol as sense.* New York: Academic Press.

Thomas, A., & Chess, S. 1976. Behavioral individuality in childhood. In L. Aronson, E. Tobach, D. Lehrman, & J. Rosenblatt (Ed.), *Development and evolution of behavior.* San Francisco: Freeman.

Wachs, T.D. 1977. The optimal stimulation hypotheses and early development. In I. Uzgiris, & F. Weizmann (Eds.), *The structuring of experience.* New York: Plenum Press.

———. 1979. Proximal experience and early cognitive intellectual development: The physical environment. *Merrill-Palmer Quarterly* 25:3–41.

———. 1983. The use and abuse of environment in behavior genetics research. *Child Development* 54:396–408.

———. 1984a. Proximal early experience and early cognitive intellectual development: The social environment. In A.W. Gottfried (Ed.), *Home environment and early cognitive development: Longitudinal research.* New York: Academic Press.

———. 1984b. *Mastery motivation as a potential individual differences parameter.* Paper presented at NICHD workshop on measurement and conceptualization of mastery motivation, Bethesda, Md.

———. 1984c. Individual differences in infant memory: Forgotten but not gone. In R. Kail, & N. Spear (Ed.), *Cognitive perspectives on the development of memory.* Hillsdale, N.J.: Erlbaum.

———. In press. Environment and the development of competence in children. *Monographs of the World Health Organization.*

Wachs, T.D., & Chan, A. 1984. *Physical and social environment correlates of three aspects of 12-month language functioning.* Paper presented at the biennial meeting of The Society for Research in Child Development, Toronto.

Wachs, T.D., Francis, J., & McQuiston, S. 1979. Psychological dimensions of the infant's physical environment. *Infant Behavior and Development* 2:155–161.

Wachs, T.D., & Gandour, M. 1983. Temperament, environment and 6 months cognitive intellectual development. *International Journal of Behavioral Development* 6:135–152.

Wachs, T.D., & Gruen, G. 1982. *Early experience and human development.* New York: Plenum Press.

Wachs, T.D., & Smitherman, C. In Press. Infant temperament and subject loss in an habituation procedure. *Child Development.*

Wohlwill, J. 1983. Physical and social environment as factors in development. In D. Magnusson & V. Allen (Eds.), *Human development: An interactional perspective.* New York: Academic Press.

Woodson, R., & daCosta-Woodson, I. 1984. Social organization, physical environment and infant-caregiver interaction. *Developmental Psychology* 20:473–476.

Yarrow, L., Morgan, G., Jennings, K., Harmon, R., & Gaiter, J. 1982. Infants' persistence at tasks: Relationship to cognitive functioning and early experience. *Infant Behavior and Development* 5:131–141.

Yarrow, L.J., McQuiston, S., MacTurk, R., McCarthy, M.E., Klein, R.P., & Vietze, P.M. 1983. Assessment of mastery motivation during the first year of life. *Developmental Psychology* 19:151–171.

Yarrow, L., Rubenstein, J., & Pedersen, F. 1975. *Infant and environment.* New York: Wiley.

Zajonc, R. 1983. Validating the confluence model. *Psychological Bulletin* 93: 457–480.

16

Parent-Infant Interaction and Infants' Social-Emotional Development

Leila Beckwith

From the beginning of human history up to the present century, the dominant issue in parenting has been to ensure the physical survival of the infant—to feed, to clothe, to protect. Only recently has "fun morality" emerged as a significant dimension to be considered in parenting and infant care (Wolfenstein, 1955). What the baby wants and what gives him/her pleasure is now as legitimate a demand as what the baby needs.

Fun morality, as identified by Wolfenstein (1955), permeates American culture today. Play, amusement, fun, enjoying oneself is no longer considered, as the Puritans did, potentially wicked. The fear of being too impulsive has been replaced by lowered self-esteem occasioned by failure to have fun. Play and work, which in the past were more separate, with the danger of sin associated with one and virtue with the other, are now more fused. Personal relations, which in the past were irrelevant to work, are now mandatory or, at least, desirable with work associates. Personal qualities such as likability or warmth, also formerly irrelevant to work, are increasingly required to get along in the corporate structure. Play is now judged by standards of achievement previously used only in regard to work: play must be done with skill; play is beneficial.

Infant rearing, which in the past was characterized as serious work, is now increasingly characterized in terms of pleasure. Patience and self-control as psychological requirements for parents have been replaced by a required quality of enjoyment. Parents must not only do the right thing but they must do it with the right feeling.

Infants' wishes, which in the past were distinguished from infants' needs, are now explicitly equated. Hedonic impulses, for example, "affectance pleasure," are now seen to organize and propel infant development. Infants' play thereby becomes intermixed with infants' work, which is to explore the environment and to learn.

The new fun morality has an increasing emphasis in developmental research. This chapter addresses one aspect of that burgeoning interest, parent-infant social play and its implications for infant social and emotional development. From the earliest months of an infant's life, an infant and its parents are likely to play together. What they choose to play and how may be exquisitely tuned to the infant's developing cognitive and motoric capacities and both reflect and enhance developing social competence.

Position of Social Play in Parent-Infant Interaction

Multiple Functions of Parent-Infant Interaction

The importance of social experience for infants' development is no longer questioned, but which aspects and with what consequences are unclear. Attachment theory argues that the essential function of the primary social relationship between parent and infant is to promote the physical survival of the infant, especially by protecting him from predators (Ainsworth, 1973; Bowlby, 1969).

Positive affect is central to Bowlby and Ainsworth's conceptualizations of the attachment system, but it is negative affect that tends to be emphasized. The parent in her attachment behavior reassures, consoles, and provides comfort. By her behavior and presence, she reduces stress and anxiety. If the infant shows avoidance and resistance to physical contact with the parent after separation, then insecure attachment is indicated. If the infant fusses or cries in the mother's presence in a strange environment, then insecure attachment is also likely (Ainsworth, Blehar, Waters, & Wall, 1978). However, if the infant is securely attached and conditions for activation of attachment behavior are absent or at a low level, then the infant is likely to turn from the parent to engage in exploratory play in the environment.

The emphasis in social play between parent and infant is to interest and delight one another. If social play is characterized by high affective level, mutual pleasure, and shared codes of conduct, then does it have different consequences for infant development than other social exchanges between parent and infant? Is it a subset of attachment behavior or is it a separate behavioral system characterized by affiliative behavior and sociability (Lamb, 1982)?

Infrequency of Social Play

Social play is relatively infrequent. When parents are videotaped in a laboratory situation and specifically asked to play with their infants, they may do so at an increased rate, but social play at home probably occupies only a small part of an infant's day. Does the small amount of time spent diminish the consequences for the infant? I suggest that the impact is neither negligible nor in proportion to its frequency. Mutual visual regard also occurs infrequently, even at its height in 3- to 4-month-old infants, but its occurrence has far-reaching consequences in the link to the development of secure attachment (Blehar, Lieberman, & Ainsworth, 1977), and to increased competence (Beckwith & Cohen, 1984).

Difficulty of Differentiating the Influence of Social Play from Other Parent-Infant Exchanges

On a practical level, it is difficult to differentiate the influence of social play from the influence of infant-parent social exchanges that occur in other than play contexts. While parents differ widely in their repertoire of games, the sensitivity with which they play them, and their propensity to do so (Stern, 1974), it is likely that those differences are reflected in the degree to which caregivers are attentive, sensitive, and contingently responsive to infant signals in other contexts.

Research supports that conjecture. In one study, social play was found to load on an "optimal" maternal factor (Clarke-Stewart, 1973). Our own study (Beckwith, Cohen, Kopp, Parmelee, & Marcy, 1976) loaded on a factor named "social" that explained most of the variance in caregiver-infant interaction. In another study social play was found to correlate with a high frequency of stimulation with objects and a generalized intensified maternal involvement (Pettit & Bates, 1984)

Tutoring and Social Play

Social play itself may have several functions, including promoting cognitive skills. Although it is difficult to identify and separate a parent's goals, either in helping the infant master the environment or in eliciting and sharing positive affect, it is useful to differentiate the tutoring relationship (Bruner, 1982) from purposefully playful interaction. First, since social play is a more potent elicitor of positive affect than is play with toys (Yarrow, McQuiston, MacTurk, McCarthy, Klein, & Vietze, 1983), it is likely that the intensity of affect will differ. Second, the present emphasis on competence, particularly in the middle-class, may diminish parents' engagements in social games in favor of educational stimulation. It may be that the emphasis on mastering the environment may slow the process of learning affect regulation and communication. While there is evidence that infants are in some ways more developmentally advanced now than in the past, we do not know if that extends to the mastery of social/affective information.

Multiple Functions of Social Play

There are several very important ways in which play between infants and parents promotes social competence. Social play allows passive experience in social situations to be turned into active mastery by selecting one part of the infant's life for the infant to practice with pleasure rather than with the negative feelings that accompany the real life event (Sutton-Smith, 1974, 1980). For example, in the game of peekaboo, in which the issue is disappearance and return, the parent does not really separate from the infant and the infant does not show separation distress. Social play, thereby, helps the child master tension-arousing experiences as well as helps the child understand the boundary between real and make-believe (Bruner & Sherwood, 1976).

To play is not only to learn actions but to practice emotions, like surprise, anticipation, excitement, and climax. Parents alter their play behavior in accord with the infant's affective signals and their signs of attention or inattention (Stern, 1974). The affective systems of infant and parent are the primary means of regulating joint exchanges (Tronick, 1982). The infant signals its affective state; the parent responds to those signals; the infant responds to the parent's signals. Prior to verbal communication, the infant's affect is the only reliable representation of the saliency and meaning of events and thereby constitutes the primary medium of communication.

Social play is a cooperative interchange in which infants learn to influence others (Ross & Kay, 1980). In social play, infants' gestures and actions are responded to and acquire meaning. Repetition, a salient aspect of social play, also allows infants to anticipate and thereby control the parents' behavior (Gustafson, Green, & West, 1979).

Social play also preempts attention. One partner becomes the focus of attention of the other, or both share the same focus of attention, thereby promoting the basis of joint exchanges (Spitz, 1972).

Social play involving organized integrated sequences of actions is rule governed. Infants in the acquisition of game skills amplify their understanding of rules and foster their acquisition of rules of language (Lewis & Cherry, 1977; Ross & Kay, 1980).

Process of Parent-Infant Social Play

Parents Help Infants

Parents select games to play before their infant has the necessary skills to do so, and the parent enables the infant to play the game. Furthermore, it is likely that parents' play (face-to-face interaction, gonna get you, pat-a-cake, horsie, peekaboo, ball, build tower–knock down, give and take, point and name, so big, and other pretend play) is finely tuned to the infant's developmental level. To the extent that this is so, it indicates an acute awareness on the adult's part of an infant's emerging skills.

The parent provides the scaffold for the infant's emerging skills (Bruner,

1982) in what is done, when it is done, and the affect with which it is done. Initially, minimal participation on the part of the infant is accepted. Infants are only expected to show attention and amusement. Kaye (1982) describes the way in which a parent interprets anything a young infant does as a turn in the game. If the infant does nothing, then the parent takes the turn or tries to coax one out of the infant.

The parent models the climax of the game as well as the subroutines, and does so slowly and with conspicuous affect and vocal marking. The parent pauses for the infant to take a turn, and by repetitive verbalizations marks the end of the parent's turn and the beginning of the infant's turn (Bruner, 1977).

Parents use attention-getting behaviors in early rounds of a game. They position the child and limit the child's arena so that the child focuses on the game. The parent gives clues as to the child's role, for example, in the game of roll the ball, holding out a hand to clue the child to return the ball to the adult (Hodapp, Goldfield, & Boyatzis, 1984).

Games Change as the Infant Matures

As the necessary active infant skills in a game emerge, that game becomes more frequent, reaching its height when the necessary infant skills converge. Face-to-face interaction is at its maximum at 3 to 4 months of age when the major skills of gaze, externally generated smiling, and cooing become integrated (Stern, 1974). In those early months, games of tickling, horsie, or I'm going to get you, in which the infant's part is to attend and to enjoy but not to be motorically active, are common (Gustafson, Green, & West, 1979). From 4 months on, games become motorically more complex as the infant achieves greater motor skills (Crawley, Rogers, Friedman, Iacobbo, Criticos, Richardson, & Thompson, 1978). Peekaboo and pat-a-cake, in which infants have an active motoric role, become frequent from 7 to 12 months, peaking at 8 months and decreasing by 12 months. Only at 12 months do games with toys, such as give and take, build and smash, and point and name occur (Crawley & Sherrod, 1984).

A particular game goes into a refractory period when the infant achieves competence in it, although the structure of that game may emerge later in the infant's invention of a new game. Thus, face-to-face interaction decreases by 5 months as the infant turns his attention outward to manipulating objects. Children resist playing peekaboo from 11 to 14 months, but then can be observed to play hiding objects on their own (Bruner, 1982).

Even in the same game, infants become more active participants as they mature. In peekaboo, for example, 6-month-olds never initiate hiding. It is the parent who mainly hides herself and who removes the cover. At 8 months, infants assume an active role about half of the time. By 14 months, infants initiate the hiding most of the time, both hiding themselves, and removing the cover (Ratner & Bruner, 1978). By 15 to 18 months infants invent new games, such as hiding objects.

Games Promote Positive Affect

One of the major goals for the parent in social play is to maintain an optimal range of attention and arousal in which the infant is most likely to manifest positive affect (Stern, 1974). Brazelton, Koslowski, and Main (1974) describe how very young infants in the early game of face-to-face interaction, when interacting with a sensitive adult, proceed through a predictable sequence of increasing involvement culminating in positive affect expression. Young infants 8-week-olds emit about equal numbers of happy, interested, and sad expressions during face-to-face interaction with their mother, but by 12 weeks they emit approximately twice the number of happy as interested and sad expressions. Surprised expressions occur very infrequently, and angry, afraid, and ashamed expressions never occur (Field & Walden, 1982). Adults elicit and reinforce positive affect in infants. They do so by emitting happy expressions more frequently than negative expressions and by reinforcing positive affect rather than negative affect in the infant. Whereas infants in face-to-face play displace a wide range of expressions and a very high rate of change, maternal expressions are limited to positive emotions, especially toward young infants. Mothers respond contingently to only about 25 percent of infant expressive changes and tend not to acknowledge infant negative expressions (Malatesta & Haviland, 1982).

Infants Enjoy Games

The degree to which games with parents interest and delight infants has been studied by ingenious experimental interventions in which games are interrupted or altered by changing contingencies or the partner's affect. It is evident that infants enjoy playing games, particularly with their parents, and are unhappy about disruptions in the parent's pacing, contingency, and affect. For example, 2-month-olds were videotaped in face-to-face interaction with their mother and then in her absence, as well as in face-to-face interaction with a stranger and then in the stranger's absence (Fogel, Diamond, Langhorst, & Demos, 1982). Already at 2 months, infants showed more distress and crying when their mother interrupted the game than when the stranger did. In another study, when the parent was asked to maintain a silent unresponsive face after a bout of more natural face-to-face interaction (Tronick, Als, Adamson, Wise, & Brazelton, 1978), infants, after a few unsuccessful attempts to regain the mother's participation, looked away and shrank down in their seats.

An even clearer demonstration of the importance of the maternal affective display to the infant's affect was shown in studies in which the mother was asked to engage in face-to-face interaction in a depressed way with a depressed face (Cohn & Tronick, 1982; Tronick, Ricks, & Cohn, 1982). During the depressed condition, 3-month-old infants were more wary, protested more, and hardly played. The differences persisted even after the mothers resumed their normal interactions, indicating that infants paid attention to their partner's affective displays and that the partner's affect regulated the infant's affect.

Although in general infants may prefer play with their parent to play with a strange adult, even with strange adults infants become unhappy at interruption. In a study with 12-month-old infants involved in play with strangers, the infants' behavior during bouts of uninterrupted play were compared to that during and after an imposed ten-second interruption, in which the strange adult stopped playing but maintained a pleasant expression. During the interruption, infants showed less positive affect.

Infants Discriminate Affect

Young infants discriminate facial expressions and prefer happy expressions to all others. Field and Walden (1982) reported a study with neonates in which an examiner, using a trials-to-criterion habituation paradigm with a Latin square order, maintained each of three affect expressions, happy, sad, and surprised, for as many trials until the infant looked at the examiner's face for less than two seconds. Longer looking time was observed for the happy than the sad or surprised expressions, and the infants required a greater number of trials to habituate to the surprised expression. Using a habituation recovery paradigm with slides of facial expressions of happiness, sadness, and surprise, 3-month-old infants discriminated between the happy and surprised expressions and occasionally between the surprised and sad expressions (Young-Browne, Rosenfeld, & Horowitz, 1977). Seven-month olds have been able to make generalized discriminations of facial expressions of more than one model, thereby noting the invariant features that characterize an expression, even when the other stimulus features of the face change (Caron & Caron, 1981). In this paradigm infants do discriminate between happy and negative expressions. They show a faster rate of habituation to happy expressions, and more frequently discriminate among positive faces (happy, surprise) than among negative faces (sad, angry, fearful).

Additional information that the infant appraises the affect displays of the parents and uses it as a mediator, elicitor, and regulator of the infant's own emotions and behavior is shown in the studies of social referencing (Emde & Sorce, 1983), which emerges in the 5- to 9-month period (Campos & Sternberg, 1981). Although social referencing occurs in situations of uncertainty, as contrasted with social games marked by positive affect, social referencing is a further demonstration of the significance of the parent's affect in regulating the infant's affect.

Relationship of Parental Play and Positive Affect to Infant Attachment

Several studies indicate that infants are more involved with parents who are more fun. The more playful a mother, the more positive affect she displays during interaction with the infant, the more the infant will be socially responsive to her and the more he will show positive affect. When mothers were asked to play with their 5- and 8-month old infants in a laboratory situation, those mothers who played more games with their infants had infants who engaged in more mutual visual regard with them and who, at 8 months, smiled more at them (Crawley et al., 1978). Clarke-Stewart (1973) found that mothers who showed more positive emotion to their toddlers had children who expressed more happiness and were more positively involved with their mothers (See figure 16–1).

Infants who have had more fun with their mothers become more securely attached. Mothers who during naturalistic home observations were noted to be more playful and more emotionally expressive during face-to-face interactions with their young infants had infants who smiled and bounced more in face-to-face bouts and who, nine months later, were more likely to be securely attached (Blehar, Lieberman, & Ainsworth, 1977). Thus, securely attached infants were more likely to have mothers who were more playful and who paced their behavior more contingently during early face-to-face interaction, whereas insecurely attached infants were more likely to have mothers who were abrupt, acted in a routine manner, and were silent and unsmiling.

Securely attached infants may during early face-to-face interactions be building up a model of a responsive partner, one with whom the infant makes positive efforts to be engaged. Tronick et al. (1982) found that infants who at 12 months were judged to be securely attached had at 6 months, in a laboratory situation in which their mothers were instructed to maintain a still face, made many more positive elicitations of their mother than had insecurely attached infants.

Similar to the association of maternal positive affect and infant secure attachment, is the association found between maternal negative affect and infant insecure attachment. Mothers who were rated more tense and irritable in their early interactions with their infants were later more likely to have infants who were judged to be anxiously attached and specifically avoidant (Egeland & Farber, 1984).

Main (1973), analyzing the narrative report data from Ainsworth's study of attachment (Ainsworth, 1979) found that mothers whose babies at 12

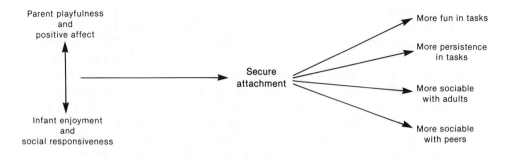

Figure 16–1. Positive Affect, Attachment, Task Behavior, and Sociability

months were noted to be insecurely/avoidantly attached had been significantly less emotionally expressive during interaction with their child throughout the whole of the first year than were mothers whose children were securely attached. Mothers of avoidant babies displayed a remarkable lack of facial expression when watching or in interaction with their infants. The interpretation was made that repressed or suppressed anger or rigidity and compulsiveness inhibited emotional expressiveness as well as interfering with sensitive responsiveness.

Relationship of Infant Attachment to Infant Affect and Sociability

Securely attached infants later have more fun in tasks and are more persistent. Infants who at 12 months were judged to be securely attached were found to be more playful at 21 months during administration of the Bayley mental scale (Main, 1973). Similarly, infants who at 18 months were judged to be securely attached were, at 24 months more enthusiastic in a problem-solving task, showed more positive affect, and were more persistent (Matas, Arend, & Sroufe, 1978).

Securely attached infants are likely to be more sociable with adult strangers. Security of attachment and sociability to adult strangers were assessed with infants at 12 months and again at 19 months. At each age, a subset of securely attached infants were the most sociable with the stranger, whereas insecurely attached (both avoidant and resistant) infants were the least sociable (Thompson & Lamb, 1983). However, the degree of sociability was only stable over time when the attachment classification also remained stable.

Securely attached infants are more sociable later with peers. Securely attached infants at 12 months were, at 21 months, friendlier to peers and participated more in play with peers (Main, 1973). They were also more likely to share, to give, and to show toys to peers (Lieberman, 1977). The increased sociability persisted even to age 3. Children who at 1 year had been judged securely attached made more complex and more successful bids to peers in a day camp setting at age 3. They were also rated as more socially competent with both peers and adults (Kennedy & Bakeman, 1984). Similarly, infants who at 15 months were judged to be securely attached, at age 3½ were more likely to be a leader with peers, to be less hesitant to engage with peers, to be less socially withdrawn, to have other children seek out their company, to be more sympathetic to peers' distress, and to attract more attention from peers (Waters, Wippman, & Sroufe, 1979).

Further Evidence that Affect Regulation between Parents and Infants is a Risk Marker

When biologically at-risk infants, those born preterm or postterm, are compared to infants born healthy at term, the biologically at-risk infant-parent dyads show decreased positive affect. The phenomenon was noted in the pioneering research of Leiderman, Leifer, Seashore, and Barnett (1973) and replicated in several other studies (Crnic, Ragozin, Greenberg, Robinson, & Bashaw, 1983; Parmelee, Beckwith, Cohen, & Sigman, 1983).

Microanalytic techniques indicate that the deviation in affect regulation occurs in both the parent and the at-risk infant. At 4 months after expected date of delivery, preterm, postterm, and term infants and their parents were videotaped during play (Field, 1979, 1982). The mothers of preterm and postterm infants engaged in significantly less game playing and a lesser variety of games during interaction with their infants, and their infants enjoyed the interactions less. They showed fewer happy facial expressions, made fewer contented vocalizations, and made more frowns and cries. They required a greater number of game trials before they achieved laughter and were more likely than were term infants to avert their gaze and to cry.

Since animated stimulation appears to have differential effects in normal and at-risk infants, Field suggests that at-risk infants may have more difficulty in modulating arousal. Appropriate levels of stimulation may differ for these infants, creating a more difficult task for their parents in fine-tuning the intensity and amount of stimulation.

It is not yet known whether the decreased enjoyment of at-risk infants with their parents is reflected in later emotional organization, such as in the organization of attachment. But at-risk infants do show decreased enjoyment when engaging with inanimate stimuli. By the second year of life, preterm infants have been noted to show less pleasure in task mastery, even when equally successful.

Conclusion

The data are still limited for individual differences among normal parent-infant dyads, but persuasive evidence exists that deviant parent-infant dyads, such as biologically at-risk and neglected infants, differ markedly from normal dyads in their enjoyment during play (Egeland, Sroufe, & Erickson, 1983; Schneider-Rosen & Cicchetti, 1984).

It is now quite clear that parenting involves reciprocity and sensitivity to the infant's cues and signals. Sensitive responsiveness is the essence of parent-infant interactions that lead to secure attachment in the infant. Yet, it is likely that parents differ in their degree of playfulness and joy, even when equally sensitive and responsive to their infants. It is not only how much parents play, but how they play. Whereas in general parents' choices of games reflect an exquisite fine tuning to the infant's increasing cognitive and motoric skills, this is not always so. Some parents keep their child passive in games for extended periods of time, as in tickling or in teasing. Similarly, whereas most parents seek to maintain an optimal range of arousal in which their infant is likely to manifest positive affect, infants differ in their state organization and parents differ in their sensitivity and skill in maintaining their infants in an optimal range of arousal.

Although the data are just beginning to accumulate, it seems that the more parents and infants are playful and enjoy their interactions with one another, the more likely the infant will later be securely attached, enjoy problem-solving tasks, and be sociable with adults and with peers.

References

Ainsworth, M.D.S. 1979. Attachment as related to mother-infant interaction. In J.S. Rosenblatt, R.A. Hinde, C. Beer, & M. Busnell (Eds.), *Advances in the study of behavior* (Vol. 9). New York: Academic Press.

———. 1973. The development of infant-mother attachment. In B.M. Caldwell & H.N. Ricciuti (Eds.), *Review of child development research* (Vol. 3). Chicago: University of Chicago Press.

Ainsworth, M.D.S., Blehar, M.C., Waters, E., & Wall, S. 1978 *Patterns of attachment*. Hillsdale, N.J.: Erlbaum.

Beckwith, L., & Cohen, S.E. 1984. Home environment and cognitive competence in preterm children during the first five years. In A.W. Gottfried (Ed.), *Home environment and early cognitive development: Longitudinal research*. New York: Academic Press.

Beckwith, L., Cohen, S.E., Kopp, C.B., Parmelee, A.H., & Marcy, T. 1976. Caregiver-infant interaction and early cognitive development in preterm infants. *Child Development* 47:579–587.

Blehar, M.C., Lieberman, A.F., & Ainsworth, M.D.S. 1977. Early face-to-face interaction and its relation to later infant-mother attachment. *Child Development* 48: 182–194.

Bowly, J. 1969. *Attachment and loss* (Vol. 1). London: Hogarth; New York: Basic Books.

Brazelton, T.B., Koslowski, B., & Main, M. 1974. The origins of reciprocity: Early mother-infant interaction. In M. Lewis & L. Rosenblum (Eds.), *The effect of the infant on its caregiver.* New York: Wiley.

Bruner, J.S. 1977. Early social interaction and language acquisition. In H.R. Schaffer (Ed.), *Studies in mother-infant interaction.* London: Academic Press.

———. 1982. The organization of action and the nature of the adult-infant transaction. In E.Z. Tronick (Ed.), *Social interchange in infancy: Affect, cognition, and communication.* Baltimore: University Park Press.

Bruner, J., & Sherwood, V. 1976. Peekaboo and the learning of role structures. In J. Bruner, A. Jolly, & K. Sylva (Eds.), *Play: Its role in development and evolution.* New York: Basic Books.

Campos, J.J., & Sternberg, C.R. 1981. Perception, appraisal and emotion: The onset of social referencing. In M.E. Lamb & L.R. Sherrod (Eds.), *Infant social cognition: Empirical and theoretical considerations.* Hillsdale, N.J.: Erlbaum.

Caron, A.J., & Caron, R.S. 1981. Processing of relational information as an index of infant risk. In S. Friedman & M. Sigman (Eds.), *Preterm birth and psychological development.* New York: Academic Press.

Clarke-Stewart, K.A. 1973. Interactions between mothers and their young children: Characteristics and consequences. *Monographs of the Society for Research in Child Development* 38, Nos. 6 and 7.

Cohn, J.F., & Tronick, E.Z. 1982. Communicative rules and the sequential structuring of infant behavior during normal and depressed interaction. In E.Z. Tronick (Ed.), *Social interchange in infancy: Affect, cognition, and communication.* Baltimore: University Park Press.

Crawley, S.B., & Sherrod, K.B. 1984. Parent-infant play during the first year of life. *Infant Behavior and Development* 7:65–75.

Crawley, S.B., Rogers, P.P., Friedman, S., Iacobbo, M., Criticos, A., Richardson, L., & Thompson, M.A. 1978. Developmental changes in the structure of mother-infant play. *Developmental Psychology* 14:30–36.

Crnic, K.A., Ragozin, A.S., Greenberg, M.T., Robinson, N.M., & Bashaw, R.B. 1983. Social interaction and developmental competence of preterm and full-term infants during the first year of life. *Child Development* 54:1199–1210.

Egeland, B., & Farber, E.A. 1984. Infant-mother attachment: Factors related to its development and changes over time. *Child Development* 55:753–771.

Egeland, B., Sroufe, L.A., & Erickson, M. 1983. The developmental consequence of different patterns of maltreatment. *Child Abuse and Neglect* 7:459–469.

Emde, R.N., & Sorce, J.F. 1983. The rewards of infancy: Emotional availability and maternal referencing. In J.D. Call, E. Galenson, & R.L. Tyson (Eds.), *Frontiers of infant psychiatry.* New York: Basic Books.

Field, T. 1979. Games parents play with normal and high-risk infants. *Child Psychiatry and Human Development* 10:41–48.

———. 1982. Affective displays of high-risk infants during early interactions. In T. Field and A. Fogel (Eds.), *Emotion and early interaction.* Hillsdale, N.J.: Erlbaum.

Field, T.M., & Walden, T.A. 1982. Production and perception of facial expressions in infancy and early childhood. In H.W. Reese and L.P. Lipsitt (Eds.), *Advances in child development and behavior* (Vol. 16). New York: Academic Press.

Fogel, A., Diamond, G.R., Langhorst, B.H., & Demos, V. 1982. Affective and cognitive aspects of the 2-month-old's participation in face-to-face interaction with the mother. In E.Z. Tronick (Ed.), *Social interchange in infancy: Affect, cognition, and communication.* Baltimore: University Park Press.

Gustafson, G.E., Green, J.A., & West, M.J. 1979. The infant's changing role in mother-infant games: The growth of social skills. *Infant Behavior and Development* 2:301–308.

Hodapp, R.M., Goldfield, E.C., & Boyatzis, C.J. 1984. The use and effectiveness of maternal scaffolding in mother-infant games. *Child Development* 55:772–781.

Kaye, K. 1982. Organism, apprentice, and person. In E.Z. Tronick (Ed.), *Social interchange in infancy: Affect, cognition, and communication.* Baltimore: University Park Press.

Kennedy, J.H., & Bakeman, R. 1982. The early mother-infant relationship and social competence with peers and adults at three years. *Journal of Child Psychology and Psychiatry* 23:185–190.

Lamb, M.E. 1982. Individual differences in infant sociability: Their origins and implications for cognitive development. In H.W. Reese & L.P. Lipsitt (Eds.), *Advances in child development and behavior* (Vol. 16). New York: Academic Press.

Leiderman, P.H., Leifer, A.D., Seashore, M.J., & Barnett, C.R. 1973. Mother-infant interaction: Effects of early deprivation, prior experience and sex of infant. In J.N. Nurnberger (Ed.), *Biological and environmental determinants of early behavior.* Baltimore: Williams and Wilkins.

Lewis, M., & Cherry, L. 1977. Social behavior and language acquisition. In M. Lewis & L.A. Rosenblum (Eds.), *Interaction, conversation, and the development of language.* New York: Wiley.

Lieberman, A.F. 1977. Preschoolers' competence with a peer: Relations with attachment and peer experiences. *Child Development* 48:1277–1287.

Main, M. 1973. Exploration, play, and level of cognitive functioning as related to child-mother attachment. Unpublished doctoral dissertation, Johns Hopkins University, Baltimore, Md.

Malatesta, C.Z. 1982. The expression and regulation of emotion: A life-span perspective. In T. Field & A. Fogel (Eds.), *Emotion and early interaction.* Hillsdale, N.J.: Erlbaum.

Malatesta, C.Z., & Haviland, J.M. 1982. Learning display rules: The socialization of emotion expression in infancy. *Child Development* 53:991–1003.

Matas, L., Arend, R.A., & Sroufe, L.A. 1978. Continuing of adaptation in the second year of life. The relationship between quality of attachment and later competence. *Child Development* 49:547–556.

Parmelee, A.H., Beckwith, L., Cohen, S., & Sigman, M. 1983. Social influences on infants at medical risk for behavioral difficulties. In J.D. Call, E. Galenson, & R.L. Tyson (Eds.), *Frontiers of infant psychiatry.* New York: Basic Books.

Pettit, G.S., & Bates, J.E. 1984. Continuity of individual differences in the mother-infant relationship from six to thirteen months. *Child Development* 55:729–739.

Ratner, N., & Bruner, J. 1978. Games, social exchange and the acquisition of language. *Journal of Child Language* 5:391–401.

Ross, H.S., & Kay, D.A. 1980. The origins of social games. In K. Rubin (Ed.), *New directions for child development*. San Francisco: Jossey-Bass.

Schneider-Rosen, K., & Cicchetti, D. 1984. The relationship between affect and cognition in maltreated infants: Quality of attachment and the development of visual self-recognition. *Child Development* 55:648–658.

Spitz, R.A. 1972. Fundamental education. In M.W. Piers (Ed.), *Play and development*. New York: Norton.

Stern, D.N. 1974. The goal and structure of mother-infant play. *Journal of the American Academy of Child Psychiatry* 13:402–421.

Sutton-Smith, B. 1980. Children's play: Some sources of play theorizing. In K. Rubin (Ed.), *New directions for child development*. San Francisco: Jossey-Bass.

Sutton-Smith, B., & Sutton-Smith, S. 1974. *How to play with your children (and when not to)*. New York: Hawthorn/Dutton.

Thompson, R.A., & Lamb, M.E. 1983. Security of attachment and stranger sociability in infancy. *Developmental Psychology* 19:184–191.

Tronick, E.Z. 1982. Affectivity and sharing. In E.Z. Tronick (Ed.), *Social interchange in infancy. Affect, cognition, and communication*. Baltimore: University Park Press.

Tronick, E.Z., Ricks, M., & Cohn, J.F. 1982. Maternal and infant affective exchange: Patterns of adaptation. In T. Field & A. Fogel (Eds.), *Emotion and early interaction*. Hillsdale, N.J.: Erlbaum.

Tronick, K.E., Als, H., Adamson, L., Wise, S., & Brazelton, T.B. 1978. The infant's response to entrapment between contradictory messages in face-to-face interaction. *Journal of the American Academy of Child Psychiatry* 17:1–13.

Waters, E., Wippman, J., & Sroufe, L.A. 1979. Attachment, positive affect, and competence in the peer group: Two studies in construct validation. *Child Development* 50:821–829.

Wolfenstein, M. 1955. Fun morality: An analysis of recent American child-training literature. In M. Mead & M. Wolfenstein (Eds.), *Childhood in contemporary cultures*. Chicago: University of Chicago Press.

Yarrow, L.J., McQuiston, S., MacTurk, R.H., McCarthy, M.E., Klein, R.P., & Vietze, P.M. 1983. Assessment of mastery motivation during the first year of life: Contemporaneous and cross-age relationships. *Developmental Psychology* 19:159–171.

Young-Browne, G., Rosenfeld, H.M., & Horowitz, F.D. 1977. Infant discrimination of facial expressions. *Child Development* 48:555–562.

17
Mother-Child Play Interaction and Children's Educational Achievement

Phyllis Levenstein

Through its development and research of the Mother-Child Home Program over sixteen years, the Verbal Interaction Project (VIP) had an unusual opportunity to study the influence of mothers' interactive behavior in play sessions on their children's educational achievement as well as their intellectual and social-emotional competence. The verbal and other interactions of low-income (education high school or below, occupation semi-skilled or lower) mothers in play with their young children was observed during the program's home sessions and on laboratory videotapes. In addition, the children's intellectual and academic skills and classroom behavior were evaluated after the program ended and in follow-up studies, thus making it possible to investigate whether mothers' verbal interaction was related to their children's achievements.

The program was the result of a 1965 pilot study (Levenstein & Sunley, 1968) and was based on suppositions about the kinds of parent behaviors which should be encouraged in children's preschool years in order to prevent the cumulative school disadvantage seen in low-income pupils. We postulated the latent presence in all families of a parent-child network which could be strengthened in low-income families by play-oriented interaction to support the growth of children's competencies in preparation for school years. A voluntary, home-based early education/parent education program for low-income 2- to 4-year-olds and their mothers evolved. Called the Mother-Child Home Program, its theory and method as it developed were inspired by numerous studies (for example, Bronfenbrenner, 1968; Brown, 1958; Bruner, 1966; Hess & Shipman, 1965; Hunt, 1961; Sapir, 1921; Vygotsky, 1962) and are described in detail elsewhere (for example, Levenstein, 1976, 1977).

The Mother-Child Home Program

The mother-child dyad was in the Mother-Child Home Program for two school years, starting when the child was 2. Home visitors, called toy demonstrators, modeled interactive skills around gifts of toys and books for the mother in play sessions conducted at home. Without benefit of the subsequently written child development literature of play (Rubin, Fein, & Vandenberg, 1983), our definition of play followed *Webster*'s "Recreational activity, especially the spontaneous activity of children."

The half-hour home sessions occurred twice a week for seven months for some dyads, and once a week for others (allowing for individual differences), each within a year, for a maximum of ninety-two play sessions over the two years. Every week, regardless of the number of home sessions, a new toy or book selected on the basis of explicit criteria (twenty-three for the toys, eleven for the books) was presented to the dyad. The fun-oriented curriculum materials included a developmentally appropriate guide sheet written for each new toy or book around a stable list of concepts (such as colors, shapes, and numbers) and concept-related activities (fitting, matching, and choosing). Each guide sheet ended with the same reminder: "Have a good time with the [toy or book], the child, and the mother!"

The verbal interaction possibilities introduced in each guide sheet were modeled for the mother by the toy demonstrators who were paid or volunteer women with a wide range of education and background. Some were former program participants or teachers, but as toy demonstrators they did not teach, preach, or become a close friend of the mother. They kept their relationships light with the children, too. In home sessions they participated in the children's spontaneity and enjoyment while unobtrusively introducing or reinforcing verbally symbolized concepts. They also followed explicit rules and practiced special techniques to preserve confidentiality and to protect the family against unintended intrusiveness on the part of the program (Levenstein, 1980).

The program's theory was (and still is in sixteen program replications) that cognitive and social-emotional growth is fostered, and future educational and emotional problems prevented, by the young child's and his mother's language and other positive interactions in mutually enjoyable play around interesting, conceptually rich material. ("Mother" may be any adult who has a primary, nurturing, and enduring relationship with the child.) The interaction must be playful, not didactic, for a maximum benign effect on the child and on the mother-child relationship (Clarke-Stewart, 1973), and it must exclude the experts as far as possible (Bronfenbrenner, 1974). Thus, the intrinsic motivation of child's and mother's interest in play and in each other will be facilitated, as well as the extrinsic motivation provided for the child by the mother's praise, for both by the play materials, and for the mother by the sense of affectance conveyed by the child's good development (White, 1963).

Outcomes

Research from 1967 through 1972 with an experimental design which minimized the self-selection of mothers (treatments assigned by location-randomization rather than by subject-randomization), and thus much of the subject bias resulting from such self-selection (Rosenthal & Rosnow, 1975; Madden, O'Hara, & Levenstein, 1984), demonstrated the success of the program in preventing educational disadvantage for its child graduates (Lazar & Darlington, 1982; Madden, Levenstein, & Levenstein, 1976). However, a question remained as to whether the program graduates' normal school achievement was linked to their mothers' verbal interaction with them through the Mother-Child Home Program.

One way we attempted to answer the question was to measure the verbal interaction in videotaped play sessions of all the mothers in the 1976 cohort (one of four cohorts studied in subject-randomized experiments) by counting the number of times they displayed program-related verbal and other interactive behaviors toward their children on the ten-minute videotapes. The results were computed by a blind rater and recorded on the VIP-created Maternal Interaction Behavior (MIB) measure. The 1976 mothers' videotaped behavior was rated on ten MIB items (categories of maternal interactive behavior) immediately after the program ended in 1978, and again a year and a half later in 1980, when the children were almost six years old and finishing kindergarten. The ten 1978 MIB scores for the combined treatment groups of 1976 mothers were then correlated with their children's kindergarten-level outcomes in multiple regression predictions. The measured outcomes were reading and mathematics scores achieved on the Wide Range Achievement Test (WRAT), the three factor scores and the total scores for the Child's Behavior Traits (CBT), a VIP-created twenty-item measure of social-emotional skills (Johnson, 1976), and intellectual competence as measured by a Stanford-Binet IQ. Similar multiple regressions were performed to correlate the mothers' 1980 MIB item scores with the kindergarten-level follow-up with the children's outcomes near the end of second grade (WISC IQ). Tables 17–1 and 17–2 summarize each of the two sets of multiple regressions. To simplify the tables, only those variables that entered into the prediction equation were also entered into the tables, by their positive or negative correlation signs. The significance levels, of course, take into account both positive and negative correlations (Levenstein & O'Hara, 1983).

The regressions, as can be seen on both tables 17–1 and 17–2, produced some puzzling and even contradictory results. For example, why should a mother's direct encouragement of her child to talk by soliciting information from him have consistently negative effects on his social-emotional development at both stages? Why should mothers' verbalized praise have a positive effect on their children's IQ at kindergarten age and a negative one by the time they reach second grade? These and other questions have not yet been answered, although rare suppressor effects among the correlations have been suggested as the cause (Nunnally, 1967).

It is possible that the MIB measure was too crude to measure the specific verbal interaction components which could predict children's school success, perhaps flawed by the limitations of including only items which were likely

Table 17–1
Multiple Regressions of MIB Items (Postprogram, 1978) on Children's Outcomes at Kindergarten Level in 1980 (Treatment Groups Combined)

MIB Item	WRAT		CBT				
	Reading	Math	Total Scores	Social Responsibility	Task Orientation	Self-Confidence	IQ
1. Label information	−						
2. Color information						+	
3. Verbalizes actions					−		
4. Number and shape		−	−	+		−	−
5. Questions (not "yes" or "no")			−	−	−	−	
6. Verbalizes praise				+		−	+
7. Stimulates divergent use of toy		+	+	+			+
8. Smiles and positive gestures	+	+	+	+	+	+	
9. Replies to child						+	+
10. No reply to child	−		−	−	−	−	
R	.41	.64	.57	.50	.70	.69	.66
R^2	.17	.41	.33	.25	.49	.48	.43
F	1.48	5.25	2.27	1.89	4.43	3.51	4.46
df	(4,30)	(4,30)	(6,28)	(5,29)	(6,28)	(7,27)	(5,29)
p	NS	.01	NS	NS	.01	.01	.01
Adjusted R^2	.05	.33	.18	.12	.38	.34	.34

Note: Tabled signs indicate signs of MIB (Maternal Interactive Behavior) item beta values (correlation sign) for only those variables which enter into prediction equation. N = 35.

[a] Treatment effects were partialled out prior to entering MIB items into the prediction. This procedure used 1 *df*. The independent treatment variable R^2s were .07 for IQ, .10 for WRAT Arithmetic, .01 for CBT Task Orientation, and .00 for all other variables. The R^2s presented in the table include the treatment effect.

Table 17–2
Multiple Regressions of MIB Items (1980) on Children's Outcomes at Grade Level in 1982 (Treatment Groups Combined)

MIB Item	WRAT			CBT			
	Reading	Math	Total Scores	Social Responsibility	Task Orientation	Self-Confidence	IQ
1. Gives label information							−
2. Gives color information						−	
3. Verbalizes actions	−						
4. Gives number and shape information				+			
5. Questions/solicits information			−	−	−	−	−
6. Verbalizes praise		−	+	+	+		
7. Stimulates divergent use of toy		+	+				
8. Smiles and positive gestures	+		+	+	+	+	+
9. Replies to child	+		+			+	+
10. No reply to child	−		−			−	
R	.61	.56	.47	.47	.36	.52	.74
R^2	.38	.31	.22	.22	.13	.27	.55
F	2.93	4.82	1.38	1.74	1.14	1.82	7.23
df	6.29	3.32	6.29	5.30	4.31	6.29	5.30
p	.05	.01	NS	NS	NS	NS	.01
Adjusted R^2	.25	.25	.06	.10	.02	.12	.47

Note: Values across MIB (Maternal Interactive Behavior) item rows are standardized beta weights. A value is given for only those items which entered into the predictions of children's variables prior to a preselected cutoff point. The regression summary statistics are presented for the prediction including only the variables for which beta weights are given (not for all MIB items). N = 36.

[a] Treatment effects were partialled out prior to entering MIB items into the prediction. This procedure used 1 df. The independent treatment variable R^2s were .02 for CBT Social Responsibility and .00 for all other variables.

to be displayed by the mothers in a ten-minute videotape. Nevertheless, the mothers' general verbal responsiveness ("replies to child") in 1978 predicted their children's degree of self-confidence and social responsibility, and math skills in kindergarten (table 17–1). As can be seen in table 17–2, mothers' 1980 verbal responsiveness predicted the children's 1982 reading scores and IQs as well as their degree of social responsibility and self-confidence. Equally influential was "Mother smiles and/or makes other positive gesture," which also entered into the prediction equation both times and was associated with children's competencies in a consistently positive direction. An almost as consistent negative influence was the contribution of "Mother does not reply" to all outcomes. There was one exception: Mothers' not replying to their children in the 1978 tapes inexplicably predicted their children's IQs at kindergarten age!

However inexact the MIB measure was for identifying the microingredients of the parental verbal interaction antecedents of children's school age competencies, the overall message appears unambiguous. Mothers who show responsiveness by replying verbally to their children and who spontaneously demonstrate their warm feelings toward their youngsters (smiles and hugs) are likely to positively influence their children's school success. Further, mothers' general responsiveness and warmth are much more important to children's school success than the mothers' attempts to teach specific information.

No video camera or other intrusive equipment had been used in a previous study of mothers' interactive behavior in the natural settings of their own homes. Mothers who had entered the program in 1972 were rated by their toy demonstrators on their home session interactive parenting behavior during the last six weeks of the program in 1974. (Because the observations were by toy demonstrators and took place in home sessions, they could be conducted only with program mothers.) The toy demonstrators recorded their global ratings of mothers' interactive behavior on a project-created twenty-item instrument called Parent and Child Together (PACT). Five of the twenty PACT items concerned parents' verbal interaction behavior. The same toy demonstrators similarly rated the program children's social-emotional behavior in home sessions by means of the Child's Behavior Traits (CBT), described earlier. Not surprisingly, the concurrent correlations between the scores for the five PACT verbal interaction items and the twenty CBT items were high, since they were scored by the same observer. Out of one hundred possible concurrent correlations, seventy-one were significant, as can be seen in tables 17–3 and 17–4, showing the 1974 correlations (when the children were 3½ years old).

Somewhat more surprising were the concurrent correlations found between the 1972 program children's postprogram IQs and the total scores for both their mothers' parenting interactions and their own social-emotional

Table 17–3
Correlations of Mothers' Home Verbal Interaction with Children's Independence, Cooperation, and Emotional Stability at Age 3½
(Pearson's r, N = 45)

Children's Independence, Cooperation, and Emotional Stability at Age 3½ (Home Observations)	Mothers' Home Verbal Interaction				
	Responds Verbally to Child's Request	Verbalizes Expectations of Child	Verbalizes Approval of Child	Tries to Converse with Child	Verbalizes Reasons for Obedience
Responsible Independence					
Accepts, asks for help		.31*	.38**		
Protects own rights				.39**	
Self-confident	.42***	.47***		.30**	
Refrains from physical risks	.38***	.40**			.37*
Social Cooperation					
Refrains from physical aggression	.33*	.40**			.32*
Cooperates with adults	.31*	.58***	.37**		.45***
Follows rules	.32*	.65***	.38**		.41**
Puts own needs second		.34*	.44***		.40**
Emotional Stability					
Cheerful and content	.38**	.32*			
Spontaneous, not explosive	.32*	.30*			
Tolerates frustration		.44***	.50***	.34*	.41***
No sudden mood changes	.37**	.48***	.34*		.41**

*p ≤ .05.
**p ≤ .01.
***p ≤ .005.

competence in home sessions (Levenstein & Madden, 1976). The children's IQs were evaluated independently in the project office by a psychologist who had no connection with the program and was blind to the children's treatment status, as well as to any information about them except their ages. The correlation between the children's mean IQ and their mothers' interactive parenting behavior as measured in home sessions by toy demonstrators on PACT was .40, significant at the .01 level. The correlation between the children's mean IQ and their home session social-emotional behavior as measured in home sessions by toy demonstrators on CBT was .56, also significant at the .01 level. Thus there appeared to be a reliable relationship between children's intellectual development and their mothers' interactive

Table 17–4
Correlations of Mothers' Home Verbal Interaction with Children's Task and Cognitive Orientation at Age 3½
(Pearson's r, N = 45)

Children's Task and Cognitive Orientation at Age 3½ (Home Observations)	Mothers' Home Verbal Interaction				
	Responds Verbally to Child's Request	Verbalizes Expectations of Child	Verbalizes Approval of Child	Tries to Converse with Child	Verbalizes Reasons for Obedience
Task Orientation					
Initiates goal-directed activities	.37*	.31*	.35*	.50***	.48***
Completes tasks	.33*		.52***	.41***	.47***
Enjoys mastering new tasks	.38**	.37*	.49***	.43***	.36*
Attentive and concentrates		.33*	.48***	.43***	.50***
Cognitive Orientation					
Well-organized	.43***	.38*	.45***	.54***	.52***
Expresses ideas in language	.57***	.30*		.52***	.42***
Differentiates between facts and make-believe	.37*	.37*	.39**	.34*	.43***
Creative, inventive	.32*	.33*	.41**	.49***	.48***

*$p \leq .05$.
**$p \leq .01$.
***$p \leq .005$.

behavior with them by age 3½, as well as a link between children's IQ and their social-emotional skills at the same age. In other words, the data indicated the presence of a triadic relationship between maternal interactive behavior, children's IQ, and children's social-emotional competence.

Even more removed from children's and mothers' 1974 home session behavior were the observations of the 1972 program children's first-grade teachers in 1977, when the children were 6½ years old. The teachers rated the children on their classroom social-emotional behavior using the CBT as the toy demonstrators had done in home sessions three years earlier. The teachers had no knowledge of whether a child had been a program subject in the Verbal Interaction Project. However, the children's social-emotional skills were rated under different conditions in the classroom. They were measured within their first grade peer groups in the classroom. The ratings were global, by competent observers (their teachers) who had no connection with the VIP. These first-grade ratings were correlated with a narrowed segment of the mothers' earlier home session behavior—the five PACT items comprising their verbal interaction behavior.

Nevertheless, as can be seen in table 17–5, the results of the first grade study indicate that mothers' 1974 home session verbal interactive behavior had considerable influence on the children's classroom attitudes in 1977. This was especially true of "Mother responds verbally to child's request," "Mother tries to converse with child," and "Mother verbalizes reasons for the child's obedience." It was primarily these three 1974 maternal items which correlated with eleven of the twenty 1977 CBT items. Altogether there were twenty-seven significant correlations between mothers' early verbal interaction with the children and four CBT categories: responsible independence (accepts appropriate help, protects own rights, is self-confident, task orientation (enjoys mastering new tasks), cognitive orientation (is well organized, expresses ideas in language, understands difference between facts and make believe, is creative and inventive, and emotional stability (is cheerful and content, is spontaneous not explosive). The correlation coefficients were distributed fairly evenly among these categories.

This was the last of five separate correlational studies of relationships between maternal parenting behavior in play situations and children's competencies described in this chapter. Three (using simple correlations) followed the 1972 program dyads from 1974 to 1977, that is, from near the end of participation in the Mother-Child Home Program into the children's first-grade classrooms. Two (using multiple regression predictions) followed the 1976 cohort of dyads from 1978 to 1982, from the program's end to the children's second-grade classrooms. Whether the dyads' behavior was measured during program home sessions, or more intrusively, by means of laboratory-made videotapes of mother and child together, or by observations of former child subjects in classrooms, the major results were the same. Mothers' interactions during play with their young children (especially verbal and often nurturing interactions) predicted their children's social-emotional and intellectual (including academic) achievements.

Hence, a mother's parenting behavior can be considered to precede her child's intellectual and social-emotional development. The data indicate that these latter two major aspects of children's personalities are linked to each other, and also that each is significantly related, in turn, to the mother's interactive behavior in play with her child.

Conclusion

The inter-correlations among mother and child behaviors in every study affirm the existence of a triadic relationship between a mother's parenting and her child's intellectual and social-emotional growth. The three parts of this triad form what perhaps are the main cables of a supportive mother-child network. Connecting them are countless strands of specific reciprocally reinforcing behaviors, leading not only from mother to child but from child

Table 17–5
Correlations of Mothers' Home Verbal Interaction with Children's Independence, Task and Cognitive Orientation, and Emotional Stability in First Grade at Age 6½
(Pearson's r, N = 39)

Children's Independence, Task and Cognitive Orientation, and Emotional Stability in First Grade At Age 6½ (School Classroom Observations)	Mothers' Home Verbal Interaction				
	Responds Verbally to Child's Request	Verbalizes Expectations of Child	Verbalizes Approval of Child	Tries to Converse with Child	Verbalizes Reasons for Obedience
Independence					
Accepts, asks appropriate help	.38*			.38*	
Protects own rights	.33*				
Self-confident	.47***			.49***	
Refrains from physical risks					
Task Orientation					
Initiates goal-directed activities					
Completes tasks				.35*	
Enjoys mastering new tasks	.48***			.54***	.36*
Attentive and concentrates					
Cognitive Orientation					
Well-organized	.39*			.41**	.35*
Expresses ideas in language	.48***			.48***	
Differentiates between facts and make-believe	.61***	.34*		.61***	.52***
Creative, inventive	.40*			.52***	.44***
Emotional Stability					
Cheerful and content	.33*			.39*	.33*
Spontaneous, not explosive	.42**			.47***	.34*
Tolerates frustration					
No sudden mood changes					

*$p \leq .05$.
**$p \leq .01$.
***$p \leq .005$.

to mother. The process seems to be a good illustration of Bronfenbrenner's (1974) conclusion from his analysis of data from over 150 studies on the effects of early environmental deprivation and stimulation in animals and humans:

In the early years of life, the psychological development of the child is enhanced through his involvement in progressively more complex, enduring patterns of reciprocal contingent interaction with persons with whom he has established a mutual and enduring emotional attachment. (p. 26)

The data furnish empirical evidence not only for other chapters of this book, but also for suppositions underlying the creation of the Mother-Child Home Program. They confirm that a parent-child network, strengthened in the child's early years and perceived most visibly in the mother's verbal and nurturing responsiveness to her young child, provides a foundation for the child's later school achievement. The elements of the mother's interactions with the child, the child's IQ, and the child's classroom attitudes and academic skills are so interwoven as to suggest that the mother's interactive behavior is at the apex of the triad that may be of crucial importance to children's school achievement.

The data also stand as a warning to mothers who see the latent presence of the parent-child network as a mandate to barrage their children with a flood of didactic instruction. The contradictory aspects of the multiple regression predictions indicate that the supportive parent-child network formed through mothers' play interactions is a delicate one. It can be torn apart by mothers' insistence on the child's learning until it becomes boring and no longer play. The successful network is formed by the mother's general responsiveness, whether verbal or silently nurturing. The probability is that mothers who approach the young child's learning through play with spontaneous joy will have a child who continues to find joy in learning.

References

Bronfenbrenner, U. 1968. Early deprivation: A cross-species analysis. In G. Newton & S. Levine (Eds.), *Early experience and behavior.* Springfield, Ill.: Charles C. Thomas.

———. 1974. *Is early intervention effective? A report on longitudinal evaluations of preschool programs* Vol. II. Washington, D.C.: U.S. DHEW, OHD 74–25.

Bruner, J.S., Olver, R., & Greenfield, P. 1966. *Studies in cognitive growth.* New York: Wiley.

Brown, R. 1958. *Words and things.* Glencoe, Ill.: The Free Press.

Clarke-Stewart, K.A. 1973. Interactions between mothers and their young children: Characteristics and consequences. *Monographs of the Society for Research in Child Development* 38, Nos. 6 & 7.

Hess, R.D., & Shipman, V.C. 1965. Early experience and the socialization of cognitive modes in children. *Child Development* 36:869–886.

Hunt, J.M. 1961. *Intelligence and experience.* New York: Ronald Press.

Johnson, O.G. (Ed.). 1976. *Tests and measurements in child development, handbook II.* San Francisco: Jossey-Bass.

Lazar, I., & Darlington, R. 1982. Lasting effects of early education: A report from the consortium for longitudinal studies. *Monographs of the Society for Research in Child Development,* 47, No. 195:2–3.

Levenstein, P. 1976. Cognitive development through verbalized play: The Mother-Child Home Program. In J.S. Bruner, A. Jolly, & K. Sylva (Eds.), *Play—Its role in development and evolution.* New York: Basic Books.

———. 1977. The Mother-Child Home Program. In M.C. Day & R.K. Parker (Eds.), *The preschool in action.* 2d ed. Boston: Allyn and Bacon.

———. 1979. The parent-child network. In A. Simmons-Martin & D.R. Calvert (Eds.), *Parent-infant intervention.* New York: Grune & Stratton.

———. 1980. Ethical considerations in home-based programs. In M. Bryce & J.C. Lloyd (Eds.), *Treating families in the home.* Springfield, Ill.: Charles C. Thomas.

Levenstein, P., & Madden, J. 1976. *Progress report to Carnegie Corporation of New York, 1973–1976.* Freeport, N.Y.: Verbal Interaction Project (Mimeographed).

Levenstein, P., & O'Hara, J. 1983. *Tracing the parent-child network.* Final Report: 9/1/79–8/31/82, Grant No. NIE G 800042, National Institute of Education, U.S. Department of Education.

Levenstein, P., & Sunley, R. 1968. Stimulation of verbal interaction between disadvantaged mothers and children. *American Journal of Orthopsychiatry* 38: 116–121.

Madden, J., Levenstein, P., & Levenstein, S. 1976. Longitudinal IQ outcomes of the Mother-Child Home Program. *Child Development* 47:1015–1025.

Madden, J., O'Hara, J., & Levenstein, P. 1984. Home again. *Child Development* 55:636–647.

Nunnally, J.C. 1967. *Psychometric theory.* New York: McGraw-Hill.

Rosenthal, R., & Rosnow, R.L. 1975. *The volunteer subject.* New York: Wiley-Interscience.

Rubin, K.H., Fein, G.G., & Vandenberg, B. 1983. Play. In E.M. Hetherington (Ed.), *Handbook of child psychology.* New York: Wiley.

Sapir, E. 1921. *Culture, language, and personality.* Reprint. Berkeley: University of California Press, 1962.

Vygotsky, L.S. 1962. *Thought and language.* Cambridge: Massachusetts Institute of Technology Press.

White, R.W. 1963. Ego and reality in psychoanlalytic theory. *Psychological Issues* 3:Monograph II.

18
The Significance of Parent-Child Interaction in Children's Development

Bettye Caldwell

Developmental Aspects of Play

Some years ago, Brian Sutton-Smith (1976) wrote about certain basic characteristics of play. He said that children's play, first, should be spontaneous and self-generated—in effect, intrinsically motivated. Second, it should not be too serious. Third, it should have no set rules—that is, it should be flexible. Fourth, particularly for young children, it should be nonliteral and involve fantasy or imagination to some extent.

Play is thought of by children in a couple of other ways. For children, play is something you don't have to do too well. They will say, "We're just playing." It's rather like being a housewife: "I'm *just* a housewife; I'm *just* playing." In other words, "Don't take me too seriously. Don't expect too much of me. I don't have to do it well because I'm playing." Play is also fun to children. When you ask them what they want to do they say, "I want to go play." What's your favorite period in school? "Recess." What do you do in recess? "We play." Regardless of what they mean by it, most children say that play is fun.

What happens to play as we develop toward adulthood? The reverse happens. First, for adults play is never spontaneous. Adults play because they need exercise or because it's the thing to do. The only playful thing that I had ever done before taking up tennis two weeks ago was run. Running has to be the most sickeningly difficult task that anybody could ever do. It also has its own rituals—acquiring the right shoes, certain kinds of running shorts and tops. These are just some of the things that take all the fun out of it, if ever indeed there could have been any fun in it. Second, it's deadly serious. Marriages are broken up over missed shots in doubles. Marriages are broken when you trump your spouse's ace or refuse to bid when your spouse opens with two no trump because you think that's not a force. Adult play does more to destroy the family than many types of work do. Third, there is absolutely no flexibility in the way adults play. In tennis, I am pleased to find that you no longer have to play in whites. But the rules are still precise: where you stand to serve, how you should move, and so on. Fourth, the play of adults is very, very literal. There is no fantasy, or only a little bit, when you want "to kill" your victorious opponent. Fifth, we adults have to play incredibly well. If we don't, then we aren't allowed to play. You don't go to the Quebec River unless you fly-fish and know exactly how to do it.

Finally, it's not fun. Play that is fun is considered to be for kids. These developmental trends, if you will, suggest that we have professionalized play, not just in our society but in growing up. As we make a profession out of it, it looses its spontaneity, its flexibility, its fun.

The Paradox of Play

These differences between child and adult play lead to my main point, which I've called the paradox of play. In this book, we talk about having adults, who don't know how to play, teach children, who know quite well, how to play. In other words, if we want to improve the play of children, we're using the wrong teachers. We're using people whose play is not at all playful, according to the criteria of Sutton-Smith and every kid on the block.

What are the implications of this paradox for studies aimed at helping parents know how to play pleasurably, informatively, and educationally, with their children? One major implication is that the adults in charge need a little bit of retooling in order to do a decent job.

I have four suggestions for parents.

1. They should teach children to play divergently as well as convergently. A lot of adults, because they're so used to playing by rules, are oriented only toward play in a convergent way. Most of the development tests we use, including intelligence tests, are convergent, such as the Bayley and Cattell. In such tests, the child is given eight or ten blocks and a tin cup, and only if he puts the blocks in the cup does he get credit. The child who piles them up, turns the cup upside down on top of them, and pushes it around gets no credit. The only allowable response is to put the blocks in the cup, which is a convergent type of activity.

Many parents get very upset when they see their 3-year-old son or daughter playing "the wrong way," as by pulling the little train over the couch and up the bookcase, and so say, "Why don't you run the train on the tracks? Play with it right." It's a clear statement that there is a type of play (convergent) that is acceptable and that the children have to conform to it.

The educational implications of what happens to play developmentally is that we need to encourage parents to value divergent play, in which doing a large number of things with an object or varying the activity would actually be the more desirable type of response.

2. Parents need to be aware that not all toys are for play as children

define play. Puzzles are really not for play. You don't play a puzzle, you work a puzzle. You don't really play with a lotto game. You learn words from lotto. If you want to play, you get a truck, or playdough, or things like that. With dramatic type toys or toys that stimulate sociodramatic play, you really can play. You can meet all four of Sutton-Smith's criteria and the one I added, fun. This is very important for parents to realize. The HOME scale (discussed by Bradley in chapter 14 of this book) does include some toys that are just for play. Most of the toys selected for the functions we think are instrumental in helping children develop, either cognitively or socially. But there are also teddy bears, cuddly toys just to hold, paints or clay that the child can "play with," and so on.

3. A third suggestion for parents is that they realize some play will just happen, without parental interaction. Parents just don't seem to know that intuitively, and need to be taught that somewhere along the way children will get bored if there's not some social stimulation to keep their play with other children as well as with adults.

4. Children like to play with other children as well as with adults. In the minds of most children play is eminently social. It's something you do with other kids. I tell mothers who worry about having their children in child care programs that the best thing group child care has going for it is other kids. Children love to be around other children and to play with them. This is a very important thing for parents to realize.

Means-End Relationships

The next point I want to make is a bit broader. Many of the contributions in this book deal with play sometimes as a means and sometimes as an end. In research on play, play is sometimes used as an independent variable and at other times as a dependent variable. Brian Sutton-Smith in his early writings used play as a dependent variable, as an activity in and for its own sake. This is something that we want to facilitate in children. But in many of the studies cited here, play has been regarded as a means to an end. Does play increase a child's intelligence? Is play associated with more creativity? Does play with tools and objects in an unstructured way lead to better problem-solving? Play as a means is an adult's view of play. For the young child, play is an end in itself. Some children also develop means-ends concerns in relation to play, but like the baby Cicchetti described, who while being held in the air kept looking back, the end goal was social interaction, not improvement of kinesthetic sensitivity or the ability to hold up the head when it's not adequately supported. The reason babies like to play is that it's a great experience, it's fun to do, and the play of preschoolers is often exactly that. We have so overweighted our research toward play as a means to an end that we have lost the essence of what play means in the life of the young child. My point is simply that our research on play must not ignore play as an end while investigating play as a means to an end.

The Physical Environment

Theodore Wachs, in chapter 15, discussed seven dimensions of the physical environment: availability of stimulus materials, variety of stimulus materials, responsivity of the physical environment, ambient background noise, over-crowding, regularity of scheduling, and physical restraints on exploration. These dimensions can be used in designing and assessing the physical environment of a good child care program and are under the control of people running the program to some extent. For example, availability and variety of stimulus materials are high in most programs, except that they are stereo-typed. The same toys are always available and there are set places for the doll corner, the sand box, and the snack tables. I used to recommend to teachers that they have three full sets of toys and that they never let everything out at once. Children need to be offered change and variety. But people seldom do that in a child care program. Ambient background noise is very difficult to control when you have a lot of children, though architects can design the environment in ways that minimize it. Overcrowding is also hard to deal with. Regularity of scheduling is a big problem in some of our programs because it leads to monotony.

The key question is whether it is possible to improve the quality of the play environment by slight regulations of these aspects of the physical envi-ronment. There is more stereotyping in the physical environments we create for young children than in our own. We have several styles of houses: ranch, colonial, Cape Cod, and so on. But virtually all early childhood programs look just alike. You could blindfold me in any state in the union and I could find you the doll corner, or the bathrooms or where the puzzles are stored, because they were the same way in the last center I visited. And I know just where the tires are going to be on the playground, and the little rope swings, and all those things that kids never play with but that architecture students think are great for livening up an environment. In many parts of the world, landscape and interior architects are much more creative about trying to design the physical space in ways that children will find useful and interest-ing. That's an area where we need a real renaissance in this country.

Changes in Attitudes of Parents

My final point relates to Leila Beckwith's question about changes over time in adult play with children (chapter 16). I've already said there are changes as we age in the way we play, but I think also there have been changes over time in the attitudes of parents toward play. Today, there is an orientation on the part of many parents to impose an adult concept of play upon children. This is related to the tremendous recent stress on cognitive development in children. Many parents, particularly middle-class parents, have been sold on what we professionals have preached for the last twenty years. Parents have listened, and now they have baby gyms and know ways to build super babies, but this is also why mothers are deadly serious about play. They play with their babies the same way they play tennis and bridge, and that's no way to play with a baby.

These patterns do change. In my own years as an adult professional, I have seen an extreme swing from a social and emotional emphasis to a cognitive one. Furthermore, I remember that when the stress was on social and emotional development we used to say we really are also concerned about intellectual development, but nobody paid attention. Now we continually say that though we want to help children cognitively, we are just as concerned about their social and emotional development, and nobody is hearing that. But playful play is related to all the things that we want children to learn to do. The data from Beckwith's study (chapter 16) and the others that she cited show that early playfulness in the relationship between parent and child is associated with secure attachment, which, in itself, is associated with creative use of play materials, enjoyment of peers, and so on. This is the kind of thing that we have to get into the public consciousness.

Allison Clarke-Stewart (1973) has reported that fathers are more playful with their children than mothers, which doesn't surprise me. Mothers work all the time with their children. It's very nice that some children have a father figure who can play with them, but think of all the children growing up without fathers and all the mothers growing old, if you will, without the enjoyment of beautiful, mutually pleasurable reciprocal play with their babies and young children. I really believe that mutually enjoyable play between parent and child is one of the most important foundations for social development, as well as cognitive development.

Returning to my point about the paradox of play, it's not always fun to play with a child. It isn't fun to hold a baby in the air and be wet upon, if the game turns into that. It's not fun to play something that a child wants to do 130 times. Then there are other children who won't play. They look away, or they have a bland expression and won't smile when they're supposed to. We need to keep in mind that it is difficult to play with some infants.

But if we encourage parents to keep it light, then they will not feel badly if their child doesn't want to play or wants to play the same game forever and ever. We need to help parents learn about the paradox of play, the developmental paradox that children's play is different from our own. But mostly we need to show parents that much play with young children should be spontaneous and flexible, involving some fantasy, and most of all, it should be fun for both parent and child.

References

Clark-Stewart, K.A. 1973. Interactions between mothers and their growing children: Characteristics and consequences. *Monographs of the Society for Research in Child Development,* 38, nos. 6 & 7.

Sutton-Smith, B. 1976. *Play and learning.* New York: Gardner Press.

Part VI
Overview

19
Play Interactions and Developmental Processes

Brian Sutton-Smith

Play Materials

Play materials have attracted less attention by psychologists than by the public at large. The public takes its play materials very seriously, either as toys or playgrounds. These are two very large industries. For example, 800 toy companies sell about 150,000 kinds of toys utilizing 250,000 tons of plastics and 200,000 tons of metal, through 150,000 retail outlets (Toy Manufacturers of America, 1984). This same public has very strong views about the meaning of such things as war toys, anatomically correct dolls, Barbie dolls, defecating dolls, and sex-stereotyped toys. Even famous intellectuals have strong feelings about the impact of play materials. Roland Barthes, the noted French structuralist and semiotician, talks about the effect of modern toys, "made of graceless material, the product of chemistry, not of nature," in his book pertinently entitled pertinently *Mythologies* (1957):

> Faced with this world of faithful and complicated [toys] . . . the child can only identify himself as owner, as user, never as creator; he does not invent the world, he uses it: there are, prepared for him, actions without adventure, without wonder, without joy. . . . They are supplied to him ready-made: he has only to help himself, he is never allowed to discover anything from start to finish. However, the merest set of blocks, provided it is not too refined, implies a very different learning of the world . . . He creates forms which walk, which roll, he creates life, not property: objects now act by themselves, they are no longer an inert and complicated material in the palm of his hand. But such toys are rather rare. (p. 54)

The same point of view is to be found in a 1980 UNESCO French publication on children's play:

> More serious still is the fact that an industrially made toy, stereotyped and technically perfect, forfeits much of its value as a plaything. It is a closed object, setting up a barrier against creativity and imagination. In almost all

instances an elementary plaything is preferable, be it stick or pebble, which the small player can turn into a musical instrument, a tool, a weapon, a car or a boat, a doll or an animal, as his mood dictates. (p. 11)

Interesting and widespread as these views are, there is no evidence that the modern child either is or is not more creative with his current plastic playthings than were his predecessors with bits of wood or stones. We do know that today's child is somewhat more domesticated than were his predecessors of the last century, somewhat less cruel and savage than they were with their toys and their play activities. The writers of these two quotations assume that one can simply look at the characteristics of toys and make predictions as to how they will be used and what their effects will be on human creativity. It is very doubtful if that is possible. One needs to know the context in which the toys are used to know much at all about their effects.

We could ask ourselves whehther our own work with play materials is in anyway relevant to the issues of such claimed public relevance. I believe the proto/nonprototypical distinctions made about toys by some contributors probably are. Realism in play material appears to facilitate pretense at an earlier developmental level, but not at a later one if we can generalize from Greta Fein's classic study (1984).

Parental Involvement in Play

We psychologists take the issue of parental involvement more seriously than the issue of play materials. Here we are ahead of the public rather than behind in our serious practical concerns. We could probably claim that either parental or peer involvement is the greater part of the play variance in the first two years of life, that there is not much solitary play at all unless it has been so shared or modelled. There may be a lot of solitary intelligent activity, exploration and mastery, but there's not much play. Piaget (1951) cites only a dozen or so examples of play for the child's first year, but hundreds of examples of sensory-motor activity in his works on intelligence. Some of us use the word *play* rather globally for almost anything that children do, while others separate play from mastery, imagination, and exploration. I favor these latter, more specific differentiations. We implicitly deny infants their intelligence and realism by calling everything play. I'm not sure whether we do this because of the difficulty in making these discriminations or as a part of some other parent-child myth which makes us want to idealize all child activity as play.

The Origins of Play

Vandenberg (in chapter 1 of this book) has passed beyond ethology to an insistence upon the importance of fantasy in human life in a rather metaphysical sense. His assertion of the primacy of fantasy in human affairs is refreshingly different within the kind of research which is typical in the immediate field of our concern. However, this may be the old cultural evolutionary argument about the primacy of primitivity, its recapitulation in children (as savages), and its replacement by mature thought. The Freudian and Jungian passage from primary to secondary process had similar evolutionary overtones.

Still the assertion of primacy doesn't need to carry those historical residues. Bruner (1984) is also satisfied to give fantasy equal time with logic as a mode of thought. Making narrative or fantasy a *mode* of thought has its limitations. It suggests a psychologistic encapsulation for fantasy. It could be just another mentalistic mechanism (along with traits, IQs, egos and the like). There are broader views. Anthropological narratologists like Bruner follow a social constructionist line in which self and society are not sundered in that way, and the narrative as mythic or ideological is both person and society. Historians, who have been the major carriers of universal narratives these past several hundred years (presumably since the Christian eschatological story began to wane), sometimes now regard narrative as neither empirically possible nor culturally interesting because modern commercial societies, unlike agrarian societies, are oriented to change rather than conservation. Similarly, some narratologists argue that narratives are implicitly conservative; that they mystify our understanding and provide us with a false sense of coherence and society. Others argue contrarily that there can be rebellious as well as conservative stories (Eagleton, 1983).

The most important implication of the Vandenberg story is the primacy given to fantasy as an *epistemological form,* rather than as literality. After two-thousand years of Platonic disenfranchisement, this new emphasis on fantasy is well taken. Still there are some other considerations. Vandenberg uses a *human centric* focus to come up with a central metaphor for his myth of fantasy. Huizinga (1955) used human centric focus for his central play metaphors of *contest* and *representation,* as did Czikszentmihalyi (1977) for his central metaphors of *flow* and *control.* There are many metaphors for play besides that of problem solving (Sutton-Smith, 1979). The history of play provides a positive shower of potential play or fantasy metaphors including *irrationality* as in the early Greek idea of the gods playing randomly with our lives; *usefulness* as in the Platonic epistemology; *dissimulation* as in the Renaissance advocacies and parodies of Machiavelli and Castisglione on the one hand and Rabelais and Cervantes on the other; and *childishness* as in the industrial disenfranchisement of children from the world of work which produced a generational or disjunctive view of play as belonging to the innocent world of children, and even child and adult play are quite distinct. From *Romanticism* we get the metaphor of play and art as especially sublime, as a world where we create "boojum" (what ifs) not just allegories (what as) (Holquist, 1969). When the "boojum" replaces the allegory, creativity is favored over imitation. Most importantly, Romanticism also gives us the metaphors of voluntarism and "autotelia" as key concepts. Our current concept of intrinsic motivation owes as much to Schiller and Wordsworth as to our own empiricism. Valid as it may be as a modern metaphor, I am intrigued by our almost desperate concern to have it associated with children's play. Why must freedom be so important to our conceptions of childhood? In the last century it was attached to the artist as the only truly free and therefore authentic being (Trilling, 1971). Now we give it to children. Why? To deliver them from our own sense of inauthenticity?

Bateson's (1972) alternative of play as metacommunication applies to both animals and humans. Evaluating it on the scientific criterion of its fertility or its comprehensiveness, (because it is a metaphor applied to play derived from some signalling behavior) I prefer it to Vandenberg's use of fantasy to provide hope. I see play as a kind of communication—a way of paradoxical talking–and what gets into the talk depends on what the conflict-full issues are for the groups doing the talking, issues like power, primary process, hope and dread. In this view, play is a neutral semiotic system, not quite as irrevocable as talking, but more elementary than that since animals do it.

What's play's function in all this? Again I favor Bateson's identification of paradox with primary process. For him the reason for the paradox was the special combination of secondary and primary process. But this view, even if we adopt it, is limited by the individualism which is naturally a part of our twentieth-century condition. If one takes Backtin on Rabelais, for example, what gets into play is a *collective* kind of primary process—a depravity of the lower functions seen as the analogue to seasonal processes. It is antithetical to normative process as in its manifestation of carnivolia, bachanalia. In general, I favor the view that play is a dialectical resolution of normative and antithetical behavior induced by either social or individual pressures. Still, when you get to such antithetical metaphors, the problem with animals become quite substantial.

Schwartzman (in chapter 2 of this book) provides the healing power that anthropologists always do with their negative examples. One such contrary example and our universals collapse to the ground. Her assertions are that:

1. Child work doesn't preclude child play. Of course she is right. However, I doubt if anyone put the matter quite that dichotomously. Obviously,

child work affects the amount of time left over for play, and the energy one has for play. I have the unpublished tables from the Whitings' six-culture study showing a very clear negative relationship between the number of chores and the amount of observed play. I imagine television affects the amount of street play in the same way, though it may also increase solitary imaginative play in front of the television.

2. Disadvantaged children do not play less complexly nor less imaginatively. Again, this cannot be settled by a case here or there. Shirley Heath and I (Sutton-Smith & Heath, 1981) have taken the approach of seeking to differentiate between kinds of imaginative play, instead of defining it only in ethnocentric middle-class terms. There is a difference between the decontextualized literacy fantasies we induce in our children, and the more contextualized ones of some nonliterate peoples. In the latter, narratives do not stand aside from speaker and hearer but include them in the content. Their narratives are more a mix of personal narratives and personal fictions rather than the purer case of fictional narratives. When talking of narratives, or even scripts, I think it pays to at least differentiate between personal narratives, personal fictions, and fictional narratives.

3. Multiage groups are more collaborative than single-age peer groups. This is well taken, although my own historical examples are full of multiage group cruelties as well. The issue may really be that multiage groups operate in a frame of some kind of constraint.

4. As for needing space and toys to be imaginative, and children throughout the world doing well without either of them, this is like the proposition about work and play earlier. Did anyone ever say it in this singular way, or was it a small significant piece of the variance in a modern sample, as for example, it was in Jerome Singer's work (1973)?

Most interesting to me is the anomaly that though play objects are world-wide, sex differences in object play have some regularity, and SES differences are present with some regularity in modern conditions, in the few cases Schwartzman cites these differences do not seem to make much difference anyway. I find this a considerable puzzlement. In the past fifty years "sensory stimulation" has become a vogue term. For good or for bad we psychologists have convinced many people that their children can be hastened forward with the right kinds of parental and object stimulation. From a scattering of findings like those of Caldwell (chapter 18), Bradley (chapter 14), and Wachs (chapter 15) in this book, we learn that the right kind of objects can be correlated with the right kind of growth. The series of books and systems of baby toys sold by Johnson & Johnson take for granted this wisdom of object stimulation. Yet, our textbooks in child psychology, or even publications on toys by toy designers such as Dick Chase or Burton White (1975) reveal how limited this information actually is. Books are full of the technology of human growth in perception, motor skills, and so forth, and full of claims about the difference the social environment makes (such as SES and mother stimulation), but there is almost no systematic work on the environment as specific objects (the two somewhat related subjects are known as "sensory deprivation" and "object constancy"). In short, although ours is a technological society, high on the technology of mind and body, there is no technology of objects, although we pour them on and around our infants en masse.

There is a sense that specific objects do not make much difference. This may represent the same status reaction to the crassness of the commercial world that Roland Barthes (1972) discusses. This reaction against the bourgeois commercial plastic culture has been a note of intellectual and artistic self-satisfaction since the middle of the last century and owes much of course to Morris and Ruskin. Still, whatever its origins, it is an anomaly.

My own empirical reconciliation to date is that there is evidence both that some toys make little difference and some make a lot of difference. In my recent study (Sutton-Smith, 1985) I found it useful to distinguish between three classes: toys of acquaintance, toys of stereotype, and toys of identity. The last group of these, at least as reminisced about by their owners, made an enormous difference. Identity toys included such heterogeneous objects as tennis racquets, music recorders, first-aid toy kits, bicycles, Barbie dolls, and many kinds of soft toys that were cuddled in bed for decades.

Greta Fein (see chapter 3 of this book) has added depth to her years of study of pretense through her more recent longitudinal data. Some of her formulations are most exciting. My only quarrel is with such metaphors as "autotelic devices," "transformational mechanism," "affective templates," all of which impute an aggregate of internal psychologistic mechanisms, whereas the data she supplies is a dialogic series of happenings between a dyad (or triad, and so forth) of players alternately using, with great fluidity, centripetal or centrifugal moves. I believe she has now really left Piaget behind and needs Bakhtin (1981), whose dialogic theory of the imagination seems a more fitting paradigm. I would rather like a set of descriptive metaphors more like the rules for fantastic interaction in game theory recently generated by Giffin (1984). The excitement of Giffin's (and Bretherton's, see chapter 8) work is that their metaphors are focused on play rather than on cognition, and in consequence are methodologically more productive for understanding play.

It has been difficult for twentieth-century play theorists not to reduce child play to some socialization function. There is no theory that doesn't claim such functionality, whereas we know much play is, in comparative and historical terms, often dysfunctional. Animals and humans die and suffer injury while at play. Fein's data have some of this dynamism and danger, but her template metaphors lead inquiry into cognition, rather than into play. I find this limiting for the understanding of play, whatever it may be for the understanding of minds.

Despite Schwartzman's (1978) earlier caution that play theorists should not use games as their metaphor because games are too structured and too much of a male concern, I suggest that in the present context some studies of games produce appropriate metaphors, such as those which show the way games are embedded in metacommunicative contexts. However, the metaphors are as susceptible to manipulation as the games themselves (Hughes, 1983). As far as a 2-year-old's symbolic play is concerned, I would prefer not to study this as an epiphenomenon of cognitive operations as Piaget does, nor even as a transformation of event structure as Bretherton (chapter 8) does. More likely its lineage is with the prior enactive play of parents with their infants as described by Beckwith in chapter 16 of this book; the excitements, anticipations, and climaxes of their theatric mode (Sutton-Smith, 1979); their chameleon funny faces and changing gestures and body postures; their affect arousals and modulations. These many shifting practical frames of action and frames of mood seem much more likely to provide the paradigms for what later becomes the subtle symbolic frame shifting described by Fein in chapter 3. But her excellence study of *interaction* is a paradox in that its leading concepts are not interactive so much as monistic, after Piaget. My comment here anticipates those of Dunn (see chapter 9 of this book).

In sum, the origins of play as presented by several authors in this book stress (1) the omnipotence of fantasy; (2) the relativity of our concepts; and (3) the existence of a metacognitive sphere of play sui generis, quite unpredictable by our usual modes of thinking about the subject as cognitions or as literal scripts.

Developmental Processes

The many authors in this book, especially Fenson (chapter 4), Fein (chapter 3), Bretherton (chapter 8), McLoyd (chapter 11), and McCune (chapter 5), have all contributed immensely to a more detailed picture of the development of play in the first two years of life than we had before. There is exciting information here about decontextualization, decentration, decoupling and integration, about moves from structured to unstructured play, from prototypic to non prototypic responses, from single schemes to multiple schemes, from relative passivity to activity, from substitutions to inventions. There are also attempts to probe the play language and gesture relationships and discover whether play parallels or precedes language in some structural sense. Wach's (chapter 15 of this book) differentiation between object- and socially oriented children also applies to other researchers presented herein. Some want to see this issue in solitary play, object-related terms as originally presented by Piaget. Others see play in social terms.

My major criticism of all of this preliminary mapping is that it is both beneficially influenced and instigated by Piaget, but at the same time limited by his structuralist metaphors of human development. Whatever he may say about interaction, Piaget's work is within the main structuralist traditions of this century as exemplified in linguistics (Jacobsen), in anthropology (Levi-Strauss) and in narratology (Barthes). The virtue of all of this work is that it has illuminated whole areas of human behavior with much more systematic description than hitherto existed. In addition, however, this work has often (but not always) argued that underlying the description of sequential and universal systems of cognition, culture, and narrative, there are internal cognitive operations (schemas, templates, binary oppositions, functions, deep structures) which propel the whole thing forward. No matter what may be said about these mental homunculi not being apriori, not being isolated from surrounding contingencies or contexts, they nevertheless seem to end up inheriting philosopher Whitehead's misplaced concreteness and become reified as relatively autotelic mentalisms. And what this does in practice is what has been illustrated here by the contributions: it leads to a belief in the virtue of tracing structural sequences, not just for a beginning of description, but as an end point. If one takes a lesson from the recent accumulation of criticism of Piaget, that is, that his descriptions of sequence have been artificially drawn from nonrepresentative situations (in the laboratory or of solitary children out of social context), then we conclude by contrast that children function much more competently than he realized when seen in natural context. Further, when children are seen in interactive social contexts we get a view of the mind as it usually works. The mind working in more abstract circumstances may well be a more abstractive mind, but it is by no means a typical one, nor therefore, a best source for even understanding cognition, let alone play.

Put another way, if we study children continuously as Fein did, in order to discover *processes* of individual *change* in the social or individual structurings we temporarily describe (and which we cannot avoid doing), we are much more likely to discover the course of development with all its individual variety, multilinearity, and mobility of operations (to borrow from Werner) than if we take Piaget's structural metaphor and reify as operations apparently universal cognitions derived from an aggregate of subjects in a limited array of highly abstracted human situations.

References

Bakhtin, M. 1981. *The dialogic imagination.* Austin: University of Texas Press.
———. 1984. *Rabelais and his world.* Indianapolis: University of Indiana Press.
Barthes, R. 1957. *Mythologies.* Reprint. New York: Hill & Wang, 1972.
Bateson, G. 1972. *Steps to an ecology of mind.* New York: Ballantine.
Bruner, J. 1984. Narrative and paradigmatic modes of thought. Paper presented at the annual meeting of the American Psychological Association, Toronto.

Bruner, E. (Ed.) 1983. Text, play and story. *Proceedings of the American Ethnological Society.* Washington, D.C.

Csikszentmihalyi, M. 1977. *Beyond boredom and anxiety.* San Francisco, Calif.: Jossey-Bass.

Eagleton, T. 1983. *Literary theory.* Minneapolis: University of Minnesota Press.

Fein, G. 1984. The self-building potential of pretend play or "I got a fish, all by myself." In T.D. Hankey & A.D. Pellegrini (Eds.), *Child's play: Developmental and applied.* Hillsdale, N.J.: Erlbaum.

Giffin, H. 1984. The co-ordination of meaning in the creation of shared make-believe reality. In I. Bretherton (Ed.), *Symbolic play.* New York: Academic Press.

Holquist, M. 1969. What is a boojum? In P. Brooks (Ed.), *The child's part.* Boston: Beacon Press.

Hughes, L. 1983. Beyond the rules of the games: Why are Rosie rules nice? In F. Maning (Ed.), *The world of play.* West Point, N.Y.: Leisure Press.

Huizinga, J. 1955. *Homo ludens.* Boston: Beacon Press.

Piaget, J. 1951. *Play, dreams and imitation in childhood.* Translated by C. Gattegno and F.M. Hodgson. London: Routledge & Kegan Paul. Norton. (Originally published 1945.)

Schwartzman, H. 1978. *Transformations: The anthropology of children's play.* New York: Plenum Press.

Singer, J. 1973. *The child's world of make-believe.* New York: Academic Press.

Sutton-Smith, B. 1979. Play as meta-performance. In B. Sutton-Smith (Ed.), *Play and learning.* New York: Gardner Press.

Sutton-Smith, B., & Heath, S.B. 1981. Paradigms of pretense. *Quarterly Newsletter of the Laboratory of Comparative Human Cognition* 3, no. 3, 41–45.

Sutton-Smith, B., & Kelly-Byrne, D. (Eds.) 1983. *The masks of play.* West Point, N.Y.: Leisure Press.

Sutton-Smith, B. 1985. *Toys as culture.* New York: Gardner Press.

The Toy Industry Fact Book. 1984. Toy Manufacturers of America, New York.

Trilling, L. 1971. *Sincerity and authenticity.* Cambridge: Harvard University Press.

UNESCO. 1980. The child and play. Theoretical approaches and teaching application. Paris.

White, B. 1975. *The first three years of life.* New York: Prentice-Hall.

Whiting, B.B., & Whiting, J.W. 1975. *Children of six cultures.* Cambridge: Harvard University Press.

20

Characteristics, Consequences, and Determinants of Play

Jay Belsky

There is general agreement that the investigation of play is a good idea and that it may serve as a window on a variety of aspects of the child's world, including his or her cognitive and motivational abilities, social skills, and relations with others. According to Inge Bretherton (in chapter 8 in this book) play actions reveal much about the child's ability to represent events and thereby tell us a great deal about his or her cognitive functioning. Hence play can serve as a window on the child's notions of roles, actions, and objects. By analyzing play in this manner her work is related to the work of Larry Fenson and Lorraine McCune (chapters 5 and 6). All share a focus on cognitive functioning and things done by most children at different ages.

While Bretherton, Fenson, and McCune consider the characteristics of object play, Judy Dunn (chapter 9) looks at another aspect of play—its social side. It is striking to discover, although we should already know this, that siblings and mothers are quite different as playmates; the child obviously lives in at least two social worlds. The people in these different worlds know him or her in different ways and, as a result of this knowledge and their own agenda for what they want to do, relate to him differently. However, there is coherence in the different patterns of play observed with the same person in different situations. And as we search for such coherence the issue that repeatedly comes to mind concerns the benefits that accrue from playing with one partner rather than another of different social status (sibling, mother) and from playing with a particular mother or sibling.

One of the most intriguing of Dunn's (chapter 9) findings involves the variability in pretend play across mother-child pairs. Is it possible that mother and child negotiate the play domains they engaged in, with some selecting pretense and other focusing more on spatial phenomena, for example, or one partner leading and the other following? Hopefully, each relationship finds a play activity in which each one can enjoy and learn things about the other and the world.

The best method for investigation depends upon the question. If one wants to know, as does Dunn, what the child's everyday experiences are, then the naturalistic context of the home environment is the place to be. But the lab can also be useful, as Bretherton and others demonstrate, for controlling the scope of activities to learn what the child may be capable of doing.

Play, as described by Ken Rubin (chapter 10), occurs not only in the lab and in the home, but beyond the family as well, in peer groups. Play is ubiquitous. By modifying Parten's (1932) traditional peer play categories, Rubin introduces an entirely new arena: Is play a window on the emergence of developmental psychopathology? Stated in terms of my framework for discussion, I am raising questions about the consequences of play. I am persuaded by Rubin's data that the answer to this question may well be yes. Some of the socially withdrawn children in the study were avoiding social contact, not merely showing greater interest in the nonsocial world. Perhaps the two groups of withdrawn children could be distinguished by psychophysiological measurements. The internal feeling states and the concomitant physiological indicators of the truly withdrawn children might show them to be quite anxious and even lonely. What we do not know, of course, are the mechanisms that lead to socially withdrawn behavior. Do these children lack skills to engage others, or do they make attributions about others and themselves that keep them from socializing, such as "I can't do that," "They don't like me," "They won't want me to join them"?

In Dunn's (chapter 9) work, some children play well with mothers, others with siblings, and others with peers. But what happens when we find children whose play across all partners lacks the enthusiasm, ease of action, and fun that we come to think about when we use the term *play*? Is it possibly the that play, or its absence, with one set of partners is more developmentally informative than play with another set?

In considering Rubin's different types of players, even more than knowing where children are going developmentally (their consequences), we need to know why (their determinants). Where does a socially withdrawn style come from? It is possible that different social orientations are temperamental, inborn, even heritable. There is evidence that sociability is inherited. Kagan, a proponent of the temperamental argument, contends that extreme inhibition in the face of arousing stimuli, including unfamiliar age-mates, is biologically based and relatively stable over time.

While I am sure that there is some truth to this, particularly with the extreme groups Kagan studies, I am also persuaded by Cicchetti's (chapter 12) and others' theory that the origins of the withdrawn social style may lie in the early mother-infant relationship. This is not to say the attachment relationship dictates the child's eventual relations with peers, but only that there is a linkage. It seems conceivable that the social skills and trust learned in a harmonious reciprocal parent-infant relationship—the breeding ground of a secure attachment—would carry over to some extent to relations with age-mates.

Because development is plastic, even well-established developmental trajectories are susceptible to deflection and redirection. A major question which this raises, then, is whether the arena of peer play, or play with others, can be used not only to diagnose risk for later problems but also as a target for clinical intervention. This possibility has been argued for a long time by play therapists. That play can be used even with short-term goals in mind to support functioning is demonstrated by Jeriann Wilson (chapter 13). Scientists studying play have contributed in practical ways to fostering the well-being of children. But we have to be careful not to intervene too quickly. Good intentions alone are not sufficient. But by the same token it is often more appropriate to act and try than to do nothing at all. Play is probably an arena in which to act.

Finally, I would like to underscore Vonnie McLoyd's (chapter 11) critical evaluation of social class studies of play. Social class offers very little as an explanatory construct, whether we are trying to account for variation in play or some other behavioral phenomenon. While SES may enable us to predict behavior—and McLoyd's review suggests otherwise—social class effects are difficult to define, for they require fewer macroconstructs, such as attitudes, housing, socialization practices, and the like. Using these as determinants would be better. As the research has shown, the variation within and across social classes is very great. And when we look beyond this macrosociological construct we not only get more precise prediction, but better explanation as well.

References

Parten, M.B. 1932. Social participation among preschool children. *Journal of Abnormal and Social Psychology* 27:243–269.

21

The Relationships of Play Materials and Parental Involvement to Young Children's Cognitive Development

Allen W. Gottfried

I would like to present data from contemporary longitudinal studies in North America dealing specifically with the contribution of play materials and parental involvement to cognitive development in infants and preschoolers (see Gottfried, 1984). The data are based on the studies by Bradley and Caldwell (1984); Gottfried and Gottfried (1984); Barnard, Bee, and Hammond (1984); Johnson, Breckenridge, and McGowan (1984); and Siegel (1984). These studies are selected because the researchers have chosen similar home and developmental assessments and subjects of the same ages on which to conduct the assessments. This provides the unique opportunity to examine comparability of findings across studies, as well as to make integrative analyses. There is also considerable variation among the studies in sample demographics, which offers further opportunity for analysis.

The Bradley and Caldwell study is based on a predominantly black lower-class population in Little Rock, Arkansas. The Gottfrieds' study is being conducted in southern California with a middle-class, predominantly white population. The population in the Barnard et al. study is predominantly white, middle-class, all first-born, and residing in the Seattle, Washington, area. Johnson et al. conducted their study with a lower-class population of Mexican-Americans in Houston, Texas. The study by Siegel was conducted in Ontario, Canada, and involved premature and full-term children from a white, blue-collar population.

These studies have all used the infant version of the HOME (Home Observation for Measurement of the Environment) scale. Developed by Caldwell and Bradley (1979), this scale was designed to measure the socio-emotional and cognitive supports in the home. The HOME contains forty-five items forming six subscales and has a total score based on all items. Higher scores indicate a greater quality and quantity of home stimulation. The six subscales are (1) emotional and verbal responsivity of mother, (2) avoidance of restriction and punishment (sometimes referred to as acceptance of the family), (3) organization of the physical and temporal environment, (4) provisions of appropriate play materials, (5) maternal involvement with the child, and (6) opportunities for variety in daily stimulation. Play materials and maternal involvement are the focus of the analysis. The play materials scale include such items as child having toys that involve pulling or pushing, eye-hand coordination, fitting together, building, role-playing, music or literature, and so on. It is important that the toys must be readily available to the child. Items in the maternal involvement scale include such activities as parent structures play periods, provides toys that challenge child to develop new skills, invests maturing toys with value via her attention, and encourages developmental advances.

Studies have proven empirically that home environment correlates with developmental status (Gottfried, 1984; Wachs & Gruen, 1982). Recently, psychologists have begun to pursue this issue in greater depth. Among the many new issues are (1) identifying the relationship between demographic factors and home environmental variables, and (2) determining the specific home environmental variables that are most highly and pervasively correlated with young children's cognitive development.

One of the most consistent findings concerning the relationship between demographic factors and home environment involves the covariation of socioeconomic status (SES) and home environmental variables. In all of the studies, a positive significant correlation resulted between SES and home environment. The relationship emerges as early as 4 months of age (Barnard et al., 1984; also see Beckwith & Cohen, 1984). Hence, children from relatively higher SES families receive an intellectually more advantageous home environment. This holds regardless of race, for white, black, Hispanic children, as well as for children born preterm and full-term.

The association of play materials and maternal involvement by SES across studies are presented in table 21–1. The studies are hierarchically arranged according to population SES. The Johnson et al. population is the lowest; the Bradley and Caldwell population is next; the Siegel population is third; and the equivalent populations of Barnard et al. and Gottfried and Gottfried are the highest. Table 21–1 displays the mean scores for play materials and maternal involvement (along with the other HOME scales) at 1 year of age. These data reveal that middle-class parents, in contrast to parents of relatively lower SES, make available a greater amount of play materials and are more involved with their children, particularly in play-oriented activities.

Determining the home environmental variables that are most highly and pervasively correlated with young children's cognitive development is a central issue of both theoretical and applied significance. Conceptually, it is important to ascertain the specific environmental factors that possibly regulate developmental status. With respect to applied aspects, having knowledge of the specific home environmental variables that correlate with developmental status has direct implications for the design of early childhood intervention programs.

Table 21-1
Means and Standard Deviations on 1-Year HOME Scales across Studies

	Johnson, Breckenridge, & McGowan	Bradley & Caldwell	Siegel	Barnard, Bee, & Hammond	Gottfried & Gottfried
Responsivity	8.5 (2.1)[a]	8.0 (2.1)	9.0 (1.9)	9.7 (1.6)	8.7 (1.5)
Restriction and punishment	5.4 (1.5)	5.3 (1.6)	6.2 (1.3)	5.4 (1.7)	6.4 (1.1)
Organization	4.5 (1.3)	4.9 (1.2)	5.1 (1.0)	4.8 (1.0)	5.2 (0.9)
Play materials	4.6 (2.1)	6.4 (2.4)	7.2 (1.8)	7.9 (1.5)	8.6 (0.7)
Involvement	3.4 (1.6)	3.3 (1.6)	3.8 (1.9)	5.0 (1.3)	4.0 (1.2)
Variety	2.6 (1.2)	3.0 (1.1)	3.1 (1.3)	3.4 (1.2)	3.4 (1.1)
Total	28.9 (6.7)	31.9 (7.6)	34.4 (5.9)	36.3 (5.6)	36.4 (3.7)
N	367	67	170	169	129

Source: Adapted from Gottfried (1984), p. 331. Reprinted by permission of Academic Press.
[a]Standard deviations in parentheses.

To determine which environmental variables correlated most highly and pervasively with cognitive development from infancy through the preschool years, a meta-analysis was conducted. The purpose of the meta-analysis is not to alter the integrity of the findings from the individual studies, but to provide a statistical integration of findings across studies. It serves to establish the magnitude of the relationships that can be anticipated collapsing across diverse populations.

The results of the meta-analysis are shown in tables 21–2 and 21–3. Table 21–2 presents the correlations between the 1-year HOME and cognitive development measured at 1, 2, 3, and 3½ to 5 years of age. The mean correlation for each HOME scale are presented for each age of testing. The mean correlation with the 1-year Bayley ranged from .02 to .18. The HOME subscales that correlated most highly at this age are maternal responsibility, play materials and maternal involvement. With the 2-year Bayley, the mean correlations ranged from .16 to .32. Play materials, maternal involvement, and variety correlated most highly. The mean correlations with cognitive development assessed at 3 years and 3½ to 5 years, ranged from .11 to .34 and .16 to .38, respectively. At both ages, play materials, maternal involvement, and variety correlated most highly. A grand mean based on seventeen size effects was computed to provide an overview of the relationships between home environment assessed at age 1-year and cognitive development between 1 and 5 years. The grand mean correlations ranged from .12 to .30,

Table 21-2
Correlations between 1-Year HOME and Cognitive Development[a]

HOME	1-Year Bayley						2-Year Bayley				
	BC	GG	BBH	JBM[b]	S[c]	Mean r	GG	BBH	JBM	S[d]	Mean r
Responsivity	.15	-.04	.10	.27*	.18	.12	.09	.29*	.19	.13	.17
Restriction and punishment	.01	-.06	.19*	.01*	-.05	.02	.08	.20*	.28	.14	.16
Organization	.20	-.07	.09	.22*	.10	.10	.00	.37*	.28	.08	.17
Play materials	.28*	-.13	.27*	.39*	.15	.18	.02	.36*	.12	.35*	.23
Involvement	.28*	-.05	.18*	.22*	.12	.14	.10	.39*	.25	.24*	.25
Variety	.05	.12	.20*	.02	.07	.10	.31*	.27*	-.03	.25*	.24
Total	.30*	-.07	.26*	.35*	.09	.17	.20*	.45*	.29	.32*	.32
N	77	129	165	85	170	626	128	155	24	148	455

	3-Year Intellectual Performance[e]					3½–5-Year Intellectual Performance[f]					
	BC	GG	JBM	S[g]	Mean r	BC	GG	BBH	S[h]	Mean r	Grand Mean r[i]
Responsivity	.39*	.18*	.18	.18	.23	.34*	.11	.27*	.00	.19	.17
Restriction and punishment	.24*	.11	−.09	.12	.11	.21	.11	.29*	.15	.19	.12
Organization	.39*	.03	.02	.10	.13	.34*	.01	.18*	.16	.16	.14
Play materials	.56*	−.05	.11	.35*	.24	.52*	−.04	.32*	.41*	.29	.23
Involvement	.47*	.31*	.36*	.22*	.33	.36*	.16*	.35*	.14	.26	.24
Variety	.28*	.36*	−.14	.28*	.24	.32*	.40*	.18*	.24*	.28	.21
Total	.58*	.33*	.17	.27*	.34	.53*	.26*	.44*	.29*	.38	.30
N	77	119	36	133	365	77	118	153	56	404	1850

Source: Adapted from Gottfried (1984) p. 340. Reprinted by permission of Academic Press.

[a]BC = Bradley & Caldwell; GG = Gottfried & Gottfried; BBH = Barnard, Bee, & Hammond; JBM = Johnson, Breckenridge, & McGowan; S = Siegel.

[b]Correlations based on control and program groups combined.

[c]Correlations based on full-terms, preterms, and cohorts combined [corrected for sample sizes]; see table 7 in Siegel chapter for significant correlations; a single significant correlation was reported for each subscale across the groups.

[d]Correlations taken from Siegel (1981, table 4).

[e]Based on Stanford-Binet IQ, except for GG, which was based on McCarthy General Cognitive Index.

[f]Based on Stanford-Binet IQ, except for GG and S, which were based on McCarthy General Cognitive Index.

[g]Correlations based on full-terms, preterms, and cohorts combined (corrected for sample sizes); see table 15 in Siegel chapter.

[h]Correlations based on full-terms, preterms, and cohorts combined (corrected for sample sizes); see table 16 in Siegel chapter.

[i]Grand mean based on average of foregoing means and based on 17 size-effects and 1,850 subject entries.

*Indicates that the correlation reached a statistical level of significance in that particular study.

Table 21-3
Correlations between 2-Year HOME and Preschool Cognitive Development

	BC^a	BC^b	BBH^c	JBM^d	Mean r
Responsivity	.49*	.50*	.42*	.01	.38
Restriction and punishment	.41*	.28*	.56*	− .21	.29
Organization	.41*	.33*	.05	.04	.21
Play materials	.64*	.56*	.21*	.04	.37
Involvement	.55*	.55*	.37*	− .01	.38
Variety	.50*	.39*	.20*	− .01	.28
Total	.71*	.57*	.60*	− .04	.50
N	77	77	133	47	334

Source: Adapted from Gottfried (1984) p. 341. Reprinted by permission of Academic Press.
[a]36-month Stanford-Binet IQ, Bradley & Caldwell.
[b]54-month Stanford-Binet IQ, Bradley & Caldwell.
[c]48-month Stanford-Binet IQ, Barnard, Bee, & Hammond.
[d]36-month Stanford-Binet, IQ on control group, Johnson, Breckenridge, & McGowan.
*Indicates that the correlation reached a statistical level of significance in that particular study.

with the correlation of the greatest strength found with play materials, maternal involvement, and variety.

In table 21-3 the correlations are shown for each study contributing data on the relationship between the 2-year home and preschool cognitive deveopment (36 to 54 months). The average correlations ranged from .21 to .50. Maternal responsivity, play materials, and maternal involvement yield the highest relationships.

Two major conclusions can be drawn from the meta-analyses of these longitudinal studies. First, the relatively most potent and most pervasive home environmental variables during the early years that correlated with cognitive development during infancy and the preschool years are play materials and maternal (parental) involvement. Second, with advancement in age, the relationships between play materials and maternal involvement and cognitive development become increasingly stronger.

References

Barnard, K.E., Bee, H.L., & Hammond, M.A. 1984. Home environment and cognitive development in a healthy, low-risk sample: The Seattle study. In A.W. Gottfried (Ed.), Home environment and early cognitive development: Longitudinal research. New York: Academic Press.

Beckwith, L., & Cohen, S.E. 1984. Home environment and cognitive competence in preterm children during the first 5 years. In A.W. Gottfried (Ed.), *Home environment and early cognitive development: Longitudinal research.* New York: Academic Press.

Bradley, R.H., & Caldwell, B.M. 1984. 174 children: A study of the relationship between home environment and cognitive development during the first 5 years. In A.W. Gottfried (Ed.), *Home environment and early cognitive development: Longitudinal research.* New York: Academic Press.

Caldwell, B.M., & Bradley, R.H. 1979. *Home observation for measurement of the environment.* Little Rock: University of Arkansas Press.

Gottfried, A.W. 1984. Home environment and early cognitive development: Integration, meta-analyses, and conclusions. In A.W. Gottfried (Ed.), *Home environment and early cognitive development: Longitudinal research.* New York: Academic Press.

Gottfried, A.W., & Gottfried, A.E. 1984. Home environment and cognitive development in young children of middle-socioeconomic-status families. In A.W. Gottfried (Ed.), *Home environment and early cognitive development: Longitudinal research.* New York: Academic Press.

Johnson, D.L., Breckenridge, J.N., & McGowan, R.J. 1984. Home environment and early cognitive development in Mexican-American children. In A.W. Gottfried (Ed.), *Home environment and early cognitive development: Longitudinal research.* New York: Academic Press.

Siegel, L.S. 1981. Infant tests as predictors of cognitive and language development at two years. *Child Development* 52:545–557.

Siegel, L.S. 1984. Home environmental influences on cognitive development in preterm and full-term children during the first 5 years. In A.W. Gottfried (Ed.), *Home environment and early cognitive development: Longitudinal research.* New York: Academic Press.

Wachs, T.D., & Gruen, G.E. 1982. *Early experience and human development.* New York: Plenum Press.

Index

List of Contributors

Leila Beckwith, Professor, Department of Pediatrics, University of California

Jay Belsky, Associate Professor, Division of Individual and Family Studies, Pennsylvania State University

Robert H. Bradley, Associate Professor and Research Director, Center for Child Development and Education, University of Arkansas

Inge Bretherton, Associate Professor, Human Development and Family Study, Colorado State University

Bettye Caldwell, Conaghey Professor of Education, College of Education, Center for Child Development and Education, University of Arkansas

Dante Cicchetti, Associate Professor, Department of Psychology and Social Relations, Harvard University

Judy Dunn, Research Scientist, MRC Unit, University of Cambridge, Sub Department of Animal Behaviour

Greta G. Fein, Professor of Education, Department of Curriculum and Instruction, College of Education, University of Maryland

Larry Fenson, Associate Professor, Department of Psychology, San Diego State University

Adele Eskeles Gottfried, Professor, Department of Educational Psychology, California State University, Northridge

Daniel W. Kee, Associate Professor, Department of Psychology, California State University, Fullerton

Phyllis Levenstein, Adjunct Associate Professor, Social Sciences Interdisciplinary Program, State University of New York at Stony Brook, Executive Office, Verbal Interaction Project, Inc.

Lorraine McCune, Associate Professor, Education/Psychology Department, Graduate School of Education, Rutgers University

Vonnie C. McLoyd, Associate Professor of Psychology, University of Michigan

Kenneth H. Rubin, Professor and Head, Graduate Program in Developmental Psychology, University of Waterloo

Helen B. Schwartzman, Associate Professor, Department of Anthropology, Northwestern University

Brian Sutton-Smith, Professor, Graduate School of Education, University of Pennsylvania

Brian R. Vandenberg, Assistant Professor, Department of Psychology, University of Missouri

Theodore D. Wachs, Professor, Department of Psychological Sciences, Purdue University

Jerriann M. Wilson, Director, Child Life Department, John Hopkins Hospital; Instructor in Pediatrics, School of Medicine, Johns Hopkins University

About the Editors

Allen W. Gottfried is professor of psychology at California State University, Fullerton, and clinical professor of pediatrics at the University of Southern California School of Medicine. He is the author of numerous scientific publications and an internationally recognized authority on the impact of early environment on young children's development. His recent books include *Home Environment and Early Cognitive Development: Longitudinal Research, Infant Stress under Intensive Care: Environmental Neonatology,* and *Maternal Employment and Children's Development: Longitudinal Research* (forthcoming). He has been an editorial board member of *Child Development, Infant Behavior and Development,* and the *Journal of Pediatric Psychology* as well as an editorial consultant to many other scientific journals.

Catherine Caldwell Brown is a freelance science writer and editor.